Nebraska
Symposium on
Motivation
1978

Nebraska Symposium on Motivation, 1978, is Volume 26 in the series on CURRENT THEORY AND RESEARCH IN MOTIVATION

University of Nebraska Press
Lincoln/London 1979

Nebraska Symposium on Motivation 1978

Human Emotion

Herbert E. Howe, Jr.	*Series Editor*
Richard A. Dienstbier	*Volume Editor*
James R. Averill	*Professor of Psychology* *University of Massachusetts* *Amherst*
Joseph V. Brady	*Director, Division of Behavioral* *Biology* *Department of Psychiatry and* *Behavioral Sciences* *The Johns Hopkins University* *School of Medicine*
Marianne Frankenhaeuser	*Research Professor of* *Experimental Psychology* *Swedish Medical Research Council* *Karolinska Institute and* *Department of Psychology* *University of Stockholm*
C. E. Izard	*Professor of Psychology* *University of Delaware*
Silvan S. Tomkins	*Professor Emeritus* *Livingston College* *Rutgers University*
Richard A. Dienstbier	*Professor of Psychology* *University of Nebraska-Lincoln*

Preface

This year's edition of the Nebraska Symposium on Motivation is dedicated to the memory of Harry K. Wolfe, one of America's early psychologists. A student of Wilhelm Wundt, Professor Wolfe is credited by many with establishing the first undergraduate laboratory in the United States at the University of Nebraska. It is especially appropriate that funds donated to the University of Nebraska Foundation in the memory of this pioneer psychologist by his late student, Dr. Cora L. Friedline, are used to support the Symposium. The editors thank the University of Nebraska Foundation for its support.

This volume represents the beginning of the second twenty-five years of the Nebraska Symposium. In this context, it is particularly fitting that the volume contains a history of the first twenty-five years of the Symposium compiled by Dr. Ludy Benjamin, formerly of Nebraska Wesleyan University, who is now Educational Affairs Officer of the American Psychological Association, and by Dr. Marshall Jones, founder and first editor of the Symposium.

The volume editor for this session of the Symposium has been Dr. Richard Dienstbier. His thoughtful development of the topic and selection of the speakers is greatly appreciated as is the energy he has shown in carrying the Symposium to completion and publication.

HERBERT E. HOWE, JR.
General Editor

Contents

From Motivational Theory to Social Cognitive Development: Twenty-five Years of the Nebraska Symposium[1]

Ludy T. Benjamin, Jr.
Nebraska Wesleyan University
Marshall R. Jones
University of Miami

T his volume, marking the completion of twenty-five years of the Nebraska Symposium on Motivation, seems an appropriate place in which to provide a brief history of its origin and development. As the longest-lived topical series in American psychology, with a national and international reputation, the symposium and its history reflect, at least in part, the development of academic psychology in this country during those years. Indeed, the list of speakers reads like a "Who's Who" of American psychology. Fourteen of those speakers have served as president of the American Psychological Association (APA). Another indicator of the quality of the participants is the fact that of the 68 Distinguished Scientific Contribution Awards given by APA since 1956, 24 of the recipients have been Nebraska Symposium speakers.

1. Some of the material for this paper was taken from records of the University of Nebraska Press and from the correspondence of David Levine, Abraham Maslow, and T. C. Schneirla which is part of the manuscript collection of the Archives of the History of American Psychology, University of Akron, Akron, Ohio. The description of the founding of the symposium is taken almost entirely from oral history, since documents surrounding the origin are essentially nonexistent.

Ludy T. Benjamin, Jr., is now Educational Affairs Officer of the American Psychological Association. Marshall R. Jones, founder and first editor of the *Nebraska Symposium on Motivation*, is currently Professor Emeritus, University of Miami.

When Marshall Jones, the editor of the first eleven volumes of the symposium, became Director of the clinical psychology training program at the University of Nebraska in 1949, there were only eight other faculty members in the psychology department. A major concern for the graduate program was to be able to expose students to a wider scope of ideas and orientations than could be represented by a faculty of that size. Some thought was given to the possibility of accomplishing this by inviting a variety of psychologists to the campus for colloquia and conferences, and in 1950, when the grant for clinical training was being prepared for the U. S. Public Health Service, a modest sum was included for that purpose. When these funds became available during the 1951–52 academic year, six distinguished psychologists with a wide variety of interests—Roger Barker, Bruno Bettelheim, Leon Festinger, Dale Harris, Robert Sears, and Muzafer Sherif—were invited to present colloquia. Because each speaker came to the campus individually, there were six separate sessions, and due to scheduling difficulties, all sessions took place in the spring semester. Each of these psychologists spent two days conferring with students and faculty about problems and viewpoints in their particular areas of interest, and the colloquia were enthusiastically received. However, it was obvious that some integration was necessary: the six sessions created problems in the meeting of other academic obligations, and a lack of continuity among the presentations was noted.

Therefore, in planning for the 1952–53 academic year, it was decided to choose one general topic and to invite three visitors at a time to discuss their research and theoretical formulations on this topic over a two-day period. There were to be two of these symposia during the year, both during the spring semester and separated by eight to ten weeks, with each participant having approximately half a day to present a formal paper and to discuss it with the audience. The fourth half-day was to be used for the discussion, first among the participants, with comments on each others' papers,[2] and then among the participants, students, and faculty. With one exception (the 1975–76 symposium on personal construct theory), this format has remained reasonably consistent during the past twenty-five years, except for the rescheduling of the two sessions in separate academic semesters, a policy begun during the twelfth year of the symposium.

2. Formal comments on each of the papers by the other participants were included in the volumes published between 1953 and 1962, and in the 1964 volume.

The topic of motivation was selected as a focus, and the speakers who came to the campus in 1953 were Judson Brown, Harry Harlow, and Leo Postman in January, and O. Hobart Mowrer, Theodore Newcomb, and Vincent Nowlis in March. The publication of their papers, however, was not part of the original plan; it was suggested to Jones in the interim between the sessions by the chancellor of the university, Reuben Gustavson. Jones was in Gustavson's office on other business, and Gustavson asked casually about the first session. When Jones described the interest and enthusiasm that had been generated, and his sense of the importance and value of the material that had been presented and discussed, Gustavson asked him to investigate the possibility of publishing the papers through the University of Nebraska Press.

The director of the press, Emily Schossberger, did not share the chancellor's enthusiasm about the symposium as a publishing venture, but she agreed to publish the volume when the chancellor indicated that his office would reimburse the press for any financial loss. Because there was not at this point a commitment to a series publication, the first volume appeared without a series number, simply as *Current Theory and Research in Motivation: A Symposium*. It was published in October, 1953, and sales far exceeded the expectations not only of the press but also of the organizers of the symposium.

Motivation was selected as the central topic of the symposium because of several concerns. First, there was no graduate course in motivation at the University of Nebraska, an omission which Jones considered to be serious. Second, he wanted the topic to be an integrating concept in psychology, one which could bring together research and theoretical work from areas such as personality, physiological psychology, learning, and social psychology. In his introduction to the first volume (1953), Jones wrote:

> The problems of motivation are significant for and relevant to practically every phase of contemporary psychology. Motivation provides a central theme around which a vast amount of experimental data from many divergent sources can be assembled and evaluated. It is also an area of great current theoretical interest and endeavor. (p. iii)

When the U. S. Public Health Service continued to fund the symposium as part of the clinical training program, motivation was again selected as the theme for the 1954 sessions, with John Atkinson, I. E. Farber, and Benbow F. Ritchie in the first session, and Leon Festinger, George Klein, and Henry Nissen in the second. The Nebraska Press, somewhat reluctantly, agreed to publication, again with a financial guarantee from the chancellor, and published the 1954 issue as Volume 2 in the series, but the first with the present series title, *Nebraska Symposium on Motivation*.[3]

This volume, like its predecessor, sold well—and thus created an unexpected problem. Since the symposia were conceived as part of the clinical training grant and financed by the U. S. Public Health Service, it seemed inappropriate and probably illegal for the University to profit from the sale of the volumes. Therefore, an informal agreement was arranged in which the Nebraska Press was reimbursed for the expenses of publication and distribution, and any additional profits were divided equally and paid to the participants in the form of royalties.

By the time the third volume was to be published, the Nebraska Press was strongly encouraging a formalized royalty arrangement, to which Jones objected on the grounds that it would violate the conditions of the training grant. When he obtained an opinion from the U. S. Public Health Service supporting his interpretation, the existing informal agreement was continued, with the symposium participants labeled "profit sharers." None of the participants was ever able to retire on the money they earned this way, but many of them did receive annual checks for several years, since the publication of each new volume seemed to stimulate anew the sales of the previous volumes.

Knowledge of the symposium began to spread. Standard orders for large numbers of copies from university book stores were an indication that the volumes were being used in the classroom. Volume 2 also apparently attracted wider interest: In May of 1955, the Basic Book Club purchased 250 copies of the second volume and requested that another 200 copies be set aside for possible reorder. Interest in the series was also reflected in reviews. Beginning with the third volume, the symposia were annually, and almost always enthusiastically, reviewed in the journal *Contemporary Psychology*.

3. For the first eight volumes, and for Volumes 10, 11, 12, and 14, the year in the title of the volume is also the year of publication. Volumes 9, 13, 15, and all subsequent volumes, however, carry a publication date one year later than the date in the title; for example, *Nebraska Symposium on Motivation 1968* (Vol. 16) was published in 1969. To avoid possible confusion, it is recommended that citations carry both dates, as well as the volume number. Some of the more recent volumes also carry subtitles.

For example, John Atkinson (1961) wrote a combined review of volumes 6 and 7, in which he described the symposium as follows:

Now in its eighth year, the Nebraska Symposium on Motivation, edited by Marshall R. Jones, continues to satisfy an important need by keeping attention focused on a field in a state of conceptual upheaval . . . . The symposium represents one of the more creative uses of training grants offered by the U. S. Public Health Service. (p. 91)

The *Harvard List of Books in Psychology* (1964 and 1971) described the series as "by far the best source of information on modern American thinking and experiments in the field of motivation" (p. 50).

Dr. Robert Felix, a psychiatrist who was director of NIMH, also had high praise for the series. In a public meeting at Stanford University in the early 1960s, Felix said he considered the funds NIMH spent on the Nebraska Symposium the most productive money in the whole agency.

Another indication of interest in the series was a survey by Norman Sundberg (1960). In 1958–59, only five years after the publication of the first Nebraska Symposium volume, Sundberg wrote to graduate departments of psychology requesting copies of reading lists for doctoral candidates. When the results of that survey were published, Nebraska Symposium was in the category of books recommended by one third to one half of the departments. The volumes even began to attract attention outside of psychology as evidenced by a series of reviews published in the *Quarterly Journal of Speech* (Weaver, 1959, 1960, 1961, 1963).

Not until the end of the 1960s was there evidence that the influence of the symposium was beginning to diminish. In a replication of the 1960 survey of graduate reading lists, Solso and Johnson (1967) had found that the symposium had maintained its position of being recommended by one third to one half of the graduate departments surveyed; however, when the survey was repeated by Solso (1971), the Nebraska Symposium was no longer listed in any of the categories. Appearing in its place was the text by Cofer and Appley (1964) entitled *Motivation: Theory and Research*.

At least part of the difficulty seemed related to the change in the status of motivation as a topic of central concern. Doubts about the utility of motivational concepts had begun to be discussed by American psychologists in the late 1950s and had been raised in some of the early symposium papers (Benbow F. Ritchie, 1954;

Robert C. Bolles, 1958). Leo Postman (1956), in his review of the 1955 volume, asked "Is the concept of motivation necessary?" (p. 229). Rather than eliminating the term, however, the interpretation of the concept was broadened as the symposium moved into the sixties: Many of the papers viewed motivation as a peripheral event, rather than according it the central status which had been more rigidly demanded in the early volumes.

In the 1962 volume Jones addressed the issue in print:

There seems to be increasing evidence over the years that the motivational concept as such has reached the end of its usefulness as a scientific construct . . . . However, even though the problems relating to the energetics and directions of behavior are now recognized as being so complex and varied that a single term such as "motivation" has so little specificity as to be of little use, except in the most casual language, it is abundantly apparent that there still are many complex and challenging problems left to cope with in understanding these aspects of behavior. (p. viii)

In a review of that volume, Irwin Sarason (1963) discussed the implications of Jones' remarks for future symposia. He indicated that whatever the outcome with respect to the term itself, he considered it important that the series should continue "to be an invaluable collection for psychologists working in a variety of areas" (p. 422). That is indeed what happened. The theoretical emphases of the papers shifted to such topics as personality, social psychology, and cognition as speakers sought to identify the motivational underpinnings of those theories. Not everyone applauded the change, however; Cofer (1968) in his review of the 1967 volume, found the papers provocative, but lamented the lack of material dealing with the systematic and theoretical nature of motivation.

In the 1962 volume, Jones had suggested that the series title might be changed, a suggestion that had been considered for some time. When George Kelly (1962) had spoken at the symposium in 1961, he had suggested a number of alternatives to the current name: "Snakes in Ireland" or "What in the World is Mankind About to do to Itself?" or "Isn't There any Other Way of Coping With a Problem Besides Lying Down and Being Treated for It?" or the "Nebraska Symposium on What Now." For a time more serious alternatives were considered, but now that the title has accomplished the transition from conceptual to historical significance, a change is no longer felt to be necessary.

In the summer of 1963, Marshall Jones left the University of Nebraska. He considered taking the symposium with him to the University of Miami, if the Nebraska faculty had been uninterested in continuing it. But they wished to retain it, and NIMH, which had taken over funding of the training grant the year before, continued to support it. David Levine, as Director of the clinical training program, was selected to be Jones's successor as editor of the symposium.

Some of Levine's problems with the symposium are documented in his letters. For example, when he invited Donald Campbell for 1964, Campbell declined, indicating he would be in Kenya. Levine reissued the invitation for 1965, and the correspondence during the next year was a disaster: Levine could not get mail to Kenya, and Campbell, who had no carbon paper in Kenya, complained in each letter that he could not remember what he had written in previous letters. (Campbell did participate in 1965). The following year Levine invited Vincent Dethier, who declined. The affirmative reply to the next years' invitation, however, was so ambiguous that Levine had to write again for clarification. There were also last-minute readjustments, but no shocks equal to that received by Marshall Jones when Sigmund Koch called a week before he was scheduled to speak to ask if the dates for the symposium had ever been set!

The editor's real job, however, began *after* the symposium sessions were held. Getting the papers ready for the volume was the greatest of tasks—in fact, on some occasions they were never received at all. Henry Murray (who presented his paper in 1963) decided not to prepare it for publication, and Daniel Lehrman (who spoke at the 1967 symposium) kept his editors waiting for over three years before he and they decided to give up. Editors sent numerous reminders to dilatory authors; Levine would close his with "worst regards." One editor even threatened murder in a letter of encouragement to a symposium delinquent. Then, with the papers ready for the printers, the printers were not always ready for the papers. The volumes were put into print by the university's print shop, which also printed the university's football programs. David Premack, who had participated in the 1965 symposium, wrote to Levine in November of that year to inquire if the volume would be published by Christmas. Levine replied to him: "In regard to your question, . . . you must know that when the football team is having an undefeated season, printing programs takes place over science" (Levine, Note 1). While the delays were numerous, most of the papers were eventually published—a total of 154 in the first twenty-five years.

When he was planning for the 1967 symposium, Levine made a change in format that had been recommended by a large number of individuals. For example, in reviewing the 1964 symposium, John Cotton (1966) had written:

> Now one thought about the volume as a whole: Do these six papers have the unity to form a true symposium? Despite a tradition of tangentially related papers, the excellent Nebraska series might be strengthened by planning one year's program to cover a certain somewhat narrow topic and the next to cover another. (pp. 53–54)

In the 1967 symposium, one session dealt with comparative psychology and the other with social psychology. This rather loose grouping of topics, oriented to areas of psychology (such as personality, social, or physiological psychology) rather than to specific topics, continued through Levine's years as editor (1964–1967) as well as those involving William Arnold (1968–1970). Typically the fall and spring session represented different fields. A more concerted effort for topical organization began in 1971 when James Cole became the editor. In his first year he organized sessions on child development and nonverbal communication. During the next two years, both sessions of each year were organized around a single theme: aggression in 1972, and sexuality in 1973.

Despite the financial problems involved there have been participants from overseas. The first foreign participant was Heinz Heckhausen, in 1968, from Germany; others have followed, including Margaret Donaldson from Scotland, in 1971, David Bromley from England in 1977, and, most recently, Marianne Frankenhaeuser from Sweden in 1978.

Another innovation in recent years has been to invite speakers whose primary training is outside of psychology and whose work is not well known by psychologists. In the last six years this group has included a zoologist (Robert Bigelow, in 1972), a sociologist (John Gagnon, in 1973) and a philosopher (Stephen Toulmin, in 1975). Non-psychologists had been invited in earlier years, but these were people whose work was well known to psychologists (for example, H. W. Magoun in 1963).

Selection of speakers has always been primarily the prerogative of the editor. The earlier symposia sought to invite well-known speakers who were active in research, and their prestige was no doubt partially responsible for the very rapid rise to prominence which the symposium enjoyed. In recent years there have been more attempts to include some speakers whose work is promising but not necessarily widely known as yet.

There have been other changes too in recent years, some of which are not readily apparent. NIMH withdrew its funding of the symposium in 1976, so funds must now come from other sources, notably a number of sources within the University of Nebraska. With rising costs of book production and declining sales, payments to speakers from sales of the volumes have been discontinued for several years. Although speakers receive an honorarium for their contribution, profits from the sale of the volumes are used to support the continuation of the symposium.

Looking back over the past twenty-five years, what have these symposia accomplished? Undoubtedly, they have been important to the graduate students and faculty at the University of Nebraska in terms of opportunities for intellectual growth. They have brought prestige to that university on both a national and international level among psychologists and others related to behavioral sciences; they have brought credit to the University of Nebraska Press.

For years the symposium was the major forum for material in motivation and after the decline of the importance of motivational issues it continued to be an important source for a wide variety of theoretical material. In its earlier years it offered a rare publishing opportunity to researchers, a vehicle in which to present a paper too long and comprehensive for an article, too short for a book. It allowed one to report the results of a number of years of research and thinking in a more complete and integrated fashion than was possible elsewhere, and to see it in print without lengthy delays. Today the symposium is only one of many such forums for publication; twenty-five years ago it was nearly unique in this country.

The symposium volumes are important sources of material for graduate education. In their comprehensive treatment of one or two topics, they are useful as textbooks: During the last two years there have been 23 orders from university bookstores for 15 or more copies of a particular volume. This list includes colleges across the entire country, with the 23 orders involving 11 different volumes. Apparently even the older volumes are used as texts: For example, in the last two years there have been four orders of 20 copies or more for the 1960 volume (which contains the papers of Roger Barker, Donald Taylor, Walter Toman, Robert W. White, Fritz Heider, and David Rapaport). One of those orders was from a university in Denmark.

The founding of this symposium required imagination and vision; its survival required the flexibility to adapt to a changing concept of motivation and the changing shape of psychology itself. It has already earned a place of significance in the development of psychology. The combination of the strength of tradition and the capacity for change will likely insure its future.

REFERENCE NOTE

1. Levine, D. Letter to D. Premack, November 23, 1965 (in Archives of the History of American Psychology, University of Akron, Akron, Ohio)

REFERENCES

Atkinson, J. W. Review of *Nebraska Symposium on Motivation*, Vols. 6 and 7. *Contemporary Psychology*, 1961, **6**, 91–94.

Bigelow, R. The evolution of cooperation, aggression, and self-control. In J. K. Cole & D. D. Jensen (Eds.), *Nebraska Symposium on Motivation 1972* (Vol. 20). Lincoln: University of Nebraska Press, 1973.

Bolles, R. C. The usefulness of the drive concept. In M. R. Jones (Ed.), *Nebraska Symposium on Motivation 1958* (Vol. 6). Lincoln: University of Nebraska Press, 1958.

Cofer, C. N. Review of *Nebraska Symposium on Motivation*, Vol. 14. *Contemporary Psychology*, 1968, **13**, 52–53.

Cofer, C. N., & Appley, M. H. *Motivation: Theory and Research*. New York: Wiley, 1964.

Cotton, J. W. Review of *Nebraska Symposium on Motivation*, Vol. 12. *Contemporary Psychology*, 1966, **11**, 52–54.

Feldman, C. F., & Toulmin, S. Logic and the theory of mind. In J. K. Cole & W. J. Arnold (Eds.), *Nebraska Symposium on Motivation 1975: Conceptual Foundations of Psychology* (Vol. 23). Lincoln: University of Nebraska Press, 1976.

Gagnon, J. H. Scripts and the coordination of sexual conduct. In J. K. Cole & R. Dienstbier (Eds.), *Nebraska Symposium on Motivation 1973* (Vol. 21). Lincoln: University of Nebraska Press, 1974.

The Harvard List of Books in Psychology, 3rd & 4th editions. Cambridge: Harvard University Press, 1964 & 1971.

Jones, M. R. (Ed.). *Current Theory and Research in Motivation: A Symposium*. Lincoln: University of Nebraska Press, 1953.

Jones, M. R. (Ed.). *Nebraska Symposium on Motivation 1962* (Vol. 10). Lincoln: University of Nebraska Press, 1962.

Kelly, G. A. Europe's matrix of decision. In M. R. Jones (Ed.), *Nebraska Symposium on Motivation 1962* (Vol. 10). Lincoln: University of Nebraska Press, 1962.

Levine, D. (Ed.). *Nebraska Symposium on Motivation 1967* (Vol. 15). Lincoln: University of Nebraska Press, 1967.

Magoun, H. W. Central neural inhibition. In M. R. Jones (Ed.), *Nebraska Symposium on Motivation 1963* (Vol. 11). Lincoln: University of Nebraska Press, 1963.

Postman, L. Review of *Nebraska Symposium on Motivation*, Vol. 3. *Contemporary Psychology*, 1956, **1**, 229–230.

Ritchie, B. F. A logical and experimental analysis of the laws of motivation. In M. R. Jones (Ed.), *Nebraska Symposium on Motivation 1954* (Vol. 2). Lincoln: University of Nebraska Press, 1954.

Sarason, I. G. Review of *Nebraska Symposium on Motivation*, Vol. 10. *Contemporary Psychology*, 1963, **8**, 420–422.

Solso, R. L. Recommended readings in psychology during the past 17 years. *American Psychologist*, 1971, **26**, 1083–1084.

Solso, R. L., & Johnson, J. E. A survey of recommended readings in psychology. *Psychological Reports*, 1967, **20**, 855–857.

Sundberg, N. D. Basic readings in psychology. *American Psychologist*, 1960, **15**, 343–345.

Weaver, A. T. Review of *Nebraska Symposium on Motivation*, Vols. 1–6. *Quarterly Journal of Speech*, 1959, **45**, 325–330.

Weaver, A. T. Review of *Nebraska Symposium on Motivation*, Vol. 7. *Quarterly Journal of Speech*, 1960, **46**, 215–216.

Weaver, A. T. Review of the *Nebraska Symposium on Motivation*, Vol. 8. *Quarterly Journal of Speech*, 1961, **47**, 432.

Weaver, A. T. Review of *Nebraska Symposium on Motivation*, Vol. 9. *Quarterly Journal of Speech*, 1963, **49**, 94–95.

Introduction

*I*n the several years since each volume of the Nebraska Symposium on Motivation has been devoted to a single topic, this is the first to be devoted entirely to human emotion. A number of this year's participants expressed surprise at that fact, because from their perspective human emotional functioning is central in human motivation. While not all of the authors in this volume are equally explicit about the interrelationships between emotion and motivation, the attention paid to the motivation concept is characteristic of the volume and provides a unifying theme between the chapters; despite the symposium title, there has not been such a consistent and direct concern with that concept for some time in the series. (For a more complete discussion of this issue, see the brief history, above, by Professors Ludy Benjamin and Marshall Jones.)

Although the participants in this symposium would probably not agree on all details, they would probably agree that the study of human emotion at the most interesting conceptual levels depends upon taking into account human symbolic or cognitive capacity. This thread runs clearly throughout the chapters by Professors Averill, Izard, Tomkins, and Dienstbier; Professor Frankenhaeuser also acknowledges this interrelationship, relying upon attributional and appraisal approaches to understand the relationship between the catecholamines and emotional experience. While Professor Brady is least explicit on this topic, some of the relationships demonstrated in his research involving interactions of sex of subject with motivational contingencies and emotional reactions in social situations may be best explained by different conceptualizations of the situation by the two sexes. Beyond those broad considerations, however, the chapters of this volume do not all fit into similar molds; each offers a unique view of human emotion.

Professor James Averill, after exploring the usefulness of a "role-metaphor" approach to emotional functioning (in contrast to a "syndrome" approach), and the necessity of considering the impact of cognitive approaches in determining the emotional experience, considers the implications of regarding emotional experience as

xxi

"passion" in which responsibility for action is eliminated. His analysis of anger as passion and as a conflictive emotion leads to consideration of the treatment of anger in the diverse areas of other contemporary cultures, historical Rome, and the American judicial system. It is in the legal arena that Professor Averill's role-metaphor approach to anger becomes a most powerful conceptual tool. As a passion, anger may provide a role structure for allowing an individual to perform acts which have some social justification, but which would otherwise be illegal. The research which Professor Averill presents in the later section of the chapter provides an analysis of the causes and the meaning of incidents of anger by those citizens of a New England town who reported on their most significant anger experiences during the period of one week. His data lead to the clear conclusion that anger is typically regarded as far from the destructive impulse which psychologists have often thought it to be, that it may instead provide the basis for structuring improvements in social relationships.

In the next chapter, Professor Joseph Brady stresses the interrelationship between the concepts of emotion and motivation by noting that occasions, behaviors, and consequences relating to a specific emotional or motivational sequence may affect the occasions, behaviors, and consequences of other emotional and motivational sequences. He suggests analysis of the somatic, associative, and hedonic dimensions to ease the "mind-boggling" complexity of motivational-emotional interrelationships. A major section of Professor Brady's chapter describes his research with small groups of resident volunteer human subjects. Behavioral programs restricting access to activities were established, creating an environment in which emotion and motivation could be studied in a controlled human setting. In some studies work contingencies had to be fulfilled in order to achieve access to social contact; in others, subjects worked to earn financial payment and to avoid the withdrawal of that payment; in still others, contingencies were established so that individual efforts contributed to group reward (appetitive situations), with that situation alternating with contingencies in which a lack of individual effort cost the group its previously earned payments (aversive situation). During appetitive situations, such arrangements led to cooperation and group cohesiveness, whereas during aversive conditions work patterns changed to more lumped performance with mood and group cohesiveness declining. This research clearly demonstrates the different effects of appetitive and aversive contingencies on emotional responses and resultant social interactions.

Professor Marianne Frankenhaeuser depends primarily upon an analysis of sympathetic-adrenal-medullary responses to environmental stressors to explicate the concepts of stress and coping. Her approach is based upon the premise that neuroendocrine responses are primary indicators of the impact of stressors on the individual's experience of emotion and on the individual's cognitive appraisal of the situation. She discusses catecholamine infusion and beta-blocking research which provides support for her basic premise, and then presents research to show that the study of secretion patterns in epinephrine, norepinephrine, and cortisol in response to varied parameters allows an assessment of the differential impact of those hormones. This approach leads to an assessment of the meaning of potential stressors to individuals through an analysis of hormonal patterning. The dimension of perceived and actual control is explored through studies of laboratory and natural settings, including schools, travel, and occupational environments. Professor Frankenhaeuser's findings linking efficiency and effort to *increased* catecholamine secretion are particularly noteworthy, while those measuring catecholamines across long time periods suggest responses of long duration. She also notes sex differences in hormonal patterning, and differences among those who adopt variations from traditional sex roles. Synthesizing her laboratory and field findings, Professor Frankenhaeuser offers an analysis of occupational requirements which are most identified with hormonally-indicated stress responses.

In his chapter, Professor C. E. Izard considers the parallel evolution of rational capacity and emotions toward greater complexity and differentiation in the human. The evolution of more discrete emotions is seen as enhancing survival since the discrete emotions motivate specific categories of responses. Because diverse responses are needed as the organism is engaged in an increasingly complex environment, emotional differentiation is required. With emotion always present at varying levels, motivation is usually best conceptualized as a function of emotion; in this approach emotion also assumes the role of a major organizing force for human consciousness. The motivational and consciousness-organizing functions of emotion are seen most clearly in the human infant: Professor Izard charts the development of the discrete emotions through affective, affective-perceptual, and affective-cognitive developmental levels.

The relationship between facial expression and emotional experience is discussed, with a review of relevant cross-cultural research and psychophysiological studies. Furthermore, attention is devoted to the ways in which emotional expression of the infant motivates others, as in the role this social interaction plays in mother-infant attachment. Finally, the role of developing discrete emotions in the organization of personality is considered.

Professor Tomkins' chapter begins with an updating of his theory of affect as presented in his 1962 volumes *Affect, Imagery, Consciousness*. The four points of modification of that approach include the recognition, first, that affect is an amplifier of drive states in an analogue fashion, by providing an additional source of arousal and motivation which resembles the drive state but which is nevertheless separate. A second modification suggests that the skin of the face rather than the face musculature is the major mechanism for the analogic amplification. Thirdly, restrictions imposed by culture, family, and specific training require that humans normally suppress the complete expression of their affects, causing a change in the experience and duration of the emotions termed "backed-up" affect. Fourth, the affects are postulated to amplify not only the activator of the affect, but to amplify as well the further responses prompted by the affects. Professor Tomkins then suggests that the interrelationships between stimuli, affects, and responses are organized through scripts. Changing levels of meaningfulness and importance of the individual script depend upon "magnification"—repetitions of the scene and script with modifications. A description and elaboration of this process comprises a major part of the chapter.

In the concluding chapter, Professor Richard Dienstbier considers emotion-attribution theory as part of a larger system of emotion theory, reviewing research from areas of emotion which relate to the validity of the underlying assumptions. He then presents a series of principles of emotion-attribution theory which relate to the impact on emotion attributions of different characteristics of eliciting stimuli, cultural, social, and personal influences, and differences in arousal patterns of different emotions. The impact of those parameters is examined at three levels: The role of emotional-attribution processes in socialization techniques and on later emotional experience is considered; the impact on later emotional experience of short-term arousal carried between situations is considered; finally, emotion-attribution concepts are used to explain the relationship of long-term emotion differences (temperament) on personality development. Attention is devoted to alienation, authoritarianism, moral socialization, the impact of tangible reinforcement on motivation, and the process of reducing emotional responses to increasingly familiar stimuli. Research is presented relating emotional arousal to increases and decreases in attraction (depending upon characteristics of the stimulus person), and finally, research critical of emotion-attribution theory is reviewed and evaluated, with the limitations of the theory discussed.

RICHARD A. DIENSTBIER
Professor of Psychology

Anger[1]

James R. Averill
University of Massachusetts, Amherst

*I*n recent years there has been a veritable avalanche of books and monographs on the topic of aggression, including an entire issue of the Nebraska Symposium (Cole & Jensen, 1972). One might assume that little is left to be said on the topic. However, a perusal of published work on aggression reveals a notable gap, namely, an almost complete absence of any discussion of the emotion of anger. Anger is not even listed in the indexes of several recent books on aggression, such as those by Baron (1977), Fromm (1973), Lorenz (1966), and Montagu (1976). In other instances, anger is treated as an intervening variable (drive) or hypothetical construct (physiological arousal) of little substantive interest in its own right (e.g., Bandura, 1973; Berkowitz, 1962, 1969). The treatment of anger in the periodical literature is not much better. In the decade prior to 1968, the *Psychological Abstracts* listed only 50 entries under the heading of "anger" (an average of 5 per year); in 1968, the heading was dropped entirely from the index, and it did not reappear until 1974. In the last several years, matters seem to be changing, with 20, 23, and 34 entries for the years 1974, 1975, and 1976, respectively. However, this still represents only a small percentage of the total number of articles (approximately 500 per year) which deal with other aspects of aggression. As a final example of the paucity of interest in anger, a recent bibliography of aggressive behavior by Crabtree and Moyer (1977) may be noted. This bibliography contains 1,779 references to human aggression, of which only 40 (2.2%) are cross-listed under the topical heading of anger.

The preoccupation of psychologists with aggression (as opposed

1. Preparation of this paper was supported, in part, by a grant from the National Institute of Mental Health (MH22299). Thanks are due Sy Epstein and Bonnie Strickland for their helpful comments on an earlier version of the manuscript.

to anger) is understandable. The threat (and sometimes actuality) of war, social anarchy, and other kinds of widespread violence has hung over the present generation like a Damoclean sword. And it is not clear how or where the emotion of anger fits into this pantheon of violence. Yet there are good reasons for not neglecting anger. Historically, perhaps no other emotion has been the subject of more debate and conflicting sentiment. Plato, for example, believed that anger is fundamental to the organization of the individual and the state (cf. *The Republic*); on the other hand, the Roman philosopher Seneca (ca. 40–50 A.D./1963) considered anger to be "the most hideous and frenzied of all the emotions" (p. 107). Anger (e.g., the wrath of God) also is an important concept in many of the world's great religions, especially Judaism as represented in the Old Testament, Zoroastrianism, and Mohammedanism (Stratton, 1923).

Whatever anger is, its prominent place within the Western intellectual tradition would indicate that it should not be lightly dismissed by contemporary psychologists. But aside from its historical interest, the study of anger is also of practical and theoretical importance. The practical importance of studying anger needs little documentation. As will be discussed more fully below, many homicides are ultimately adjudicated as "crimes of passion," e.g., due to anger. And that is just the tip of the iceberg: battered children, wives, and even husbands; broken marriages and friendships; lost hours spent ruminating over real and fancied insults—the list of misdeeds committed in the name of anger is almost endless. Moreover, it is not only the expression of anger which causes problems. The inability to become justifiably angry can also be a personal and social handicap, a fact which is reflected in the current popularity of "assertiveness training" (cf. Holmes & Horan, 1976).

On a more theoretical level, the study of anger is important for two major reasons. First, it has implications for theories of emotion, and second, it has implications for research on aggression. The relevance of anger for the former may appear self-evident: no one would deny that anger is an emotion. However, most contemporary theories of emotion are not based on the observation of emotional behavior; rather, they represent extensions to the area of emotion of theories originally designed to account for other kinds of behavior. For example, most "drive" theories are based primarily on studies of learning (cf. "fear" as a learned drive in avoidance conditioning, and its analogue, "anger," in the case of aggression). Other theories, such as psychoanalysis, are based primarily on the study of psychopathology. And theories which emphasize physiological mechanisms are based primarily on animal research, where the application of emotional concepts is often metaphorical at best. At the risk of overexaggeration for the sake of emphasis, it may be said that many theorists have studiously avoided any reference to everyday emotional reactions as experienced by normal human beings. Against this background, the assertion that the study of anger is relevant to theories of emotion is not as trivial as it first appears. In any case, one purpose of the present analysis is to explore the dynamics of emotional behavior, using anger as a paradigm case.

The relevance of the study of anger for research on aggression is also not as self-evident as it might at first appear. Consider, for example, the assertion by Kaufmann (1970) that, when the concept of anger is introduced, "the basic question [of aggression] has been encumbered by another term; but we still do not have insight into the relationships among antecedent events, inner states, and behavior" (p. 43). One can well sympathize with this assertation, especially in view of the fact that not all aggression can be characterized as "angry," and anger does not always involve aggression. But this does not mean that one can ignore anger when studying aggression. Quite the contrary, as a recent experiment by Konečni (1975) illustrates. The goal of the study was to "contrast the arousal-level and cognitive-labeling (anger) interpretations of aggressive behavior." Konečni found that repeated exposure to aversive auditory stimulation—which presumably increased the level of arousal—did not enhance aggressive behavior unless the subjects also were insulted and reported (labeled) themselves as angry. Konečni therefore concluded that aggression is *not* enhanced by stimulation which is not also conducive to the label of anger. (Similar findings have been reported by other investigators; for a comprehensive review of this and related issues, see Rule & Nesdale, 1976.)

In short, "anger" is not just another term, the understanding of which would provide no insight into the relationship among antecedent events, inner states, and aggressive behavior. Rather, the self-attribution of anger is an important determinant of aggression, at least under certain circumstances.

The importance of anger for research on aggression can be illustrated in still another way. As already noted, anger has seldom been the topic of experimental research in its own right, yet there is reason to believe that it has played an important role in many laboratory studies of aggression. In Bandura's (1973) extensive review of aggression research the induction of anger is described many times in connection with individual experiments, as for example when the subject is provoked by insult, the arbitrary administration of electric shock, or the like (see also Baron, 1977). Bandura gives the topic of anger little explicit consideration in the interpretation of experimental results, however, because he defines anger simply as a nondirected state of arousal. But as the above-mentioned study by Konečni (1975) illustrates, subjects in psychological experiments do not have such a sanitized view of anger. And it is the subject's conception—not the experimenter's—that determines experimental outcomes.

Under what conditions do people (including experimental subjects) typically become angry? What is the relationship between anger and aggression? And what functions does anger serve, both for the individual and for society? These are some of the questions which I hope to answer during the course of the present discussion.

In summary, the object of this presentation is twofold: first, to illustrate the dynamics of emotional behavior, using anger as a paradigm case; and, second, to explore the meaning and functional significance of anger, in both its destructive (aggressive) and constructive aspects. The method of analysis will be primarily inductive. I will not start with an operational definition of anger which strips the concept of its everyday nuances. Rather, during the course of analysis, I will attempt to uncover the implicit theory of behavior which gives this concept its meaning. The analysis will be based on three kinds of data: (a) historical teachings on anger; (b) the treatment of anger in courts of law; and (c) the everyday experience of anger. Based on these data, I will offer a formulation for anger which emphasizes its functional significance within Western societies.

Although primarily inductive, the present analysis does not start without presuppositions, especially with regard to the nature of emotion. Therefore, let me begin by summarizing briefly the general view of emotion on which the present analysis is based.

THEORETICAL BACKGROUND

Emotional reactions are familiar to everyone from observation and personal experience; nevertheless, there is surprisingly little agreement among psychologists regarding the nature of emotion, even on a descriptive level. Personally, I find two metaphors helpful in approaching this issue (cf. Averill, 1976; in press). According to one metaphor, emotions are complex syndromes; according to the other, they are transitory social roles. In this section, I will illustrate briefly the relevance of each metaphor to the study of emotion. I will then describe two features which help distinguish the emotions from other psychological phenomena, namely, the process of appraisal and the experience of passivity. Finally, I will distinguish among several kinds of emotions, thereby placing some limits on the scope of the present analysis.

Two Metaphors of Emotion

Emotions as Syndromes. The concept of a syndrome is familiar to most people from its use in medicine. A disease is a syndrome, definable in terms of a specific etiology (when known), symptomatology, and/or prognosis (course of development). But the concept of a syndrome is not limited to medical applications. Broadly speaking, a syndrome is any *set* of responses which covary in a *systematic* fashion.

Let us apply this definition of a syndrome to the emotions. The set of responses which comprises an emotional syndrome may involve physiological changes, expressive reactions, subjective experiences, and instrumental coping responses. Some responses may, of course, be more symptomatic of emotion than are others (e.g., expressive reactions as opposed to instrumental responses), but *no single response, or subset of responses, is essential to an emotional syndrome*. Rather, one instance of a syndrome (e.g., any given episode of anger) may involve one subset of responses while another incident may involve a quite different subset. People who are angry, for example, may strike out at their antagonists, or they may withdraw from the situation; they may experience a high degree of physiological arousal, or they may coolly retaliate; their subjective experiences may vary from exhilaration to depression; and, under some conditions, they might not even realize that they are angry. Of course, individuals must do or experience something, or else we would not consider them to be angry. The important point, however, is that anger—or any other emotion—cannot be identified with any single subset of responses.

The great variability in emotional reactions is due to the fact that the various elements which comprise a syndrome are under multiple control. Physiological reactions, for example, are influenced by homeostatic mechanisms, and hence are not free to vary simply as a function of emotional reactivity. Similarly, overt behavior during emotion is subject to a variety of nonemotional constraints. And yet the elements of a syndrome cannot operate completely independently of one another; rather, they must covary in a systematic fashion. One of the major problems posed by a syndromic conception of emotion is, therefore, the specification of the mechanisms or "rules" which govern the selection of, and covariation among, various response elements. Historically, the mechanisms which bind emotional syndromes together have been viewed primarily in biological terms. The present analysis, by contrast, is based on the assumption that the emotions are primarily social constructions or institutionalized systems of behavior. To explicate this latter point of view, a second metaphor of emotion is helpful.

Emotions as transitory social roles. A social role, like a syndrome, might also be defined as a "set of responses which covary in systematic fashion." However, the connotation of the two metaphors is quite different. Because of its close association with medicine, the syndrome metaphor has biological or physiological overtones. The role metaphor points in a different direction: A role is part of a script or drama; and, in the case of social roles, the script is dictated by society.

Perhaps the best way to illustrate the role metaphor as it applies to emotion is by considering a concrete example, such as falling in love. In all cultures, there are rules regulating courtship and mating. These rules stipulate, among other things, who is eligible to mate, the proper forms of courtship, when and how sexual intercourse can be performed, what obligations the couple has toward one another and toward any children which might be conceived, and so forth. Through observation and experience in concrete situations (e.g., adolescent play), as well as through formal and informal didactic means (e.g., direct instructions, songs, literature, myths) couples learn how and when to apply the rules, so that their behavior follows an appropriate "script." In order to complete the script, of course, each participant must play his or her role according to the relevant subset of rules. In the case of falling in love, which is only one of a variety of scripts relevant to mating, these roles are temporary—the young couple typically "recovers." However, if the love-script follows its conventional course within our own culture, it usually results in a more permanent set of roles, such as that of husband and wife. (For a more detailed discussion of sexual scripts in general, and falling in love in particular, see Gagnon, 1974; Simon, 1974; and Averill & Boothroyd, 1977.)

The role metaphor has several important implications for the study of emotion. For the sake of brevity, I will mention only one. A major theme underlying much contemporary research is that the experience of emotion is basically an interpretation of one's own behavior. Although this theme is most closely associated with attribution theory (cf. Nisbett & Valins, 1971; Schachter, 1971), it is not limited to any theoretical position. From a phenomenological point of view, for example, Schutz (1968) has argued that the experience of behavior as deliberate or emotional is not inherent to the response but is a meaning reflectively bestowed on spontaneous activity; similarly, but from a behaviorist point of view, Bem (1972) has suggested that emotional reactions, like other responses, may be emitted spontaneously or unselfconsciously, only to be interpreted in the light of antecedent and consequent events. And, starting from a psychoanalytic position, Schafer (1976) has suggested that emotions can be viewed as "disclaimed actions," i.e., as responses which the individual performs but for which he disclaims responsibility.

There is, however, a certain ambiguity in the assertion that the experience of emotion represents an interpretation of one's own behavior. The nature of that ambiguity can be illustrated by the role metaphor. When an actor interprets a role, two things must occur. First, he must understand the meaning of the role, or how it fits into the drama as a whole; and, second, he must monitor his own behavior to assure that it conforms to the meaning of the role. Most research on the self-attribution of emotion has focused on the second (self-monitoring) aspect only. For example, experiments have shown how the interpretation of a response as emotional may vary as a function of physiological arousal (Valins, 1970), situational cues (Schachter, 1971), overt behavior (Bem, 1972), expressive reactions (Laird, 1974), and/or response outcomes (Averill, DeWitt, & Zimmer, 1978). The main issue, however, is not *which* cues are used in interpreting a response as emotional, but *why* such an interpretation is made at all. And in order to answer the latter question, we must understand the part that emotions play within the broader social drama.

On mixing metaphors. Although the syndrome metaphor and role metaphor emphasize different aspects of emotional behavior, they are by no means incompatible. This may be illustrated by noting the importance of role expectations on the manifestation of disease syndromes. The symptomatology of most "organic" disorders is influenced by the sick role the patient adopts (Segall, 1976). This is particularly evident in the case of mental illness, where the role expectations of the patient may outweigh organic factors in determining the nature of the syndrome. And when we consider "functional" syndromes, such as hysterical reactions, organic factors are by definition absent or minimal. In the latter case, the syndrome is constituted by the role being played; or, stated differently, the syndrome is a manifestation of the role as interpreted by the patient.

Extending the above line of reasoning to the emotions, it may be said that any given emotional syndrome represents the enactment of a transitory social role. This is not to deny the importance of biological factors in many—if not most—emotional syndromes. It does mean, however, that emotional syndromes are not simply "instincts" or remnants from our phylogenetic past; nor can they be explained in strictly physiological terms. Rather, the emotions are social constructions, and their meaning or significance can be fully understood only by including a social level of analysis.

Differentiating Emotions from Other Psychological Phenomena

Simply saying that emotions are like syndromes and/or social roles does not take us very far; a similar statement could be made with regard to many other psychological phenomena. Some differentiae must therefore be added. These have to do with the appraisal of emotional stimuli and the experience of passivity.

The appraisal of emotional stimuli. Traditionally, emotions have been viewed as noncognitive or physiological ("gut") reactions which are relatively independent of higher mental activity. This traditional view may be contrasted with so-called cognitive theories of emotion. Fundamental to the latter is the proposition that all emotions are based upon an individual's evaluation (appraisal) of the situation (cf. Arnold, 1960; Lazarus, 1966; Mandler, 1975). People cannot be angry, afraid, proud, etc., in the abstract; they must be angry at something, afraid of something, proud of something, and so forth. This means that the emotions cannot be conceptualized simply as a set of responses strung together in a certain manner; rather, they express a judgment about the situations in which individuals find themselves. Indeed, some analysts (e.g., Solomon, 1976) have argued that *emotions are judgments*, and as such they may or may not be accompanied by subjective feelings, physiological changes, etc. But that, I believe, is going too far, or becoming too restrictive, in the direction of cognition.

Although not the *sine qua non* of emotion, cognitive appraisals must be taken into consideration when differentiating emotional from nonemotional responses, and also when differentiating one emotion from another. With regard to differentiating emotions as a group, one example will suffice to illustrate the point. Traditionally, the emotions often have been linked conceptually with such deficit drive states as hunger and thirst. But although the latter are strongly influenced by cognition, their origins are not primarily cognitive. If a person goes without a drink for several hours, he or she is liable to become thirsty. The situation is quite different in the case of emotion. People may become angry because of the way they appraise the situation they are in, but not because they have been deprived of fighting for a certain period.

The way a person appraises the situation also helps to distinguish among emotional responses. This is easily illustrated by the following thought experiment. Try to distinguish among three closely related emotional states, such as anger, envy, and jealousy. Each may involve the same kind of response (e.g., attacking another person). How, then, may they be distinguished? The answer is in terms of the underlying cognitive appraisals. Very briefly, it may be said that anger involves the appraisal of some injustice or wrongdoing. Envy, on the other hand, is based on the appraisal that another is better off than oneself, whether rightfully or wrongfully. Jealousy differs from both anger and envy in that the appraisal necessarily implicates a third person (or object). Thus, a suitor may become envious if he believes a rival to be more handsome than himself, but he may become jealous if he believes that his girlfriend also considers his rival to be more handsome.

Of course, a person may appraise a situation as unjust, and even aggress against (punish) the offender, without being angry. Still another differentiating criterion must therefore be added before we have a working description of emotional syndromes.

Emotions and the experience of passivity. Colloquially speaking, a person "falls" in love, is "paralyzed" by fear, "gripped" by anger, "carried away" with joy, etc. Such expressions imply that emotions are something which happen to us (passions) and not something we do (actions).

The term "passion," which is the traditional name for the emotions, derives from the Latin *pati*, as do such other terms as "passivity" and "patient." Thus it may be said that emotions are experienced passively—not in the sense that emotional reactions lack energy or vigor but rather in the sense that they are interpreted as beyond personal control. (For a more detailed discussion of emotions as passions, see Averill, 1974; Peters, 1962, 1969; Solomon, 1976.)

The interpretation of emotional responses as passions rather than as actions leads to a certain paradox. Being something which happens to a person, a passion is in a sense alien to the self. Yet states such as anger, fear, love, hope, and sorrow are generally considered among the truest reflections of the self. Most theories of emotion have attempted to resolve this paradox by treating the emotions as remnants of our biological heritage, or as responses mediated by the autonomic nervous system and its central representations (e.g., hypothalamic and limbic structures). Since the basic assumption underlying the present analysis is that emotional syndromes are social constructions, one of the major tasks of the discussion which follows must be to account for the experience of passivity within a social rather than a biological framework.

The argument that anger is a biologically and not a socially constituted response is based on two assumptions: (a) that anger is closely related to aggression, and (b) that aggression is a biologically based response. Both assumptions deserve a brief comment, starting with the latter. Although it has become quite popular to view human beings as innately aggressive (e.g., Ardrey, 1976; Storr, 1972), the validity and even the meaning of this assumption has been vigorously debated (cf. Fromm, 1973; Montagu, 1976). Space does not allow—nor does the present argument require—a detailed discussion of this complex issue. A simple statement of my bias will have to suffice. I believe the evidence is pretty convincing that there is a propensity toward aggression in human beings, and that this propensity may be based on one or more biological systems (Moyer, 1976). This does not mean, however, that any particular form of aggression is "prewired" into the human organism, or that there is a basic "drive" toward aggression which somehow must be expressed regardless of the past socialization and present circumstances of the individual. Certainly, there is no evidence to suggest that anger is isomorphic with any kind of aggression observable in infrahuman animals. To equate human anger with animal aggression is analogous to equating a particular human language—such as English or Chinese—with some communication system on the animal level.

This last observation is also pertinent to the assumption that anger is closely related to aggression. Aggression (like human language) may take many forms, of which anger is only one. Conversely, anger may be expressed in a great variety of ways, nonaggressive as well as aggressive. To equate anger only with aggression is to confuse the whole (an entire emotional syndrome) with some of its parts (a particular subset of common—but highly variable and not even necessary—symptoms).

To understand anger, the entire syndrome must be viewed from a sociocultural perspective. This is not to deny the importance of biological factors. However, even a cursory review of the ethnological literature reveals a wide variety of aggressive syndromes that are obviously the product of sociocultural and not biological evolution. Some examples are running amok in Malaysia (Carr & Tan, 1976; Westermyer, 1972), "being a wild pig" in New Guinea (Langness, 1965; Newman, 1964; Salisbury, 1967), *to nu* among the Kaingang indians of Brazil (Henry, 1936); and various kinds of witchcraft (Colson, 1974). Syndromes such as these vary not only in form, but also in function. To say that they reflect some innate propensity toward aggression, while possibly correct, is not very informative.

Kinds of Emotion

The analysis of one emotion, such as anger, need not apply to other emotions, such as fear, say, or grief. In concluding these introductory comments, I therefore want to draw some distinctions among various types of emotion. This will help delimit the scope of our analysis.

As explained above, when a response is interpreted as a passion it is related to the self in a certain way, i.e., it is not regarded as self-initiated or under self-control. A response may be regarded as beyond self-control for any of three reasons, and this fact allows us to distinguish among three kinds of emotion—transcendental, impulsive, and conflictive (Averill, in press).

In the case of transcendental emotions, the cognitive systems which help define the self are disrupted, e.g., through psychological or physical trauma, drugs, sensory deprivation (or overload), meditation, etc. When this occurs, there can be no action, only passion. Or perhaps more accurately, the categories of both activity and passivity are transcended and the individual becomes engulfed in an undifferentiated flood of experience. Anxiety and mystical experiences are good examples of such transcendental emotional states (cf. Lazarus & Averill, 1972; Averill, 1976).

In contrast to transcendental emotional states, impulsive and conflictive emotions presume well-integrated ego boundaries. The class of impulsive emotions includes straightforward desires (or aversions) which have never become fully integrated with the self-as-agent. Examples are grief, joy, hope, sexual desire, and certain common fears. Some impulsive emotions are based largely on biological predispositions; others are the result primarily of sociocultural evolution; while still others are the product of idiosyncratic learning history of the individual. Most commonly recognized impulsive emotions are the product of all three factors, a fact well illustrated by grief and mourning (cf. Averill, 1968, 1979).

While impulsive emotions are analogous to states of strong motivation, conflictive emotions are analogous to hysterical or conversion reactions. In the case of a hysterical reaction, the individual wishes to engage in some behavior which conflicts with personal norms or standards. The result is a compromise or symbolically transformed response, the meaning of which is dissociated from the self. For example, a man suffering from hysterical paralysis may be greatly troubled by his affliction and go to great lengths to seek help. On a deeper level of analysis, however, the paralysis is a product of his own intrapsychic conflicts. It is a way of coping which the person cannot recognize or condone as such, and yet which fulfills a definite function in maintaining psychological equilibrium. By analogy standard conflictive emotions can be viewed as hysterical-like phenomena on a cultural as opposed to an individual level. That is, the source of the conflict, and the "script" for the expression of the response, are to be found within the social system, and are not due to intrapsychic conflicts peculiar to the individual.

As will become evident during the discussion which follows, anger is representative of the class of conflictive emotions. This is not to imply that a typical episode of anger contains no impulsive elements (e.g., straightforward aggressive tendencies) or even transcendental aspects (the extreme frustration that sometimes accompanies anger can, for example, result in a breakdown in cognitive organization—cf. de Rivera, 1976). The distinction between transcendental, impulsive, and conflictive emotions is primarily analytical; any actual emotional syndrome may contain elements from all three classes, albeit in varying degrees.

An example of a conflictive emotion from another culture. Since conflictive emotions involve compromise and/or obfuscating justifications, their meaning is often obscure. Before beginning an analysis of anger, therefore, it might be helpful to illustrate some of the dynamics of this kind of emotion with an example from another culture. The syndrome "being a wild pig," observed among the Gururumba of New Guinea, serves this purpose well.

As Newman (1964) has described it, "being a wild pig" involves a variety of aggressive acts, such as looting, shooting arrows at bystanders, and so forth. Serious harm is seldom done, however. The episode is typically allowed to run its course for several days, after which time the affected individual disappears into the forest where he disposes of his stolen goods (mostly inconsequential objects left for him to take). Generally, he then returns in a normal state, not remembering anything of his previous behavior. If, however, he should return still in the wild state, he is captured and subjected to a ritual which fosters recovery.

The Gururumba believe that "being a wild pig" is caused by the bite of a ghost and that the responses exhibited reflect the behavior of people before the achievement of culture. Not everyone is equally likely to be bitten by a ghost, however. The syndrome is limited primarily to men between the ages of 25 and 35. This is an especially stressful period for the Gururumba male. Not only must he give up the freedom of his youth, but he must also assume considerable economic and social obligations upon which his prestige—and that of his clan—depend. According to Newman, "being a wild pig" is one way a man can call attention to difficulties in meeting such obligations.

Like most New Guinea societies, the Gururumba form a closely knit group which requires a great deal of conformity from its members. This makes it difficult for an individual to engage in actions which run counter to group expectancies and values. Thus, if a man wishes to renounce certain debts, be rid of a wife (marriages are prearranged and often unstable at first), move to another location, etc., he may find himself in considerable conflict. "Being a wild pig" provides a resolution of the conflict; following an episode, members of the society tend to re-evaluate the affected individual, bringing expectancies more into line with reality.[2]

"Being a wild pig" must thus be viewed as a way of declaring psychological bankruptcy. And like financial bankruptcy in our own society, it should be due to circumstances ostensibly beyond a person's control. Such a procedure, it is important to note, works to the advantage of society as well as the individual. By providing an involuntary "out," the group can maintain pressure on individual members to conform voluntarily to social norms. Of course, if a syndrome such as "being a wild pig" is to serve this function, its true meaning and significance must be hidden or symbolically transformed. No longer is it the action of a normal human being; rather, it is the manifestation of primordial, animal-like impulses.

Using a metaphor introduced earlier, it may be said that "being a wild pig" is a transitory social role which certain persons are allowed to enact under particular circumstances. The experience of passivity (being overcome) and acting in a wild fashion are part of the role. In actuality, the behavior of the affected individual is well-attuned to the situation and, on a deeper level of analysis, could almost be described as deliberate.

Not all emotional syndromes are as dramatic as "being a wild pig." This is an unusual form of behavior even among the Gururumba. Nevertheless, some of the major features we have noted with respect to "being a wild pig" are also features of standard conflictive emotions within our own culture; for example, the presence of an underlying conflict; the existence of a transitory social role to help resolve the conflict; the interpretation of behavior as a passion rather than as an action; and even an emphasis on the presumed animal-like qualities of the response.

With the above considerations as background, let me turn now to a detailed analysis of anger. I will begin by examining some historical teachings on the topic. These teachings will help illuminate three main issues: (a) the instigations to and consequences of anger; (b) the reasons for interpreting anger as a passion (beyond self-control) rather than as an action (a deliberate response); and (c) the nature of the conflict underlying anger. In turn, these three issues provide insights into the possible social functions of anger.

---

2. Langness (1965) and Salisbury (1967) have offered somewhat different interpretations for "being a wild pig" and related syndromes. These alternative interpretations do not, however, affect the basic thrust of the present analysis.

HISTORICAL TEACHINGS ON ANGER

It may seem somewhat out of place to refer to historical teachings in a symposium which typically is devoted to the latest research findings. I do so for several reasons. First, examining an issue historically is like examining it cross-culturally; the preconceived notions which sometimes misdirect our thoughts are more readily apparent when viewed through the eyes of a historical figure. Second, one of the primary concerns of this analysis is with the social norms which help constitute the syndrome of anger. These norms are largely ethical in nature; that is, they involve not only what *is*, but also what *ought* to be. The notions of "is" and "ought" are, of course, not independent. What is is often regarded as what ought to be; and what ought to be often becomes what is. But be that as it may, most historical teachings on anger were written explicitly with ethical concerns in mind. They are thus directly relevant to an analysis of social norms. In fact, to the extent that historical teachings have been incorporated into the general cultural matrix, they *are* the norms which help constitute anger.

Space does not allow a broad sampling of historical teachings on anger. But that fortunately is not necessary, for the general themes quickly become redundant. I will therefore focus on three early works: the first by Seneca, who condemned anger without reservation; the second by Lactantius, who believed that anger was given by God for the preservation of humankind; and the third by Aquinas, who attempted to reconcile such conflicting views in a single formulation.

Seneca

The first complete work devoted solely to the topic of anger was written by Seneca (40–50 A.D./1963), perhaps the greatest of the Roman Stoics. Born in the year 4 B.C., Seneca had a distinguished public career, amassing great wealth and becoming confidant to emperors. But it also was a career marked by calamity. In the year 39, he was all but condemned to death by the emperor Caligula; he was supposedly saved by ill health, which it was thought would bring an early death anyway. In the year 41, Seneca was banished to Corsica by the emperor Claudius on a charge of adultery with the latter's niece. He was recalled to Rome in 49 and became tutor to the young

Nero. After Nero's accession in 54, Seneca continued to be one of his chief advisors; but nine years later he was accused of a conspiracy and ordered to commit suicide—which he did with Stoic fortitude.

It would seem that Seneca had ample personal reasons for condemning anger. But his personal views were also informed by his Stoic philosophy. The Stoics considered the emotions to be diseases of the soul, analogous to diseases of the body. They did recognize certain affective states as beneficial, such as cheerfulness, discretion, fear of dishonor, and the like. But these affects were distinguished from the more turbulent passions, which the Stoics regarded as perverted or false judgments. The wise man should strive to be rid of the passions by forming correct judgments.

Of all the passions, Seneca believed that none should be avoided more than anger. Realizing that such an unreserved condemnation of anger would meet with objection, Seneca attempted to answer his critics in advance by posing a number of rhetorical questions. The following examples illustrate the flavor of his argument.

Does not anger spur the warrior to bravery during battle? Sometimes, admits Seneca, but so too does drunkenness, lunacy, and even fear. Moreover, since anger is contrary to reason and self-control, it more often hinders than helps the individual when he is faced with danger. For warriors, "skill is their protection, anger their undoing" (p. 133).

Should not a man become angry in defense of others, e.g., if his father is murdered or his mother outraged before his eyes? No, replies Seneca. "To feel anger on behalf of loved ones is the mark of a weak mind, not of a loyal one. For a man to stand forth as the defender of parents, children, friends, and fellow-citizens, led merely by his sense of duty, acting voluntarily, using judgment, using foresight, moved neither by impulse nor fury—this is noble and becoming" (p. 139).

Should not a good man become angry at evil? Again, the answer is no. The good man should try to rehabilitate the evil-doer, just as the physician tries to heal the sick. And if that is not possible, then the evil-doer must be removed from society. "Mad dogs we knock on the head; the fierce and savage ox we slay; sickly sheep we put to the knife to keep them from infecting the flock; unnatural progeny we destroy; we drown even children who at birth are weakly and abnormal. Yet it is not anger, but reason that separates the harmful from the sound" (p. 145).

But don't we have to be angry in order to punish wrongdoing? When inflicting punishment, Seneca advises that we act in the spirit of the law. Reason, the foundation of law, grants a hearing to both sides, and then seeks to postpone action in order that it may sift out the truth. Anger, by contrast, is precipitate. "Reason wishes the decision that it gives to be just; anger wishes the decision which it has given seem the just decision. Reason considers nothing except the question at issue; anger is moved by trifling things that lie outside the case" (p. 153).

These, and many other similar arguments offered by Seneca, may be summarized in a single statement: Anything that can be done in anger can be done better with reason and deliberation. The problem, then, is how to avoid becoming angry. Seneca's advice in this regard is remarkably similar to that of modern cognitive-behavior therapists (e.g., Novaco, 1975). Specifically, we must first determine the kind of appraisals which lead to anger, and then we must learn to appraise events differently. The two general conditions under which anger is typically aroused are (a) if we think we have received an injury; and (b) if we think we have received it unjustly. With regard to the first condition, Seneca means by "injury" only harmful events which are done *intentionally or through negligence*. Thus, we ordinarily do not become angry at an inanimate object or at dumb animals, for although they can harm us they cannot injure us. The same is true of most accidental events caused by other persons.

With regard to the second condition, an intentional harm (e.g., punishment) may still be deserved; anger occurs when the injury also is appraised as unjust. Seneca offers many examples of how an injury which might superficially be appraised as unjustified can actually be interpreted differently. For example, many offenses may be turned into farce or jest, others can be ignored as unworthy of attention, and still others can be justified on some grounds, or at least forgiven. Seneca maintained that "the really great mind, the mind that has taken true measure of itself, fails to revenge injury only because it fails to perceive it" (p. 267). Of course, there are cases where an injury is unjust, and it would be foolish to appraise it otherwise. In such cases, the initial promptings to anger will be aroused, but a person need not yield to such promptings. Instead, reason should determine what, if any, retribution is called for.

At first, it might seem difficult to argue with Seneca's assessment of anger. His analysis, however, does contain several questionable assumptions. On the one hand, for example, he explicitly restricts the concept of anger to only those states in which the individual completely loses control of his actions. Thus, he states that if "anger suffers any limitation to be imposed upon it, it must be called by some other name—it has ceased to be anger; for I understand this to be unbridled and ungovernable" (pp. 130–131). At the same time, however, Seneca extends the notion of anger to cover all forms of brutality, even those which on the surface appear to be quite deliberate. At one point he even defines anger as "the tumult of a mind proceeding to revenge by choice and determination" (p. 173). How can a response which is "unbridled and ungovernable" proceed by "choice and determination"? As if to anticipate criticism of this apparent self-contradiction, Seneca explicitly draws a distinction between anger and cruelty. The latter, he says, presupposes no prior injury, and it is done for pleasure rather than vengeance. However, there is a close relationship between anger and cruelty, according to Seneca. If too often repeated or indulged in, anger destroys mercy and the bonds which unite human beings. And when this happens, what was originally done out of anger may subsequently be done for pleasure.

In spite of the above distinction, most of the instances of anger cited by Seneca could just as well be classified as deliberate cruelty. For example, he tells the story of Cambyses, King of Persia, who was much addicted to wine. At a banquet one of his closest friends, Praexaspes, urged him to drink more sparingly, declaring that drunkenness is disgraceful of a king. Taking affront, Cambyses drank even more heavily. He then ordered that Praexaspes' son come before him, and in order to demonstrate to the father that the wine did not affect his performance, Cambyses unerringly shot the son through the heart with an arrow.

In light of the above example, and many others cited by Seneca, the assertion that anger is always unbridled and ungovernable would seem to be inconsistent. The inconsistency disappears, however, when one considers Seneca's definition of a passion as "only the transformation of the mind toward the . . . worse" (p. 127). In other words, the distinction between actions and passions was for Seneca more a value judgment than a psychological assessment. Behaviors which Seneca regarded as unwise, immoral, and detrimental were almost automatically treated as passions, for no truly wise man would engage in them. We shall have much more to say about this issue shortly.

Lactantius

Stoicism was the major philosophical school of the Roman empire, but it was ultimately replaced by Christianity. Lactantius was an important figure in this transition. Though little is known of his life, he is often praised as the Christian Cicero because of the eloquence of his style. He was born sometime around 250–260, received a classical pagan education, and became a teacher of Latin rhetoric. He converted to Christianity about the year 300, and most of his major works were written after that date. As a religious philosopher, Lactantius exerted considerable influence during the formative years of Christianity. One indication of his renown even during his own lifetime is the fact that he became a spokesman for the Emperor Constantine and tutor to his son.

By way of background to Lactantius' analysis of anger, it should be noted that anger has often been the subject of praise within the Judeo-Christian religious tradition. Jehovah of the Old Testament is a wrathful God, inflicting severe punishment on those who disobey His will. The 58th Psalm, for example, reads in part:

Break the teeth of these fierce lions, O God.
May they disappear like water draining away;
may they be crushed like weeds on a path.
May they be like snails that dissolve into slime;
may they be like a baby born dead that never sees the light.
Before they know it, they are cut down like weeds;
in his fierce anger God will blow them away while they are still
    living.
The righteous will be glad when they see sinners punished;
they will wade through the blood of the wicked.
People will say, "The righteous are indeed rewarded;
there is indeed a God who judges the world."

(Good News Bible)

In the New Testament, the emphasis on the wrath of God is tempered, and greater stress is placed on the virtues of meekness, forgiveness, and love. But not even Christ is depicted in the Bible as immune from anger; it was in anger that he cast out the merchants from the Temple and overthrew the tables of the moneychangers.

How could such biblical teachings be reconciled with the types of argument against anger raised by Seneca and other philosophers influenced by Stoicism? This question was a source of embarrassment for the early Christian apologists, and it provided the impetus for Lactantius to undertake an analysis of anger.

Referring to the definition of anger offered by Seneca (and also Aristotle), Lactantius (313–314/1965) criticizes the notion that anger is the desire to avenge injury, or to return pain for pain. That, at best, refers to what Lactantius calls "unjust" anger. Such anger does not exist in God, who cannot be injured or suffer pain. Nor should it exist in man, where it can be the source of great evil. It can, however, be found in dumb beasts. "Just" anger, by contrast, is not marked by vengeance. Rather, it is "a movement of a mind arising to the restraint of offenses" (p. 102). This kind of anger "ought not to be taken from man, nor can it be taken from God, because it is both useful and necessary for human affairs" (p. 102). In fact, without the threat of just anger, civilized life would not be possible. Man would no longer consider his fellow man, but would seek his own selfish interests. Disorder and confusion would be prevalent and brute force would rule. Society would be reduced to chaos, as each man sought his own advantage, safe in the knowledge that he would reap no punishment. According to Lactantius, just anger is directed especially at those over whom we have authority. "When we see these offend, we are aroused to improve them. For it is necessary that things which are bad should displease one who is good and just, and he to whom evil is displeasing is moved when he sees it done. Therefore, we rise to punishment, not because we have been injured, but in order that discipline be preserved, morals corrected, and license suppressed" (p. 101).

But what about the objection raised by Seneca that there is no need for anger since—as in a court of law—punishment can be better administered, and offenses corrected, in a reasoned and dispassionate way. Lactantius observes that offenses brought before a judge have been committed elsewhere, and the guilt of the defendant must be proved, not assumed. Moreover, the judge must be moved, not by his own opinions, but by the opinions of the law. The situation is somewhat different when the offense is committed directly before one's own eyes. "There is no one who is able to watch calmly a person guilty of committing an offense. . . . He who is not moved at all, either approves of the faults, which is more shameful and unjust, or he avoids the bother of correcting them, bother which a calm spirit and quiet mind shuns and rejects unless anger has goaded and aroused it" (pp. 102–103).

Lactantius seems to recognize that this argument is not entirely

convincing on strictly logical grounds. For those who remain skeptical he therefore suggests that they consult their own feelings. They
will then recognize that the exercise of authority would be difficult,
if not impossible, without the assistance of anger. In Lactantius'
own words, "where there is not anger, there will not be authority
either" (p. 114).

But even if one were to accept the argument that anger is necessary for the maintenance of social order, Lactantius was still faced
with another kind of dilemma. Anger is a passion. By definition,
only a mutable object can suffer a passion, i.e., have something
"happen" to it. But God is presumably immutable and all-powerful.
It would therefore seem to follow that God is not capable of experiencing anger, except perhaps in a metaphorical sense. According to Lactantius, however, we are not speaking metaphorically
when we attribute anger to God; but neither do we mean that God is
passively affected, or overcome, by anger. "Since God is possessed
of the highest virtue, we ought to understand that He has His wrath
in His power and is not ruled by it, but that He Himself governs the
wrath as He wishes, which is not at all repugnant to a higher being"
(p. 109). The situation is different in the case of man. In contrast to
God, man is a feeble being, who cannot always govern himself while
angry. The fact that anger is sometimes experienced passively is
thus more a commentary on the nature of man than on the nature of
anger.

Shortly, we shall compare the conception of a passion offered by
Lactantius (as due to the animal in human nature) with that offered
by Seneca (as due to a false judgment). But first, I wish to consider
one additional historical treatment of anger.

Aquinas

Starting in the twelfth century, the works of Aristotle were reintroduced into the Latin West, first through Arabic sources and
then in the original Greek. This set the stage for Thomas Aquinas
(1225–1274), whose thought continues to influence psychological as
well as ethical treatments of emotion (cf. Arnold, 1960; O'Brien,
1948).

In his analysis of anger, one of the first issues addressed by
Aquinas is whether this emotion involves the use of reason. He
concludes that it does, in the sense that reason reveals the provoca-

tion that leads to anger. Citing a remark by Aristotle, he observes "that those who are so drunk that they have lost all rational capacity do not become angry; they are angered when they are slightly drunk, capable of reasoning, at least imperfectly" (*Summa Theologiae*, 1a2ae. 46, 4). (This and all subsequent references to the *Summa Theologiae* are cited by part, question, and article number.)

What kind of provocations lead to anger? Some form of injustice, according to Aquinas. Moreover:

> The greatest injustice is to injure someone by deliberate intent or effort, with conscious malice, as we read in [Aristotle's] *Ethics*. That is why we are especially angry at those whom we believe have made a deliberate effort to injure us. If we think that the injury was done out of ignorance or emotion we are not angry with them, or at least not violently so. The injury is not as serious if it is motivated by ignorance or emotion and in a sense calls for mercy and forgiveness. But those who do injury deliberately seem to be guilty of contempt, which is why they anger us so intensely. Aristotle says that *we feel no anger, or comparatively little, with those who themselves acted through anger; apparently, at least, they did not intend to slight us*. (1a2ae. 47, 2)

Since only human beings can perform actions which are just or unjust, deliberate or nondeliberate, it follows that anger can properly be directed only at other persons. Aquinas recognizes that we—as well as "brute" animals—sometimes aggress against inanimate objects that injure us. But such aggression, Aquinas suggests, is an automatic reaction to painful stimulation. It is the animal analogue of anger, being based on "natural instinct," the animal analogue of reason.

Anger also involves "a desire to punish another by way of just revenge" (1a2ae. 47, 1). However, desire alone is not enough; revenge must also be possible. For example, if the person who provoked us is of very high station, then the reaction may be sadness rather than anger. It is important to note that Aquinas is not simply saying that anger will be suppressed when faced with powerful opposition, but that the actual provocation will be appraised in a fashion incompatible with anger.

Assuming that some kind of retribution is possible, under what conditions is anger virtuous (beneficial), and under what conditions is it vicious (harmful)? Anger is virtuous, according to Aquinas, when it conforms to reason, for then its object (revenge) may be considered the application of a temporary good (punishment) to an evil (the provocation). On the other hand, anger is vicious if the desire for revenge does not conform to reason. In particular, it is wrong "to seek to punish one who does not deserve it, or more than he deserves, or not according to the legitimate process of law, or not with the right intention, which is the correction of fault and the maintenance of justice" (2a2ae. 158, 2).

And what about the passionate element in anger? Aquinas argues that a person cannot appraise an act as unjust, and desire to correct the injustice, without also experiencing certain feelings and undergoing physiological changes. This is because the lower "powers" of the soul (the sensory appetites) naturally follow the higher (reason and will). Such being the case, "sensory feelings of anger cannot be wholly absent except the will's motion of anger be withdrawn or weak. As a consequence the lack of high-tempered feeling will be wrong, as also the lack of the will to vindicate according to the judgment of right reason" (2a2ae. 158, 8).

In some instances, however, the bodily changes which normally accompany anger may become so tumultuous as to impede the use of reason. The person is then "overcome" by anger. Such a condition is to be avoided, for it can lead to excessive or inappropriate behavior. But since people cannot be held fully responsible for actions performed when reason is impaired, neither can they be held entirely responsible for acts committed during anger.

Summary and Implications

As mentioned at the outset of this discussion, historical teachings on anger may illuminate three main issues of contemporary concern: (a) the instigations to, and consequences of anger; (b) the reasons for interpreting anger as a passion rather than as an action; and (c) the nature of the conflict underlying anger.

Instigations and consequences. Seneca, Lactantius, and Aquinas all agree that anger involves a judgment that some harm has been committed, and that the harm was either deliberate and unjustified, or else due to negligence. As we shall see in a subsequent section on the everyday experience of anger, these are the conditions under which people usually do become angry. Although this fact is not particularly surprising, it does have several implications worth considering.

For one thing, the above considerations imply that the target of anger will typically be—as Aquinas emphasized—another human being, for predicates such as deliberate, unjustifiable, and negligent apply only to human behavior. This further suggests that inanimate objects, or events such as simple frustration, are not sources of anger except under unusual circumstances. A second implication is that anger is a human emotion, for only persons can make complex judgments regarding such matters as deliberateness, justifiability, and negligence. Animals may, of course, become aggressive in a manner that is reminiscent of human anger (just as animals may communicate in a manner that is reminiscent of human language), but the concept of anger when applied to animals is derivative and metaphorical. Perhaps Seneca expressed this matter best when he observed that "wild beasts and all animals, except man, are not subject to anger; for while it is the foe of reason, it is nevertheless born only where reason dwells" (p. 115).

There are important disagreements as well as agreements in the works of Seneca, Lactantius, and Aquinas. Seneca saw anger primarily as malicious, and of little social value. Lactantius and Aquinas, on the other hand, believed that anger is not only benefi-cial, but also necessary for the maintenance of a just social order. Of course, they—like Seneca—recognized that anger may be abused, as when it is engaged in for personal gain or for the sheer pleasure of revenge. In such cases, anger is itself subject to punishment and condemnation. To this last point, however, Aquinas added an im-portant proviso: If a person commits an offense out of anger, even though the anger may have been excessive or unjustified, he will be judged less harshly than if the offense were committed deliberately.

Offenses committed in anger are treated more leniently than similar offenses committed deliberately because anger is a passion, and passions are supposedly beyond a person's control. But in what sense is anger a passion?

Reasons for interpreting anger as a passion. If anger has a positive social function, as Lactantius and Aquinas maintained, then it is somewhat paradoxical that anger should be interpreted as a pas-sion. How can justice be maintained by behavior which is ostensibly beyond personal control? Seneca resolved this paradox by denying that anger has any value. Specifically, he arbitrarily restricted the concept of anger to cases where the retribution is "irrational," e.g., inappropriate or excessive. But this only begs the question. In the first place, such a restriction does not conform to ordinary usage;

and, in the second place, it does not even conform to Seneca's own usage. Recall the example of Cambyses, who shot his critic's son through the heart. If Cambyses' purpose was to demonstrate the steadiness of his hand, while at the same time intimidating his critic, then his response was quite rational. The issue here is not one of rationality but of value. What Seneca considered to be wrong or immoral he also regarded as a "foe of reason," and hence a passion rather than an action.

Lactantius solved the dilemma of classifying anger as a passion in a somewhat different fashion. For theological reasons, he could not simply restrict the concept of anger as did Seneca. He therefore distinguished between two kinds of anger, just and unjust. Just anger is not only reasonable, but even God-like. Unjust anger, by contrast, is an attribute of animals, and of the animal in man. But this is also a value judgment. Uncontrollable anger may be "brutish," "bestial," and "inhumane"; it is not, however, nonhuman.

Aquinas' explanation for the passionate element in anger was in some respects similar to that of Lactantius. That is, anger is a passion because it involves the so-called sensory appetite, which is common to animals and humans. Aquinas did not, however, create a sharp gulf between human and animal nature, and hence between two kinds of anger. Rather, all anger involves a certain amount of physiological arousal. It is only when such arousal becomes too extreme that anger obscures reason and hence becomes uncontrollable. But this solution is not satisfactory either. For one thing, anger can be excessive and unreasonable without involving a great deal of physiological arousal. (Even mild anger is inordinate in the absence of an adequate provocation; and intense anger may sometimes proceed with relatively little physiological involvement, as when one humiliates an opponent with a sarcastic remark, or passively retaliates by withdrawing affection.) For another thing, physiological arousal (as induced, say, by exercise) does not necessarily becloud reason. These considerations suggest that the "irrational" or passionate element of anger lies in the appraisal process (as Seneca maintained), and not in our animal (Lactantius) or physiological (Aquinas) make-up. But we already have noted the inadequacies of the former (Seneca's) position.

In attempting to explain why anger is interpreted as a passion rather than as an action, we seem to be caught in a vicious cycle. In order to break out of this cycle, we must cease to focus on individual dynamics (whether cognitive or physiological) and focus instead on anger as a social phenomenon. As a working hypothesis, I would like to propose that anger is interpreted as a passion so that an individual need not be held responsible for behavior (interpersonal aggression) which is generally condemned by society, but which is also encouraged under certain circumstances.

This working hypothesis turns around the traditional assumption that anger is inherently a passion, i.e., that it is the passionate element in anger that frees the individual from responsibility. Actually, we are dealing here with an issue of which came first, the chicken (the attribution of responsibility) or the egg (the passionate element in anger). By emphasizing the priority of the chicken, I do not wish to minimize the importance of the egg. Rather, I simply wish to focus attention on certain aspects of anger that too often have been ignored.

The nature of the conflict in anger. The above hypothesis implies that anger is the product of conflicting social norms. The contrasting views of Seneca and Lactantius on the value of anger may be used to illustrate the nature of this conflict. But first, it might be helpful to reiterate and further clarify the general distinction between conflictive and impulsive emotions, using for comparison a somewhat similar distinction made by Aquinas.

Aquinas divided the emotions into two broad categories—the concupiscible and the irascible. The concupiscible emotions (love, desire, joy, hate, aversion, and sorrow) represent unobstructed tendencies toward or away from objects appraised as good or bad. In the case of the irascible emotions, direct approach or avoidance is blocked. The dominant emotion which results is anger (*ira*), from whence the name of the class is derived. But other emotions may also ensue (namely, hope, despair, courage, or fear), depending upon the circumstances.

What I have called impulsive emotions are basically the same as the concupiscible emotions as defined by Aquinas, i.e., both represent straightforward tendencies toward or away from some object. The same is not true, however, in the case of the irascible and conflictive emotions. In a sense, the rationale behind the irascible emotions represents a medieval version of the frustration-aggression hypothesis. If an impulse toward or away from some goal is frustrated, people may try to overcome the obstacle by aggression, or they may give up in despair, etc. Frustration, however, is a much broader concept than is conflict. People need not experience conflict simply because they fight to overcome an obstacle, or give up in despair. Conflict arises only if a person believes that in a given situation aggression is wrong or dangerous, say, or that despair is contemptible. In other words, conflict involves incompatible response tendencies, and not simply the frustration of goal-directed activity.

The difference between frustration and conflict can be expressed somewhat differently. Frustration may give rise to new impulses (e.g., toward aggression); conflict, however, involves a transformation of behavior due to incompatible impulses. Sometimes, the response to conflict may resemble one of the original impulses, i.e., it may appear that no transformation has occurred. But the resolution of a conflict always requires some compromise, or at least some justification as to why one impulse is acceded to while the other is not. In this respect, conflictive emotions are more like defense mechanisms in a Freudian sense than they are like irascible emotions in a Thomistic sense.

In the case of anger, the incompatible impulses reflect conflicting social norms. Consider again the condemnation of anger by Seneca, and the counter-arguments by Lactantius. Seneca assumed that people are basically good, that reason is humankind's highest faculty, and that punishment should be administered only after a careful weighing of evidence. Lactantius, on the other hand, assumed that people are prone to evil (as the result of original sin), that human reason is limited in scope, and that swift punishment is often necessary for the maintenance of a just social order. Of course, there are countervailing themes in each author, for neither completely rejected the assumptions of the other. Thus, Seneca had no compunction about recommending the execution of criminals and even the drowning of malformed infants—provided such acts of homicide were done in accordance with reason and for the long-term benefit of society. And for his part, Lactantius embraced the Christian teachings of forgiveness, mercy, and love, not to mention a belief in the ultimate sanctity of human life.

In short, the disagreement between Seneca and Lactantius reflects two sets of norms, both of which are deeply ingrained within Western intellectual and moral traditions. One set condemns deliberate acts of violence as inhumane, while the other set calls for the forceful retribution of injustice. A number of social institutions have evolved which help resolve this conflict. Courts of law are a primary example. Here transgressors may be punished, even executed, in the name of society. This is the kind of institution favored by Seneca.

However, most transgressions are too minor to be adjudicated in courts of law, while others may be of such a nature as to require immediate action. Lactantius offered his defense of anger in recognition of these latter types of situations.

Substituting Seneca's *imitatio iudicii* for Lactantius' *imitatio Dei*, the following conclusion is suggested: Anger is an institutionalized means of social control; it is a personalized judiciary, so to speak, that operates in situations where more formal legal proceedings are either not warranted or are impractical. This conclusion also helps to clarify the proposal made earlier, namely, that anger is interpreted as a passion so that individuals need not be held responsible for their behavior. By interpreting anger as a passion, and hence as beyond personal control, the norms encouraging retribution (an eye for an eye) can be upheld on a personal level without violating the norms which prohibit *deliberate* acts of violence.

ANGER AND THE LAW

Although metaphorical, the above reference to a personalized judiciary implies that anger is in some respects complementary to the legal system. The purpose of the present section is to explore that implication further. We will focus on instances where anger is expressed so violently as to result in the death of another person. The legal treatment of such "crimes of passion," and of the related plea of temporary insanity, tells us much about the social dynamics involved in the interpretation of a response as anger. But first, let us review briefly the law of homicide and its relationship to general cultural norms.

The Law of Homicide

When committed by a private citizen not in the performance of any official duty, a killing may be placed in one of four legal categories: justifiable homicide (e.g., self-defense), homicide due to insanity, manslaughter, and murder. The first two categories represent noncriminal offenses, while the latter two imply some culpability on the part of the killer. Murder and manslaughter are often further divided into subcategories. First-degree murder is a killing committed with "malice aforethought," a rather misleading legal phrase which includes not only premeditation, but also such things as a killing committed during the perpetration of another felony. Second-degree murder is a vaguely defined category which takes into account the presence of mitigating circumstances, such as provocation or the absence of deliberation. Manslaughter also may be divided into two categories, voluntary and involuntary. Voluntary manslaughter is the typical "crime of passion," as will be discussed more fully below. Involuntary manslaughter includes those homicides committed by accident or misfortune, but where there is culpable negligence on the part of the slayer. (The number and names of these categories may differ somewhat from one jurisdiction to another, but the present list is representative and will be used throughout this discussion for the sake of consistency.)

A study by Wolfgang (1958) provides some data on the incidence of the various forms of homicide. He studied all cases of potentially criminal homicides recorded in the city of Philadelphia during the five-year period from 1948 to 1952. There were 588 such cases, approximately 90% of which resulted in the arrest of one or more suspects. Of the 607 suspects arrested, 64% (387) were convicted and sentenced by a court of record, 20% were acquitted, and the remaining 16% were disposed of in some other fashion (e.g., dismissal due to lack of evidence, a finding of insanity, the natural death of the defendant). Considering only the 387 suspects who were convicted, the distribution by degree of criminal homicide was as follows: first-degree murder, 20%; second-degree murder, 29%; voluntary manslaughter, 36%; and involuntary manslaughter, 15%.

After reviewing similar statistics from various sources, Wolfgang concludes that "most reported distributions of convicted offenders according to degree of homicide is more like than unlike the distribution in Philadelphia" (p. 310). He also cautions, however, that the variability is great from one jurisdiction to another, and from one time to another.

This last point can be illustrated by a recent study of homicide in Houston. Lundsgaarde (1977) reviewed 268 cases of potentially criminal homicide on file for the year 1969. Approximately 90% of these cases were "solved" with the apprehension of 239 suspects. However, of those apprehended, 106 (44%) were acquitted (i.e., no charges were brought, the charges were subsequently dismissed, or the suspect was found not guilty by a jury). In most instances, the reason for the acquittal was that the homicide was ultimately deemed justifiable. In commenting on such a high acquittal rate, Lundsgaarde notes that the Texas penal code still embodies some of the norms of the "Old West." For example, in contrast to the situation in many other states, a Texan who is attacked need not retreat in order to avoid the necessity of killing his or her assailant. Norms such as this, together with the ready availability of weapons, help account for many "justifiable" homicides.

In addition to those acquitted, 102 suspects (43% of the total) were convicted of some crime, while 31 (13%) of the cases were disposed of in some other fashion. Lundsgaarde does not indicate the proportion of suspects convicted of various degrees of criminal homicide. However, he does report the sentences received. Of the 102 persons convicted, 23 received probation, 19 received jail sentences of four years or less, 55 were sentenced to jail for five years or more, and 5 were sentenced to death. In view of the probation and light sentences (four years or less) received by approximately 40% of the convicted suspects, it appears that many of the homicides were considered to be due either to negligence or passion. A light sentence, probation, or outright acquittal was especially likely if the killing occurred during the course of an argument between peers (e.g., marriage partners, lovers, friends, or acquaintances).

According to Lundsgaarde, patterns of homicide indicate the involvement of "at least two kinds of sanctions: (1) the organized negative sanctions of criminal law and the public sentiment prohibiting and forbidding the taking of human life; (2) the diffuse positive sanctions that approve of individual aggression and violence, including killing, given specific situations and acceptable motivational circumstances" (p. 17). He also notes that the Texas laws regarding excusable homicide "practically eliminate the need for police, judges, and any form of third party authority as long as one can convincingly establish that the killing was a response to a threat against person or property" (p. 164).

The two kinds of sanctions mentioned by Lundsgaarde correspond to the conflicting norms discussed earlier in connection with historical teachings on anger. And although Lundsgaarde does not refer to anger per se, his descriptions of individual cases make it clear that anger was a significant factor in many of the Houston homicides. Therefore, let us turn to a more specific consideration of the relationship between anger and the law.

Crimes of Passion

Lundsgaarde emphasizes the complementarity between certain kinds of homicide and the legal system. That is, homicides which uphold community standards, and which do not pose a threat to the public order, are often excused, if not encouraged. However, one function of the law is to supplant, or make unnecessary, personal violence. The individual who "takes the law into his own hands" may thus find himself in legal jeopardy; and the most likely charge in such cases is voluntary manslaughter, i.e., a crime of passion.

In the study of Philadelphia killers by Wolfgang, it will be recalled that 36% of the convictions were for voluntary manslaughter. This suggests that the crime of passion is the most common form of criminal homicide—at least in jurisdictions where few willful (nonaccidental) homicides are considered justifiable. The gist of the legal conception of a crime of passion is contained in the following definition:

"Passion," as used in a charge defining manslaughter as voluntary homicide committed under the immediate influence of a sudden passion arising from an adequate cause, means any of the emotions of the mind known as "anger," "rage," "sudden resentment," or "terror," rendering the mind incapable of cool reflection (*Words and Phrases*, 1957, Vol. 31A, p. 94).

Actually, terror is seldom used as a defense for voluntary manslaughter. If a person is so terrorized as to kill another, and the terror is justified, then he or she might as well plead self-defense. For the most part, then, the typical crime of passion is a homicide committed in anger, rage, or sudden resentment.

But how is it determined whether or not the defendant was in a state of passion at the time of a killing? As will become evident below, the answer to this question bears directly on the hypothesis proposed earlier; namely, that a response is interpreted as a passion so that the person need not be held (fully) responsible for his or her behavior, rather than vice versa.

Criteria for interpreting a response as a passion. In order for a homicide to be considered a crime of passion, four criteria must be met: (1) the provocation must have been adequate; (2) the response must have been in the heat of passion; (3) there must not have been sufficient time for the passion to cool before the killing; and (4) the provocation, the passion, and the killing must have been causally linked. Let us consider each of these briefly.

(1) The most important criterion for the attribution of emotion in courts of law is the adequacy of provocation. This criterion traditionally has been satisfied by the so-called "reasonable-man" test. That is, would such a provocation arouse passion in an ordinary person under similar circumstances? This test is considered "objective" because it refers to a hypothetical norm and not to the psychological state of the individual. If the defendant does not happen to be reasonable (e.g., because of insanity), then his or her defense must be based on grounds other than passion.

Until recently, the "reasonable man" (according to Anglo-American common law) could be provoked to homicide only by a small range of circumstances (e.g., a man's catching his wife in the act of adultery, or a violent assault upon one's person). However, the Model Penal Code (1962/1974) would grant the "reasonable man" considerable leeway in how he or she appraises events. Specifically, it states that criminal homicide constitutes manslaughter when:

> A homicide which would otherwise be murder is committed under the influence of extreme mental or emotional disturbance for which there is reasonable explanation or excuse. The reasonableness of such explanation or excuse shall be determined from the viewpoint of a person in the actor's situation under the circumstances as he believes them to be. (Article 210.3)

The older statutes, by specifying in advance what constitutes adequate provocation, tended to restrict the kind of evidence which could be presented to the jury. However, these restrictions were often circumvented in one way or another. The Model Penal Code simply recognizes what has been the case, namely, that an adequate provocation is what the members of the community—represented by the jury—consider it to be.

Of course, few people are ever provoked to homicide. Some individuals may not even become angry at situations which are considered highly provocative by a "reasonable" person. Conversely, other individuals may become extremely angry—even to the point of homicide—at relatively minor provocations. For certain purposes, therefore, it is necessary to distinguish between a socially adequate and a psychologically effective provocation. The former is dependent upon social norms and customs as interpreted (in court proceedings) by the jury; the latter is dependent upon the individual's own appraisal of the situation, and is a function of his or her particular psychological make-up. For the well-socialized individual, however, there is a close correspondence between socially adequate and psychologically effective provocations to anger. And when such a correspondence is lacking—in everyday affairs, as well as in courts of law—the claim of anger may be disallowed or else punished as unjustified.

(2) For murder to be mitigated to manslaughter, not only must the provocation be adequate, but the homicide must also have been committed in the "heat of passion." This latter criterion refers to the psychological state of the defendant at the time of the killing, and not to some hypothetical "reasonable man." But how is the jury to determine whether a person is in a state of passion? One basis, of course, is the nature of the response. A response which is exceptionally cruel, "cold-blooded," or idiosyncratic might be taken to indicate that more is involved (e.g., malice aforethought) than simple anger. It is important to note, however, that a great deal of physiological arousal need not be manifested, as in violent rage, in order for a response to be interpreted as passionate. Rather, a passion "is principally a state of mind in which there is an absence of design to cause death and an absence of a deliberate implementation of such a design" (*People v. Lewis*, 1953). An "absence of design" implies irrationality, and an "absence of deliberate implementation" implies spontaneity. These, then, are the standards by which the "heat of passion" is judged.

(3) The third criterion for a homicide to be classified as a crime of passion is insufficient cooling time. Like adequacy of provocation, insufficient cooling time is judged by the "reasonable-man" test. That is, the decision is based on what a reasonable person would or should do under similar circumstances, as well as on what the defendant actually did do. Not surprisingly, the more extreme the provocation, the longer the delay that is considered reasonable. However, time alone is not the critical factor. Rather, it is what the person does during the period between the provocation and the slaying. If he or she engages in deliberate, well-planned acts (especially if they are not related to the provocation, such as making a business call), then these acts may be taken as a sign that the passion has cooled, no matter how short the time (Perkins, 1946). On the other hand, notions such as suppressed anger may be used to bridge

the gap between provocation and act, even over extended periods of time (*Drye v. State*, 1944).

(4) The final requirement for a crime of passion is that there be a causal link between the provocation, the passion, and the crime. For example, there can be no mitigation if the intent to kill was formed before the provocation, or if the wrath was vented on some innocent bystander. This requirement appears simple enough, although in actual practice it may be very difficult to apply. Most homicides involve relatives, friends or acquaintances, and often are preceded by a long history of antagonism and resentment (cf. Lundsgaarde, 1977; Wolfgang, 1958). In such situations, there may be a long-standing predisposition to kill, which only requires some provocation to be activated. Sometimes, the individual who becomes angry may actually have goaded his or her victim into making the final provocation, in which case the passion may be considered partly intentional, and hence not legitimate.

Let us now consider briefly how the above four criteria bear upon the hypothesis presented earlier, namely, that a response is interpreted as a passion so that people need not be held (fully) responsible for their behavior, rather than vice versa. The first thing to note in this connection is the fact that two of the criteria (adequacy of provocation and insufficient cooling time) do not refer to the psychological state of the individual defendant at the time of the killing, but to what a supposedly "reasonable" person would do under similar circumstances. This means that the attribution of anger in courts of law is more a matter of social norms and customs than it is of individual psychology. In fact, only one of the four criteria (in the heat of passion) specifically refers to the psychological state of the individual. But even here, social custom would seem to be the determining factor in making an emotional attribution. In fact, until recently psychiatric testimony regarding the individual's state of mind at the time of a killing was not even allowed in most courts (although the defendant's own testimony was considered relevant). This tradition has been overturned by the Pennsylvania Supreme Court (*Commonwealth v. McCusker*, 1972). Writing the majority opinion, Justice Roberts noted that psychiatry has made "tremendous advancements" during the past several decades, and hence ruled that psychiatric testimony is competent and admissible under certain circumstances. In a dissenting opinion, however, Justice Eagen expressed the fear that "from now on in Pennsylvania every pet theory advanced by a psychiatrist will have probative value in determining criminal responsibility." Justice Eagen evidently would prefer to rely on the "practical wisdom" of the jury in determining whether or not a homicide was committed in the heat of passion. "Practical wisdom" is, of course, little more than a euphemism for social custom.

Justice Eagen's fears are not entirely without foundation, in view of the lack of agreement among psychiatrists and psychologists regarding the nature of emotion. But whatever one's theoretical (and/or political) orientation, there can be little disagreement with the contention that the primary function of the courts is the assignment of responsibility, and that the attribution of emotion is secondary to that function. The fourth criterion for a crime of passion (that there be a causal link between the provocation, passion, and homicide) may be considered in this light. If the causal link is deemed absent, then the individual may be held responsible for his behavior regardless of his mental state at the time of the killing. As applied to certain cases (e.g., where the killer prods the victim into making the "adequate" provocation), this criterion reflects the practical wisdom that what is a passion on one level of analysis may still be considered a deliberate or purposeful act on another level.

The attribution of anger in courts of law is not a trivial matter, for if the claim of passion is accepted as legitimate, then the defendant will be treated with leniency (a short prison term, perhaps, as opposed to life in prison or the death sentence). This brings us back to our original question: Are some homicides treated leniently because they are interpreted as due to passion? Or are some homicides interpreted as due to passion so that they may be treated leniently? Recognizing that there is no unequivocal answer to either question, the bulk of the evidence reviewed thus far strongly suggests an affirmative answer to the second. To recapitulate briefly, the interpretation of a response as a passion is not based on the psychological state of the individual at the time of the killing. Rather, it is based on the presumed state of mind of a hypothetical "reasonable man" when similarly provoked. To meet this test, the defendant must be seen as upholding certain community standards. Of course, a reasonable person is not supposed to kill. Therefore, a kind of subterfuge is necessary: The "reasonable man" is judged temporarily unreasonable (in a state of passion) and hence not entirely responsible for his or her behavior.

Temporary Insanity

Additional light can be shed on the above process by considering the legal treatment of temporary insanity. A plea of temporary insanity is much broader than a plea of anger; however, the concepts of anger and insanity have much in common. Colloquially speaking, for example, to be "mad" may mean to be angry or to be insane. This association of anger with insanity is also quite ancient. Nearly two thousand years ago, Seneca observed that "certain wise men have claimed that anger [iram] is temporary madness [insaniam]" (p. 107). This way of speaking also has been incorporated into Anglo-American law, in which anger is defined as a "short madness, and when provoked by a reasonable cause excuses from the punishment of murder" (Words and Phrases, 1953, Vol. 3, p. 658).

There are, of course, important differences between anger and temporary insanity from a legal point of view. In theory, for example, a crime of passion is to be judged by the standards of the reasonable-man test, which does not take into account the idiosyncrasies of the individual defendant. In contrast, the plea of temporary insanity focuses explicitly on the mental state of the defendant and asks whether the slaying was the product, not of adequate provocation, but of mental disease. Moreover, a plea of passion can only mitigate a homicide from murder to manslaughter; the defendant is still subject to punishment if found guilty. Insanity, on the other hand, is a complete defense, exonerating the defendant from all criminal liability; and if the insanity was only temporary, then release may be immediate.

In spite of the above differences, the legal distinction between passion and temporary insanity is often vague and indistinct. For one thing, the hypothetical reasonable person, by whose standards the crime of passion is judged, often becomes endowed with the characteristics of the specific defendant at trial, thus making this standard almost indistinguishable from the more "subjective" (individualized) standard used in the insanity defense (Goldstein, 1967). For another thing, the law is intentionally vague with regard to what constitutes a "mental illness" (Hardisty, 1973). Hence, a homicide which is prosecuted as a crime of passion in one court may be treated as temporary insanity in another.

For our present purposes, the legal criteria for identifying temporary insanity are less important than the way this plea is sometimes used in homicide cases. One famous example is that of

Remus, who killed his wife during the course of divorce proceedings (*State v. Remus*, 1927). No immediate provocation was involved, and hence it could not be claimed that this was a crime of passion. By setting up a defense of insanity, however, Remus was able to introduce evidence of his wife's infidelity and of a plan by her and another man to deprive him of his property. Expert witnesses for the prosecution unanimously declared Remus to be sane, but the jury found him not guilty by reason of insanity. In commenting on this case, Guttmacher and Weihofen (1952) have observed:

> Cases such as this must be accepted as a normal concomitant of the jury system. Indeed they can be said to be the justification of the jury system. No one would claim that a jury is more competent than the judge to pass upon the literal correctness or truth of the testimony presented; the only justification for getting a jury's reaction is that we want a community consensus. Taking the verdict of the jury allows the rule of law to be tempered by the public sense of justice in hard cases. This has in fact nothing to do with the defense of insanity as such. It is merely the case of a jury unwilling to apply the law as written, and using any excuse that happens to be at hand. (pp. 399–400)

Szasz (1968) has stated the matter even more dramatically. Referring to the novel *Anatomy of a Murder*, in which a husband is acquitted of the murder of his wife's lover on the grounds of temporary insanity, Szasz writes that:

> While this sort of crime has, in my opinion, nothing to do with insanity, the jury's refusal to convict the defendant makes sense. Such a trial is a kind of modern morality play. Its message is to uphold the sanctity of marriage. The husband who kills his wife's lover is like the soldier who protects the fatherland from the enemy. If society wishes to promote this kind of morality, it will sanction this type of murder. The game is reasonable, although not necessarily one in which we might wish to participate. (p. 139)

The simile of a soldier protecting the fatherland highlights the institutionalized nature of this kind of homicide. In the case of the soldier, however, there is no question of his breaking the law when he kills the enemy. In the case of the husband who kills his wife or her lover, the situation is quite different. He does need an excuse, one which will leave intact the general proscription against the deliberate and malicious killing of another (murder). Temporary insanity provides such an excuse, as does the plea of passion.

Summary and Implications

In this section, evidence has been presented which suggests that anger can be viewed as an informal means of social control complementary in some respects to the legal system. To place this suggestion in broader perspective, it might be noted that the widespread use of police and other law enforcement agencies is of relatively recent origin, at least as far as the great masses of people are concerned. For most of Western history, it has been up to the individual to assure that justice is done in the conduct of daily affairs. Even today, only about half of the criminal offenses that are committed are actually reported to the police by the victims. And it goes without saying that criminal offenses are numerically small in comparison to the vast number of irritations and provocations encountered in everyday interpersonal relations. Some informal means of social control, such as anger, is still necessary and useful.

Even when anger is expressed so violently as to result in homicide, the killing may be considered justifiable in situations where law enforcement is weak and/or the provocation is particularly great. More typically, however, homicide is treated as a criminal offense. But if the provocation is considered "adequate," a defendant may still plead that the killing was done in a state of passion (or, perhaps, temporary insanity); and if the plea is accepted, the defendant will be treated with leniency.

The defendant who enters a plea of passion, or temporary insanity, is in effect asking the jury to judge his or her behavior, not by the set of norms which prohibit the deliberate killing of another, but by the set of norms (often called the "unwritten law") which encourages the protection of home and honor. There is a problem, however. The norms against homicide do not allow many exceptions, except as noted above. The act itself must therefore be redefined. No longer is it the act of a normal human being; rather, it is the result of an irrational, animal-like impulse (anger) or the symptom of a disease (temporary insanity).

The process of redefining or legitimizing a response as anger involves a third set of norms (i.e., in addition to those which prohibit violence, on the one hand, and those which call for retribution, on the other). These "norms of anger" specify the conditions under which, and the manner in which, anger may be expressed. In courts of law, the norms of anger are embodied in the "reasonable-man" test. That is, would an ordinary person become provoked under similar circumstances and to a similar degree? If the reasonable-man test is not met, the claim of passion may be disallowed and the person punished accordingly.

In the case of temporary insanity, the norms that help legitimize the response are more vague and imprecise (e.g., there are no historical teachings on how and when to become insane, as there are in the case of anger). But this vagueness and imprecision is somewhat illusory. Since the concept of mental illness has no well-defined meaning, testifying psychiatrists and psychologists often define temporary insanity by reference to social norms rather than medical guidelines. Yet the medical connotation of mental "illness" places a scientific disguise on a social occurrence (cf. Hardisty, 1973). Such an obfuscation is, of course, necessary if the insanity defense is to provide an excuse for homicide.[3] But there is a certain danger in this process. Given appropriate social encouragement and rationale, people may come to experience their own behavior as beyond control, and to act in a manner befitting the cultural stereotype of a temporarily insane person. I would suggest that something of this sort has occurred in the case of anger, albeit on an informal level.

The preceding argument may be summarized by the statement that anger is a socially constituted form of temporary insanity. This statement obviously involves some hyperbole. At best, it applies only to extreme instances of anger, such as those which result in crimes of passion. There are not, however, two fundamentally different kinds of anger, one intense and the other mild; hence many of the same considerations that apply to crimes of passion may also apply to the everyday experience of anger. That is the issue we shall examine next.

---

3. I do not wish to imply that temporary insanity is always—or even typically—used *merely* as an excuse for homicide. Under conditions of extreme stress, or due to neurological disorder (e.g., brain tumor or lesion), a person may commit homicide while temporarily insane in a literal sense (psychologically speaking).

THE EVERYDAY EXPERIENCE OF ANGER

In the preceding section, the norms of anger were defined with reference to the "reasonable man." But, of course, a reasonable person does not commit homicide. Therefore, if we are to examine the norms of anger in any detail, we should consider how reasonable people behave in more reasonable settings. At whom, and for what reasons, do people typically become angry? How is anger customarily expressed? And what are the actual and expected consequences of anger? In the present section, I will report some results of a recent survey designed to answer questions such as these.[4]

Participants in the survey were recruited from the city of Greenfield, Massachusetts, and surrounding communities. Greenfield itself has a population of 18,000 and is located 20 miles north of the University of Massachusetts, Amherst. Incorporated in 1753, it is the county seat and a center for agriculture and light industry (tap and dies, cutlery, hand tools, and the like). More than most communities, it is a microcosm of New England.

Participants were recruited in the following manner. Names were selected randomly from the Greenfield area telephone directory, and letters were sent explaining the project. After allowing time for receipt of the letters, each potential subject was contacted by phone. If he or she agreed to participate, a questionnaire was sent together with a $4.00 check as remuneration.

A goal was set to obtain 80 subjects (40 men and 40 women) who were: (a) native-born Americans, (b) between the ages of 21 and 60; and (c) married (although widowed and divorced subjects also were included). One hundred and fifty-six persons (78 men and 78 women) who met these criteria were contacted by letter and telephone. Of these, 44 (28%) refused to participate, while another 23 (15%) agreed to participate but either returned the questionnaire unanswered, or did not return it at all. Five persons (3%) returned questionnaires which were improperly filled out. Of the remaining 84 subjects (54% of those eligible) who returned usable questionnaires, 40 were men and 44 women. Four of the women were eliminated at random in order to equalize the groups at the desired number (40 subjects each).

4. I wish to thank Patricia Jeney for her invaluable assistance with the construction of the questionnaire used in this survey and with the collection of the data; thanks are also due Doug Frost for his assistance with the analysis of the results.

The Questionnaire

On the written questionnaire, subjects were asked to describe the most intense episode of anger experienced during the preceding week (or, if the person did not become angry during the week, then the most recent experience of anger). The topics covered by the questionnaire included, among other things, the object or target of the anger; the nature of the instigation; the impulses felt and responses actually made; the "motives" for becoming angry, i.e., what the subject thought he or she might accomplish; the reactions of the instigator to the subject's anger; and the reactions of the subject to his or her own anger.

The questionnaire consisted of a mixture of objective (ratings scales, multiple-choice items, etc.) and open-ended questions. The objective questions were based on extensive pilot testing, so that they included the most common responses made by people as well as other alternatives which were logically possible. These objective questions were grouped according to topic (e.g., the nature of the instigation, responses, motives, etc.). After each group of objective items, subjects were asked to explain in an open-ended fashion the reasons for their responses.

Although the questionnaire was quite lengthy (approximately 90 items, depending upon how the various response options are counted), it was not difficult to complete. (The average time of completion was between one-half and one hour.) Moreover, the majority of subjects reported that they found the questionnaire interesting and helpful in understanding their anger. Many even expressed appreciation for the opportunity to describe their feelings. This perhaps accounts for the 54% rate of return, which is remarkably high for a questionnaire of this complexity (cf. Linsky, 1975).

The Sample

The ages of subjects ranged from 21 to 60 years, with a mean of 40. Throughout this age-range, the distribution of subjects was approximately rectangular. Most of the subjects (94%) were currently married; one man and two women were divorced, and one man and one woman were widowed. Most (75%) of the men and women also had children living at home.

As far as educational background is concerned, 11% of the sample never completed high school, 46% were high-school graduates, 20% had some training beyond high school, 11% were college graduates, and 11% had some training beyond college. Nearly half the men (47%) could be classified as blue-collar workers (mechanics, carpenters, police and firemen, and factory workers). White-collar workers (salesmen, clerical workers, etc.) comprised 30% of the male sample, and 18% could be classified as professional. (The remaining 5% could not be classified.) The majority (70%) of the women in the sample also held a job outside the home (i.e., only 30% described their occupation as housewife). Of the 28 working women, 7 were employed in teaching, 6 in nursing and health-related professions, and the remainder in a variety of different positions.

The Incidents Described

As mentioned earlier, subjects were asked to describe the most intense incident of anger which had occurred during the preceding week, or the most recent incident before that. The purpose of this was not only to assure that memory of the episode would be fresh, but also that the incident would be fairly typical (i.e., not an extreme or unusual event). Nearly three-quarters of the subjects (58) did report on an incident which had occurred during the preceding week, and the remaining subjects (22) reported on incidents which had occurred within the month.

In order to determine the representativeness of the incidents described, subjects were asked to rate how typical the precipitating incident was "to what makes people in general angry," and how typical their responses were to "how other people generally respond when angry." With regard to the precipitating incident, 23 thought it very typical, 44 thought it somewhat typical, and only 13 believed it to be not at all typical. With regard to their angry responses, the corresponding numbers were 18, 57, and 5. A large majority of the subjects obviously believed that the incidents described were fairly representative of anger in general. An inspection of the open-ended descriptions provided by subjects leaves no reason to doubt this conclusion.

Although the incidents were considered by subjects to be fairly typical, they were by no means regarded as trivial. This is indicated by the rated intensity of the episodes. On a 10-point scale ranging from "very mild" (1) to "very intense; as angry as most people ever become" (10), the mean rating of all episodes was 6.7. The majority of the responses (69%) fell above the midpoint of the scale.

There is not space here to discuss all aspects of the anger incidents as described in the questionnaires. Therefore, the remainder of this discussion will focus on five major issues: (a) the target of anger (At whom or what do people typically become angry?); (b) the nature of the instigation (What is the typical provocation to anger?); (c) the motives for anger (What do people accomplish by becoming angry?); (d) the expression of anger (What responses are made during anger?) and (e) the consequences of anger (Does the expression of anger lead to beneficial or harmful outcomes?).[5]

The Target of Anger

If anger is an institutionalized means of social control, as postulated above, then it should be directed primarily at other human beings (as opposed to nonhuman objects). Moreover, it should be directed at individuals (a) whom the angry person wishes to influence and (b) whom it is possible to influence.

Human versus nonhuman targets. Of the 80 subjects, 71 (89%) indicated that the target of their anger involved another person or persons. In 17 of these cases, some nonhuman object also was involved in a complex set of circumstances. But even in these latter instances, where a nonhuman object helped "cause" the anger, the response tended to become focused on some person associated with the incident.

There were only 9 episodes in which the target did not involve another person. But 2 of these episodes did involve a human institution; and in 2 other episodes the individuals became angry, in part, at their own selves, although they directed their anger at an inanimate object. This leaves only 5 episodes which did not involve a human being or human institution in some way. And several of these episodes are of interest because of the anthropomorphism

5. Few differences in anger were found as a function of the age, education, or sex of the subject. At least in the case of sex, this relative lack of difference is of some theoretical interest in its own right, and has been discussed elsewhere (Frost & Averill, Note 1).

exhibited. One woman, for example, became angry at her cat for fighting in the middle of the night—after the animal had been spayed specifically to stop such behavior. Another woman became angry at being seriously ill and actually hallucinated a little man (personifying her illness) at whom she could direct her anger. And a plumber became angry at a trap he had installed when it developed a hairline leak. He described his response to the leak as follows: "I made the hole in [the trap] bigger, as if to say—'That's what you should look like if you're going to leak.' " When describing his motives, he added: "Silly, but if I'm doing my job, why can't the trap do its job."

The type of person who becomes a target. If we limit consideration to the 71 episodes which involved another person, we may ask: What was the relationship between the angry individual and the target? In almost half the cases, the target was either a "loved one" (27 instances) or "someone you know well and like" (8 instances). "Acquaintances" (e.g., business colleagues, neighbors) represented another 22 cases. "Strangers" (8 instances) and "someone you know well and dislike" (6 instances) comprised the remainder.

There are at least four major reasons why a person is more likely to become angry at loved ones, friends, and/or acquaintances, as opposed to strangers and/or disliked others: (a) Close and continual contact with loved ones (friends, etc.) increases the opportunity for anger; (b) transgressions committed by loved ones are more likely to be cumulative and distressing; (c) there is a stronger motivation to get loved ones to change their ways; and (d) knowledge of what to expect from loved ones leads to greater confidence in the expression (and experience) of anger.

The above four reasons are not independent, and each is undoubtedly important under certain circumstances. But be that as it may, the mere fact that nearly 50% of the subjects reported becoming angry at a loved one or friend, while another 28% reported becoming angry at an acquaintance, is of theoretical interest in its own right. Most psychological theories—if they consider the matter at all—tend to associate anger with hate. The present data would suggest, however, that anger is more often associated with love. Of course, if the provocations which lead to anger are repeated often enough, i.e., if anger is not effective in inducing change, then love may turn to hate (cf. McKellar, 1950). But that is not the ordinary course of events.

The relationship between the angry person and the target of his or her anger can also be examined in terms of relative status. In the present sample, 34 persons (48% of the incidents involving another person) became angry at an equal or peer; another 22 (31%) became angry at a subordinate (child, employee, etc.); and 14 (20%) became angry at a superior. It is difficult to evaluate the significance of these figures in a statistical sense, for there is no way to determine the base rate of provocations among the various status conditions. However, it seems unlikely that the relative lack of anger at superiors—e.g., employers or other persons in authority at the time of the incident—can be attributed entirely to a lack of provocation (objectively speaking). For one thing, the majority of subjects in the present sample were employed in blue- or white-collar positions, where normal on-the-job frustrations and frequent contact with a supervisor might provide ample opportunity for anger. For another thing, a variety of laboratory and field investigations (e.g., Cohen, 1955; Doob & Gross, 1968; Graham, Charwat, Honig, & Weltz, 1951; Harris, 1974) have found that anger is less likely to be aroused by the actions of persons of high status than by similar actions on the part of peers and subordinates. Finally, this pattern of results is consistent with historical teachings on anger, and hence seems to reflect general social norms (cf. especially Lactantius and Aquinas, who emphasized the instructional and deterrent uses of anger).

In short, status and authority confer on an individual a certain immunity from anger. On a psychological level, this effect is probably mediated in two ways. First, a provocation by a superior is more likely to be appraised as justified or legitimate than a similar provocation by a peer or subordinate; and, second, even if a provocation by a superior is appraised as unjustified, it may lead to indifference or depression, rather than anger, if retaliation is not a viable response.

The Nature of the Instigation

As described earlier, emotions can be distinguished from other psychological phenomena, and among themselves, largely on the basis of the appraisals involved. The nature of the instigation, as perceived by the subject, is therefore of primary importance for an analysis of anger. Because of this importance, I will devote some space to a review of previous attempts to classify the instigations to anger. I will then present data from the present study.

In an early survey of anger experiences, Richardson (1918) asked

12 persons (10 graduate students at Clark University and 2 others) to observe and keep daily records of their anger for a period of at least three months. A total of 600 incidents were recorded. Richardson divided the instigations into two broad categories—irritation (frustration, pain, etc.) and negative self-feelings (humiliation, hurt feelings, etc.). He found that the latter type of instigation was more directly and immediately related to anger, although no exact figures are given.

Several other attempts to classify the instigation to anger are presented in Table 1. In each of these studies, subjects were asked to keep a daily record of their anger, or to provide a brief open-ended description of recent incidents. The instigations were then divided into mutually exclusive categories. Gates (1926) and Meltzer (1933) treated all instances of anger as the result of some kind of frustration or thwarting; however, they distinguished between the thwarting of routine activities (e.g., the interruption of sleep or habitual responses) and the thwarting of self-assertive impulses. Following a scheme developed by Woodworth (1921), self-assertion was further divided into three subcategories: (a) "defensive reactions to persons," provoked by threats to self-esteem, attempts at domination by others, and the like; (b) "aggressive reactions to persons," provoked by disobedience, refusals of a request, or other attempts by the target to resist the influence of the angry person, and (c) "defensive reactions to things," provoked by inanimate objects (e.g., equipment malfunction), which interfered with "mastery" or ego-involving behavior.

As can be seen from Table 1, most of the instigations reported by Gates and Meltzer involved frustration of self-assertive activities. This is particularly true of the Meltzer study. (The difference between the two studies in this regard may be due to the fact that Meltzer defined frustration of routine activities somewhat differently—and more narrowly—than did Gates.) According to Gates, a defensive reaction to persons is particulary characteristic of the most intense episodes of anger.

Anastasi, Cohen, and Spatz (1948) did not impose a logically consistent classification on their data; rather, they attempted "to adhere as closely as possible to the subject's own reports." The result was a fivefold classification: thwarted plans; inferiority or loss of prestige (e.g., sarcastic comments); school work (e.g., lengthy assignments); family relations (e.g., sibling rivalry); and abstract problems (e.g., seeing a classmate cheat or witnessing intolerance

Table 1

The Instigations to Anger as Classified in Previous Studies

Study	Sample	Number of incidents reported	Nature of the instigation	Percentage frequency
Gates (1926)	51 college students; female	All incidents during 1 week; total = 145	Frustration of routine activities	36.5
			Frustration of self-assertive activities a) defensive reactions to persons (35.8%) b) assertive reactions to persons (6.9%) c) defensive reactions to things (20.7%)	63.5
Meltzer (1933)	93 college students; male & female	All incidents during 1 week; total = 393	Frustration of routine activities	13.7
			Frustration of self-assertive activities a) defensive reactions to persons (37.7%) b) assertive reactions to persons (13.4%) c) defensive reactions to things (35.2%)	86.3
Anastasi, Cohen, & Spatz (1948)	38 college students; female	All incidents during 1 week; total = 598	Thwarted plans	52.0
			Inferiority and loss of prestige	20.9
			School work	12.7
			Family relationships	9.9
			Abstract problems	4.5
McKellar (1950)	200 adult education students; male & female	1 or 2 recent incidents; total = 379	Need situations	46.7
			Personality situations	53.3

toward others). These five categories accounted for 52%, 20.9%, 12.7%, 9.9%, and 4.5%, respectively, of the anger reported by subjects.

As a final example, McKellar (1950) distinguished between "need situations" and "personality situations" in the instigation to anger. Need situations, which accounted for approximately 47% of the incidents analyzed by McKellar, included any interference with the pursuit of a goal, such as missing a bus. Personality situations, which accounted for 53% of the instigations, included the imposition of physical or mental pain, or the encroachment upon personal values, status, possessions, etc. Examples of such situations were the criticism of ideas, work, clothing, or friends.

From this brief review of previous research, it is evident that the classification of "typical" instigations to anger is no simple matter. Most classifications seem to be either too broad (e.g., the dichotomies of Richardson and McKellar) or too specific to a given population (e.g., the "school work" category of Anastasi et al.); or they are based on a priori schemes of questionable validity (e.g., the trichotic division of self-assertive needs used by Gates and Meltzer). One source of difficulty has been the tendency to focus on the specific kinds of incidents which arouse anger (e.g., the interruption of some activity, criticism, an extended work assignment, and so forth), as opposed to the manner in which such incidents are evaluated by the individuals involved. For example, is the interruption (criticism, etc.) considered justified, or could it have been avoided with a little care and foresight?

When we turn from surveys of everyday experience to the results of experimental research, little additional light is shed on the nature of the instigation to anger. Following publication of the frustration-aggression hypothesis by Dollard, Doob, Miller, Mowrer, and Sears (1939), most investigators focused on frustration as the major source of aggression, and all kinds of provocations—from physical pain to the loss of pride—were simply interpreted as frustrating. It was quickly pointed out by critics, however, that frustration does not always lead to aggression. In his 1962 revision of the frustration-aggression hypothesis, Berkowitz therefore postulated that frustration leads to anger, an emotional drive state, and that aggression is a joint function of the intensity of the anger and the presence of aggressive cues in the environment. (For further revisions of this hypothesis, see Berkowitz, 1969, 1974.)

Below, I will have more to say about the role of frustration in the instigation to anger and aggression. But first, I want to review briefly one line of research which was stimulated by the frustration-aggression hypothesis and which provides relevant background to our present concerns. Numerous laboratory studies have demonstrated that provocations such as frustration are less likely to lead to anger and/or aggression if they are accompanied by mitigating circumstances (e.g., Burnstein & Worchel, 1962; Cohen, 1955; Pastore, 1952; Worchel, 1974; Zillman & Cantor, 1976). Controversy surrounding this body of research centers on two main issues: (a) Does the existence of mitigating circumstances influence the appraisal of threat, or does it merely inhibit the expression of aggression? and (b) what constitutes a mitigating circumstance?

With regard to the first question, a recent experiment by Zillman and Cantor (1976) indicates that if mitigating circumstances (in this case, the pressure of an impending examination) are known before a provocation (rude and obnoxious behavior), then subjects will tend *not* to appraise the situation in an angry fashion (as indicated by a relative lack of physiological arousal following the provocation). If, however, the mitigating circumstances are not discovered until after the provocation has occurred, then subjects may reappraise the situation in a non-angry fashion, but previously formed tendencies to aggress may still be expressed. Of course, if the mitigating circumstances are such that aggression is made socially inappropriate, then such response tendencies may be inhibited or expressed only indirectly (cf. Burnstein & Worchel, 1962).

With regard to the second question, few investigators have addressed the issue of what constitutes a mitigating circumstance. Most have been content with the demonstration that "arbitrary" provocations are more likely to instigate anger and/or aggression than are "nonarbitrary" provocations. But a provocation can be arbitrary in many different ways. For example, a random event is arbitrary. However, in a rather ingenious experiment, Worchel (1974) found that ostensibly random events did not lead to anger even when they involved frustration or disappointment; on the other hand, willful arbitrariness on the part of the experimenter which limited the freedom of subjects, but which had no other negative consequences, did tend to provoke anger. In a somewhat similar vein, a number of experiments have demonstrated that the intentions of a provocateur are more important in the instigation to anger than is the actual harm done (Epstein & Taylor, 1967; Green-well & Dengerink, 1973).

To summarize this brief background review, laboratory research indicates that the existence of mitigating circumstances affects the appraisal of threat, not just the expression of aggression, and that mitigation depends upon how an individual evaluates the intentions and motives of the provocateur. However, like the results of prior surveys of everyday experience, laboratory research has not greatly clarified the nature of the instigation to anger. One reason for this has been noted by Pepitone (1976). "In the research conducted by psychologists over the past 35 years," he observes, "there is scarcely any reference to *normative values and beliefs* associated with roles and cultural groups as to the origin, direction, inhibition, and form of aggression" (p. 645, italics added).

Let us turn now to the results of the present survey. Subjects were asked to evaluate the incident that made them angry first in terms of its justification, and then in terms of its specific characteristics. With regard to the former, four mutually exclusive categories were presented in the questionnaire, and subjects were asked to select the category which best described the incident that made them angry. The results are presented in Table 2. The vast majority of subjects indicated that the incident was either voluntary and unjustified (50%) or a potentially avoidable accident or event (30%). Relatively few persons became angry at events which they considered voluntary but justified (12.5%) or unavoidable (7.5%).

The fact that half the subjects appraised the event that made them angry as "voluntary and unjustified" suggests that moral fault or blame is commonly involved in the instigation to anger. This finding is, of course, quite consistent with the historical teachings on anger reviewed earlier. It also is consistent with incidental observations made by Richardson (1918), who noted that irritation is more likely to develop into anger if there is a breach of fairness or justice. Richardson further observed that "in some extreme cases the subject may assume a make-believe attitude and trump up reasons to suit his own ends regardless of the facts" (p. 17). McKellar (1950) also has reported that anger is likely to be severe, and may even develop into long-term attitudes of resentment and hatred, if the instigation involves a morally unjustified act.

Moral fault or blame is not, however, the only factor involved in the instigation to anger. Nearly one-third of the subjects indicated

Table 2

The Instigation to Anger Described in Terms of Justification

Justification	Number of incidents	Percentage
1. Voluntary and unjustified: The instigator knew what he was doing, but he had no right to do it.	40	50.0
2. Potentially avoidable accident or event: the result of negligence, carelessness, or lack of foresight.	24	30.0
3. Voluntary and justified: The instigator knew what he was doing and had a right to do it.	10	12.5
4. Unavoidable accident or event: it could not have been foreseen or was beyond anyone's control.	6	7.5

that they became angry at a "potentially avoidable accident or event." This suggests that anger is commonly used to correct behavior, even when moral wrong is not implied. Pursuing the legal analogy used earlier, it might be said that anger appraisals are like judgments rendered in civil as well as criminal cases.

The above considerations illustrate one reason why it is so difficult to specify with any precision and finality the nature of the instigation to anger. Almost any potential harm may provoke anger if it is appraised as unjustified and/or avoidable. Conversely, any circumstance which makes an event appear justifiable and/or unavoidable will help mitigate the instigation. And it should go without saying that what is considered justifiable (or unavoidable) is dependent in large measure on social norms and customs, and hence may vary from one group to another, from one context to another, and from one time to another.

This does not mean that the specific nature of the precipitating event is devoid of practical or theoretical interest. If anger serves as an informal means of social control, as was suggested earlier, then certain kinds of instigations should be more important than others, regardless of their justification. Violations of social and/or personal norms, for example, should be more important than the thwarting of routine activities. To gather data on this issue, six specific factors were described in the questionnaire, and subjects were asked to rate *each* on a 3-point scale depending upon whether it was "not at all" (0), "somewhat" (1), or "very much" (2) involved in the incident that made them angry. The six factors are listed in Table 3, rank-ordered by degree of involvement.

Frustration, or the interruption of some ongoing or planned activity, was the single factor most frequently mentioned. This is not particularly surprising. As the foregoing review of survey and laboratory research illustrates, frustration has often been postulated as a major—if not a necessary—condition for anger. However, the relationship between frustration and anger is far from clear. Laboratory research has shown that frustration—when unconfounded by other factors such as arbitrariness—sometimes increases (Geen, 1968), sometimes decreases (Gentry, 1970; Rule & Hewett, 1971), and sometimes has no effect (Buss, 1966; Taylor & Pisano, 1971) on subsequent aggression. This has led Baron (1977) to conclude that frustration "is not a very common or important [antecedent of anger or aggression] and is probably far less crucial in this respect than has widely—and persistently—been assumed" (p. 92).

Controversy regarding the importance of frustration requires that we examine more closely the way this factor was involved in the incidents reported by subjects in the present survey. Of the 63 subjects (80% of the total) who mentioned frustration, 62 indicated that one or more of the following factors also was somewhat or very much involved in their anger: violation of important personal expectations or wishes (46 subjects), violation of socially accepted ways of behaving (40 subjects), a loss of personal pride (39 subjects), possible or actual property damage (14 subjects), and possible or actual physical injury (12 subjects).

The violation of personal and social norms, the loss of pride, etc., could be interpreted as causes of frustrations, varieties of frustration, or factors in addition to frustration. These different interpretations are possible because "frustration" is one of those rubberband concepts that can be stretched to fit almost any circumstance or be reduced to a rather small perimeter for the sake of appearance. This is certainly true of the concept in ordinary language; and, in spite of

Table 3

The Instigation to Anger Described in Terms of Intrinsic Characteristics

Factors involved in the instigation to anger	Mean rating[a]	Number of subjects marking "somewhat" or "very much"	
		Total	Percentage
1. Frustration or the interruption of some ongoing or planned activity	1.26	63	78.8
2. Violation of expectations and wishes which are important to you but which may not be widely shared by others	1.10	58	72.5
3. An event, action, or attitude which resulted in a loss of personal pride, self-esteem, or sense of personal worth	.99	51	63.8
4. Violation of socially accepted ways of behaving or widely shared rules of conduct	.93	50	62.5
5. Possible or actual property damage	.33	18	22.5
6. Possible or actual physical injury and/or pain	.24	13	16.3

[a]0 = not at all; 1 = somewhat; 2 = very much

avowals to the contrary, it is also true in psychological discourse. For scientific purposes, it might be helpful if we could be rid of the concept of frustration entirely. That, however, is not likely to occur. The safest conclusion would therefore seem to be that frustration is an important but seldom sufficient condition for anger.

After frustration, the second most frequently mentioned factor (by 73% of the subjects—see Table 3) was "the violation of expectations and wishes which are important to you but which may not be widely shared by others." As mentioned above, this factor could be construed as a variety of frustration, or perhaps as a cause of frustration. However, the examples which were used to illustrate the item in the questionnaire emphasized such incidents as someone disregarding "one of your pet likes or dislikes," a child or spouse not acting "in line with your expectations," or dislike for "a neighbor's life style." In line with these examples, the kinds of incidents which subjects most frequently described in connection with the item were the breaking of family rules or understandings (especially by children); being let down by friends or coworkers; disagreeing with the opinions and attitudes of another; and the like. The thrust of these responses is thus more toward the violation of personal norms or standards than toward the interruption of activity.

The third and fourth most frequently mentioned factors were the loss of self-esteem and the violation of socially accepted ways of behaving (each mentioned by about 63% of the subjects). The loss of self-esteem has been frequently noted as an important instigation to anger and requires little further comment here. The violation of social norms does, however, deserve brief discussion. This factor corresponds roughly to the "abstract problems" category used by Anastasi et al. (see Table 1). However, Anastasi et al. found that only 4.5% of the instigations fell into this category. The reason for the wide discrepancy between the results of Anastasi et al. and the present findings is twofold. In the first place, people do not often become very angry at the violation of social norms unless such violations affect them personally, e.g., by interfering with some planned activity or by threatening their self-esteem. Therefore, when Anastasi et al. divided the instigations into mutually exclusive categories on the basis of the most important factor involved, relatively few fell into the category of abstract problems. In the second place, the subjects in the present survey—and not the experimenter as in Anastasi's study—chose what factors were involved in the instigation. It is apparent from the open-ended responses that many subjects viewed nearly any frustration, chastisement, or threat to the self as a violation of social norms, provided that it also was regarded as unjustified and/or avoidable.

For the sake of completeness, note should also be made of the relatively low incidence of possible or actual physical injury and property damage as precipitating factors (see items #5 and #6, Table 3). Obviously, this does not mean that such factors are unimportant when they occur. However, they occur relatively infrequently in everyday affairs, whereas psychological and/or interpersonal threats are quite common.

To summarize this discussion briefly, normative standards are involved in the instigation to anger in at least two ways. First, the instigation may represent a violation of some specific social and/or personal norm. A breach of etiquette or the breaking of an agreement would be examples. Second, any inconvenience, humiliation, or threat of physical injury may violate general social norms if the incident is unjustified or avoidable (e.g., due to negligence, lack of forethought, etc.). The function of anger, it is here proposed, is to inhibit such violations, whether on the specific or more general level.

The Motives for Anger

If anger helps to regulate interpersonal relationships by upholding personal and social norms, this fact should be reflected in the motives people give for becoming angry. Unfortunately, most of the data currently available on this issue come from clinical populations where selfish and antisocial motives are likely to be predominant. In the present survey, therefore, a special effort was made to assess the motives people typically have—or think they have—for becoming angry. It was explained to subjects that:

Sometimes when we become angry, we may simply want to get back at the person or thing that angered us. Often, however, additional motives are involved in our anger. For example, we may become angry at a child for running into the street in order to protect him from injury; or we may become angry in order to get someone to help us out with some work. Although such motives are quite common, *we typically are not fully aware of them at the time of our anger*. It may only be in looking back and thinking carefully about the incident that we may come to realize all that was involved in our anger.

Subjects were then asked to read through a list of 11 motives, each of which was accompanied by several examples. After reading the entire list, subjects rated each motive on a 3-point scale, indicating how much it was involved in their anger (0 = not at all; 1 = somewhat; and 2 = very much). The list of motives, ranked according to the mean ratings, is presented in Table 4.

As can be seen, the most frequently endorsed motive was "to assert your authority or independence, or to improve your image." The second and third most frequently mentioned motives were "to

Table 4

The Motives Subjects Offered for Becoming Angry

Motive	Mean rating[a]	Number of subjects marking "somewhat" or "very much"	
		Total	Percentage
1. To assert your authority or independence, or to improve your image	.95	55	68.8
2. To strengthen a relationship with the instigator	.84	47	58.8
3. To bring about a change in the behavior of the instigator primarily for his or her own good	.84	44	55.0
4. To get back at, or gain revenge on, the instigator for the present incident	.75	44	55.0
5. To bring about a change in the behavior of the instigator primarily for your own good	.73	40	50.0
6. To "let off steam" over miscellaneous frustrations of the day which had nothing to do with the present incident	.49	30	37.5
7. To get even for past "wrongs" by the instigator	.49	29	36.3
8. To express your general dislike for the instigator	.38	20	25.0
9. To get the instigator to do something for you	.28	18	22.5
10. To break off a relationship with the instigator	.28	15	18.8
11. To get out of doing something for the instigator	.19	18	22.5

[a]0 = not at all; 1 = somewhat; 2 = very much

strengthen a relationship with the instigator" and "to bring about a change in the behavior of the instigator primarily for his or her own good." From these responses, it would appear that the typical episode of anger was not motivated by a desire to harm or injure the instigator; rather, it was intended to enhance one's own position and/or to strengthen a relationship by bringing about a change in the instigator's behavior (ostensibly for his or her own good). Of course, not all anger is so constructively motivated. A significant minority of the subjects (approximately 20% to 25%) admitted that they wanted to express dislike for the instigator (#8), to get the instigator to do something for them (#9), to break off a relationship with the instigator (#10), and/or to get out of doing something for the instigator (#11).

Before analyzing the above results further, a possible objection should be considered. Self-reports of psychological—and especially motivational—processes have long been suspect. Adding to this suspicion, Nisbett and Wilson (1977; see also Nisbett & Bellows, 1977) have recently reviewed a considerable amount of research which indicates that self-reports are often based on presuppositions or "a priori theories" about the causal links between a stimulus and a response. Following this line of reasoning, a critic might argue that the reasons offered by subjects for becoming angry reflect, not true motives, but post hoc rationalizations for their behavior. Space does not allow a complete discussion of this issue here. However, several comments are in order.

First, the validity of self-reports depends not only on their accuracy but also upon the use to which they are put. One of the main purposes of the present analysis is to help identify the norms of anger (or what Nisbett would call a subject's "a priori theory" of anger). From this perspective, it is not crucial whether or not a subject's self-report is an accurate reflection of underlying cognitive processes. I do assume, however, that on the average, or over the long run, people tend to conform to the norms in which they believe. (The cognitive mechanisms by which norms influence behavior are poorly understood. This problem has, however, been the subject of considerable recent research and speculation in at least one area of psychology, viz., altruism—see Schwartz, 1977; Staub, 1978, Ch. 5.)

Of course, people often become angry for reasons that do not conform to social norms; and, to the extent that the present analysis is relevant to how people actually behave, as well as to how they think they should behave, the psychological accuracy of the self-reports is still a concern. This brings me to the second point. It cannot be said how accurately subjects were able to report the "real" motives for their anger; hence, the relative ratings of motives presented in Table 4 may be somewhat distorted. However, only if such distortion were major would it affect the *patterns* of relationships among motives, or between motives and other aspects of the angry episodes that will be described below. There is no reason to assume that the self-reports were distorted to such a major degree. From their open-ended responses, it is evident that subjects made a sincere effort to describe their motives candidly. There was, in particular, little evidence of dissimulation for the sake of appearance.

Returning now to the list of motives presented in Table 4, most subjects indicated that more than one motive was involved in their anger. To help identify common patterns of motivation, ratings of the 11 motives were intercorrelated, and a factor analysis (principle components) was performed. Four factors had eigenvalues greater than unity, and these were rotated orthogonally using the varimax method. The fourth factor was defined primarily by one motive, "to get out of doing something for the instigator." However, this motive and several others ("to get the instigator to do something for you" and "to break off a relationship") were endorsed by less than one-fourth of the subjects. Since these items might have distorted the factor structure, a second analysis also was performed on the eight most frequently endorsed motives. Three factors emerged from this second analysis with eigenvalues greater than unity, and these corresponded closely to the first three factors obtained using all eleven variables. The factor loadings from both analyses are presented in Table 5.

The first factor seems to represent a kind of *malevolent* anger. It is best characterized by such motives as "to express dislike," "to gain revenge for the present incident," and "to break off a relationship." "To assert your authority or independence," "to get even for past wrongs," and "to bring about a change in the instigator for your own good" also had moderately high loadings on this factor. These latter motives are not, however, unique to malevolent anger.

The second factor represents a more *constructive* use of anger. "To strengthen a relationship," "to bring about a change for your own good," and "to bring about a change for the instigator's good" are the motives which best characterize this dimension.

The third factor is not as well defined as the first two. It involves

Table 5

Rotated Orthogonal Factor Loadings for the Complete List of Eleven Motives (The loadings obtained from a factor analysis of a reduced list of eight motives are included in parentheses.)

Motive	Rank-order of endorsement	Factor A Malevolent anger	Factor B Constructive anger	Factor C Fractious anger
To express dislike for the instigator	8	78(41)	-13(-44)	
To break off a relationship[a]	10	57(—)		
To gain revenge for the present incident	4	47(62)		
To assert authority or independence	1	48(31)		44(60)
To get even for past wrongs	7	37(42)	40(17)	
To bring about a change for your own good	5	35(67)	62(35)	
To bring about a change for the instigator's good	3		42(42)	
To strengthen a relationship	2		43(54)	43(20)
To let off steam over miscellaneous frustrations	6			34(23)
To get the instigator to do something for you[a]	9			41(—)
To get out of doing something for the instigator[a]	11			

Note. Loadings are not presented if the values from *both* analyses were less than .30.

[a]These motives were not included in the second analysis, the results of which are presented in parentheses.

"asserting authority or independence," "letting off steam over miscellaneous frustrations," and "getting the instigator to do something for you." This last motive suggests a selfish quality. However, "to strengthen a relationship" also had moderate loadings on this factor. In general, this third kind of anger seems to be more focused on the angry person and his or her frustrations than on the precipitating incident. For lack of a better term, I will call it *fractious* anger.

On a priori grounds, one might expect the motive for anger to be related to the target; e.g., malevolent anger—if it is truly malevolent—should be directed toward those we dislike whereas constructive anger should be directed toward those we care for. To test this possibility, analyses of variance were performed in which subjects were divided into groups depending upon whether the target was a loved one, someone the subject knew well and liked, someone the subject knew well and disliked, an acquaintance, or a stranger. Analyses which reached the .05 level of significance are presented in Table 6. (Because the size of the groups varied considerably—from 6 to 27—and due to nonhomogeneity of variance, the significance levels reported in Table 6 must be considered only approximate.)

Three motives which had high loadings on the malevolent dimension ("to express dislike for the instigator," "to break off a relationship," and "to get even for past wrongs") had the highest ratings when the target of anger was someone who was known well but disliked. On the other hand, only one constructive motive ("to strengthen a relationship") differed reliably as a function of the target, it being rated most highly when the anger was directed at a loved one. Another constructive motive ("to bring about a change for the instigator's good") also was rated most highly when the target was a loved one or friend (1.15 and 1.13, respectively), but these ratings did not differ significantly from those in which the incident involved someone who was disliked (.66), an acquaintance (.86), or a stranger (.50). Evidently it is easier to become constructively angry at strangers and enemies than it is to become malevolently angry at loved ones and friends.

With regard to fractious anger, the motives with unique loadings on this dimension ("to let off steam" and "to get the instigator to do something for you") received approximately equal ratings regardless of the target. The failure of these motives to differentiate among

Table 6

Differences among the Mean Ratings[a] *of Motives as a Function of the Target of the Anger*

Motive	Loved one	Know well & like	Know well & dislike	Acquaintance	Stranger	F-ratio (df=4,66)
Express dislike	.04	.13	1.50	.36	.50	9.96***
Break off a relationship	.11	.00	1.17	.32	.38	5.09***
Get even for past wrongs	.41	.25	1.33	.55	.38	2.72*
Strengthen a relationship	1.33	.89	.50	.68	.50	3.92**

[a] 0 = not at all; 1 = somewhat; 2 = very much

*p < .05
**p < .01
***p < .001

targets supports the observation made earlier that fractious anger has more to do with the frustrations and concerns of the angry person than with the precipitating incident.

Although the three kinds of anger described above—malevolent, constructive, and fractious—make good logical as well as empirical sense, it should also be noted that together they account for only 50% of the variance in the 11-item factor analysis, and 60% of the variance in the 8-item analysis. It thus appears that many subjects had their own idiosyncratic pattern of motives for becoming angry.

The Expression of Anger

Regardless of the motive involved, anger may be expressed in a variety of different ways. Eleven possibilities were described in the questionnaire. For ease of discussion, these can be grouped into the following categories:

A. Direct and indirect aggression
   1. Verbal or symbolic aggression or punishment directed at the offender.
   2. Denial or removal of some benefit customarily enjoyed by the offender.

3. Physical aggression or punishment directed at the offend-er.
4. Aggression, harm, or damage to someone or something important to the offender.
5. Telling a third party in order to get back at the offender, or to have the offender punished. (Hereafter this response will be referred to as *malediction*.)

B. Displaced aggression

6. Taking your anger out on some *person* other than the offender; that is, aggression (physical, verbal, or other-wise) toward an individual who was not related to the instigation.
7. Taking your anger out on, or attacking, *some nonhuman object or thing* not related to the instigation.

C. Nonaggressive responses

8. Talking the incident over with the offender without exhibiting hostility.
9. Talking the incident over with a neutral, uninvolved party, with no intent to harm the offender or make him/her look bad.
10. Engaging in calming activities (e.g., going for a walk).
11. Engaging in activities opposite to the expression of anger (e.g., being extra friendly with the instigator).

Subjects were asked to read through the entire list and then rate each item on two 3-point scales. One scale referred to how much the subject felt like making the response (0 = not at all, 1 = somewhat, 2 = very much), and the second scale referred to what the sub-ject actually did. The mean ratings for both scales are depicted in Figure 1.

Seventy-five (94%) of the subjects either felt like aggressing or actually did aggress—directly or indirectly—against the instigator. And of the remaining five subjects, two displaced their aggressive tendencies on some uninvolved person or object. The most common form of aggression—both felt and actually expressed—was verbal and/or symbolic. The denial of some benefit, and malediction (tell-ing a third party about the incident with hostile intent), were the next most common modes of aggression. Though the impulse to physical aggression was often felt, it was seldom expressed.

The expression of physical aggression deserves special comment. Ten subjects indicated that they responded in this way. In five of these instances, the target of the aggression was a young child, and

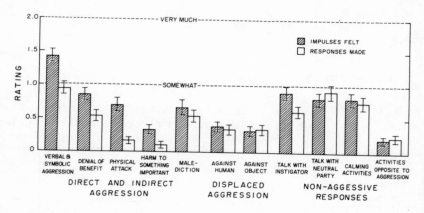

FIGURE 1. Mean Ratings (and Standard Errors of the Mean) of Impulses Felt and Responses Made While Angry

in one instance it was an adolescent (the angry person's 17-year-old daughter). This confirms the observations of Richardson (1918) and McKellar (1949) that when anger results in physical aggression, it is usually directed at a child in the form of punishment. This tendency becomes even more apparent when it is realized that children were involved in only 16 of the 80 episodes of anger included in the present survey. Thus of all the episodes involving physical aggression, 50% were directed against children; and, conversely, of all episodes involving children, 30% resulted in physical aggression.

The above percentages should not be taken to mean that child beating or some other form of malignant aggression is common during anger. The aggression involved in these episodes was quite mild (a spank, shove, or slap), and under ordinary circumstances probably would not even be labeled "aggressive." The stated intent was to instruct and/or deter the child, not to harm.

Referring again to Figure 1, it is also evident that aggression is not the only kind of response typical of anger. All but six of the subjects felt like, or actually engaged in, some nonaggressive behavior. More specifically, of the 71 incidents where another person was involved in the instigation, 60% of the subjects felt like talking it over with the instigator without displaying hostility. However, nearly half of these subjects were not able to do so, at least not to the extent they wished. The most common nonaggressive responses actually made were calming activities and talking the incident over with a neutral third party.

Table 7

Correlations among Response Tendencies and the Motives for Anger

Impulses felt and responses made			Malevolent				
			Express dislike	Break off relationship	Revenge for present incident	Assert authority	Get even for past wrongs
Direct and Indirect Aggression	Verbal & symbolic aggression	I					.30
		R					
	Denial of benefit	I	-.25				
		R					
	Physical attack	I					.24
		R					
	Harm to something important	I	.31	.41			
		R	.40				
	Malediction	I	.26	.30	.28	.34	
		R	.22	.39	.28	.31	
Displaced Aggression	Against person	I	.22			.27	
		R	.29				
	Against object	I					
		R					
Non-aggressive Responses	Talk with instigator	I					.27
		R					
	Talk with neutral party	I			.23		.23
		R		.26	.23		.23
	Calming activities	I					
		R					
	Activities opposite to aggression	I					
		R					

Note. Only correlations that were significant at the .05 level of confidence (two-tailed test) are listed.

	Constructive			Fractious		
	Change for your own good	Change for instigator's good	Strengthen relationship	Let off steam	Get instigator to do something for you	Get out of doing something for instigator
	.29	.23				.27
		.30				
		.22	.28			
			.24			
		-.22				
		-.23				
	.25			.23		
	.30					
					-.22	
			.28			
	.27		.33			

How does the expression of anger relate to the motives a person gives for becoming angry? In order to examine this issue, the responses were intercorrelated with the motives described in the previous section. The results are presented in Table 7.

Intuitively, it might be thought that malevolent anger (defined in terms of the motives involved—see Table 2) would be more associated with aggressive responses, whereas constructive anger would be more associated with nonaggressive responses. An inspection of Table 8 indicates that such is not the case. All the correlations between motives and responses were relatively small, and each kind of response was related (if at all) to several kinds of motives. However, the distribution of correlations does form a meaningful pattern. Indirect modes of aggression (malediction and harming something important to the instigator) were most associated with motives indicative of malevolent anger, whereas direct aggression (verbal and physical attack, and the denial of benefits) was most associated with constructive anger. This makes logical sense. If anger is to be constructive, it must be communicated to the instigator, often in an emphatic (aggressive) way. On the other hand, if the intent is malevolent, then indirect aggression may not only be more hurtful but also safer.

The Consequences of Anger

The evolution of behavior, whether in a biological or social sense, depends ultimately on consequences. Behavior that is beneficial for the species or the society will be maintained, while harmful responses will be extinguished. This fact has presented a paradox for commentators on anger. Most people consider anger to be a "bad" or "unpleasant" emotion, e.g., when rated on the evaluative scales of the Semantic Differential (Averill, 1975). As we have seen in the case of Seneca, social theorists also have frequently condemned anger as detrimental to the common weal. And, finally, the expression of anger is frequently punished, especially if it is directed at authority figures. In view of all this negative evaluation and reinforcement, why is anger such a prevalent response? The answer most commonly given to this question is that anger was at one time biologically adaptive, but that it is no longer so. Like the vermiform appendix, which typically is benign but which often becomes inflamed, even sometimes fatally so, anger is presumed to be a remnant of our evolutionary past.

Table 8

Reactions of the Target (N = 60) to the Subject's Anger

Target's reaction	Mean rating[a]	Number of subjects marking "somewhat" or "very much"	
		Total	Percentage
Indifference or lack of concern	.55	25	41.6
Defiance	.53	25	41.6
Apology or other sign of contrition	.53	24	40.0
Anger or hostility	.48	22	36.7
Denial of responsibility	.48	20	33.3
Hurt feelings	.47	21	35.0
Surprise	.37	15	25.0
Rejection	.30	15	25.0
Jokes, frivolity, or silliness	.13	7	11.6

[a] 0 = not at all; 1 = somewhat; 2 = very much

But there is another possible explanation for the persistence of anger, namely that it continues to serve a function within the social system. Therefore, let us look more closely at the consequences of anger as perceived by the subjects in the present sample. Three kinds of consequences are of interest. The first has to do with the instigator's reactions to the subject's anger; the second with the subject's reaction to his or her own anger; and the third with the overall beneficial or harmful effects of the episode.

The reactions of the instigator. Sixty subjects indicated that the instigators knew that they (the subjects) were angry. The major reactions exhibited by the instigator in these instances are shown in Table 8. (Each reaction was rated on a 3-point scale with 0 = not at all, 1 = somewhat, 2 = very much.) Most often, the instigator reacted with indifference and/or defiance. However, an apology or other sign of contrition was about equally forthcoming. A denial of responsibility for the instigation, a return display of anger, and hurt feelings were also common reactions.

From the subject's point of view, of course, an apology from the instigator would be the most desirable consequence. An overt apology, however, is not necessary for a beneficial outcome. An instigator who responds with defiance, for example, may still be hesitant to repeat the provocation on a subsequent occasion.

The reactions of the subject. Subjects also were asked to rate on 3-point scales how they felt about their own anger after their initial response. The results are presented in Table 9. As can be seen, the subjective after-effects of anger are overwhelmingly negative—that is, subjects tended to feel irritable, depressed, and/or anxious after their initial response. Relatively few subjects (between 10% and 20%) reported feeling good or triumphant.

The interpretation of these results is unfortunately ambiguous. Although subjects were asked to rate how they felt *about their own anger*, it seems likely that most subjects also described their continuing mood following the episode. This mood undoubtedly reflected their original appraisal of the instigation and the subsequent reactions of the instigator, as well as an evaluation of their own behavior. For example, a person who feels that he or she has been treated unjustly, or who has suffered a loss of self-esteem, is likely to feel irritable, depressed, and anxious for a considerable period of time following the incident, especially if the instigator responds with indifference or defiance rather than with an apology. The present data suggest that anger is not a very effective way of alleviating such negative feelings, and may even exacerbate them.

The overall beneficial or harmful effects. As the final question regarding their anger, subjects were asked:

> Everything considered (the nature of the instigation, your response to it, the consequences of your anger, etc.), do you believe that this episode of anger was adaptive (beneficial) ＿＿＿ or maladaptive (harmful) ＿＿＿?

The ratio of "adaptive" to "maladaptive" responses was almost 3 to 1. Specifically, 52 subjects found the incident beneficial, 18 found it harmful, and 10 indicated that it was neither or both.

Approximately 65% of the subjects who rated the episode as beneficial indicated that it helped to rectify the situation. This was accomplished primarily by getting the instigator to change his or her attitudes and/or behavior toward the angry person, or by increasing mutual understanding. However, some subjects (7 to be exact) indicated that the change for the better occurred primarily on their own part. For example, the angry person either increased his or her resolve to overcome the difficulty, or came to reappraise the situa-

Table 9

Reactions of the Subject to His or Her Own Anger

Reaction	Mean rating[a]	Number of subjects marking "somewhat" or "very much"	
		Total	Percentage
Irritable, hostile, aggravated	.96	51	63.8
Depressed, unhappy, gloomy	.83	46	57.5
Anxious, jittery, nervous	.66	41	51.3
Ashamed, embarrassed, guilty	.43	23	28.8
Relieved, calm, satisfied	.41	28	35.0
Good, pleased, glad	.21	15	18.8
Triumphant, confident, dominant	.14	10	12.5

[a]0 = not at all; 1 = somewhat; 2 = very much

tion differently, realizing perhaps that it was not so important or that the fault must be shared.

A number of subjects also indicated that their anger served to release tension. Approximately 20% of those who considered the episode to be beneficial gave this as the reason. (The remaining explanations—15%—for the beneficial outcomes were too vague to be classified.)

With regard to the 18 subjects who considered the incident maladaptive or harmful, 40% explained that it accomplished nothing, 30% believed that it had a detrimental effect on their relationship with the instigator, 20% indicated that the experience was itself unpleasant or led to unwarranted (e.g., aggressive) behavior, and 10% said that they failed to express their anger. These figures must, of course, be viewed as only approximate because of the small number of subjects involved.

To recapitulate briefly, the typical episode of anger is no more likely to elicit an apology on the part of the instigator than it is to elicit a reaction of indifference, defiance, or hostility. Moreover, following his or her initial response, the angry person is likely to feel irritable, depressed, or anxious. Nevertheless, the overall consequences of anger appear to be positive by a margin of almost 3 to 1. And if only those episodes which lead to an actual improvement in the situation (as opposed to a simple release of tension) are compared with those episodes which result in an actual deterioration of the situation (as opposed to accomplishing nothing or simply resulting in an unpleasant experience), then the ratio of beneficial to harmful outcomes increases to approximately 7 to 1.

Summary and Implications

The typical instigation to anger involves a potentially harmful event which is appraised as unjustified or at least avoidable. The exact nature of the potential harm is not crucial, although frustration (the interruption of some ongoing or planned activity), a loss of self-esteem, and the violation of personal and/or social norms are the most common factors involved.

The person who instigates or becomes the target of anger is most likely to be a loved one, friend, or acquaintance. Opportunity is undoubtedly an important factor here: We tend to avoid contact with those whom we dislike, and strangers seldom threaten us. But opportunity does not negate the fact that anger is more frequently associated with those we love (e.g., a parent, child, spouse) than with those we hate.

In terms of the motives involved, it is possible to distinguish among three kinds of anger—malevolent, constructive, and fractious. Malevolent anger is often expressed indirectly (e.g., in the form of malediction) at those whom we dislike. It is less frequent than constructive anger, which tends to be expressed openly (and aggressively) toward those whom we like. Fractious anger is a diffuse response, a kind of "letting off steam," and perhaps should not even be called anger except in a metaphorical sense.

These results—that anger typically is initiated by an appraised wrong, is directed toward a loved one or friend, and is constructively motivated—strongly support the hypothesis that anger serves a positive social function by helping to regulate interpersonal relations.

Of course, the final criterion by which the functional significance of anger must be judged has to do with consequences. Few people enjoy becoming angry, for if their anger is justified, then they probably have suffered some wrong. Likewise, few people enjoy being the target of anger, not only because they may become the object of aggression, but also because anger is an implied accusation of wrongdoing. In view of this latter fact, it is not surprising that anger often elicits a show of indifference, a denial of responsibility, or even a return display of anger. But in spite of often negative reactions on the part of the instigator, as well as the unpleasantness of the experience for the angry person, most people feel that the final outcome of a typical episode of anger is more beneficial than harm- ful.

A FORMULATION FOR ANGER WITHIN WESTERN SOCIETIES

On the basis of the considerations presented thus far, I would like to offer the following definition of anger. *Anger is a socially constituted response which helps to regulate interpersonal relations through the threat of retaliation for perceived wrongs, and which is interpreted as a passion rather than as an action so as not to violate the general cultural proscription against deliberately harming another.* A brief discussion of each aspect of this definition will serve to summarize and conclude this discussion.

Anger is a Socially Constituted Response

Most contemporary theorists would probably agree with Izard's (1977) observation that "in the human being the expression of anger and the experiential phenomenon of anger are innate, pancultural, universal phenomena" (p. 64). Izard and others who share this view recognize, of course, that the conditions which elicit anger, and the overt responses displayed while angry are subject to cultural influence. Nevertheless, the tendency has been to treat such cultural differences as a mere patina on a more basic biological substratum. The present analysis assumes, by contrast, that there are no core biological features (whether expressive reactions, subjective experience, and/or neurological circuits) in terms of which anger can be defined without reference to sociocultural factors.

This last statement does not deny the possibility that some biologically based elements (e.g., related to aggression) may become incorporated into a complex emotional syndrome such as anger. However, anger transcends any biological imperatives related to self- or species-preservation, and it assumes cognitive capacities which exceed in complexity anything observable on the infrahuman level. Seneca was undoubtedly correct when he maintained that anger is "born only where reason dwells."

The assertion that anger is a socially constituted response also implies that it may be specific to a given culture. That is why the present formulation is only for anger within Western societies. However, since the proposed function of anger—to regulate inter-personal relations—is a necessary aspect of any society, anger-like responses may also be universal. But it is important to keep in mind the qualifying phrase, "anger-like," for there are important differences as well as similarities in the ways that societies have devised to regulate interpersonal relations. Such differences clearly exist on the level of formal institutions (e.g., legal systems), and there is no reason to believe they are any less important on the emotional level.

Anger Helps to Regulate Interpersonal Relations Through the Threat of Retaliation for Perceived Wrongs

Theories which emphasize the biological bases of anger also tend to emphasize the destructive aspects of this emotion. Anger evolved, so the reasoning goes, under conditions which are far different than those which obtain at the present time. And although anger may have been adaptive for our hominid ancestors, it is maladaptive in today's world. By contrast, the conception of anger as a socially constituted response focuses attention on the functions which anger may now be serving within the social system. Social evolution is much faster than biological evolution; and if anger were not serving some social function, it would have become "extinct" because of its often harmful consequences.

The hypothesis that anger helps to regulate interpersonal relations, as here proposed, is hardly novel. As we have seen, this was the central thesis of Lactantius' analysis. We rise to anger, he maintained, "not because we have been injured, but in order that discipline be preserved, morals corrected, and license suppressed." Nearly a thousand years later, Aquinas was echoing a similar theme, namely, that the proper goal of anger "is the correction of fault and the maintenance of justice." Among contemporary psychologists, the constructive aspects of anger have been commented upon by Holt (1970) and Rothenberg (1971), among others. It is fair to say, however, that most contemporary theories of emotion have viewed anger as primarily dysfunctional.

The constructive aspects of anger are also reflected in the motives people give for becoming angry; the stated intent is seldom to do harm or violence but rather to express displeasure in a very emphatic way. Of course, there is a threat of violence implied in anger. And like any threat or deterrent, the display of anger must carry with it the real possibility of attack. Hence some episodes of anger do spill over into acts of violence, of which crimes of passion are extreme examples. But for the most part, the everyday expression of anger is designed to make a harmful attack unnecessary.

Anger is Interpreted as a Passion Rather than as an Action so as Not to Violate the General Cultural Proscription against Deliberately Harming Another

Most societies have strong proscriptions against deliberately harming one's fellow citizens, clansmen, etc. These proscriptions are often couched in highly moralistic tones which would seem to allow few exceptions. However, most societies also encourage interpersonal aggression in defense of certain rights and principles. How is this conflict resolved? One way is to establish special roles—such as the military, police, executioners, etc.—for those who must commit aggression in the service of society. Another way is to establish special occasions—ritual sacrifices, duels, competitive sports, and the like—during which the norms prohibiting aggression are temporarily suspended. But formal exemptions such as these do not begin to cover the innumerable cases of quarreling which occur in connection with everyday interpersonal relations. This is where anger enters the picture, at least in our own culture.

For reasons having to do primarily with the attribution of responsibility, if a person retaliates out of anger, then the response will be interpreted as a passion rather than as an action. But before retaliation can be interpreted as a passion, it must satisfy the norms of anger. For example, the provocation must meet socially defined criteria of adequacy; the response must be proportional to the provocation; and the mode of expression must conform to certain standards of legitimacy (e.g., it should not be malicious or long delayed). If these conditions are not met, the claim of anger may be disallowed entirely; or, if some but not all of the conditions are met, the response may be judged as unjustifiable anger and hence subject to punishment.

These last remarks might seem more applicable to extreme outbursts of anger, such as those which result in crimes of passion, than to the everyday experience of anger, which seldom goes beyond a verbal rebuke or the denial of some benefit. However, many of the same considerations that apply to crimes of passion also apply to everyday experiences. For instance, crimes of passion may sometimes be quite "deliberate," in the sense that the individual knows and plots in advance what he or she is going to do. Nevertheless, if the provocation is considered adequate, the act may still be classified as passion, thus diminishing the defendant's responsibility. Similarly, in everyday affairs, if a person's anger is justified (e.g., the provocation violates social norms or mutual understandings) then responsibility for the episode is placed on the instigator and not on the angry person. Consider the familiar warning: "Don't do that again; it makes me angry, and I won't be responsible for what happens." The angry person may actually be planning an appropriate response, just in case the warning is ineffective. Yet he or she is also disclaiming in advance any responsibility for a planned action by attributing it to anger, a passion. Of course, most people do not plan in advance the responses they will make when provoked. Typically, when a provocation occurs, people simply respond. Only afterwards, if they feel the need to account for or explain their behavior, are they likely to interpret the response as either an action (and hence accept responsibility) or as a passion (and hence disclaim responsibility). The latter interpretation is facilitated if the response was especially aggressive and/or accompanied by physiological arousal, but those are not necessary nor sufficient conditions for the attribution of anger.

A FINAL COMMENT

In the foregoing analysis, I have emphasized the positive as opposed to the negative aspects of anger. Such an emphasis seems to be dictated by the data. However, I do not wish to gloss over the fact that anger is often the source of great harm and suffering. It was not without reason that Seneca condemned this emotion so vehemently. However, if we wish to understand anger on a theoretical level, an exclusive focus on its negative aspects will not lead us very far. And even on a practical level, any attempt to reduce anger must take into account the positive functions which it serves. Anger as we know it will be eliminated only when those functions are no longer necessary, or until they are met in some other fashion. That has not happened in the nearly 2,500 years since the first speculations on anger were recorded; nor is it likely to happen in the near future. In the meantime, therefore, it might be well to heed the words of Aristotle:

Anyone can get angry—that is easy; . . . but to do this to the right person, to the right extent, at the right time, with the right motive, and in the right way, that is not for everyone nor is it easy; wherefore goodness is both rare and laudable and noble. (*Nichomachean Ethics*, 1109a25)

REFERENCE NOTE

1. Frost, W. D., & Averill, J. R. *Sex differences in the everyday experience of anger*. Paper presented at the meeting of the Eastern Psychological Association, Washington, D.C., March, 1978.

REFERENCES

Anastasi, A., Cohen, N., & Spatz, D. A study of fear and anger in college students through the controlled diary method. *Journal of Genetic Psychology*, 1948, **73**, 243–249.

Aquinas, T. *Summa Theologiae* (60 vols.). (Blackfriars) New York: McGraw-Hill, 1964–.

Ardrey, R. *The hunting hypothesis*. New York: Atheneum, 1976.

Arnold, M. B. *Emotion and personality* (2 vols.). New York: Columbia University Press, 1960.

Averill, J. R. Grief: Its nature and significance. *Psychological Bulletin*, 1968, **70**, 721–748.

Averill, J. R. An analysis of psychophysiological symbolism and its influences on theories of emotion. *Journal for the Theory of Social Behavior*, 1974, **4**, 147–190.

Averill, J. R. A semantic atlas of emotional concepts. JSAS *Catalogue of Selected Documents in Psychology*, 1975, **5**, 330 (Ms. No. 421).

Averill, J. R. Emotion and anxiety: Sociocultural, biological, and psychological determinants. In M. Zuckerman & C. D. Spielberger (Eds.), *Emotion and anxiety: New concepts, methods and applications*. New York: LEA–John Wiley, 1976.

Averill, J.R. The functions of grief. In C. Izard (Ed.), *Emotions in personality and psychopathology*. New York: Plenum, 1979.

Averill, J. R. A constructivist view of emotion. In R. Plutchik & H. Kellerman (Eds.), *Theories of emotion*. New York: Academic Press, in press. (a)

Averill, J. R., & Boothroyd, P. On falling in love in conformance with the romantic ideal. *Motivation and Emotion*, 1977, **1**, 235–247.

Averill, J. R., DeWitt, G., & Zimmer, M. The self-attribution of emotion as a function of success and failure. *Journal of Personality*, 1978, **46**, 323–347.

Bandura, A. *Aggression: A social learning analysis*. Englewood Cliffs, N.J.: Prentice-Hall, 1973.

Baron, R. A. *Human aggression*. New York: Plenum, 1977.

Bem, D. J. Self-perception theory. In L. Berkowitz (Ed.), *Advances in experimental social psychology*, Vol. 6. New York: Academic Press, 1972.

Berkowitz, L. *Aggression: A social psychological analysis*. New York: McGraw-Hill, 1962.

Berkowitz, L. The frustration-aggression hypothesis revisited. In L. Berkowitz (Ed.), *Roots of aggression*. New York: Atherton Press, 1969.

Berkowitz, L. Some determinants of impulsive aggression: Role of mediated association with reinforcements for aggression. *Psychological Review*, 1974, **81**, 165–176.

Burnstein, E., & Worchel, P. Arbitrariness of frustration and its consequences for aggression in a social situation. *Journal of Personality*, 1962, **30**, 528–540.

Buss, A. H. Instrumentality of aggression, feedback, and frustration as determinants of physical aggression. *Journal of Personality and Social Psychology*, 1966, **3**, 153–162.

Carr, J. E., & Tan, E. K. In search of the true amok: Amok as viewed within the Malay culture. *American Journal of Psychiatry*, 1976, **133**, 1295–1299.

Cohen, A. Social norms, arbitrariness of frustration, and status of the agent of frustration in the frustration-aggression hypothesis. *Journal of Abnormal and Social Psychology*, 1955, **51**, 222–226.

Cole, J. K., & Jensen, D. D. (Eds.). *Nebraska Symposium on Motivation 1972* (Vol. 20). Lincoln: University of Nebraska Press, 1973.

Colson, E. *Tradition and contract: The problem of order*. Chicago: Aldine, 1974.

Commonwealth v. McCusker, Pa., 292 A2d, 286 (Supreme Court of Pennsylvania, 1972).

Crabtree, J. M., & Moyer, K. E. *Bibliography of aggressive behavior*. New York: Alan R. Liss, 1977.

de Rivera, J. The structure of situations, emotion, and unreality. In J. de Rivera (Ed.), *Field theory as human-science*. New York: Gardner Press, 1976.

Dollard, J., Doob, L., Miller, N., Mowrer, O., & Sears, R. *Frustration and aggression*. New Haven: Yale University Press, 1939.

Doob, A. N., & Gross, A. E. Status of frustrator as an inhibitor of horn-honking responses. *Journal of Social Psychology*, 1968, **76**, 213–218.

Drye v. State, 184 S. W. 2d, 10 (Supreme Court of Tennessee, 1944).

Epstein, S., & Taylor, S. P. Instigation to aggression as a function of degree of defeat and perceived aggressive intent of the opponent. *Journal of Personality*, 1967, **35**, 265–289.

Fromm, E. *The anatomy of human destructiveness*. New York: Holt, Rinehart, & Winston, 1973.

Gagnon, J. H. Scripts and the coordination of sexual conduct. In J. K. Cole & R. Dienstbier (Eds.), *Nebraska Symposium on Motivation 1973* (Vol. 21). Lincoln: University of Nebraska Press, 1974.

Gates, G. S. An observational study of anger. *Journal of Experimental Psychology*, 1926, **9**, 325–331.

Geen, R. G. Effects of frustration, attack, and prior training in aggressiveness upon aggressive behavior. *Journal of Personality and Social Psychology*, 1968, **9**, 316–321.

Gentry, W. D. Effects of frustration, attack, and prior aggressive training on overt aggression and vascular processes. *Journal of Personality and Social Psychology*, 1970, **16**, 718–725.

Goldstein, A. S. *The insanity defense*. New Haven: Yale University Press, 1967.

Graham, F. K., Charwat, W. A., Honig, A. S., & Weltz, P. C. Aggression as a function of the attack and the attacker. *Journal of Abnormal and Social Psychology*, 1951, **46**, 512–520.

Greenwell, J., & Dengerink, H. A. The role of perceived versus actual attack in human physical aggression. *Journal of Personality and Social Psychology*, 1973, **26**, 66–71.

Guttmacher, M. S., & Weihofen, H. *Psychiatry and the law*. New York: Norton, 1952.

Hardisty, J. H. Mental illness: A legal fiction. *Washington Law Review*, 1973, **48**, 735–762.

Harris, M. B. Mediators between frustration and aggression in a field experiment. *Journal of Experimental Social Psychology*, 1974, **10**, 561–571.

Henry, J. The linguistic expression of emotion. *American Anthropologist*, 1936, **38**, 250–257.

Holmes, D. P., & Horan, J. J. Anger induction in assertion training. *Journal of Counseling Psychology*, 1976, **23**, 108–111.

Holt, R. R. On the interpersonal and intrapersonal consequences of expressing or not expressing anger. *Journal of Consulting and Clinical Psychology*, 1970, **35**, 8–12.

Izard, C. E. *Human Emotions*. New York: Plenum, 1977.

Kaufmann, H. *Aggression and altruism*. New York: Holt, Rinehart, & Winston, 1970.

Konečni, V. J. The mediation of aggressive behavior: Arousal level versus anger and cognitive labeling. *Journal of Personality and Social Psychology*, 1975, **32**, 706–712.

Lactantius. *The wrath of God*. In R. J. Deferrari (Editorial Director), *The fathers of the church*. Vol. 54: *Lactantius: Minor works*. Washington, D. C.: Catholic University of America Press, 1965. (Originally written 313–314).

Laird, J. D. Self-attribution of emotion: The effects of expressive behavior on the quality of emotional experience. *Journal of Personality and Social Psychology*, 1974, **29**, 475–486.

Langness, L. L. Hysterical psychosis in the New Guinea highlands: A Bena Bena example. *Psychiatry*, 1965, **28**, 258–277.

Lazarus, R. S. *Psychological stress and the coping process*. New York: McGraw-Hill, 1966.

Lazarus, R. S., & Averill, J. R. Emotion and cognition: With special reference to anxiety. In C. D. Spielberger (Ed.), *Anxiety: Current trends in theory and research*. New York: Academic Press, 1972.

Linsky, A. Stimulating responses to mailed questionnaires. *Public Opinion Quarterly*, 1975, **39**, 82–101.

Lorenz, K. *On aggression*. New York: Harcourt, Brace & World, 1966.

Lundsgaarde, H. P. *Murder in space city*. New York: Oxford University Press, 1977.

Mandler, G. *Mind and emotion*. New York: Wiley, 1975.

McKellar, P. The emotion of anger in the expression of human aggressiveness. *British Journal of Psychology*, 1949, **39**, 148–155.

McKellar, P. Provocation to anger and the development of attitudes of hostility. *British Journal of Psychology*, 1950, **40**, 104–114.

Meltzer, H. Students' adjustments in anger. *Journal of Social Psychology*, 1933, **4**, 285–309.

Model penal code. Reprinted in *Uniform laws annotated*, Vol. 10. St. Paul, Minn.: West Publishing Co., 1974. (Originally published by the American Law Institute, 1962.)

Montagu, A. *The nature of human aggression*. New York: Oxford University Press, 1976.

Moyer, K. E. *The psychobiology of aggression*. New York: Harper & Row, 1976.

Newman, P. L. "Wildman" behavior in a New Guinea highlands community. *American Anthropologist*, 1964, **66**, 1–19.

Nisbett, R. E., & Bellows, N. Verbal reports about causal influences on social judgments: Private access versus public theories. *Journal of Personality and Social Psychology*, 1977, **35**, 613–624.

Nisbett, R. E., & Valins, S. Perceiving the causes of one's own behavior. In E. E. Jones et al., *Attribution: Perceiving the causes of behavior*. New York: General Learning Press, 1971.

Nisbett, R. E., & Wilson, T. D. Telling more than we can know: Verbal reports on mental processes. *Psychological Review*, 1977, **84**, 231–259.

Novaco, R. W. *Anger control: The development and evaluation of an experimental treatment*. Lexington, Mass.: Lexington Books/D. C. Heath, 1975.

O'Brien, V. P. *The measure of responsibility in persons influenced by emotion*. Washington, D. C.: Catholic University of America Press, 1948.

Pastore, N. The role of arbitrariness in the frustration-aggression hypothesis. *Journal of Abnormal and Social Psychology*, 1952, **47**, 728–731.

People v. Lewis, 123 N. Y. S. 2d, 81 (Supreme Court, Appellate Division, 1953).

Pepitone, A. Toward a normative and comparative biocultural social psychology. *Journal of Personality and Social Psychology*, 1976, **34**, 641–653.

Perkins, R. M. The law of homicide. *Journal of Criminal Law and Criminology*, 1946, **36**, 391–454.

Peters, R. S. Emotions and the category of passivity. *Aristotelian Society Proceedings*, 1962, **62**, 117–134.

Peters, R. S. Motivation, emotion, and the conceptual scheme of common sense. In T. Mischel (Ed.), *Human action. Conceptual and empirical issues*. New York: Academic Press, 1969.

Richardson, F. *The psychology and pedagogy of anger*. Baltimore: Warwick & York, 1918.

Rothenberg, A. On anger. *American Journal of Psychiatry*, 1971, **128**, 454–460.

Rule, B. G., & Hewitt, L. S. Effects of thwarting on cardiac response and physical aggression. *Journal of Personality and Social Psychology*, 1971, **19**, 181–187.

Rule, B. G., & Nesdale, A. R. Emotional arousal and aggressive behavior. *Psychological Bulletin*, 1976, **83**, 851–863.

Salisbury, R. [Reply to L. L. Langness]. *Transcultural Psychiatric Research*, 1967, **4**, 130–134.

Schachter, S. *Emotion, obesity, and crime*. New York: Academic Press, 1971.

Schafer, R. *A new language for psychoanalysis*. New Haven: Yale University Press, 1976.

Schutz, A. On multiple realities. In C. Gordon & K. J. Gergen (Eds.), *The self in social interaction* (Vol. 1). New York: Wiley, 1968.

Schwartz, S. H. Normative influences on altruism. In L. Berkowitz (Ed.), *Advances in experimental social psychology* (Vol. 10). New York: Academic Press, 1977.

Segall, A. The sick role concept: Understanding illness behavior. *Journal of Health and Social Behavior*, 1976, **17**, 162–169.

Seneca. On anger. In J. W. Basore (Trans.), *Moral essays*. Cambridge, Mass.: Harvard University Press, 1963. (Originally written ca. 40–50 A. D.)

Simon, W. The social, the erotic, and the sensual: The complexities of sexual scripts. In J. K. Cole & R. Dienstbier (Eds.), *Nebraska Symposium on Motivation 1973* (Vol. 21). Lincoln: University of Nebraska Press, 1974.

Solomon, R. C. *The passions*. Garden City, N. Y.: Anchor Press/Doubleday, 1976.

State v. Remus, No. 29969 (Ohio Com. Pleas, 1927); also, *Ex parte Remus*, 162 N. E. (Supreme Court of Ohio, 1928).

Staub, E. *Positive social behavior and morality: Personal and social influences.* New York: Academic Press, 1978.

Storr, A. *Human destructiveness.* New York: Basic Books, 1972.

Stratton, G. M. *Anger: Its religious and moral significance.* New York: Macmillan, 1923.

Szasz, T. S. *Law, liberty, and psychiatry.* New York: Collier Books, 1968.

Taylor, S. P., & Pisano, R. Physical aggression as a function of frustration and physical attack. *Journal of Social Psychology,* 1971, **84**, 261–267.

Valins, S. The perception and labeling of bodily changes as determinants of emotional behavior. In P. Black (Ed.), *Physiological correlates of emotion.* New York: Academic Press, 1970.

Westermeyer, J. A comparison of amok and other homicide in Laos. *American Journal of Psychiatry,* 1972, **129**, 703–708.

Wolfgang, M. E. *Patterns of criminal homicide.* Philadelphia: University of Pennsylvania Press, 1958.

Woodworth, R. S. *Psychology: A study of mental life.* New York: Holt, 1921.

Worchel, S. The effect of three types of arbitrary thwarting on the instigation to aggression. *Journal of Personality,* 1974, **42**, 301–318.

Words and Phrases. St. Paul, Minn.: West Publishing Co., 1953 (Vol. 3), 1957 (Vol. 31A).

Zillman, D., & Cantor, J. R. Effect of timing of information about mitigating circumstances on emotional responses to provocation and retaliatory behavior. *Journal of Experimental Social Psychology,* 1976, **12**, 38–55.

Behavior Analysis of Motivational and Emotional Interactions in a Programmed Environment[1]

Joseph V. Brady
and
Henry H. Emurian[2]

The Johns Hopkins University School of Medicine

*T*he historical precedents established by this distinguished symposium series, spanning a quarter century of theoretical and investigative endeavor, bear eloquent testimony to an abiding concern with the motivational and emotional attributes of behavior. While the observations to which these terms refer are not easily denied, many subtleties in the phenomena continue to be obscured by the semantic, linguistic, and taxonomic conventions which determine their popular use and abuse. Even the technical and quasi-technical usage of the terms as unitary behavioral referents tends to confuse a number of fundamental distinctions. Not the least of these ambiguities arises in the context of differentiations between motivational and emotional functions based upon attributions which are, for the most part, response-inferred. The need, thus revealed, to base independent variable distinctions upon dependent variable designations should warn against the obvious perils to sound theory.

1. Supported by NASA Grant NGR–21–001–111, Contract N00014–77–C–0498 from the office of Naval Research, and NIDA Grant DA–00018.
2. Henry H. Emurian is Assistant Professor of Behavioral Biology, The Johns Hopkins University School of Medicine.

The ultimate validity of the concepts which focus attention upon motivational and emotional functions must nonetheless be sought, if anywhere, among behavioral indicators which can be related and distinguished on the basis of lawful variation in parametrically analyzed experimental situations. Such an interbehavioral analysis would provide the essential foundation of a unifying operational framework encompassing motivational and emotional functions. A basic building block for this systematic formulation is suggested by the "three-term contingency" analysis (Skinner, 1969) which identifies and specifies controlling relations between "occasions," "behavior," and "consequences." The dominant relationship between these component terms emphasizes the governance of action (i.e., the likelihood of "behavior") by the contingently occurring effects of that action (i.e., its reinforcing "consequences"). Emergent relations between "occasion" and "behavior" components are also specified to the extent that "behavior-consequence" contingency relations are dependent upon the occurrence of occasioning events. More complex *interrelationships* between the terms can, of course, be elaborated (e.g., "rule" or "schedule" relations) and must necessarily enter into the precise definition of behavioral contingencies. Within the context of these *common* empirical referents, motivational and emotional functions can be usefully analyzed and *differentiated* in terms of their effects upon distinguishable components (and/or relations between components) of the three-term contingency.

An analysis of *motivational functions*, thus expressed, would proceed, in the simplest case with a primary focus upon operations which affect the potency (i.e., "potentiating operations") of the *consequence component* of a behavioral contingency. Food deprivation, for example, potentiates the consequence and increases the likelihood of consumatory behaviors. Conversely, nutritive ingestion attenuates the potency (i.e., reinforcing function) of food and defines the opposite pole of the same class of motivational procedures. In more complex instances, as elaborated in recent conceptual extensions (Goldiamond, 1978), the analysis requires attention to the effects of motivational operations upon the relations between the behavior and consequence components of the three-term contingency (e.g., schedules of food reinforcement which temporally distribute periods of ingestion and deprivation).

By contrast, the analysis of *emotional functions* within the framework of such a systematic formulation would focus upon the *occasion component* of the three-term contingency and procedures which affect the efficacy (i.e., *discriminant function*) of occasioning events. As an elementary case in point, abrupt and episodic "startle" effects may disrupt occasioning circumstances and decrease the likelihood of ongoing behavior-consequence relations (e.g., food ingestion). Conversely, "orienting" and/or "alerting" effects may augment occasioning circumstances (e.g., amplify the salience of discriminative stimuli) and increase the likelihood (e.g., decrease response latency) of a consequated performance, thus defining the opposite pole of the same class of emotional functions. More complex instances requiring analysis of the relations between occasion and behavior components of the three-term contingency have been extensively elaborated in previous experimental and conceptual accounts of emotional interactions (Brady, 1970, 1971, 1975a).

The formal simplicity of these statements, shorn of subjective unobservables and the inferred mediational terms (e.g., "drive," "fear," etc.) common in linearly causal accounts of both "motivation" and "emotion" should not obscure accommodation of the obvious "somatic" participants in such interactions. In the *motivational* case, for example, physiological interventions, specified either directly (e.g., cell dehydration) or as functional equivalents of other defineable operations (e.g., water deprivation) can be expressed in terms of making potent (i.e., potentiating) a contingency component (e.g., a consequence), the relations between contingency components, or combinations thereof. Prominent "associative" features (e.g., "acquired motivation") can as well be analyzed by specifying the operations which generate conditioned and generalized potentiating effects (e.g., "pairing" and "chaining"), and by characterizing the temporal and quantitative relations between contingency components (e.g., "delay" and "amount" of "reward," "response cost," etc.). Even the "hedonic" characteristics of motivational functions can be accommodated within the empirical framework of this conceptual analysis by appealing to the experimentally based distinctions between "positive" and "negative" reinforcement operations. The evident byproducts (e.g., "euphoria") of "appetitive" consequating relations which increase the likelihood of behavior, on the one hand, and the "dysphoric" accompaniments of "aversive" consequences which weaken behavior (or strengthen escape and avoidance performances), would seem to provide a fruitful point of departure for the experimental analysis of this eudaemonic dimension.

A similar analysis of the somatic, associative, and hedonic dimensions which characterize *emotional* functions has emphasized the prominent role of "inner events" (e.g., "feelings") in such interactions (Brady, 1975a). Significantly, if somewhat paradoxically, this "radically behavioristic" approach neither excludes internal processes nor requires their reformulation in terms of the "convergent operations" (Garner, Hake, & Eriksen, 1956) which have traditionally served to exhaust their definition (i.e., conventional operationism). The acceptance of a meaningful distinction between public and private events, however, does not impose adherence to linearly causal accounts of emotional interactions. Rather, both sets of events are emphasized within the framework of an experimental analysis which presumes only that the procedures found useful in providing a scientific account of public behavior will prove fruitful in analyzing those private events which participate so prominently in emotional interactions.

The conceptual clarity of an empirical analysis which purports to *differentiate* between *emotional* and *motivational* operations on the basis of their effects upon selective "occasion" and "consequence" components of the three-term contingency is put to its severest test in providing an articulate account of the evident interrelationships between these interacting functions in complex behavioral situations. Indeed, it could be argued that in all but the theoretically purest (and empirically rarest) of cases, the definition and differentiation of motivational and emotional influences upon distinguishable components of a behavioral contingency should be formulated in functional terms which emphasize the "primary locus" rather than the "exclusive domain" of such operations. But it would appear that the conceptual problems involved may arise more from the social conventions and cultural conditioning which burden "motivational" and "emotional" vocabularies with excess meaning than from the logic of an empirical analysis which eschews semantics ("a rose by any other name . . .") and focuses upon the differential functional properties of operations which exert unique influences upon distinguishable components of a behavioral contingency. In any event, such a formulation may provide a somewhat different and, it is hoped, more operational approach to parceling out the contributions of the functional components which make up interacting segments of ongoing behavioral transactions.

In what would appear to be a most obvious case of such interacting operations, for example, a singular event may share both motivational and emotional functions (i.e., influence both occasion and consequence components of a behavioral contingency). The sight of blood (particularly one's own!) is likely not only to affect the occasion controlling eating behavior, for example, but as well to result in somatic changes (e.g., nausea) which attenuate the potency of food as a maintaining consequence (i.e., decrease its reinforcing function). Equally common would seem to be those instances which involve the simultaneous occurrence of independent and separable (but obviously interacting) motivational and emotional operations. The context in which these distinguishable but concurrent motivational and emotional functions emerge will, of course, determine whether synergistic or antagonistic interactions result. Emotional operations which enhance the discriminability of occasioning events (e.g., alerting) may, on the one hand, interact synergistically with independently indentified motivational operations which "energize" a performance (e.g., the intensity of aversive consequences maintaining escape or avoidance behavior). The same emotional alerting functions may, on the other hand, interact antagonistically with motivational operations which potentiate the consequence of less energetic behaviors (e.g., sleep deprivation). And, of course, topographically identical operations may at one time subserve motivational functions (i.e., potentiate a consequence) and at other times subserve emotional functions (i.e., enhance occasioning circumstances).

Temporal and sequential dependencies between behavior segments can also be seen to play an important role in determining the interrelationships and functional interactions between motivational and emotional operations. Prior-occurring behavior-consequence relations and attendant motivational functions, for example, can exert powerful emotional influences upon the occasioning circumstances for ensuing behavioral contingencies (e.g., the "joy" of victory and the "agony" of defeat). Moreover, the form and extent of these interactional complexities between motivational and emotional functions, as they emerge within the context of shifting behavioral contingencies, approach mind-boggling proportions when the multiple somatic, associative, and hedonic dimensions of the participant processes are parceled out for experimental analysis. The method of dealing with such complex phenomena by resolution or reduction has a longstanding and productive history in scientific thought, and the schemata which have proven useful for most discourse within science (in the sense of public, consensual exchange) are often represented in a two-dimensional plane (i.e., xy

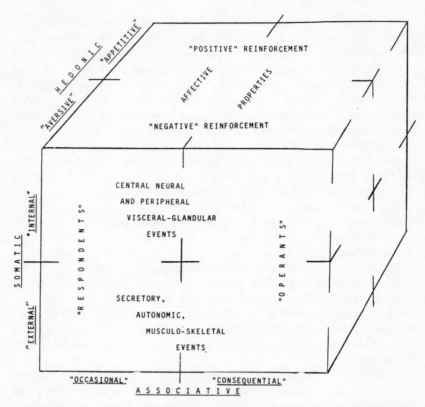

FIGURE 1. Schematic diagram of three-dimensional space encompassing the multiple somatic, associative, and hedonic parameters of motivational and emotional functions.

axes) in which verfication and falsification can take place. The interacting biological, behavioral, and psychological complexities presented by motivational and emotional functions, however, would seem to require conceptualization of a three-dimensional space within which the multiple somatic, associative, and hedonic dimensions can be encompassed.

Figure 1, for example, illustrates diagrammatically a composite topographic-functional framework for such a multidimensional schematic analysis. By way of at least preliminary specification of relevant basic constructs, the *somatic* dimension can be operationally defined in terms of the broad range of biochemical, anatomical, and physiological participants (both "inside" and "outside" the skin) which participate in motivational and emotional functions. The *associative* dimension is represented by the prominent "learning" effects (both historical and contemporary) which reflect the temporal ordering of stimulus and response events. And the *hedonic* dimension is defined by the emergent eudaemonic properties of somatic-associative interactions. As conceptualized, each of the indicated dimensions is considered to be *inclusive* in that each encompasses the entire universe of motivational and emotional events. The parameters and interactive features of these constructs, in turn, delineate the three-dimensional space within which analysis and discourse would seem to be most profitably pursued.

Indeed, essential parametric delineation of these multiple inclusive dimensions presents operational problems of formidable proportions. The evident continua which characterize such dimensional formulations will doubtless require analogical analysis for accurate and precise definition. But a first approximation "analogue-to-digital" conversion may at least serve to dichotomize such continuous arrays into operationally discriminable categories. The vast array of *somatic* (i.e., biochemical, anatomical, physiological, behavioral) events and processes involved in motivational and emotional functions, for example, may be divided into two reasonably exclusive classes based upon the distinction between operations which occur "inside" and "outside" the skin. The defining operations of the *internal* class would include measurable neurohumoral, neurophysiological, and visceral-glandular events related to motivational and emotional operations (e.g., catecholamine levels, EEG activity, autonomic responsivity, etc.). The defining operations of the *external* somatic class, on the other hand, would be constituted by measurable secretory and musculo-skeletal effects (e.g., "fight" or "flight" reactions, etc.). In general, the distinctions involved refer to the *physical locus* of motivational and emotional interactions.

A similar "digital conversion" for the *associative* (i.e., learning) processes involved in motivational and emotional functions distinguishes between two broad categories of behavioral interactions based upon the temporal ordering of environmental "stimulus" events and organismic "response" activities. The first of these parametric classes is defined by the occurrence of *antecedent* events in the environment (both internal and external) which *elicit* activities (i.e., "respondent" interactions). The defining operations of the second associative class are characterized by occurrence of *consequent* events in the internal and external environment which follow and are contingent upon *emitted* performances (i.e., "operant" interactions). These "associative" distinctions refer primarily to the *temporal relationships* involved in motivational and emotional interactions.

Somewhat more problematically (consensual validation notwithstanding), the *hedonic* (i.e., affective) properties of somatic/ associative interactions involved in motivational and emotional functions suggest a first-approximation parametric analysis in terms of experimentally based distinctions between positive and negative reinforcement operations. The positive or *appetitive* category represented in the third eudaemonic dimension of Figure 1 is defined (in obviously oversimplified form) by the occurrence of consequences (e.g., "euphoria") which strengthen the performances upon which such effects are contingent. A comparable oversimplification would identify the negative or *aversive* class with consequences (e.g., "dysphoria") which weaken the performances producing such effects or strengthen responses which prevent their occurrence. This dichotomous characterization of the "hedonic" dimension would refer primarily to the *affective valence* of motivational and emotional interactions.

A more detailed specification of the interacting components which occupy the multidimensional space outlined in Figure 1 is required to delineate the operational elements which form the empirical building blocks of this conceptual schematic. The temporal and sequential interrelationships between these component elements would provide a systematic framework for experimental analysis of both the behavioral and physiological processes which participate in complex and multifaceted motivational and emotional interactions. A range of animal laboratory studies addressing the commonalities and differences in such motivational and emotional functions have in fact begun to analyze experimentally the constituent operations involved (Brady, 1975a), and to examine in detail the interrelationships between behavioral activities and the broader patterning or balance of biochemical, anatomical, and physiological events which in concert regulate the internal milieu (Brady, 1975b; Brady & Harris, 1976; Mason, 1968). Figure 2 summarizes in diagrammatic form the integrative features of this systematic interbehavioral formulation in terms of the multidimensional determinants, both historical and contemporary, which provide the basis for an operational analysis of motivational and emotional functions.

It may, of course, be premature to suggest that any such unifying

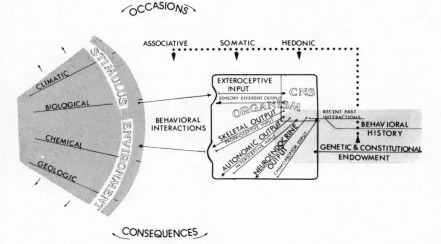

FIGURE 2. Integrative diagrammatic representation of the multidimensional historical and contemporary determinants of motivational and emotional functions.

conceptual framework can adequately encompass the full range and complexity of motivational and emotional interactions. Certainly, the model will require systematic analysis with regard to its novelty and comprehensiveness, gaps in knowledge which it reveals, and new directions of experimental inquiry which it suggests. Some heuristic value may be derived, however, from an account which proceeds without recourse to the fruitless polemic exchanges over temporal ordering and linear causality which have marred prominently reified accounts of the motivational and emotional attributes of behavior. Rather the more operational framework herein proposed would appeal to the empirical relations among and between components of the three-term contingency and the functional analysis of behavior which experimental examination of these interrelationships has provided. While such reformulation may not solve the empirical problem of "motivation" and "emotion," it does suggest a different and, it is hoped, more productive approach to conceptual and investigative analysis of both the general laws of behavior, as applied to motivational and emotional functions, and the parameter determinations required to make such laws operative in fact as well as in principle.

Indeed, it is to the latter problem of parameter values and methodological requirements for the analysis of human motivational and emotional interactions that the remainder of this discussion will be addressed. Despite evident dedication and industry, the slow and somewhat halting scientific progress in this field would appear to be attributable, at least in part, to the limited availability of effective and relevant experimental methodologies for the interactive analysis of motivational and emotional functions in naturalistic but controlled human behavior situations. In our laboratories at the Johns Hopkins University School of Medicine over the past few years, we have been developing an experimental methodology for the study of human individual and social behavior under residential "programmed environment" conditions which provide for the analysis of motivational and emotional functions (Brady, Bigelow, Emurian, & Williams, 1974; Emurian, Bigelow, Brady, & Emurian, 1975; Bigelow, Emurian, & Brady, 1975; Emurian, Emurian, Bigelow, & Brady, 1976; Emurian, Emurian, & Brady, in press). Findley and Brady (Note 1) and Findley (1966) have provided a discursive rationale and preliminary model for the application of continuously programmed environments in human research on the basis of extended experimental control, objective recording, and the maintenance of realistic and naturalistic incentive conditions for the assessment of a broad range of behavioral processes. In addition, the development and application of contingency management procedures in a variety of naturalistic social settings over the past decade (e.g., Ayllon & Azrin, 1965; Cohen, 1968) have provided an effective methodology for the experimental control, manipulation, and measurement of relevant individual and group variables in such laboratory human behavior research.

The research environment has been designed and constructed for the conduct of small-group experiments over extended time periods within the context of a self-contained laboratory programmed for continuous residency by volunteer human subjects. Groups of male and female volunteers, recruited from local college student communities, have served as experimental subjects in these studies. All subjects receive psychometric test evaluation and interview assessment by a staff psychiatrist as part of the screening procedure for acceptance as participants in the experiment. Each subject is fully informed about the research setting and about the research procedures involved. In addition, all subjects participate in several daily briefing sessions in the programmed environment prior to the start of an experiment to insure familiarization with the operational features of the laboratory. Following these briefings, but before begin-

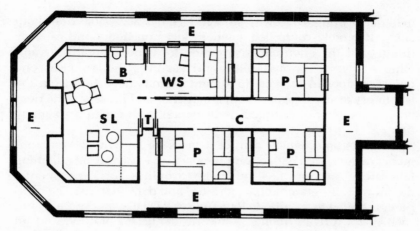

FIGURE 3. Diagrammatic representation of the overall floor plan of the laboratory and its arrangement within the external building shell.

ning an experiment, a written informed consent agreement is signed and exchanged between the subjects and experimenters. In addition, a manual of instructions detailing the experimental procedures and environmental resources is provided each subject for guidance throughout the experiment and retention thereafter for whatever reference purposes the participant may find necessary or desirable. With these procedures in effect, over 70 experimental subjects have participated in and completed upward of 30 residential studies in the programmed environment without untoward occurrence.

The residential laboratory environment is composed of a complex of five specially-designed rooms joined by an interconnecting common corridor constructed within a wing of the Phipps Clinic at the Johns Hopkins University School of Medicine. The overall floor plan of the laboratory and its arrangement within the external building shell is illustrated in figure 3. The three identical private rooms (P - each 8½' × 11') are similar to small efficiency apartments containing kitchen and bathroom facilities, bed, desk, chair, rug and other furnishings. The social living area (SL - 14½' × 22½') is equipped with tables, chairs, sofa beds, storage cabinets, and a complete kitchen facility. The workshop (WS - 8½' × 13½') contains benches, stools, storage cabinets, tools, and a washer-dryer combination. A common bath (B, Figure 3) serves the social living area and the workshop. Access to the exterior walls of the laboratory is provided by a four- to six-foot corridor between the residential chambers and the external building shell which permits transfer of supplies and materials through two-way storage facilities accessible from both sides. Remotely controlled solenoid locks on doors and cabinets throughout the environment provide for experimental programming of access to various facilities and resources, though at least one unlocked door in each compartment permits departure from the laboratory at any time in case of emergency and preserves the right of subjects to terminate their participation in an experiment at any time.

The electromechanical control devices throughout the environment are interfaced with a computer system located in an adjoining laboratory support facility which provides for experimental monitoring, programming, recording, and data analysis. The computer is linked to a Cathode Ray Tube (CRT) Display Device within each of the private rooms of the residential laboratory, and an alpha-numeric keyboard with each display unit provides for direct communication with the system control. The communication panel in each individual chamber incorporates the CRT unit and also includes a telephone intercom for exchanges between subjects within the environment and a cassette tape player. Audio and video equipment in each of the residential chambers permits continuous monitoring during conduct of an experiment.

Behavioral programming procedures have been developed to establish and maintain stable performance baselines as well as provide for systematic experimental manipulation of performance interactions during extended residential studies in the laboratory environment. A behavior program is defined by: (1) an array of activities or behavioral units, and (2) the rules which govern the relationship between these activities. Figure 4, for example, illustrates diagrammatically the fixed and optional sequences which characterize a typical behavioral program used to establish baseline performances for these experiments, as well as the array of component activities which make up such a program. Variations in this program as required for specific experimental studies will be described below. Each box in the diagram represents a distinct behavioral unit and performance requirement, with progression through the various activities programmed sequentially from left to right. Regardless of the fixed or optional sequence selected, all behavioral units are scheduled on a contingent basis such that access to a succeeding activity depends upon satisfaction of the requirement for the preceding unit.

Beginning at the far left, the fixed activity sequence is composed

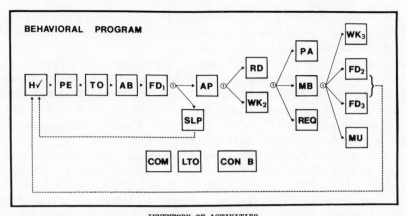

INVENTORY OF ACTIVITIES

NOTATION	FULL NAME	BRIEF DESCRIPTION
H√	HEALTH CHECK	TEMPERATURE, PULSE, WEIGHT, STATUS REPORT
PE	PHYSICAL EXERCISE	300 CORRECT PRESSES ON AUTOMATED TASK
TO	TOILET OPERATIONS	USE OF PRIVATE BATHROOM AND CONTENTS OF DRAWER CONTAINING TOILETRIES, CLEAN CLOTHING
AB	AUTOGENIC BEHAVIOR	RELAXATION EXERCISES ON TAPE
FD1	FOOD ONE	TWO SELECTIONS FROM A LIST OF LIGHT FOODS
SLP	SLEEP	UNLIMITED USE OF BED
AP	ARITHMETIC PROBLEMS	100 CORRECT SOLUTIONS OF ARITHMETIC PROBLEMS
RD	READING	ACCESS TO BOOK
WK2	WORK TWO	PROBLEMS, EXPERIMENTS, ASSEMBLY PROJECTS
PA	PUZZLE ASSEMBLY	ASSEMBLE A PUZZLE
MB	MANUAL BEHAVIOR	ACCESS TO ART MATERIALS
REQ	REQUISITION	EARN DELAYED DELIVERY OF TREATS OR REPLENISHMENT OF CONSUMABLES
WK3	WORK THREE	SOCIAL, ACCESS TO COMMUNAL WORKSHOP
FD2	FOOD TWO	PRIVATE MAJOR MEAL
FD3	FOOD THREE	SOCIAL, MAJOR MEAL IN RECREATION ROOM, GAMES
MU	MUSIC	5000 LEVER PRESSES TO EARN A CASSETTE TAPE
COM	COMMUNICATION	ACCESS TO INTERCOM
LTO	LIMITED TOILET OPERATIONS	ACCESS TO ESSENTIAL TOILET FACILITIES
CON B	CONDITION B	CHANGE IN PROGRAM CONDITION

FIGURE 4. Diagrammatic representation of a typical behavioral program governing the sequential and contingent relationship of activities.

of all activities between and including Health Check (H√) and Food One (FD1). The Health Check activity requires the subject to determine his temperature, pulse, and weight, and to fill out subjective status questionnaires. He then completes the following activities in the order displayed: Physical Exercise (PE), requiring 300 correct responses on an automated exercise task; Toilet Operations (TO), providing access to the private-room bathroom and drawers containing towels, toiletries, and a vacuum cleaner; Autogenic Behavior (AB), in which the subject is permitted to select two items from a presented list of 10 light foods such as coffee, tea, soup, cereal, etc.

When Food One is completed, the subject is eligible to select one of the following two activities: Arithmetic Problems (AP), requiring 100 solutions on a series of mathematical problems presented on a cathode-ray display screen and keyboard; and Sleep (SLP), providing access to the bed for an unlimited time period of at least 30 minutes. If the subject selects Sleep, he is required to return to the Health Check activity and fixed activity sequence at the completion of Sleep. This minimum recycling sequence is designed to maintain and assess the subject's health if he were otherwise indisposed to engage in the broader selection of opportunities.

The optional activity sequence commences with the choice of Arithmetic Problems instead of Sleep. At the completion of Arithmetic Problems, the subject is eligible to select one of the following two activities: Reading (RD), providing at least 30-minute access to books contained within a drawer; or Work Two (WK2), in which the subject completes in private various problems, experiments, or assembly projects presented in a drawer. When the selected activity is completed, the subject is eligible to select one of the following three activities: Puzzle Assembly (PA), requiring the subject to assemble a puzzle presented in a drawer; Manual Behavior (MB), providing at least 30-minute access to art supplies contained in a drawer; or Requisition (REQ), allowing the subject to press a lever to earn at least one but not more than 30 points exchangeable for treats, such as soft drinks and pastries, or for consumables, such as soap and toothpaste. On completion of the selected activity, the subject is eligible to select one of the following four activities: Work Three (WK3), providing at least 30 minutes in the workshop by one, two, or three subjects to complete assembly projects and maintenance chores: Food Two (FD2), requiring at least 30 minutes and providing the subject with a major meal to consume in the private room; Food Three (FD3), providing at least 30 minutes in the recreation room by one, two or three subjects to consume a major meal and to play games; or Music (MU), allowing the subject to press a lever to earn a cassette tape that can be played at any time. Once a subject has completed his choice among these four activities, he returns to Health Check and the fixed activity sequence, indicated by the dotted line. The optional activity sequence allows the subject flexibility in the selection and arrangement of activities, both individual and social.

At the bottom of the diagram are two activities with more general rules. The Limited Toilet Operations (LTO) activity, which allows access to essential toilet facilities, is the only activity that can be

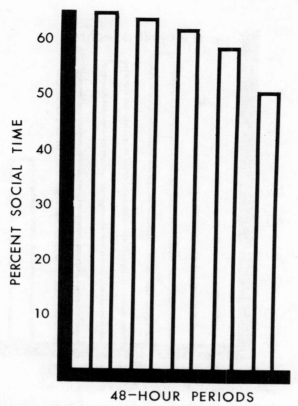

FIGURE 5. Percent of time that subjects were engaged in social activities, across consecutive 48-hour periods of the experiment.

selected at any time. The Communication (COM) activity allows access to the intercom for intersubject communications. A subject is permitted to use the intercom to initiate or answer a communication only if he is between any two program activities. Although the Communication activity is available between any activities, an actual conversation requires at least two subjects' simultaneous presence within the Communication activity. Conversing subjects, however, whether in pairs or all three at once, could be located at different sequential positions within the behavioral program. For example, a Communication and conversation might occur when one subject is between Autogenic Behavior and Food One, and another subject is between Manual Behavior and the last column of activities, and so on.

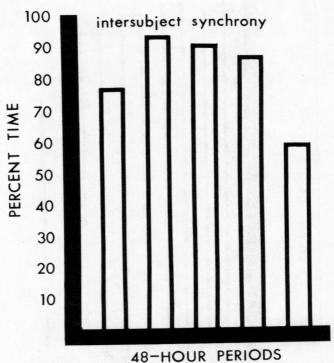

FIGURE 6. Percent of time that subjects were synchronized with respect to their positions in the behavioral program across consecutive 48-hour periods of the experiment.

The CON B notation at the bottom of the diagram refers to a program change determined by the requirements of a specific experiment, as described below. A manual of instructions detailing the program and use of environmental resources is contained in each room of the environment. An error in following the behavioral program causes a five-second blackout. Subjects follow the behavioral program throughout the periods of residence, and pairs of research assistants monitor the experimental environment continuously with audio and video equipment located, with the subject's awareness, in each room of the environment.

Initially, preliminary environmental habitability and performance programming studies (Brady et al., 1974) were conducted with groups of two and three subjects during intervals of continuous residence in the research environment ranging from 2 to 16 days. Only minimal (and basically biological) activity sequences (i.e., eat-

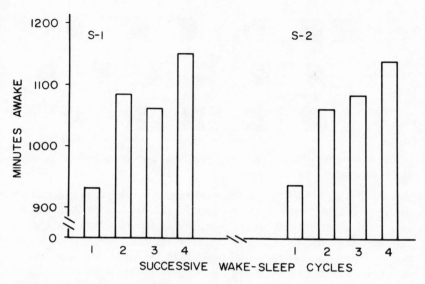

FIGURE 7. Minutes awake during successive wake-sleep cycles. Only consecutive waking periods bound both before and after by sleep are presented.

ing, sleeping, group recreational interactions, etc.) were required during the briefer exploratory periods, with gradual extensions of continuous residential periods from 1 to 3, and then to 10 days, introducing more complex programmatic sequencing of performance activities with successive groups. Figure 5, for example, shows the high and relatively stable percentage of time spent in social activities for two subjects over the course of such a 10-day residential study, and Figure 6 reflects the high degree of intersubject program synchrony evidenced by the percentage of time the same two subjects were engaged in identical individual activities or were simultaneously engaged in different individual activities within the same column of optional activities during the 10-day study period.

Based upon the finding that these small groups could not only be maintained under stress-free living conditions for extended periods of continuous residence in the experimental environment, but that the sequential contingency performance program developed in the course of these investigations was supportive of both individual and group behavioral activity (Emurian, Bigelow, Brady & Emurian, 1975), a series of program parameter studies was undertaken. The

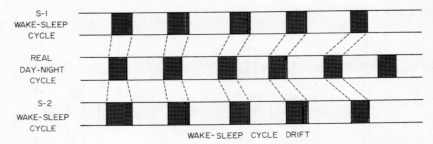

FIGURE 8. Successive wake and sleep durations across the temporal course of the experiment for both subjects.

major purpose of these experimental manipulations was to focus on the temporal determinants of behavioral interactions in the programmed environment under conditions of performance schedule "pacing" (i.e., imposed delays between activities) and upon extensions of continuous residential periods in the laboratory up to several weeks. Figures 7 and 8, for example, illustrate some of the more interesting incidental observations on orderly changes in sleep-wake cycles during one such residential study with two subjects. As shown in Figure 7, there was a progressive increase in the duration of successive wake periods with little or no systematic change in the duration of successive sleep intervals (Figure 8), resulting in a complete 12-hour reversal of the sleep-wake cycle over the 7-day residential period.

The major findings of these early studies emphasized the differential importance of selected program components (e.g., social activities) in maintaining individual and group performance and the sensitivity of behavioral interactions to experimental manipulations (e.g., program condition changes and reversals) over the course of extended residential periods. Consequently, a series of more systematic and extensive studies (Emurian, Emurian, Bigelow, & Brady, 1976) was undertaken to focus upon the motivational and emotional effects of varying social interaction conditions in five groups of three subjects each for periods up to 15 days of continuous residence in the programmed environment. The scheduled arrangement of required and optional private and social activities described above determined the individual and group baseline performances upon which the experimental social interaction conditions were superimposed. A *cooperation* condition (C) was in effect when all three subjects were required to select simultaneous access to a group area before it became available for use. This condition was programmed by requiring that either of two activities within the group area (i.e., FD3 or WK3) was accessible only when all three subjects selected it together. Typically, subjects would use the intercom several activities in advance to plan subsequent selection of a social activity. They would then pace their individual schedules accordingly to arrive at the choice point in the program at approximately the same time. Subjects almost always used the intercom immediately before FD3 or WK3 to insure that their schedules and choices were synchronized. Under the cooperation condition, subjects were also required to leave the group area at the same time, returning to their private rooms one after another.

In contrast to the cooperation contingency, a *non-cooperation* condition (NC) was in effect when FD3 or WK3 was accessible singly, without regard to the other subjects' activity selections. For example, a single subject could select FD3 or WK3 at the choice point and could then leave his private room immediately and enter the chosen group area even though the other subjects were engaged in private activities. Of course, the other subjects could also have access to the same group area at the same time, but they were not required to enter and leave together.

For Groups 1 through 5, these two conditions were investigated in the following order and number of successive days under each condition, respectively: C–NC–C (days: 4, 3, 3); NC–C–NC (days: 5, 5, 5); NC–C–NC (days: 4, 3, 3); C–NC–C (days: 4, 3, 3); and C–NC–C (days: 4, 3, 3).

A time sampling procedure was employed to monitor the occurrence of social interactions during triadic episodes. When all three subjects occupied either the social living area (FD3) or the workshop (WK3), 10-second observational samples were taken on a variable-interval schedule averaging eight minutes between samples. During each 10-second sample, each subject was rated independently on a "yes/no" dichomotization reflecting the presence or absence of a social interaction. A subject was rated as having exhibited a social interaction if he engaged in any of the following four behaviors: (1) any vocal utterance, (2) participation in social games, (3) physical contact with another subject, or (4) handling materials between subjects. The high degree of inter-rater reliability upon which these social interaction measures were based was reflected in a coefficient of correlation well above +.90.

The results of this experiment showed clearly that the systematic effects of such contingency management procedures could be dis-

Table 1

Percent of Time in Intersubject Program Synchronization

Group	Conditions[a]			
	C	NC	C	NC
1	55.5	18.6	47.4	—
2	—	24.4	27.9	20.0
3	—	35.5	48.7	54.6
4	73.8	45.7	67.8	—
5	64.6	49.3	70.8	—

[a]C=cooperation condition, NC=non-cooperation condition.

Table 2

Mean Daily Intercom Selections

Group	Subject	Conditions[a]			
		C	NC	C	NC
1	1	9.3	5.7	6.0	—
	2	5.5	0.3	2.7	—
	3	9.3	5.0	5.3	—
2	1	—	4.0	3.4	2.2
	2	—	2.4	2.2	0.8
	3	—	2.8	2.4	2.0
3	1	—	4.0	8.3	2.3
	2	—	3.8	8.0	3.7
	3	—	3.5	5.3	2.3
4	1	6.5	1.7	5.0	—
	2	5.8	3.3	4.7	—
	3	5.8	2.0	4.0	—
5	1	2.5	1.0	1.3	—
	2	2.5	1.7	1.3	—
	3	2.5	1.3	1.7	—

[a]C=cooperation condition, NC=non-cooperation condition.

Table 3
Percent of Time in Triadic Episodes

Group	Conditions[a]			
	C	NC	C	NC
1	25.8	12.5	34.9	—
2	—	4.0	8.8	1.9
3	—	21.2	17.9	14.1
4	28.2	13.1	21.4	—
5	19.8	5.8	24.2	—

[a]C=cooperation condition, NC=non-cooperation condition.

Table 4
Mean Triadic Durations (Hours)

Group	FD3				WK3			
	Conditions[a]				Conditions[a]			
	C	NC	C	NC	C	NC	C	NC
1	3.2	2.3	5.4	—	2.6	none	3.6	—
2	—	4.8	4.6	1.2	—	none	1.4	none
3	—	4.2	5.8	4.5	—	1.8	2.3	none
4	4.7	2.7	3.4	—	2.8	1.3	1.9	—
5	3.6	1.3	5.8	—	2.2	0.4	none	—

[a]C=cooperation condition, NC=non-cooperation condition.

cerned not only upon the social behavior of the group, but as well upon *collateral individual behaviors* which characterized performances within the continuously programmed environment. Enhanced levels of intersubject program synchronization (Table 1) and intercom frequencies (Table 2) were accompanied by comparable increases in the magnitude of triadic episodes during the cooperation condition. Not only the percent of total time spent in triadic social activities (Table 3), but the *durations* of triadic episodes (Table 4), combined with corresponding social interaction measures (Table 5), suggested a potentially important consequence of cooperation contingencies in maintaining more durable social interactions when

Table 5

Proportion of Samples Where Social Interactions
Occurred During Triadic FD3 Episodes

Group	Subject	Conditions[a]			
		C	NC	C	NC
3	1	—	.842	.854	.838
	2	—	.833	.878	.897
	3	—	.783	.805	.779
4	1	.774	.834	.609	
	2	.788	.750	.731	—
	3	.688	.750	.475	—
5	1	.634	.654	.420	—
	2	.653	.615	.420	—
	3	.703	.269	.375	

[a]C=cooperation condition, NC=non-cooperation condition.

continued access to the group areas accrued primarily as a result of the *frequency* of the social interactions.

Cooperation contingency effects on triadic conditions would seem to be of particular significance when considered in light of group fragmentation effects observed during non-cooperation conditions. The distribution of dyadic percent times into two high-pairing subjects and one low-pairing subject within the groups, illustrated in Figure 9, suggests development of a two-person in-group and a relative social isolate during the non-cooperation condition. And the extent to which motivational and emotional interactions participated in the social contingency effects is suggested by the results observed with the very first group when the change from cooperation to non-cooperation conditions was programmed. Within minutes after the condition change was introduced during the course of a triadic social episode at the end of day 4, Subject 2 became involved in an altercation with the other two subjects and abruptly returned to his individual chamber. During the ensuing three days of the non-cooperation condition, Subjects 1 and 3 continued to engage in frequent *dyadic* social interactions which excluded Subject 2, as illustrated in the left-hand segment of Figure 9. More importantly, the performances of Subject 2 with respect to the maintenance of "housekeeping" chores in his individual

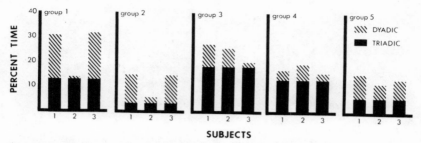

FIGURE 9. Percent of total time within non-cooperation (NC) conditions that all subjects in each group spent in triadic and dyadic episodes totalled across FD3 and WK3 activities. Where two NC conditions occurred for Groups 2 and 3, data have been combined across conditions.

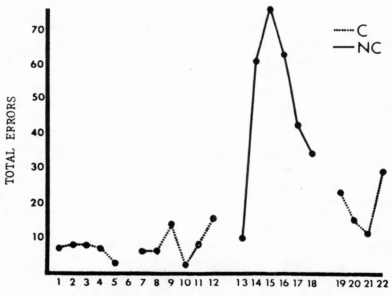

FIGURE 10. The total errors committed by Subject 2 on an arithmetic task, requiring 100 correct solutions to complete, across successive selections of the arithmetic task activity. C = cooperation condition; NC = non-cooperation condition.

chamber deteriorated and, significantly, the error rate reflected in his "private arithmetic" performances increased dramatically, as shown in Figure 10, during the period immediately following the

FIGURE 11. The progressive "shrinkage" of a series of potholders produced by the subject in the course of several successive WK3 activities.

disruptive emotional interaction (i.e., arithmetic activities 14, 15, and 16). The interacting motivational effects of delayed progress through the program can, however, be presumed operative in the equally dramatic decrease in error rate which occurred even before termination of the non-cooperation condition (i.e., arithmetic activities 17 and 18). In contrast, Figure 11 illustrates the weakening disposition of Subject 2 to engage in less consequential "hobby" activities as reflected in the progressive shrinkage of a series of pot holders produced in the course of several successive WK3 ("workshop behavior") selections during this same experiment.

A more extended analysis of such social interaction contingency effects was undertaken with four additional groups of three male subjects each who participated in a series of 10-day experiments to evaluate further the effects of subject pairing on individual and social behavior (Emurian, Emurian, & Brady, 1978). In addition to the triadic contingencies studied previously, dyadic contingencies were scheduled when simultaneous occupancy of a group area was permitted to any combination of two, and only two, subjects. Solitary access to group areas also was permitted to parcel out the reinforcing effects of social episodes, independently of those attributable to the accessibility of a larger space. Additionally, included in the behavioral program was a group task that allowed individual contributions to a group criterion that had to be satisfied before triadic or dyadic episodes could occur. This Group Arithmetic Problems (GAP) activity could be selected immediately following the completion of Private Arithmetic Problems (AP). During the GAP activity, the subject could work privately on the problems to contribute to a group criterion of 600 solutions. This criterion had to be satisfied before WK3 or FD3 could be selected by more than one subject, and a counter, present in each private room, showed cumulative contributions to this criterion by all subjects combined.

Once a subject had selected GAP, he was required to solve at least one problem correctly before selecting another activity. The GAP task was included to determine the extent to which responding could be maintained by access to different social situations (i.e., triadic or dyadic).

A triadic program condition (T) was in effect when either of two social activities within group areas (i.e., WK3 or FD3) was accessible only when all three subjects selected it together. During this condition, however, 600 counts on the group task were required before either WK3 or FD3, permitting subjects to leave their private rooms and enter the appropriate group area, could be selected by a triad.

In contrast to the triadic condition, a dyadic program condition (D) was in effect when WK3 and FD3 were accessible for social activities by any combination of two, and only two, subjects. As in the triadic condition, 600 counts on the group task were required before WK3 or FD3 could be selected by a dyad. In both conditions, subjects were required to enter and leave the group areas at the same time. Once a group area was occupied by a dyad, access to that area by the third subject was denied until the activity was terminated by the dyad.

For Groups 1 through 4, the dyadic and triadic conditions were investigated in the following order and number of successive days under each condition, respectively: T–D–T (days: 4, 3, 3); D–T–D (days: 4, 3, 3); T–D–T (days: 4, 3, 3); and D–T–D (days: 4, 3, 3). These sequences were used to control for the effects of the order in which the conditions were presented. For Groups 1 and 2, there was no upper limit on the durations of WK3 and FD3, but for Groups 3 and 4, a three-hour upper limit was in effect. Throughout social episodes in the recreation room (FD3), 10-second observational samples were taken on a variable-interval schedule averaging five minutes between samples. During each observational sample, the subjects' identification numbers (i.e., 1, 2, and 3) were recorded directly on a schematic diagram of the room by two independent observers, giving the subjects' exact location in the room and their proximity to one another. On the basis of these observations, a social distance scale was computed for each subject reflecting his physical proximity to the other two subjects during triadic social episodes. A given subject's score for a single observational sample was the sum of the distance between himself and the other two subjects. The recordings upon which the social distance scores were based showed high inter-rater reliability (correlation = +.96).

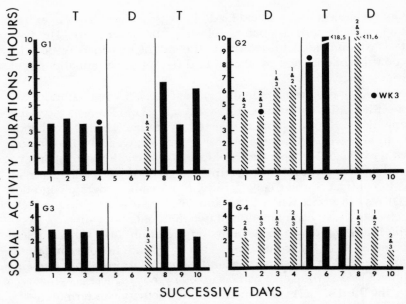

FIGURE 12. Social activity durations across successive days of the experiment for all groups. Bars represent durations of individual episodes. Numbers above dyadic durations identify the two subjects engaged in the episode. T = triadic condition; D = dyadic condition.

The results of this experiment showed that the status of a closed three-person social system changed when social opportunities were limited to *dyads* as compared to the *triad*. Under such dyadic conditions, durations of social contacts were briefer (Figure 12), and performance schedules drifted apart as reflected by decreased levels of harmony in the selection and completion of behavioral program activities (Figure 13). Additionally, daily response outputs on a task having social consequences (GAP) were more often omitted during dyadic conditions (Figure 14). These results illustrate the group fragmentation effects previously observed during a non-cooperation condition (Emurian, Emurian, Bigelow, & Brady, 1976) in a situation in which triadic social interactions were prohibited, rather than being optionally available.

Although division of group members occurred in the non-cooperation condition of the previous experiments, all subjects continued to have both dyadic and triadic social interactions, and consequently, no subject was ever completely isolated from group

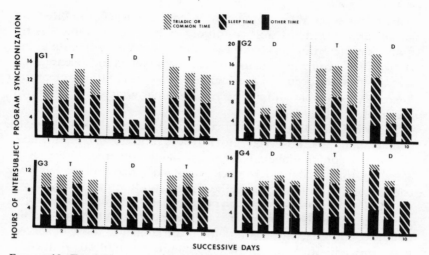

FIGURE 13. Total hours of intersubject program synchronization for each group across successive days of the experiment. T = triadic condition; D = dyadic condition.

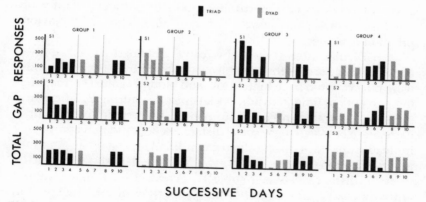

FIGURE 14. Total group-task (GAP) responses for all subjects in each group across successive days of the experiment.

activities. In the present experiment, however, group fragmentation effects were stronger during the dyadic condition than observed under the previous non-cooperation condition. Under dyadic conditions, three of the four groups in the present study had a lone member who failed to have any direct social contact for several successive days. These differences may be attributable, at least in

part, to the more demanding contingencies that were in effect for
social contact under dyadic conditions, where responding was required on the group task, and two subjects had to cooperate in the
choice of a group area before social behavior could occur. That
dyadic episodes occurred at all when free access to the large group
areas was available shows the motivational effects of even such
minimal social contact.

The triadic condition was associated with longer periods of social
contact than those observed under dyadic conditions. Under triadic
conditions, lone members were immediately integrated into social
activities that continued to occur on each successive day of the
triadic condition. In addition, the triadic condition was always associated with *more* schedule synchrony among subjects *within* a
given group in comparison to such synchrony observed under
dyadic conditions. These latter effects are similar to those observed
in the previous study in which the cooperation condition produced a
greater magnitude of synchrony than the non-cooperation condition. Enhanced synchrony observed under both cooperation and
triadic conditions in the two studies substantiates the motivational
effects of triadic social opportunities upon the reduction of intersubject discrepancies in the selection and completion of behavioral
program activities.

Of particular interest were the results obtained when the mean
social distance scores for all subjects observed over triadic episodes
were rank ordered from high to low and plotted against corresponding percents of time in dyadic social episodes during dyadic conditions, as illustrated in Figure 15. A product-moment coefficient of
correlation between these social distance scores and percents of time
in dyadic episodes during dyadic conditions revealed a significant
inverse relationship ($r = -.79$, $p<.01$). These data show that as the
physical distance between subjects increased for a given subject
within a triadic group setting, the proportion of time he spent in
social episodes decreased during dyadic conditions, predicting with
reasonable accuracy the sociability of group members under conditions requiring group fragmentation.

The robust effects of social contingencies upon the behavior of
small groups within the continuously programmed environment
has recently provided the basis for some extensions of such group
interaction analyses to investigate the role of explicitly programmed
motivational operations. Three recently completed 10-to-12-day,
three-person experiments incorporated a "work unit" completion

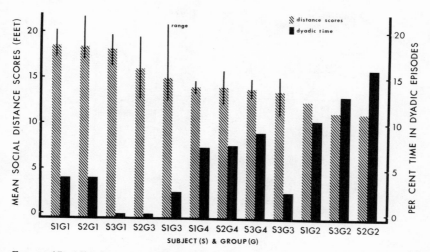

FIGURE 15. All subjects' mean social distance scores, rank ordered from high to low, plotted against corresponding percents of time in dyadic social episodes during dyadic conditions. The ranges of social distance scores between episodes are given for all groups except Group 2, which had only one triadic episode in the recreation room.

contingency determining the amount of group remuneration for participation in the study. In all previous experiments, individual subjects received a fixed per diem allowance (i.e., $25) for participation regardless of their performance. In contrast, this recent series of motivational studies provided a programmatically controlled amount of remuneration for each completed work unit by an individual subject in the form of a contribution to a group "bank account," with group earnings divided evenly among the participants upon completion of the experiment.

The basic fixed and optional components of the behavioral program continued to be in effect during these experiments with a sequence of work unit activities made available independently of the remaining sequentially arranged activities, as illustrated in Figure 16. The five work unit activities included: (1) Private Arithmetic Problems (PAP), requiring 200 correct solutions; (2) Work One (WK1), requiring 5000 lever operations; (3) Arithmetic problems (AP), requiring 50 correct solutions; (4) Physical Exercise (PE), requiring 400 correct presses; and (5) Health Check (H√), requiring completion of the health assessment battery. This work unit could

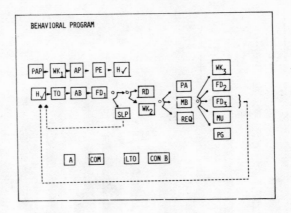

INVENTORY OF ACTIVITIES

Abbreviation	Full Name	Brief Description	Abbreviation	Full Name	Brief Description
PAP	Private Arith-metic Problems	200 correct solutions to arithmetic problems	MB	Manual Behavior	Access to art materials
WK$_1$	Work One	5000 lever operations	REQ	Requisition	Press a lever to earn treats
AP	Arithmetic Problem	50 correct solutions of arithmetic problems	WK$_3$	Work Three	Social option, access to communal workshop
PE	Physical Exercise	400 correct presses on automated task	FD$_2$	Food Two	Private major meal
H✓	Health Check	Temperature, pulse, weight, status report	FD$_3$	Food Three	Social option, access to recreation room, meal, games
TO	Toilet Operations	Use of bathroom and contents of TO drawer, toiletries, clean clothing	MU	Music	5000 lever presses to earn a cassette tape
AB	Autogenic Behavior	Relaxation exercises on cassette tape	PG	Private Games	Access to games drawer
FD$_1$	Food One	Two selections from a list of light foods	A	Audit	Free access to group "bank account" records
SLP	Sleep	Use of bed and privacy curtain	COM	Communication	Access to intercom
RD	Reading	Access to book	LTO	Limited Toilet Operations	Access to essential toilet facilities
WK$_2$	Work Two	Problems, experiments, assembly tasks	CON B	Condition B	Used to signal change in program rules
PA	Puzzle Assembly	Assemble a puzzle			

FIGURE 16. Diagrammatic representation of modified behavioral program showing sequences of independently available work unit activities arrayed upper left above the sequentially programmed behavioral activities.

be selected upon completion of any activity within the full behavioral program. Once a work unit had been selected, all five activities had to be completed before the subject could resume the behavioral program at the location where the work unit was voluntarily initiated. During a work unit, the Communication activity was unavailable, and subjects were not permitted to use the tape player for music. The parameters for the several component activities were chosen such that one to two hours were required for completion of a work unit.

The consequences of completing a work unit were systematically varied to assess the effects of alternative behavior-consequence relationships under program control. Throughout the initial four days of the first experiment, for example, a "positive" (i.e., appetitive) relationship was in effect whereby completion of a work unit by an individual subject produced a $10 deposit to the group bank account. Throughout the next four days of the experiment, a "negative" (i.e., avoidance) relationship was in effect such that work units no longer produced $10 increments in the group bank account, but rather were required of the participants in order to avoid withdrawals of similar magnitude. That is, work performance requirements for days 5 through 8 provided that a $10 withdrawal be made from the group bank account for each uncompleted work sequence below an assigned daily total (i.e., 20) determined on the basis of the group productivity sequences completed per 24 hours. This group requirement could be satisfied under any conditions of individual work scheduling or distribution decided upon by the group participants. Finally, the last two days of the experiment, days 9 and 10, were programmed as a return to the conditions in effect during the first four days.

The work unit contingency maintained substantial productivity levels for all subjects throughout the course of the experiment. No participant completed fewer than five work sequences per day with a range of 5 to 14 units. A distinguishable and relatively stable pattern of group work performances and social interactions emerged during the first four "appetitive" days of the experiment. Although all members of the group were not contributing equally to the group bank account (i.e., one of the three participants consistently completed fewer work units than the other two during this period), a high degree of group cohesiveness was reflected in the social episodes, the intercom exchanges, and the frequent use of the "audit" option available to each participant for monitoring the status of the group bank account and the individual contributions thereto.

In contrast, the second four-day segment of the experiment (i.e., days 5 through 8) with work performances aversively maintained by avoidance of group monetary resources diminution was characterized by a dramatic change in the relatively stable work-rest pattern observed during the first four days, and by a progressive

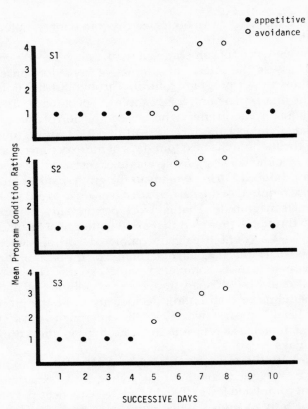

FIGURE 17. Mean ratings of the experimenters on a 4-point scale progressing from 1 ("not at all irritated at the experimenters") to 4 ("extremely irritated"), across successive days of the experiment. Ratings were obtained during each Health Check activity.

deterioration of group cohesiveness. Beginning with day 5, work schedules were drastically altered by the group, and the two productive members of the group became openly intolerant of the third participant's "below-par" performance. As a result, this low-productivity participant was progressively isolated from the group and spent days 7 and 8 alone in his private chamber. Concomitantly, all three members of the group became openly hostile and vehemently expressive of their displeasure with the program control perceived as responsible for this obviously "aversive" state of affairs, as reflected in ratings for days 5 through 8 shown in Figure 17.

Paradoxically, group productivity as grossly estimated from work

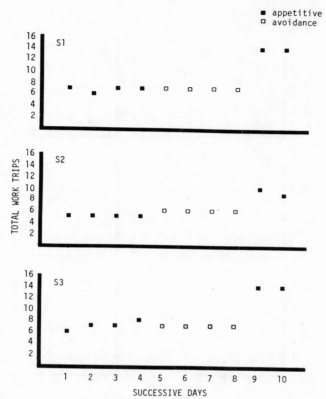

FIGURE 18. Total work units completed by all subjects across successive days of the experiment.

unit completions was not materially affected by the change from appetitive to aversive maintaining conditions, and the absolute number of work units completed by the low-productivity group member (S2) actually increased slightly during days 5 through 8 as shown in Figure 18. Both the daily work-unit frequency and the total number of hours devoted to work by the group participants were maintained at relatively stable levels throughout the two four-day intervals, and remained sufficiently high during the avoidance contingency in effect from days 5 through 8 to prevent even a single withdrawal from the group bank account. And on the basis of a more detailed analysis of the several component tasks in the work units as summarized in Figure 19, there is little evidence that performance effectiveness was differentially influenced by the two

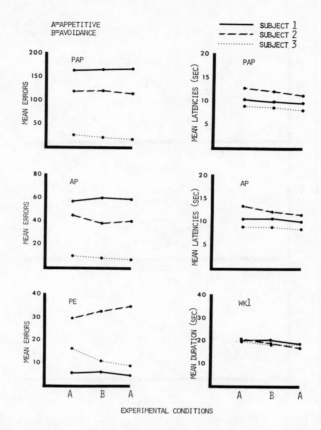

FIGURE 19. Mean performance effectiveness on the several components of the work unit across successive experimental conditions.

conditions. This finding is in marked contrast to the dramatic changes in group cohesiveness, ratings of program control conditions, and both interpersonal (e.g., "irritation") and intrapersonal (e.g., "mood") ratings recorded by the subjects during days 5 through 8.

Although these socially disruptive byproducts of the aversive control procedures in effect during the avoidance segment of the experiment did not produce obvious decrements in either individual or group effectiveness on work unit performance, changes did occur in the distribution of work units as a function of the transition from appetitive to aversive motivational conditions. These effects are presented graphically in Figure 20, which shows the distribution of

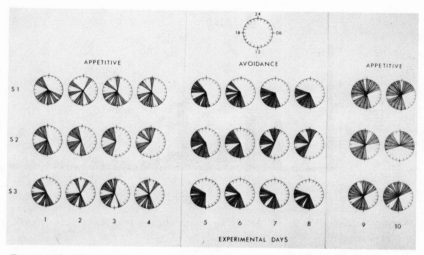

FIGURE 20. The distribution of work unit time (shaded segments) over successive days (depicted as 24-hour clocks) under each of the three program conditions.

work unit time (shaded segments) over successive days (depicted as 24-hour clocks) under each of the three program conditions. During days 1 thru 4, the completion of one or two work units was typically followed by a rest break during which a social episode (e.g., communal meal) would usually occur. Additional brief work periods would then generally occur interspersed with individual or social recreational interludes before sleep. In contrast, days 5 through 8 were characterized by a dramatic change in this work-rest pattern with comparable numbers of work units compressed into more restricted time segments as shown on the 24-hour clocks for this avoidance period. This alteration in the temporal distribution pattern effectively insured that the daily group performance requirement (i.e., 20 work units) was completed before any social or recreational episodes occurred. Significantly, the progressive deterioration of group cohesiveness, shown in Figure 21 by the progressive decrease in triadic social interaction over days 5 through 8, developed concurrently with this change in the work-rest pattern.

The extremely high work rates reflected in the 24-hour clock distribution for days 9 and 10 following reversal to the appetitive motivational conditions of days 1 through 4 probably accounts at least in part for the group fragmentation which persisted through-

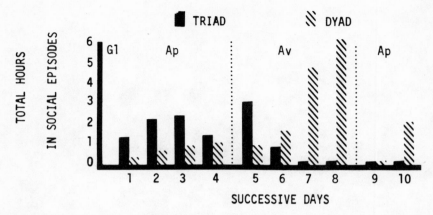

FIGURE 21. Total dyadic and triadic time in minutes over successive days of the experiment.

out these final two days of the experiment. While this final burst of work activity can be attributed to some combination of "emotional" facilitation occasioned by the condition change (i.e., from aversive to appetitive control) on the one hand, and the "motivational" potentiation produced by temporal proximity of the behavior-maintaining consequence (i.e., the "pay-off" at the end of the experiment), it is noteworthy that this extremely high work output (far exceeding those levels observed during any of the 25 previous experiments conducted in our laboratory) occurred in the absence of any deleterious side effects to the subjects. In fact, the rating data shown in Figure 17 along with the "Mood Scale" assessments obtained during each Health Check activity reflected virtually complete recovery to the positive levels which characterized the first four days of the experiment.

To provide a more detailed analysis of such motivational and emotional interactions under aversive and appetitive programming conditions, as well as to control for order effects attributable to the temporal sequence in which these diverse programming conditions were presented, two additional 12-day experiments were conducted, one with the three male participants and one with three females. The experimental methodology and general programming procedures were basically similar to those illustrated in Figure 19, with this exception: an expanded group of work unit activities (e.g., perceptual, memory, vigilance, etc.) was programmed for the second group of male subjects, and the order and number of days of

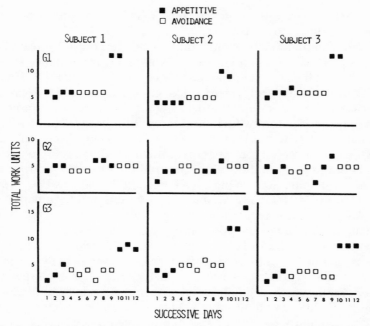

FIGURE 22. Total number of work units completed by all subjects across successive days of the three experiments.

exposure to the appetitive and aversive conditions were varied. Both groups resided in the continuously programmed environment for 12 days with the appetitive (Ap) and avoidance (Av) conditions in effect in the following order and number of successive days under each condition, respectively: Ap–Av–Ap–Av (3, 3, 3, 3), and Ap–Av–Ap (3, 6, 3).

As with the first group, the work unit contingency, requiring approximately one hour for completion, maintained substantial productivity levels for all subjects in each of these two additional groups. Figure 22, for example, summarizes the total number of work units completed by all subjects across successive days of the three group studies. No subject completed fewer than two work units per day (e.g., Subject 2 in Group 2 on Day 1) with a range of 2 to 16 units. Within all groups, the work unit outputs were more evenly distributed among subjects during the avoidance condition than during the appetitive condition. A comparison between the two conditions of the differences between the highest and lowest work frequency for all subjects in each group (under the assumption that such differences approach zero when variability is absent) showed a significant effect.

Subjects with a relatively low daily work unit output during the first appetitive condition showed a work unit performance increment during the succeeding avoidance condition (e.g., S2G1, S2G2, S3G2, and S2G3). And Group 3, like Group 1, showed a dramatic increase in daily work unit frequency when the appetitive condition was reintroduced for the final three days of the study. The less than dramatic change in this regard observed with Group 2 can probably be attributed to some combination of the more demanding requirements of the work unit activities programmed for this group (i.e., the motivational effects of increased "response cost") and the order effects produced by multiple condition reversals and termination of the study with the avoidance contingency in effect (i.e., the emotional effects of aversive occasioning circumstances).

With respect to the intrapersonal aspects of the program condition effects, almost all subjects reported mood changes between program conditions on the Depression factor of the Lorr's Outpatient Mood Scale which was administered during each Health Check activity. Eight of the nine subjects showed the highest ratings during the avoidance condition, and, for a pooled analysis, the avoidance condition was associated with significantly higher depression ratings. Additionally, Figure 23 shows that on a 4-point scale reflecting degree of irritation (1=none to 4=extreme) with the program condition, all subjects in each group displayed more irritation during the avoidance condition than during corresponding appetitive program conditions.

As with Group 1, the three male subjects in Group 2 showed local effects of the avoidance condition in the form of clear displays of aggression. Members within Group 2 evidenced destructive behaviors in relationship to laboratory property (e.g., kicking the walls and damaging the furniture) and repeatedly failed to conform to the requirements of the behavioral program. In contrast, the three female subjects in Group 3 displayed no such aggressive or hostile behaviors, even after six successive days under the avoidance contingency, though their program rating scores (Figure 23) did show a modest degree of intermittent irritation in the course of this extended exposure to the aversive avoidance condition.

The results of these several residential studies illustrate the development and application of an effective and relevant experimental methodology for the analysis of motivational and emotional interac-

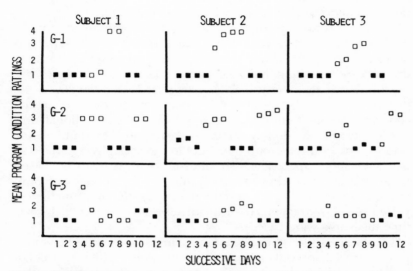

FIGURE 23. Mean daily ratings of the program condition on a 4-point scale reflecting degree of irritation (1 = none to 4 = extreme) for all subjects in each group.

tions in a continuously programmed laboratory environment. The initial observations showed clearly that small groups of individuals could not only be maintained under naturalistic experimental conditions for extended periods of continuous residence, but that the sequential contingency performance program developed for these studies was productively supportive of both individual and social behavior interactions. Moreover, these studies confirmed the sensitivity of such behavioral interactions to environmental manipulations within the time frame of a given experiment (i.e., program conditions changes and reversals), and emphasized the importance of specific program components (e.g., social activities) as maintaining consequences for the performances upon which their access was made contingent.

Motivational operations in the form of program condition changes potentiated the reinforcing functions of social consequating events, and performance enhancement was observed under circumstances which made access to group activities contingent upon cooperative behaviors. In contrast, when this cooperation contingency was not in effect (i.e., non-cooperation condition), group fragmentation and individual performance deterioriation occurred. Additionally, emotional influences upon the occasioning circumstances for both individual and group performances within the programmed environment were interactive with motivational functions. The effects of such emotional interactions were evident not only in the more dramatic disruptions of individual performance baselines (e.g., Figure 13), but as well in the less obvious relationship between social distance and dyadic social engagements observed under pairing contingency conditions (e.g., Figure 18). Operative emotional influences upon the occasioning circumstance provided by simultaneous presence of all three group members in the social living area (i.e., triadic episodes upon which social distance measures were based) were found to interact in an orderly and systematic way with motivational operations which potentiated the reinforcing functions of paired social transactions (i.e., dyadic episodes upon which social time measures were based).

The complexity of these behavioral functions was perhaps most prominently displayed in the more recent studies which have begun to address critical dimensional and parametric aspects of motivational and emotional interactions. The motivational effects of contrasting appetitive and aversive performance-maintaining consequence potentiation, for example, clearly interacted with emotional functions expressed obtrusively as effects upon interpersonal occasioning circumstances provided by program condition requirements (e.g., Figures 17 and 21). Superordinate motivational functions were nonetheless evident in the consequence potentiating effects which not only prevented work unit decrements under such aversive programming conditions (e.g., Figure 19), but in notable instances actually enhanced performance levels (e.g., Figure 18). Even more powerful motivational influences were evident in the performance enhancement observed under appetitive conditions when the behavior-maintaining monetary consequences of subject participation were potentiated by temporal proximity of the "pay-off" upon termination of the experiment (e.g., Figure 18, days 9 and 10).

Finally, of more than coincidental interest from the standpoint of a parametric analysis of such motivational and emotional interactions would seem to be the very striking, if obviously preliminary observation differentiating the behavior of the male and female group participants under essentially similar program conditions. Data limitations necessarily preclude even tentative conclusions based upon the observed variations, though the findings do suggest a potentially fruitful course for future experimental analysis of the somatic, associative, and hedonic influences, both contemporary and historical, which determine the commonalities and differences in motivational and emotional attributes of behavior.

REFERENCE NOTE

1. Findley, J. D., & Brady, J. V. *Exposure to total and continuous environmental control with a single human organism*. Symposium at the Seventh Annual Human Factors Society meeting, Palo Alto, Calif., 23 October 1963.

REFERENCES

Ayllon, T., & Azrin, N. H. The measurement and reinforcement of behavior of psychotics. *Journal of the Experimental Analysis of Behavior*, 1965, **8**, 357–383.

Bigelow, G., Emurian, H., & Brady, J. V. A programmed environment for the experimental analysis of individual and small group behavior. In C. G. Miles (Ed.), *Experimentation in controlled environments and its implications for economic behavior and social-policy making*. Toronto, Canada: Alcoholism and Drug Addiction Research Foundation of Ontario, 1975.

Brady, J. V. Emotion: Some conceptual problems and psychophysiological experiments. In M. Arnold (Ed.), *Feelings and emotions*. New York: Academic Press, 1970.

Brady, J. V. Emotion revisited. *Journal of Psychiatric Research*, 1971, **8**, 363–384.

Brady, J. V. Toward a behavioral biology of emotion. In L. Levi (Ed.), *Emotion—Their parameters and measurement*. New York: Raven Press, 1975. (a)

Brady, J. V. Conditioning and emotion. In L. Levi (Ed.), *Emotions—Their parameters and measurement*. New York: Raven Press, 1975. (b)

Brady, J. V., Bigelow, G., Emurian, H., & Williams, D. M. Design of a programmed environment for the experimental analysis of social behavior. In D. H. Carson (Ed.), *Man-environment interactions: Evaluations and applications. 7: Social ecology*. Milwaukee, Wis.: Environmental Design Research Association, Inc., 1974.

Brady, J. V., & Harris, A. H. The experimental production of altered physiological states. In W. K. Honig & J. E. R. Staddon (Eds.), *Handbook of operant behavior*. Englewood Cliffs, N. J.: Prentice Hall, 1976.

Cohen, H. L. Education therapy: A design of learning environments. *Research in Psychotherapy*, 1968, **3**, 21–53.

Emurian, H., Bigelow, G., Brady, J. V., & Emurian, C. Small-group performance maintenance in a continuously programmed environment. JSAS *Catalogue of Selected Documents in Psychology*, 1975, Vol. 5.

Emurian, H. H., Emurian, C. S., Bigelow, G. E., & Brady, J. V. The effects of a cooperation contingency on behavior in a continuous three-person environment. *Journal of the Experimental Analysis of Behavior*, 1976, **25**, 293–302.

Emurian, H. H., Emurian, C. S., & Brady, J. V. Effects of a pairing contingency on behavior in a three-person programmed environment. *Journal of the Experimental Analysis of Behavior*, 1978, **29**, 319–329.

Findley, J. D. Programmed environments for the experimental analysis of human behavior. In W. Honig (Ed.), *Operant behavior: Areas of research and application*. New York: Appleton-Century-Crofts, 1966.

Garner, W. R., Hake, H. W., & Eriksen, C. W. Operationism and the concept of perception. *Psychological Reviews*, 1956, **63**, 149–159.

Goldiamond, I. A programming-contingency analysis of mental health. *Journal of Medical Philosophy*, in press.

Mason, J. W. Organization of psychoendocrine mechanisms. *Psychosomatic Medicine*, 1968, **30**, 565–808.

Skinner, B. F. *Contingencies of reinforcement: A theoretical analysis*. New York: Appleton-Century-Crofts, 1969.

Psychoneuroendocrine Approaches to the Study of Emotion as Related to Stress and Coping[1]

Marianne Frankenhaeuser

*University of Stockholm
and Karolinska Institutet*

FRAMEWORK FOR PSYCHONEUROENDOCRINE STUDIES

One of the notions underlying the use of neuroendocrine and other physiological techniques in human stress research is that one can determine the emotional impact of specific factors in the environment by measuring the activity of the body's organ systems. Thus, one can make functional assessments of various organs that are controlled by the brain and reflect its activity and level of wakefulness. With the development of biochemical techniques that permit the determination of exceedingly small amounts of various hormones in blood and urine, psychoneuroendocrinology has come to play an increasingly important role in stress research. Two neuroendocrine systems are of particular interest in the study of stress and emotion: the sympathetic-adrenal medullary system, with the secretion of the catecholamines adrenaline and noradrenaline, and the pituitary-adrenal cortical system, with the secre-

1. This paper is based on research supported by the Swedish Medical Research Council (Project No. 997), the Swedish Council for Research in the Humanities and Social Sciences, and the Swedish Work Environment Fund (Project No. 76/49). It is a review article and contains some findings and conclusions that have appeared in previous papers by the author. For other general surveys of similar topics, see the reference section.

tion of corticosteroids. These hormones play a key role in several ways: as sensitive indicators of the stressfulness of person-environment transactions, as regulators of vital bodily functions, and, under some circumstances, as mediators of bodily reactions leading to pathological states. Whereas the catecholamines play a main role in mobilizing acute adaptive resources, corticosteroids provide more enduring support in the case of prolonged stress.

The susceptibility of the sympathetic-adrenal medullary system to psychological factors was first demonstrated by Walter B. Cannon and his associates at Harvard during the early part of this century. Results from a series of experiments on cats led Cannon (1914, 1932) to formulate the "emergency function" theory of adrenal-medullary activity, stating that many of the physiological effects of adrenaline serve the goal of preparing the organism to meet threatening situations involving fear or rage or pain. Some decades later, Euler (1946, 1956) showed that noradrenaline, the nonmethylated homologue of adrenaline, was the adrenergic neurotransmitter as well as an adrenal-medullary hormone. These findings, together with Selye's (1950) pioneering research on the part played by pituitary-adrenal cortical activity in the General Adaptation Syndrome, followed by Mason's (e.g., 1975) multihormonal, integrative approach, form the basis of today's psychoendocrine stress research.

Work in my laboratory has been focused on the psychological significance of the sympathetic-adrenal medullary system, with more recent work also including the pituitary-adrenal cortical system. (For reviews the reader is referred to Frankenhaeuser, 1971, 1975 a, b, in press–a.) An important feature of our research strategy is the combination of laboratory and field studies, both of which will be illustrated by examples. In the former type of study, specific problems are extracted from natural settings and brought into the laboratory for systematic examination. The latter takes our laboratory-based, experimental techniques into the field and applies them to persons engaged in their daily activities. Both approaches involve examining individual response patterns under controlled conditions, securing *concurrent* measures of responses at the psychological and physiological level, and relating these to more enduring characteristics of the person.

Adopting Lazarus's theoretical formulations (e.g., Lazarus, 1977a, 1977b), stress, in the present context, is regarded as a process of transactions between the individual and the environment. Techniques for measuring neuroendocrine responses are seen as tools by which new insights can be gained into the dynamics of these transactions. A key notion is that the neuroendocrine responses to the psychosocial environment reflect its emotional impact on the individual which, in turn, is determined by his or her cognitive appraisal of stimuli and events. This implies that attitudes and values are potent determinants of stress responses at the physiological level and hence are associated with the "diseases of adaptation."

CATECHOLAMINES, STRESS, AND EMOTION

Our experimental approaches to the study of catecholamines and behavior include pharmacological as well as psychological manipulations of arousal level. These approaches will be considered in turn.

Pharmacological manipulations

We have found catecholamine infusions particularly instructive in the study of quantitative relations between psychological and physiological indices of emotional arousal. Adrenaline, when infused in small or moderate doses, gives rise to changes in emotional experience and other functions that resemble, in some respects, symptoms typical of real-life stress situations. Thus, palpitation, tremor, and dryness of the mouth are common symptoms. The point is that genuine anxiety, fright, and panic are usually not experienced, but the subjects report feeling *as if* they were afraid, anxious, etc. However, Marañon (1924), who pioneered in using adrenaline injections as a means for manipulating emotions, made an interesting observation. When, following adrenaline injections, he discussed with his subjects their recent emotional experiences, such as a death in the family, they reported true affect rather than "cold" or "as if" feelings. In other words, "if appropriate cognitive support was available" (Mandler, 1975, p. 88), a full emotion developed. This observation is in accord with the views advanced by Schachter and Singer (1962) on the basis of experiments showing that, depending upon how the external situation was manipulated, the bodily symptoms induced by adrenaline injections were interpreted differently, so that either euphoria or anger was experienced. (For an excellent treatment of questions relating to cognitive factors

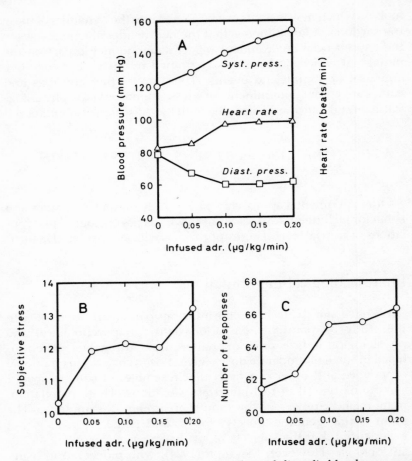

FIGURE 1. Mean values for heart rate, systolic and diastolic blood pressure (A), estimates of subjective stress (B), and performance in a concentration task (C) during infusions of a placebo solution and four doses of adrenaline. Based on Frankenhaeuser & Järpe, 1963.

and arousal the reader is referred to Mandler, 1975, pp. 65–149.)

By studying concomitant physiological, behavioral, and subjective reactions produced by adrenaline infusions, some knowledge can be gained about causal relationships between the different parameters of emotion. Figure 1 shows dose-response curves from a study (Frankenhaeuser & Järpe, 1963) where each subject had 35-

minute infusions of a placebo solution and adrenaline in four different doses. The variables examined were heart rate and blood pressure, subjective stress (as measured by the method of magnitude estimation), and performance in a continuous concentration task. For all variables, reactions increased progressively with increasing dose of adrenaline. However, this similarity in mode of response applied only to the mean dose-response curves. For any one subject the same consistent relationship between changes in different variables could not be demonstrated. Furthermore, the time-response curves for the various functions differed. Thus, heart rate and blood pressure remained relatively constant during each infusion period after the first 5–10 minutes had elapsed, whereas the degree of subjective stress was markedly higher at the beginning than at the end of the infusion period. This discrepancy indicates that the subjective changes were only partly mediated by the physiological responses, and the results are consistent with the view that cognitive factors are prime determinants of emotional responses. In this context it is also important that noradrenaline infusions induced changes in emotional experience similar in kind to those of adrenaline, but much less intense at the same dose level (Frankenhaeuser, Järpe, & Matell, 1961).

Beta-adrenergic blocking agents also provide useful tools for the study of relationships between adrenergic and psychological functions. These drugs, which are widely used in the treatment of certain cardiovascular disorders, have been found effective in the treatment of anxiety states, too (Jefferson, 1974). Moreover, some of the beta-blockers, e.g., propranolol, have been shown to reduce "basal anxiety levels" in clinically healthy subjects (Gottschalk, Stone, & Gleser, 1974). Since propranolol passes freely through the blood-brain barrier, it may exert its anxiolytic action through direct effects on brain mechanisms. Alternatively, the anxiety-reducing actions may be due to the peripheral anti-adrenergic effects, such as reduced heart rate. In a recent study (Sjöberg, Frankenhaeuser, & Bjurstedt, 1979) concerned with effects of a single dose of propranolol on psychological functions, we found that the degree of perceived effort induced by different loads of physical and/or mental work was not noticeably influenced by the propranolol-induced reduction of heart rate. This suggests that, at least in healthy persons, peripheral cues play only a minor role in the development of different motivational states.

Excretion rates of adrenaline and noradrenaline as indices of emotion

Research concerning the psychological significance of the adrenal-medullary hormones has been greatly facilitated by the development of fluorimetric techniques for estimating free catecholamines in urine (Andersson, Hovmöller, Karlsson, & Svensson, 1974; Euler & Lishajko, 1961). This means that relevant data can be obtained by sampling urine while persons are engaged in their ordinary daily activities. Thus, as first demonstrated by Euler and Lundberg (1954), these methods are well suited for the study of psychosocial influences in everyday life. Only a small fraction of the liberated amines is excreted in urine as free adrenaline and noradrenaline, but this fraction shows a high degree of intra-individual constancy over time (e.g., Johansson, Note 1; Pátkai, Note 2). For a comprehensive review of adrenal-medullary secretion and its neural control, the reader is referred to Euler (1967).

Catecholamine-excretion rates of healthy subjects are generally low during recumbency and rest. In males, adrenaline secretion doubles during daily routine activities, and rises three to five times above the resting level under conditions of "mild" to "moderate" stress. The rise is generally lower in females (see below, p. 145). Severe emotional stress elicits a further pronounced increase of adrenaline secretion, and noradrenaline may rise markedly, too. In other words, noradrenaline also reflects emotional arousal but the threshold for its release in response to psychological stimuli is higher than that of adrenaline. It is also noteworthy that, of the two amines, adrenaline shows the more pronounced diurnal variation, secretion being lowest between midnight and the early morning hours, and highest in the afternoon (Fröberg, Karlsson, Levi, & Lidberg, 1975; Levi, 1972). Some data indicate that there are interindividual differences in the diurnal pattern associated with "morningness" and "eveningness" (Pátkai, 1971a).

Provided the conditions under which urine is sampled are carefully standardized, catecholamine excretion rates constitute sensitive indices of the emotional impact of the environment. In general, stimulus conditions that are perceived as deviating from those to which the person is accustomed will induce a change in adrenaline output, whereas stimuli and events that are perceived as part of the familiar environment will not affect secretion. Novelty, change, challenge, and anticipation may be considered key components in

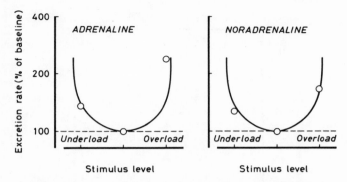

FIGURE 2. Mean adrenaline and noradrenaline excretion (log scale) at different levels of stimulation in laboratory situations. Values obtained under conditions of stimulus underload and overload are expressed as percentages of those obtained under conditions of "medium" stimulation. Based on Frankenhaeuser, Nordheden, Myrsten, & Post, 1971.

the psychosocial conditions triggering the adrenal-medullary response.

Conditions of underload and overload, although each other's opposite in terms of physical characteristics, are psychologically similar in that both are experienced as disturbing deviations from the level of stimulation to which the person is cognitively set and emotionally tuned. Insofar as this psychological resemblance dominates situational perception, one would expect the adrenal-medullary response to be the same in both conditions, and this assumption has been supported by several experiments. Results from a laboratory study (Frankenhaeuser, Nordheden, Myrsten, & Post, 1971) are presented in Figure 2, showing that underload (represented by a monotonous vigilance task) and overload (represented by a complex audiovisual choice-reaction task) both induced an increased catecholamine secretion compared with a situation designed to match the medium input level of an "ordinary" environment. Psychologically, the underload and overload situations were similar in that both induced distress and both required effort.

Another approach to the study of psychological versus situational determinants of the adrenal-medullary response is the habituation experiment, in which one monitors the reduction of stress responses accompanying repeated exposure to one and the same stressful event. Results from experiments (Frankenhaeuser, Sterky, & Järpe,

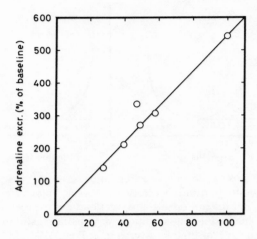

FIGURE 3. Mean values for adrenaline excretion (expressed as percentages of baselines) plotted against mean self-reports of distress in six sessions (one week apart) in a human centrifuge. Based on Frankenhaeuser, Sterky, & Järpe, 1962.

1962) in which subjects were exposed to gravitational stress on six occasions show that adrenaline excretion was almost directly proportional to the degree of subjective distress, measured by a ratio-estimation technique (Fig. 3). It is worth noting that noradrenaline was markedly elevated in all sessions and that, unlike adrenaline, it showed no tendency to decrease with repeated exposure. The dissociation between the two adrenal-medullary hormones in this particular situation is consistent with their different adaptive functions, noradrenaline being involved in maintaining cardiovascular homeostasis under gravitational stress.

It is interesting to compare the above data with results from a study of parachute jumpers (Bloom, Euler, & Frankenhaeuser, 1963). Parachute jumping is an activity which probably never becomes routine in the sense of demanding less acute attention and concentration. Unlike exposure to gravitational stress during which the person remains passive, each parachute jump requires an extreme degree of active effort. In accordance with the psychological demands inherent in this activity, our results showed that the increase in catecholamine excretion during jump periods, as compared with periods of ground activity, was as high in experienced

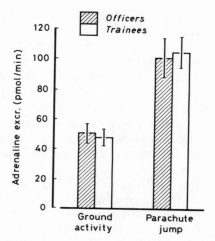

FIGURE 4. Means and standard errors for adrenaline excretion in a group of officers and a group of paratroop trainees during periods in which either ground activity or parachute jumps were performed. Based on Bloom, Euler, & Frankenhaeuser, 1963.

officers as in trainees making their first jump (Fig. 4). In other words, under conditions where a high degree of involvement was maintained, the level of catecholamine secretion remained high.

Endocrine pattern and emotional quality

As already pointed out, infusions of adrenaline and noradrenaline do not induce qualitatively different emotional changes, although the patterns of sympathetic discharge differ. Nor do our data on endogenous adrenaline and noradrenaline lend any support to the view that emotional experience would be *controlled by* the hormonal or sympathetic pattern. However, as pointed out by Mandler (1975, pp. 126 ff.), an entirely different and more controversial question is whether adrenaline and noradrenaline are selectively released in situations giving rise to different emotional experiences and behaviors. The hypothesis stating that adrenaline secretion is related to anxiety and fear, whereas noradrenaline is associated with aggressiveness and anger, has received some support (e.g., Ax, 1953; Brady, 1967; Funkenstein, 1956), but the hypothesis has been questioned by those investigators (e.g., Levi, 1965; Pátkai, 1971b) who have obtained measures of catecholamine output and self-reports of emotional experiences in one and the same situation. Levi, for example, used different films, selected with the aim of evoking feelings of either amusement, anger, fright, or equanimity. Self-reports showed that the predominant emotional state induced by each film was, in fact, of the intended quality. All the "arousing" films induced a rise in adrenaline output, regardless of the specific quality of the emotion evoked, whereas adrenaline decreased (relative to baseline) during the "tranquilizing" film session. Noradrenaline showed a similar picture, but the changes from baseline were smaller in all conditions.

Although the pattern of adrenal-medullary secretion thus appears to be the same irrespective of the quality of the emotional experience, the *overall endocrine pattern*, including adrenal-cortical as well as adrenal-medullary activity, will undoubtedly vary in high-arousal situations insofar as these are associated with demands that elicit different behaviors. An illustration will be provided in the next section by an experiment showing a differential pattern of adrenaline and cortisol secretion in an achievement situation characterized by a high degree of personal control. The model used by Henry (1976) is relevant in this context, since it emphasizes the association between, on the one hand, sympathetic-adrenal medullary activation and dominant, aggressive behavior patterns and, on the other, pituitary-adrenal cortical activation and subordinate, passive behaviors. It is also interesting that differences in the balance of these two endocrine systems have been noted between dominant "type A" persons and subordinate "type B" persons (Friedman, Rosenman, & St. George, 1969).

Personality factors obviously play an important role, since they induce the person to appraise environmental demands in divergent ways conducive to different emotions (cf. Lazarus, 1977a). In healthy subjects, positive correlations have been found between adrenaline secretion and different indices of ego strength (Roessler, Burch, & Mefferd, 1967) and emotional stability (Lambert, Johansson, Frankenhaeuser, & Klackenberg-Larsson, 1969), whereas depressive tendencies tend to be related to low adrenaline secretion during stress (Frankenhaeuser & Pátkai, 1965). In these studies, the relation of noradrenaline to personality is similar to that of adrenaline but the data are less consistent. Schildkraut (1973 a), in his review of catecholamine secretion in psychiatric patients, concludes that noradrenaline and, although less consistently, adrenaline excretion tends to be lower during periods of depression than during periods of mania and after recovery.

An interesting patterning of adrenaline and noradrenaline secretion was recently reported in a study of arrested men awaiting trial (Lidberg, Levander, Schalling, & Lidberg, 1978). There was a pronounced difference between subjects classified as high versus low in psychopathy on the basis of different personality inventories. The high-psychopathy group was characterized as impulsive, low in empathy, and low in socialization. Members of this group differed from the low-psychopathy subjects in that they did not react with an increase of either adrenaline or noradrenaline secretion as the time for their trial drew closer. In other words, they failed to show the normal anticipatory response, which is consistent with the clinical conception of psychopathic individuals as lacking in planning and foresight, being unable to use fantasy and imagination in preparing to cope with anticipated stresses. Moreover, the high-psychopathy group had conspicuously low noradrenaline/adrenaline ratios compared to the low-psychopathy group, in which the ratio between the two amines was similar to that ordinarily found in healthy persons.

THE "HELPLESSNESS-MASTERY" DIMENSION

In psychobiological stress research, opportunities for exercising control over one's own activities are recognized as a major determinant of the stressfulness of person-environment transactions. It is generally agreed that, over the long run, controllability facilitates adjustment and enhances coping effectiveness, although the effort involved in exerting control may be associated with a temporary increase in arousal (cf. review by Averill, 1973). Conversely, lack of control may have widespread negative consequences, among which is a state of "learned helplessness" (Seligman, 1975) which, in turn, may lead to depression. According to this theory (Maier & Seligman, 1976), a sense of hopelessness, paired with a reduced motivation to control, is likely to develop when a person experiences events and outcomes as independent of his or her actions.

Our psychobiological approach to the issue of personal control rests on the assumption that a person who is in a position to regulate stimulus input may be able to maintain both physiological arousal and psychological involvement at an optimal level over a wide range

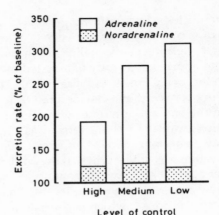

FIGURE 5. Mean adrenaline and noradrenaline excretion in three laboratory situations differing with regard to the level of control. Values are expressed as percentages of baseline level. Based on Frankenhaeuser & Rissler, 1970.

of stimulus conditions. Some aspects of controllability lend themselves well to experimental study. I shall illustrate our approach to the problem, starting with two laboratory experiments and proceeding with studies conducted in natural settings.

Control over aversive stimulation

As already emphasized, conditions characterized by uncertainty, unpredictability, and lack of control usually produce a rise in adrenaline output. In laboratory experiments with humans, the level of stimulus predictability as well as the availability of adequate coping responses can be varied systematically. An example is provided by a study (Frankenhaeuser & Rissler, 1970) concerned with the avoidance of aversive stimulation in three differently designed sessions. Figure 5 shows that under conditions of low control, i.e., when the subjects were exposed to mild but uncontrollable and unpredictable electric shocks, adrenaline excretion was about three times as high as during relaxation. The two other sessions were designed so that the subjects exercised varying degrees of control over the aversive stimuli. As seen in the diagram, adrenaline output decreased successively as the subjects' situation changed from one in which they were helpless into one that they could master.

Noradrenaline excretion was not much affected by the degree of control, but remained slightly elevated as long as the subjects were engaged in the attention-demanding activity. While peripheral noradrenaline thus appears unrelated to predictability, it is worth noting that Weiss, Stone, & Harrell (1970), using the "yoked partner" design in experiments with rats, showed that unpredictable shocks produced a more pronounced depletion of brain noradrenaline than predictable shocks.

We have used a basically similar design in human experiments for studying the influence of control over noise intensity. In a situation (using all male subjects) where the subject performed mental arithmetic under noise exposure, every other subject was offered a choice between noise intensities, while the next subject, serving as his yoked partner, had to submit to the same noise. An interesting feature of the results was that the participants tended to respond to the control versus no-control situations in accordance with their general expectations about control as assessed by the internal-external locus of control scale (Rotter, 1966). Thus, for "internals" the increase of physiological responses from baseline tended to be smaller (indicating a lower stress level) when they exerted control over noise intensity than when they did not, whereas for "externals" the pattern was reversed. It thus appears that stress responses to noncontrollable situations may be related to the extent to which persons generally tend to perceive life events as lying beyond or within their sphere of influence. This underscores the role of learning in the development of active modes of coping.

Control over work pace

The pituitary-adrenal cortical system plays a particularly interesting role in relation to the helplessness-mastery dimension. While lack of control is accompanied by a pronounced increase in the secretion of cortisol, secretion may be actively suppressed under conditions characterized *either* by a high level of control and predictability (e.g., Coover, Ursin, & Levine, 1973; Weiss, 1972) *or* by strong psychological defenses (Friedman, Mason, & Hamburg, 1963).

Recent data from our laboratory (Frankenhaeuser, Lundberg, & Forsman, Note 3) illustrate the dissociation between the adrenal-medullary and the adrenal-cortical response to an achievement situation characterized by feelings of complete mastery, safety, and control (Fig. 6). This was attained by giving each participant (again

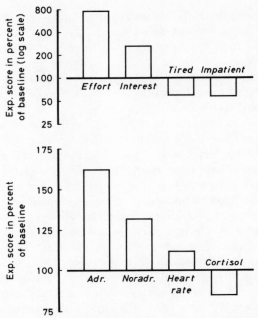

FIGURE 6. Mean changes from baseline level in mood variables (upper diagram) and physiological variables (lower diagram) in an achievement situation characterized by high controllability and "confident task involvement." Frankenhaeuser, Lundberg, & Forsman, Note 3.

all were males) a carefully designed preparatory period in which he was encouraged to try out different stimulus rates on a choice-reaction task in order to arrive at his own "preferred work pace." The task proper did not begin until the subject felt confident about the pace at which to begin a period of sustained work. Every five minutes he was then given the opportunity to modify the stimulus rate so as to maintain an optimal work pace. Hence, the situation was both predictable and controllable to a very high degree. Self-reports indicated that these experimental arrangements were successful in creating an atmosphere which was both pleasant and stimulating, providing excellent possibilities for sustained work. Under these conditions of "confident task involvement," cortisol showed a tendency to decrease to a level below the baseline. At the same time, the increase in adrenaline reflected a sustained involvement in carrying out the task. The interesting point was that, under these demanding work conditions, the sense of being in control had

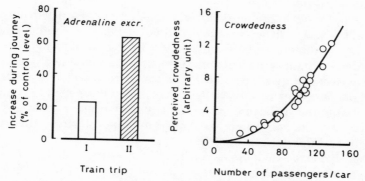

FIGURE 7. Mean increase (in percent of baseline) of adrenaline excretion during each of two train trips made under different conditions of crowdedness (left diagram) and ratings of perceived crowdedness (right diagram). Based on Lundberg, 1976.

a pronounced *deactivating* effect on one of the organism's main adaptive systems. This, together with relevant clinical data (e.g., Sachar, 1970), points to far-reaching consequences of controllability for people's health and well-being.

"Commuter stress"

Let us now consider the modifying influence of control on stress responses in a natural setting. Commuting is one of the day-to-day hassles that add to the stressfulness of urban life. Our psychoendocrine approach is well suited for identifying the stressful aspects of daily commuting by train between a suburban home and a central-city job. A brief period of gasoline rationing during the oil shortage in the winter of 1973–74 provided an opportunity to examine a group of passengers who made the same train journey under different conditions of crowdedness, i.e., before and during the rationing period (Lundberg, 1976). Although the number of passengers per train car increased by only 10 percent during rationing, adrenaline excretion was significantly higher on this occasion. In Figure 7 (left-hand diagram) adrenaline values during commuting have been expressed as percentages of Sunday values, when the subjects stayed at home.

As to the actual traveling conditions, seats were available for all passengers on both occasions. The most pronounced difference between the two trips was that the possibility of selecting a seat and choosing one's own company was much more restricted on the second occasion. In agreement with this, we found in another study (Singer, Lundberg, & Frankenhaeuser, 1978) that passengers who boarded the train at the first stop secreted less adrenaline than those who boarded midway, when the train was already crowded and seat selection more restricted. We have interpreted these results as indicating that the social and ecological circumstances, including controllability, are more important determinants of stress than the length and duration of the trip.

Perceived crowdedness, according to self-ratings made at successive points on the trip, increased as the square of the number of passengers. Figure 7 (right-hand diagram) shows the mean data for a larger group of passengers, used here mainly to illustrate the ability of "the man in the street" to quantify his experiences by a simple scaling procedure.

Further illustrations of the modifying influence of control on psychoendocrine response patterns will be given below when discussing stress in working life.

THE COSTS OF ACHIEVEMENT

Efficiency and adrenal-medullary activity

Our experiments show that among normal healthy persons, those who secrete relatively more catecholamines tend to perform better in terms of speed, accuracy, and endurance than those who secrete less. This relationship is particularly marked for adrenaline secretion under low to moderate stimulation, but tends to hold for noradrenaline secretion, too. The example given in Figure 8 shows that performance in a learning task was consistently better in high-adrenaline than in low-adrenaline subjects, i.e., subjects above and below the median adrenaline-excretion value (Frankenhaeuser & Andersson, 1974). The mechanisms relating circulating catecholamines to performance are not clearly understood, but it is known that the catecholamines cross the blood-brain barrier in some regions only. Intravenously infused adrenaline produces a transient

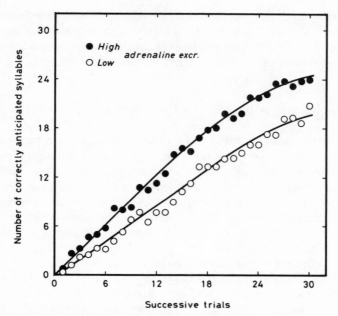

FIGURE 8. Mean performance on successive trials in a verbal-rote learning task in subjects with high (above median) and low (below median) adrenaline-excretion values. Based on Frankenhaeuser & Andersson, 1974.

EEG activation, the effect appearing in sleeping and drowsy animals only and not in those already aroused (Rothballer, 1959).

While subjects with relatively high adrenaline levels tend to perform better under monotonous conditions, those with relatively low levels perform better under conditions of audiovisual overload requiring selective attention (Frankenhaeuser, Nordheden, Myrsten, & Post, 1971). The impaired ability of high-adrenaline subjects to select relevant signals when exposed to overload is consistent with Easterbrook's (1959) interpretation of the Yerkes-Dodson law in terms of a narrowing of the range of cues utilized at high levels of arousal.

The positive relationship between adrenaline secretion and psychological efficiency at low to moderate stimulus levels is not confined to acute situations but applies to cognitive functions in general. For example, studies of children (Johansson, Frankenhaeuser, & Magnusson, 1973) show that school achievement and measures of intelligence correlate positively with catecholamine secretion. Moreover, according to teachers' ratings and self-ratings, high-adrenaline children are happier, livelier, and better adjusted to the school environment than their low-adrenaline peers.

Strategies for coping with task demands

In our studies of achievement stress, we have been particularly interested in how people cope when confronted with an increase in task demand. Basically, they may adopt one of two different strategies, either maintaining performance at a constant level by increasing their efforts, or keeping their effort constant and letting performance deteriorate. The former strategy exacts a higher "subjective cost," as reflected in self-reports of various aspects of psychological involvement. The "physiological cost" will be higher, too, as reflected in various arousal indices.

In general, the participants in our experiments, under laboratory as well as natural conditions, choose to meet situational demands by investing the effort needed to maintain a high performance level, often showing a remarkable ability to "pull themselves together" (reviewed by Lundberg, 1979). An example is provided by experiments in which a color-word conflict task (a modified form of the Stroop test) was performed at two levels of difficulty, one denoted "single conflict," the other "double conflict" (Frankenhaeuser & Johansson, 1976). In the latter case, where interfering auditory color words were added to those presented visually, the mental load was markedly higher. This was reflected in self-reports of increased distress as well as in increased adrenaline excretion (Fig. 9). In other words, the subjects met the increase in task demand by "raising the body's thermostat of defense" (Selye, 1974) and, under these circumstances, performance remained intact.

The picture was similar (Fig. 10) when subjects were exposed to one of two intensities of white noise while performing mental arithmetic. As predicted, more effort was invested in doing arithmetic at the higher noise load, physiological arousal increased, and performance remained intact. The trend was the same for all arousal indices, i.e., adrenaline, noradrenaline, and cortisol excretion as well as heart rate.

When, however, the subjects' cognitive set was manipulated so as to induce a less ambitious response style, the picture was different

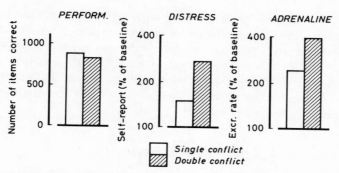

FIGURE 9. Mean performance in a cognitive task under conditions of "single" and "double" conflict, and mean changes (log scale) in subjective distress and adrenaline excretion, expressed as percentages of baseline values. Based on Frankenhaeuser & Johansson, 1976.

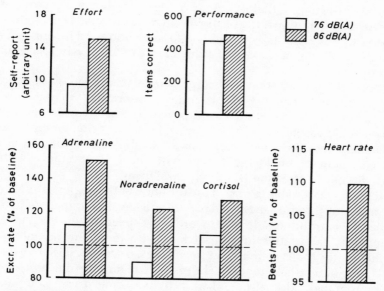

FIGURE 10. Mean scores for effort, arithmetic performance, adrenaline, noradrenaline, and cortisol excretion, and heart rate in subjects doing arithmetic under exposure to noise of 76 and 86 db(A). Based on Lundberg & Frankenhaeuser, 1978.

(Frankenhaeuser & Lundberg, 1977). In essence, this manipulation consisted of introducing the subject, right at the beginning of an experimental series, to a lower noise load than that used in the main part of the experiment. In keeping with the notion that the conditions prevailing in the initial phase of stress exposure tend to have a lasting effect on a person's mode of adjustment, the subjects responded to increased noise intensity by letting their performance drop instead of striving to meet the rise in task demand. Under these circumstances increased noise intensity was not accompanied by increased physiological arousal.

Aftereffects of achievement strivings

The results reviewed above take us to the question of relationships between psychoendocrine stress responses and health. Although direct evidence for a causal relationship between catecholamine secretion and disease is still lacking, data from several sources suggest that if periods of high secretion are prolonged or repeated frequently, the cardiovascular system may be adversely affected. This raises the question of possible undesirable long-term effects of adrenaline-mediated adjustments to the psychosocial environment.

Our results show that a healthy person who deals with acute environmental demands by "raising the thermostat" may have to pay a price in terms of increased psychological involvement and physiological arousal. We do not know, however, whether repeated adjustments to short-term demands are likely to have lasting aftereffects, reducing the ability to cope with subsequent requirements and ultimately affecting health and wellbeing.

It seems reasonable to regard the duration of the response evoked by temporary disturbances in daily life as a key determinant of their potential harmfulness. In other words, the speed at which a person "unwinds" after stressful transactions with the environment will influence the total "wearing" of the biological system. It is noteworthy that individuals tend to differ with regard to the temporal pattern of their adrenal-medullary activity during stress. Comparisons between persons classified as rapid and slow "adrenaline decreasers" support the assumption that a quick return to physiological baselines, after energy mobilization induced by a short-term exposure to a heavy mental load, implies an "economic" mode of response. Conversely, a slow return to baseline indicates poor adjustment in the sense that the person "over-responds" by spending resources that are no longer called for. In agreement with this reasoning, results from a laboratory study (Johansson & Frankenhaeuser, 1973) showed that "rapid decreasers" tended to be psychologically better balanced and more efficient in achievement situations than "slow decreasers." There is also some indication Frankenhaeuser, Lundberg, & Forsman, in preparation) that the coronary-prone behavior pattern A (see, e.g., Glass, 1977; Rosenman, Brand, Sholtz, & Friedman, 1976) may be characterized by low flexibility in physiological arousal relative to situational demands.

An equally important finding is that the time for "unwinding" varies predictably with the individual's state of general well-being. Thus, in a group of industrial workers, the proportion of "rapid decreasers" was significantly higher after than before a vacation period, which had improved the workers' physical and psychological condition (Johansson, 1976).

Cumulative effects of work overload

An interesting example of "slow unwinding" is provided in one of our recent studies of female employees in an insurance company (Rissler, 1977; Rissler & Elgerot, Note 4). We were particularly interested in their stress and coping patterns during an extended period of "overtime" at work. The extra time (an average of 73 hours per employee) was spread over two months, but most of it occurred within a four-week period. No new duties were involved, only an increase in the quantity of regular work. The employees were free to choose the schedule for their extra hours and most of them opted for work on Saturdays and Sundays, rather than doing more than eight hours on weekdays. Since these women ordinarily devoted several weekend hours to household duties, they faced a conflict between responsibilities at home and at work.

It was argued that the additional overtime load would call for intense adaptive efforts, the effects of which would not be restricted to the extra work-hours, but would also manifest themselves during and after the ordinary work-days. The results supported this hypothesis, in that adrenaline excretion was significantly increased throughout the overtime period, both during the day and in the evening. Figure 11 shows daytime and evening measures of adrenaline excretion on nine occasions, one before, six during, and two after the overtime period. The daytime values were determined in samples obtained at the place of work, the evening values in sam-

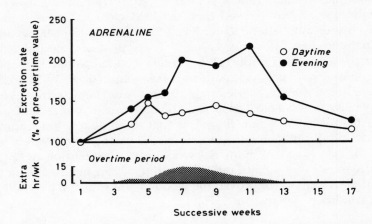

FIGURE 11. Mean adrenaline excretion in office workers during the day and evening on nine occasions before, during, and after a period of overtime at work. Values obtained during and after the overtime period are expressed as percentages of those obtained before this period. Most of the extra hours were worked at weekends, and urine samples were obtained on Tuesdays. Based on Rissler & Elgerot, Note 4.

ples taken at home. Each value during and after the overtime period was expressed as a percentage of the corresponding daytime or evening value before the overtime period. As shown in the diagram, the adrenaline level was consistently elevated during the overtime period, after which it declined and approached the levels typical of ordinary work conditions. The most remarkable finding was the pronounced elevation of adrenaline output in the evenings, which were spent relaxing at home. This was accompanied by markedly elevated heart rate as well as feelings of irritability and fatigue. It is worth noting the time lag between the work-load peak, which occurred in the middle of the overtime period, and the peak-adrenaline excretion, which came at the very end of the period. Hence, the results show that the effects of overload may spread to leisure hours, and that they may accumulate gradually, which delays their full impact.

It should also be noted that there were considerable differences between the women in their response to the overtime work. These differences, which may be partly related to constitutional factors, indicate that slow unwinding tended to be associated with various symptoms of dissatisfaction and psychosomatic disturbances.

SEX ROLES AND
PSYCHONEUROENDOCRINE ACTIVITY

Sex differences in psychoendocrine response

Most of the catecholamine data so far reported in this paper emanate from male subjects and hold only in part for females. During rest and relaxation sex differences in catecholamine excretion are generally slight (provided one allows for body weight). It is only in stressful and challenging situations that consistent sex differences appear, indicating a lesser reactivity of the adrenal-medullary system in females than in males. Thus, in a series of experimental conditions involving moderately intense stress (e.g., Frankenhaeuser, Dunne, & Lundberg, 1976; Johansson & Post, 1974) we found little, if any, increase of adrenaline excretion in women, whereas males in the same situations showed a significant rise. Figure 12 summarizes results from three experiments. Each diagram shows the adrenaline excretion in a stress condition expressed as a percentage of a baseline value obtained under conditions spent in relative inactivity, where the sexes did not differ markedly. Stress in the different experiments was induced by intelligence testing, a color-word conflict task, and venipuncture.

The common characteristic of all diagrams is the lack of adrenaline increase during stress in the females and, in contrast, the significant rise in the males. An important point is that the low adrenal-medullary activity of the females was not accompanied by inferior achievement. Thus, the females did as well as the males on the intelligence test, and on the color-word test they were, in fact slightly superior. These results fit well with our earlier data on school children (Johansson, Frankenhaeuser, & Magnusson, 1973) showing that achievement and, in particular, overachievement, tends to be positively correlated with adrenaline output in boys, but not in girls (Bergman & Magnusson, in press).

Our next step was to examine sex differences in response to more intense and long-lasting stressors, and to relate catecholamine measures to a wider range of psychological and biological parameters. To this end, we engaged in a longitudinal project concerned with various aspects of psychological and somatic development of Finnish boys and girls (Rauste, Note 5). An opportunity arose to study a group of these subjects, who were taking a final examination when matriculating from high school (Frankenhaeuser, Rauste von

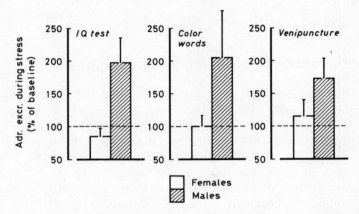

FIGURE 12. Means and standard errors for adrenaline excretion (expressed as percentages of baselines) in female and male groups during stress induced by an IQ test, a color-word conflict test, and venipuncture. The first diagram is based on Johansson & Post, 1974, the two other diagrams on Frankenhaeuser, Dunne, & Lundberg, 1976.

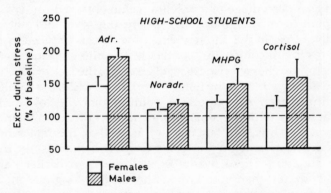

FIGURE 13. Means and standard errors for adrenaline, noradrenaline, MHPG, and cortisol excretion in female and male high-school students. Values obtained during a matriculation examination have been expressed as percentages of values obtained during a day of ordinary school work. Based on Frankenhaeuser, Rauste von Wright, Collins, von Wright, Sedvall, & Swahn, 1978.

Wright, Collins, von Wright, Sedvall, & Swahn, 1978). This real-life stress was much more severe than the experimentally induced stress in our previous studies. Not only does the outcome of the examination determine whether or not the student will be admitted to the university, it may also have a lasting influence on his and her success in competing on the labor market.

Figure 13 shows the urinary excretion of adrenaline, noradrenaline, the catecholamine metabolite 3-methoxy-4-hydroxyphenyl glycol (MHPG), and cortisol, measured in samples obtained after a six-hour examination and after ordinary school work. MHPG was measured by a massfragmentographic technique (Swahn, Sandgärde, Wiesel, & Sedvall, 1976) and cortisol by radioimmunoassay (Ruder, Guy, & Lipsitt, 1972). Examination-stress values are expressed as percentages of those obtained during ordinary school work which, of course, was also somewhat stressful. Hence, the changes are smaller than they would have been had we had access to true baseline values.

In this very challenging achievement situation, both sexes did increase their adrenaline secretion to a significant degree. But the rise was significantly greater for the males, and the rise in MHPG and cortisol was significant for the males only. In other words, under conditions of severe stress, the females did respond in a manner similar to the males, but to a lesser degree. (We should recall that the female office workers discussed above did show a pronounced adrenaline increase during the evening hours in the course of the overtime period. Presumably they were under severe stress, since the overtime at work created a conflict with their duties at home.)

As to the psychological significance of the examination-stress data, it is worth noting that MHPG is assumed to provide an index of the synthesis and metabolism of noradrenaline in the brain, and to reflect changes in the affective state of patients with manic-depressive disorders. According to the catecholamine hypothesis of affective disorders (Schildkraut & Kety, 1967), depression is associated with a functional deficit of noradrenaline at critical synapses in the brain, whereas mania is associated with a functional excess of this amine. Clinical studies have provided some support for this hypothesis (Schildkraut, 1973b), increase of MHPG excretion accompanying improvements in the state of depressed patients.

In view of these clinical data it is interesting to consider MHPG excretion during examination stress in relation to the mood and subjective state of our students. Self-reports showed that males and females experienced the examination in different ways. Feelings of success and confidence were common among males, whereas feel-

ings of discomfort, failure, and dissatisfaction with their own performance dominated in the female group. This difference on the
subjective level was, however, not reflected in objective performance, both sexes doing equally well in the examination. Rather
surprisingly, high discomfort was correlated with poor performance
in the males and, conversely, with good performance in the females.

One might speculate about the relationship between the lower
MHPG excretion in the female students and their feelings of discomfort and disappointment. Tentatively, the results suggest that
MHPG excretion could be used as an index of affective state, not
only in clinical cases, but in healthy persons, too.

Stress patterns in "nontraditional" females

The psychoneuroendocrine sex differences that we have consistently found suggest that the cost of adapting to the demands from
the psychosocial environment may be higher for males than for
females. This, in turn, leads to the speculation that sex differences in
the mode of adaptation may be associated with the greater vulnerability of the male sex, reflected in higher morbidity and mortality
rates. And this takes us to the interactions of biological and social
determinants of psychoneuroendocrine stress reactions in the two
sexes. To the extent that these responses are learned, differences
between the sexes in this respect are likely to be reduced as the social
roles of males and females become more equal.

One way of approaching this problem is by studying interindividual differences between women in different social roles, the
hypothesis being that those women who have adopted a male role
in, for instance, their professional life, would tend to exhibit the
neuroendocrine stress responses typical of men. Following this line
of thinking, a study was made (Johansson, Note 6) of the
catecholamine excretion of a female graduate student in connection
with an oral examination in which she publicly defended her Ph.D.
thesis. Figure 14 A shows a gradual increase of adrenaline excretion
during the days preceding the examination, followed by a dramatic
rise on the day of the examination. Noradrenaline (Fig. 14 B) showed
a similar, although less regular, pattern. On the psychological level,
the student coped very well and her performance was excellent.

Our next step was to compare male and female engineering students, choosing our subjects from the most male-dominated study

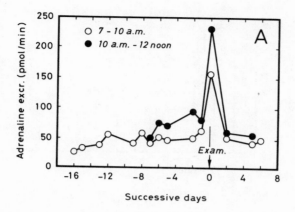

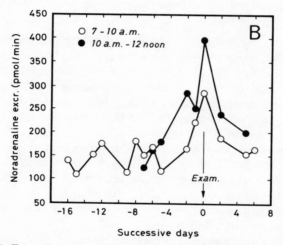

FIGURE 14. Excretion rates of adrenaline (diagram A) and noradrenaline (diagram B) in a female Ph.D. candidate during a three-week period before, during, and after the public defense of her doctor's thesis. Based on Johansson, Note 6.

courses, such as electromechanics and metallurgics, where less than 5% of the students are women (Collins & Frankenhaeuser, 1978). It was argued that insofar as the neuroendocrine sex differences are part of a learned sex-role pattern, these nontraditional females would be more like their male colleagues than the more traditional females studied in our previous experiments.

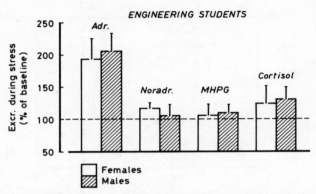

FIGURE 15. Means and standard errors for adrenaline, noradrenaline, MHPG, and cortisol excretion in female and male engineering students. Values obtained during a cognitive-conflict task have been expressed as percentages of values obtained during an inactivity period. Based on Collins & Frankenhaeuser, 1978.

Data from a laboratory experiment in which the students performed a color-word conflict task were expressed as percentages of corresponding data obtained in a control condition spent in inactivity. The results (Fig. 15) showed that adrenaline and cortisol excretion increased to nearly the same degree in the females as in the males, whereas noradrenaline and MHPG excretion was not much affected by stress in either sex.

Thus "nontraditional" females tend to be more similar to males in respect of their neuroendocrine stress reactions than the "traditional" females examined in our earlier experiments (cf. Fig. 12). While these data are suggestive, the causal relations remain obscure. We do not know to what extent a constitutional tendency to respond to stress and challenge in a "male-like fashion" had influenced the "nontraditionals" in their vocational choice, and to what extent they had acquired a masculine way of responding as a consequence of being exposed to the same challenges as their male colleagues.

With regard to psychological functions, these male and female students showed some differences, but were strikingly similar in other respects (Collins & Frankenhaeuser: in preparation). A factor scale of intellectual ability showed a clear tendency toward the well-established sex difference in intellectual profile, males being superior in spatial and reasoning abilities, females in verbal ability and perceptual speed. However, with regard to personality-related variables, males and females rated themselves very similar in terms of characteristics traditionally viewed as specifically desirable for males only ("agentic" qualities) and females only ("communal" qualities). All ratings were high, meaning that members of both sexes considered themselves to be psychologically "androgynous" persons (cf. Bem, 1974). Interestingly enough, this psychological similarity was reflected in similar neuroendocrine stress responses.

These results, when viewed in relation to the possible part played by elevated catecholamine and corticosteroid levels in the development of pathological states, prompt the question whether new sex-role patterns will serve to diminish the sex differential in disease and mortality. Although conclusive data are still lacking, it is generally assumed that the incidence of coronary heart disease is increasing among women who have acquired a more competitive life style. Less attention has been paid to the new male role and the possibility that males will acquire some of the ways of coping now considered typical of females, where emphasis is on interpersonal relations rather than on self-assertiveness and competition. The question is whether such new ways of coping among males will raise their resistance to disease. This seems a plausible hypothesis in view of the health data showing that social networks may provide protection against the damaging effects of severe environmental pressures, close emotional ties serving as a buffer.

JOB DEMANDS AND WELL-BEING

Combining psychoendocrine and social psychological approaches

The findings outlined above prompt the question whether, and if so how, we can put the knowledge gained by our psychoneuroendocrine techniques to practical use. Can it be applied to problems of real life, and perhaps used as a basis for changing adverse work conditions?

In Scandinavia, as in many of the technologically advanced countries, there is a new readiness, on the political level, to pay attention to knowledge gained by social psychological research on working life. Among important research contributions are those indicating that ill effects of psychologically unrewarding work conditions tend to spread to life outside work and hence may color the individual's total life situation (Gardell, 1976). The view that the worker would be able to compensate for a dull and boring job by stimulating and enriching activities in his or her free time is being replaced by a new insight into the strong links between a job that is circumscribed and repetitious and a leisure which is passive and psychologically unrewarding. In other words, those individuals whose work is restricted and monotonous are less likely to engage in leisure activities requiring planning, cooperation, and effort.

When viewing our experimental, psychobiological research on underload and overload in this context we were struck by the conceptual similarity between our research problems and those of the social psychology of working life, emphasizing autonomy, participation, and control over one's own work as prime determinants of job satisfaction, health, and well-being. These two areas have had little in common, but it seemed that by bridging the gap, one would strengthen the knowledge gained by each of them. Data integrating knowledge from the two areas would carry more weight with those responsible for planning the work environment.

Accordingly, we have made problems of working life part of our psychoendocrine stress research program, focusing on psychological and physiological responses to work conditions associated with advanced technology (Frankenhaeuser, 1977, in press-b; Frankenhaeuser & Gardell, 1976). As a first target we selected highly mechanized industrial work, and results from a study of sawmill workers will be reported below.

Stress on the assembly line

Data from a recent large-scale ergonomics study of sawmills in Sweden—based on experts' ratings, health surveys, and interviews—show that many jobs in the sawmill are characterized by severe physical strain and restriction of social interaction and movement (Ager, Aminoff, Baneryd, Englund, Nerell, Nilsson, Saarman, & Söderqvist, Note 7). The workers report feelings of extreme monotony, repetitiveness, nonparticipation, and coercion. The work is machine-paced, and the monitoring process demands unfailing attention, since skilled judgments of timber quality have to be made at very short intervals. A striking feature is the short work

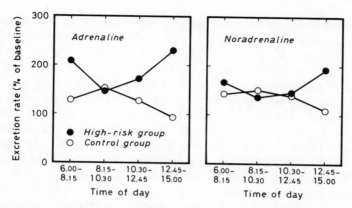

FIGURE 16. Successive mean values for adrenaline and noradrenaline excretion during an 8-hour work shift in two groups of sawmill workers. Values are expressed as percentages of baselines obtained under nonwork conditions. Based on Frankenhaeuser & Gardell, 1976.

cycle, in some cases less than 10 seconds. Great effort is required to maintain a high level of performance and attention under conditions as completely lacking in variety as these. In the case of the sawmill worker, these factors are combined with a high pace of work (set by the machine), responsibility for correct judgments, piece-work rush, and a high noise level in the saw house. In other words, the worker is exposed to conditions characterized by a pronounced lack of personal control, combined with elements of both underload and overload, i.e., exactly those conditions which have been shown to elicit sympathetic-adrenal medullary arousal. Moreover, he is a shift worker, which requires adaptation to repeated changes in the work-sleep cycle, and he is paid on a piecework basis, which adds to the rush and time pressure.

For our pilot study (Johansson, Aronsson, & Lindström, 1978) we selected a group classified as high-risk workers on the basis of the extremely constricted, machine-paced nature of their assembly-line job. This group was compared with a control group of workers from the same mill whose job was not as constricted physically and mentally. Figure 16 shows successive measurements of catecholamine excretion, taken during an eight-hour work shift and expressed as percentages of baseline values obtained under work-free conditions at home. The average adrenaline excretion was significantly higher in the high-risk group than in the controls. Furthermore, the time course was strikingly different for both amines, catecholamine release decreasing towards the end of the work day in the control group, but increasing in the high-risk group. The difference between the two groups in the last measurement of the day was significant for both amines. Such a build-up of catecholamine arousal during a long work day should be regarded as a warning signal, indicating that the organism is forced to mobilize "reserve capacity," which in the long run is likely to add to its wear and tear. In other words, the cost of adaptation may be exceedingly high. These assumptions were supported by interview data indicating that an inability to relax after work was a common complaint in the high-risk workers. Moreover, the frequency of psychosomatic symptoms as well as absenteeism were exceptionally high in this group.

The next step was to try to identify those aspects of the work process which induced the psychological and neuroendocrine stress responses. It was hypothesized that the common origin of the high catecholamine level and the high frequency of psychosomatic symptoms in our high-risk group was the monotonous, coercive, machine-paced nature of the job. In agreement with this, correlational analyses showed consistent, statistically significant relations between psychoendocrine response patterns and job characteristics referring to different aspects of monotony and constraint. These relationships were examined further by comparing subgroups of workers differing with regard to specific job characteristics, as determined by expert ratings. Most subgroups were rather small and differences between them not statistically significant, but the trends were consistent and formed a meaningful pattern (Fig. 17; for details see Johansson, Aronsson, & Lindström, 1978). Stress, as reflected in adrenaline and noradrenaline excretion and in self-reports of irritation, was most severe when the job was highly repetitious, when the worker had to maintain the same posture throughout working hours, and when the work pace was controlled by the machine.

When evaluating these results, it should be noted that conditions in the sawmill are representative of a wide range of mass-production industries. Hence, our data point to potential uses of psychoendocrine techniques in assessing the stressfulness of different aspects of technologically advanced work systems. A key question, dealt with in a study now in progress, concerns the risks and benefits involved in the transition to completely automated production systems, where the repetitive, manual elements are taken over by machines

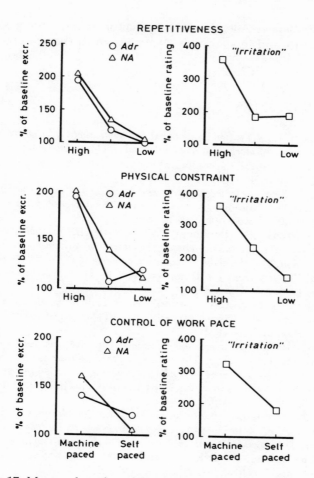

FIGURE 17. Mean values for adrenaline and noradrenaline excretion and self-ratings of irritation in a group of sawmill workers under conditions differing with regard to repetitiveness, physical constraint, and control of work pace. Values obtained during work have been expressed as percentages of baselines obtained under nonwork conditions. Based on Johansson, Aronsson, & Lindström, 1978.

and the workers are left with mainly supervisory, controlling functions. Such a set-up increases the chances for an active, participatory work role. However, at the same time it introduces new stress components associated with long, monotonous monitoring periods and with the abstract nature of the work. Knowledge gained by experimental psychoendocrinology may aid in identifying potential risk factors and in suggesting ways in which they can be prevented.

REFERENCE NOTES

1. Johansson, G. *Activation, adjustment and sympathetic-adrenal medullary activity. Field and laboratory studies of adults and children.* (Dissertation Summary.) Reports from the Psychological Laboratories, University of Stockholm, 1973, Suppl. 21.

2. Pátkai, P. *Relations between catecholamine release and psychological functions.* (Dissertation Summary.) Reports from the Psychological Laboratories, University of Stockholm, 1970, Suppl. 2.

3. Frankenhaeuser, M., Lundberg, U., & Forsman, L. *Dissociation between sympathetic-adrenal and pituitary-adrenal responses to an achievement situation characterized by high controllability: comparison between Type A and Type B males and females.* Reports from the Department of Psychology, University of Stockholm, 1978, No. 540.

4. Rissler, A., & Elgerot, A. *Stressreaktioner vid övertidsarbete [Stress reactions related to overtime at work].* Department of Psychology, University of Stockholm, Rapporter, 1978, No. 23.

5. Rauste, M. *The image of man among Finnish boys and girls.* Reports from the Department of Psychology, University of Turku, Finland, 1975, No. 41.

6. Johansson, G. *Case report on female catecholamine excretion in response to examination stress.* Reports from the Department of Psychology, University of Stockholm, 1977, No. 515.

7. Ager, B., Aminoff, S., Baneryd, K., Englund, A., Nerell, G., Nilsson, C., Saarman, E., & Söderqvist, A. *Arbetsmiljön i sågverk. En tvärvetenskaplig undersökning [Work environment in the sawmill. A multidisciplinary investigation].* Stockholm: Arbetarskyddsstyrelsen (National Board of Occupational Safety and Health), 1975, Rapport AM 101/75.

REFERENCES

Andersson, B., Hovmöller, S., Karlsson, C.-G., & Svensson, S. Analysis of urinary catecholamines: An improved auto-analyzer fluorescence method. *Clinica Chimica Acta*, 1974, **51**, 13–28.

Averill, J. R. Personal control over aversive stimuli and its relationship to stress. *Psychological Bulletin*, 1973, **80**, 286–303.

Ax, A. F. The physiological differentiation of fear and anger in humans. *Psychosomatic Medicine*, 1953, **15**, 433–442.

Bem, S. L. The measurement of psychological androgyny. *Journal of Consulting and Clinical Psychology*, 1974, **42**, 155–162.

Bergman, L. R., & Magnusson, D. Overachievement and catecholamine output in an achievement situation. *Psychosomatic Medicine*, in press.

Bloom, G., Euler, U.S.v., & Frankenhaeuser, M. Catecholamine excretion and personality traits in paratroop trainees. *Acta Physiologica Scandinavica*, 1963, **58**, 77–89.

Brady, J. V. Emotion and sensitivity of psychoendocrine systems. In D. C. Glass (Ed.), *Neurophysiology and emotion*. New York: Rockefeller University Press and Russell Sage Foundation, 1967.

Cannon, W. B. The emergency function of the adrenal medulla in pain and the major emotions. *American Journal of Physiology*, 1914, **33**, 356–372.

Cannon, W. B. *The wisdom of the body*. New York: Norton, 1932.

Collins, A., & Frankenhaeuser, M. Effects of a cognitive-conflict task on psychophysiological stress reactions in male and female engineering students. *Journal of Human Stress*, 1978, **4**, 23–48.

Coover, G., Ursin, H., & Levine, S. Corticosterone and avoidance in rats with basolateral amygdala lesions. *Journal of Comparative and Physiological Psychology*, 1973, **85**, 111–122.

Easterbrook, J. A. The effect of emotion on cue utilization and the organization of behavior. *Psychological Review*, 1959, **66**, 183–201.

Euler, U.S.v. A specific sympathomimetic ergone in adrenergic nerve fibers (sympathin) and its relation to adrenaline and noradrenaline. *Acta Physiologica Scandinavica*, 1946, **12**, 73–97.

Euler, U.S.v. *Noradrenaline*. Springfield, Illinois: Thomas, 1956.

Euler, U.S.v. Adrenal medullary secretion and its neural control. In L. Martini & W. F. Ganong (Eds.), *Neuroendocrinology* (Vol. 2). New York: Academic Press, 1967.

Euler, U.S.v., & Lishajko, F. Improved technique for the fluorimetric estimation of catecholamines. *Acta Physiologica Scandinavica*, 1961, **51**, 348–355.

Euler, U.S.v., & Lundberg, U. Effect of flying on the epinephrine excretion in air force personnel. *Journal of Applied Psychology*, 1954, **6**, 551–555.

Frankenhaeuser, M. Behavior and circulating catecholamines. *Brain Research*, 1971, **31**, 241–262.

Frankenhaeuser, M. Sympathetic-adrenomedullary activity, behaviour and the psychosocial environment. In P. H. Venables & M. J. Christie (Eds.), *Research in psychophysiology*. New York, London, & Sydney: Wiley, 1975. (a)

Frankenhaeuser, M. Experimental approaches to the study of catecholamines and emotion. In L. Levi (Ed.), *Emotions—their parameters and measurement*. New York: Raven Press, 1975. (b)

Frankenhaeuser, M. Job demands, health and wellbeing. *Journal of Psychosomatic Research*, 1977, **21**, 313–321.

Frankenhaeuser, M. Psychoneuroendocrine approaches to the study of stressful person-environment transactions. In H. Selye (Ed.), *Selye's guide to stress research*. Van Nostrand Reinhold, in press. (a)

Frankenhaeuser, M. Coping with job stress—a psychobiological approach. In B. Gardell & G. Johansson (Eds.), *Man and working life*. Wiley, in press. (b)

Frankenhaeuser, M., & Andersson, K. Note on interaction between cognitive and endocrine functions. *Perceptual and Motor Skills*, 1974, **38**, 557–558.

Frankenhaeuser, M., Dunne, E., & Lundberg, U. Sex differences in sympathetic-adrenal medullary reactions induced by different stressors. *Psychopharmacology*, 1976, **47**, 1–5.

Frankenhaeuser, M., & Gardell, B. Underload and overload in working life: Outline of a multidisciplinary approach. *Journal of Human Stress*, 1976, **2**, 35–46.

Frankenhaeuser, M., & Järpe, G. Psychophysiological changes during infusions of adrenaline in various doses. *Psychopharmacologia*, 1963, **4**, 424–432.

Frankenhaeuser, M., Järpe, G., & Matell, G. Effects of intravenous infusions of adrenaline and noradrenaline on certain psychological and physiological functions. *Acta Physiologica Scandinavica*, 1961, **51**, 175–186.

Frankenhaeuser, M., & Johansson, G. Task demand as reflected in catecholamine excretion and heart rate. *Journal of Human Stress*, 1976, **2**, 15–23.

Frankenhaeuser, M., & Lundberg, U. The influence of cognitive set on performance and arousal under different noise loads. *Motivation and Emotion*, 1977, **1**, 139–149.

Frankenhaeuser, M., Nordheden, B., Myrsten, A.-L., & Post, B. Psychophysiological reactions to understimulation and overstimulation. *Acta Psychologica*, 1971, **35**, 298–308.

Frankenhaeuser, M., & Pátkai, P. Interindividual differences in catecholamine excretion during stress. *Scandinavian Journal of Psychology*, 1965, **6**, 117–123.

Frankenhaeuser, M., Rauste von Wright, M., Collins, A., von Wright, J., Sedvall, G., & Swahn, C.-G. Sex differences in psychoneuroendocrine reactions to examination stress. *Psychosomatic Medicine*, 1978, **40**, 334–343.

Frankenhaeuser, M., & Rissler, A. Effects of punishment on catecholamine release and efficiency of performance. *Psychopharmacologia*, 1970, **17**, 378–390.

Frankenhaeuser, M., Sterky, K., & Järpe, G. Psychophysiological relations in habituation to gravitational stress. *Perceptual and Motor Skills*, 1962, **15**, 63–72.

Friedman, M., Rosenman, R. H., & St. George, S. Adrenal response to excess corticotropin in coronary-prone men. *Proceedings from the Society of Experimental Biological Medicine*, 1969, **131**, 1305–1307.

Friedman, S. B., Mason, J. W., & Hamburg, D. A. Urinary 17-hydroxycorticosteroid levels in parents of children with neoplastic disease. *Psychosomatic Medicine*, 1963, **25**, 364–376.

Fröberg, J. E., Karlsson, C.-G., Levi, L., & Lidberg, L. Circadian rhythms of catecholamine excretion, shooting range performance and self-ratings of fatigue during sleep deprivation. *Biological Psychology*, 1975, **2**, 175–188.

Funkenstein, D. H. Nor-epinephrine-like and epinephrine-like substances in relation to human behavior. *Journal of Mental Diseases*, 1956, **124**, 58–68.

Gardell, B. Technology, alienation and mental health. Summary of a social psychological research programme on technology and the worker. *Acta Sociologica*, 1976, **19**, 83–94.

Glass, D. C. *Behavior patterns, stress, and coronary disease.* Hillsdale, N.J.: Lawrence Erlbaum Associates, 1977.

Gottschalk, L. A., Stone, W. N., & Gleser, G. C. Peripheral versus central mechanisms accounting for antianxiety effects of propranolol. *Psychosomatic Medicine*, 1974, **36**, 47–55.

Henry, J. P. Understanding the early pathophysiology of essential hypertension. *Geriatrics*, 1976, **31**, 59–72.

Jefferson, J. W. Beta-adrenergic receptor blocking drugs in psychiatry. *Archives of General Psychiatry*, 1974, **31**, 681–691.

Johansson, G. Subjective wellbeing and temporal patterns of sympathetic-adrenal medullary activity. *Biological Psychology*, 1976, **4**, 157–172.

Johansson, G., Aronsson, G., & Lindström, B. O. Social psychological and neuroendocrine stress reactions in highly mechanized work. *Ergonomics*, 1978, **21**, 583–599.

Johansson, G., & Frankenhaeuser, M. Temporal factors in sympatho-adrenomedullary activity following acute behavioral activation. *Biological Psychology*, 1973, **1**, 63–73.

Johansson, G., Frankenhaeuser, M., & Magnusson, D. Catecholamine output in school children as related to performance and adjustment. *Scandinavian Journal of Psychology*, 1973, **14**, 20–28.

Johansson, G., & Post, B. Catecholamine output of males and females over a one-year period. *Acta Physiologica Scandinavica*, 1974, **92**, 557–565.

Lambert, W. W., Johansson, G., Frankenhaeuser, M., & Klackenberg-Larsson, I. Catecholamine excretion in young children and their parents as related to behavior. *Scandinavian Journal of Psychology*, 1969, **10**, 306–318.

Lazarus, R. S. Cognitive and coping processes in emotion. In A. Monat & R. S. Lazarus (Eds.), *Stress and coping.* New York: Columbia University Press, 1977. (a)

Lazarus, R. S. Psychological stress and coping in adaptation and illness. In Z. J. Lipowski, D. R. Lipsitt, & P. C. Whybrow (Eds.), *Psychosomatic medicine: Current trends and clinical applications.* New York: Oxford University Press, 1977. (b)

Levi, L. The urinary output of adrenaline and noradrenaline during pleasant and unpleasant emotional states. *Psychosomatic Medicine*, 1965, **27**, 80–85.

Levi, L. Stress and distress in response to psychosocial stimuli. *Laboratory and real life studies on sympathoadrenomedullary and related reactions. Acta Medica Scandinavica*, 1972, Suppl. 528.

Lidberg, L., Levander, S., Schalling, D., & Lidberg, Y. Urinary catecholamines, stress, and psychopathy: A study of arrested men awaiting trial. *Psychosomatic Medicine*, 1978, **40**, 116–125.

Lundberg, U. Urban commuting: Crowdedness and catecholamine excretion. *Journal of Human Stress*, 1976, **2**, 26–32.

Lundberg, U. Psychophysiological aspects of performance and adjustment to stress. In H. W. Krohne & L. Laux (Eds.), *Achievement, stress and anxiety*. Washington, D.C.: Hemisphere Publishing Corporation, 1979.

Lundberg, U., & Frankenhaeuser, M. Psychophysiological reactions to noise as modified by personal control over noise intensity. *Biological Psychology*, 1978, **6**, 51–59.

Maier, S. F., & Seligman, M. E. P. Learned helplessness: Theory and evidence. *Journal of Experimental Psychology: General*, 1976, **105**, 3–46.

Mandler, G. *Mind and emotion*. New York: Wiley, 1975.

Marañon, G. Contribution à l étude de l action emotive de l adrénaline. *Revue francaise d Endocrinologie*, 1924, **2**, 301–325.

Mason, J. W. Emotion as reflected in patterns of endocrine integration. In L. Levi (Ed.), *Emotions: Their parameters and measurement*. New York: Raven Press, 1975.

Pátkai, P. The diurnal rhythm of adrenaline secretion in subjects with different working habits. *Acta Physiologica Scandinavica*, 1971, **81**, 30–34. (a)

Pátkai, P. Catecholamine excretion in pleasant and unpleasant situations. *Acta Psychologica*, 1971, **35**, 352–363. (b)

Rissler, A. Stress reactions at work and after work during a period of quantitative overload. *Ergonomics*, 1977, **20**, 13–16.

Roessler, R., Burch, N. R., & Mefferd, R. B., Jr. Personality correlates of catecholamine excretion under stress. *Journal of Psychosomatic Research*, 1967, **11**, 181–185.

Rosenman, R. H., Brand, R. J., Sholtz, R. I., & Friedman, M. Multivariate prediction of coronary heart disease during 8.5 year follow-up in the Western Collaborative Group Study. *American Journal of Cardiology*, 1976, **37**, 903–910.

Rothballer, A. B. The effects of catecholamines on the central nervous system. *Pharmacological Review*, 1959, **11**, 494–547.

Rotter, J. B. Generalized expectancies for internal versus external control of reinforcement. *Psychological Monographs*, 1966, **80**, No. 1 (Whole No. 609).

Ruder, H. J., Guy, R. L., & Lipsitt, M. B. A radioimmunoassay for cortisol in plasma and urine. *Journal of Clinical Endocrinological Metabolites*, 1972, **35**, 219–224.

Sachar, E. J. Psychological factors relating to activation and inhibition of the adrenocortical stress response in man: A review. In D. De Wied & J. A. W. M. Weijnen (Eds.), *Progress in Brain Research* (Vol. 32). Amsterdam: Elsevier, 1970.

Schachter, S., & Singer, J. E. Cognitive, social and physiological determinants of emotional state. *Psychological Review*, 1962, **69**, 379–399.

Schildkraut, J. J. Neuropharmacology of the affective disorders. *Annual Review of Pharmacology*, 1973, **13**, 427–454. (a)

Schildkraut, J. J. Catecholamine metabolism and affective disorders: Studies of MHPG excretion. In E. Usdin & S. H. Snyder (Eds.), *Frontiers in catecholamine research*. New York: Pergamon Press, 1973. (b)

Schildkraut, J. J., & Kety, S. S. Biogenic amines and emotion. *Science*, 1967, **156**, 21–30.

Seligman, M. E. P. *Helplessness. On depression, development and death*. San Francisco: Freeman, 1975.

Selye, H. *The physiology and pathology of exposure to stress*. Montreal: ACTA, 1950.

Selye, H. *Stress without distress*. Philadelphia and New York: Lippincott, 1974.

Singer, J. E., Lundberg, U., & Frankenhaeuser, M. Stress on the train: A study of urban commuting. In A. Baum, J. E. Singer & S. Valins (Eds.), *Advances in Environmental Psychology*. (Vol. 1). Hillsdale, N. J.: Erlbaum, 1978.

Sjöberg, H., Frankenhaeuser, M., & Bjurstedt, H. Interactions between heart rate, psychomotor performance and perceived effort during physical work as influenced by beta-adrenergic blockade. *Biological Psychology*, 1979, **8**, 31–43.

Swahn, C.-G., Sandgärde, B., Wiesel, F. A., & Sedvall, G. Simultaneous determination of the three major monoamine metabolites in brain tissue and body fluids by a mass fragmentographic method. *Psychopharmacology*, 1976, **48**, 147–152.

Weiss, J. M. Psychological factors in stress and disease. *Scientific American*, 1972, **226**, 104–113.

Weiss, J. M., Stone, E. A., & Harrell, N. Coping behavior and brain norepinephrine level in rats. *Journal of Comparative and Physiological Psychology*, 1970, **72**, 153–160.

Emotions as Motivations: An Evolutionary-Developmental Perspective

C. E. Izard
University of Delaware

The emotions and the emotion system are as much a product of evolution as is our highly praised neocortex, which accounts for much of the increase in the size of the hominid brain. There are parallels in the evolution of the brain and the emotion system. Increases in the size of the brain are associated with increases in the number of discrete emotions; increases in the size of the brain and in the complexity of mental processes parallel the changes in the physiological mechanisms that capacitate emotion expressions. The comparative anatomy of living forms of different phyla and species shows a strong relationship between increases in the differentiation of the expressive musculature of the face and increases in the size of the brain and the complexity of behavior (Huber, 1931).

The reason for the strong parallel between the evolution of higher forms of life and increases in the number of discrete emotions is that the emotions played a central role in survival and adaptation. A particular emotion sensitizes the organism to particular critical features of its environment. Presence of an emotion in consciousness insures a readiness to respond to events of significance to the organism's survival and adaptation. Some emotions insure an increased vigor of physical response, while others function to increase the organism's capacity to receive and process information that is of immediate or future consequence for the individual.

In the simplest forms of life the emotion system or its precursors motivated only approach and avoidance responses. This simple beginning gave rise to the fight/flight system, which in higher forms includes expressive behaviors from which we can infer the specific emotions of anger and fear. In simple approach-avoidant or fight/ flight responses, afferent-efferent activities resulting from environmental stimulation might be described in terms of simple linear processing, reflexes or reflex-like sequences. Behavioral alternatives in response to environmental inputs were limited both by the small number of emotions or motivational qualities in the animal's repertory and by the number of channels available for relating sensory input to emotion and behavior. With the advent of each discrete emotion, brought about by selection pressures to increase the repertory of adaptive behaviors in the face of changing environmental conditions, behavioral alternatives increased, and cognitive capability for making decisions and choosing among alternatives increased concomitantly. With each new emotion came a new quality of motivation and new cognitive and behavioral tendencies. The ten fundamental emotions, their interactions with each other, with physiological needs, and with cognitions provide the human being with a vast array of motivational experiences and behavioral alternatives for survival and adaptation.

I have recently attempted to sketch the way in which each of the discrete emotions participated in human evolution (Izard, 1977). In a later section of this paper I shall attempt to show how each of the fundamental emotions figures in ontogeny. I think we shall be able to see some parallels between the processes that occur in ontogeny and those that occurred in phylogeny.

I. DIFFERENTIAL EMOTIONS THEORY IN EVOLUTIONARY-DEVELOPMENTAL PERSPECTIVE

Differential emotions theory (Izard, 1971, 1972, 1977; Tomkins, 1962, 1963) assumes that motivation is a function of emotion. Emotion includes as one of its components a distinct quality of consciousness which motivates cognition; emotion interacting with cognition specifies and directs complex behaviors. Emotion-cognition interactions and the resulting affective-cognitive structures form a virtually limitless number of motivational phenomena that characterize human consciousness. Emotion is assumed to be always present in ordinary consciousness, giving it a particular experiential quality and maintaining its purposeful flow. At no time of life is this more evident than in infancy and early childhood—the period of principal concern in this paper.

One reason why many scientists do not give emotion such a continuous role in consciousness is their reluctance to recognize as an emotion the ubiquitous interest in novelty and change displayed by human beings from birth. Several investigators (e.g., Fantz, 1966; Kagan, 1971; Wolff, 1965), have observed the manifestations of interest in infants and have used the term descriptively without conceiving it as an affective-motivational system. Others have described similar concepts like "aroused intention," which Bruner (1974) conceives as a key factor in organizing skilled actions in infants. Breger (1974) is an exception, for, like Tomkins and Izard, he sees interest as an emotion as "primary" as distress, anger, or fear. Once interest is conceived as an emotion, we have an explanation for the focusing and selectivity of attention that characterizes focal awareness and for the directedness of positive approach and exploratory behavior from birth. All the empirical research on attention and visual tracking in infancy is consistent with this position.

One might argue that selective attention in early infancy is in part reflexive. This may be so, in that the very young infant is less capable of voluntary effort to sustain attention to a given stimulus in the face of competing ones than is a 6- or 12-month-old. This does not mean that the attentional responses in early infancy are unmotivated or nonemotional or that reflex-like responses to novelty and change cannot include emotion responses. The expressive component of an emotion, as Darwin (1872) suggested, may be considered in part as a highly complex reflex. In the course of normal development such a complex reflex comes to be more under voluntary or self-control and less under stimulus control.

When an emotion other than interest achieves awareness (e.g., distress), consciousness and the resources of the individual are appropriately redirected. The exploration motivated by interest gives way temporarily to activities (e.g., a cry for help) relevant to the dominant emotion experience (e.g., distress).

With a few important exceptions (e.g., Lazarus, 1968), major theories of behavior that give any place at all to emotion consider it as having motivational properties. There is still far more theory than research on the issue of emotion-as-motivation, but more answers may be forthcoming, with the increasing interest in emotion concepts gaining a foothold in the laboratories of a number of different disciplines and various specialty areas of psychology.

I recently turned to infancy as an area for the study of emotions and emotion-cognition relationships on the assumption that infants will display the facial expressions of discrete emotions more frequently than older persons who have learned to disguise, mask, or inhibit emotion expressions according to the rules laid down by the culture and the social learning experiences of the particular individual (Izard, 1971; Ekman, 1971). Even in young infancy it is possible to observe functional relationships between stimulus situations or incentive events, specific facial expressions, and subsequent behavior (Emde, Gaensbauer, & Harmon, 1976; Emde, in press). The young infant has the capacities to provide the data to examine such relationships.

The genetic endowment of the human infant guarantees each personality subsystem a minimal set of genetically encoded programs for system interaction and for person-environment transactions. In the more traditional language of psychology, the infant is born with certain capacities to stay alive (the homeostatic system); to experience and respond to drives or physiological needs (the drive system); to experience and express the emotions of distress, interest, and enjoyment (the rudiments of the emotion system); to explore nearby objects in the environment (the rudiments of the perceptual system); and to react differentially, both affectively and perceptually, to changes in stimulation or information inputs (the rudiments of the cognitive system and the basis for affective-cognitive structures). In the language of Harlow and Mears (1978), these inborn capacities are complex, unlearned responses, and they form an important part of the basis for the development of the behavioral systems of infancy. They guarantee a minimal set of adaptive subsystem and infant-environment interactions. (Izard, 1978, pp. 389–390)

Differential emotions theory has been detailed elsewhere (Izard, 1971, 1972, 1977; Izard & Tomkins, 1966; Tomkins, 1962, 1963), so I shall only state some of the major propositions that relate to ontogenetic development and personality integration in infancy.

1. The human personality is a complex organization of six relatively independent though complexly interactive subsystems: the homeostatic, drive (physiological-need), emotion, perceptual, cognitive, and motor systems. Each of these systems has motivational properties whose salience varies at different developmental levels,

in different environmental contexts, and in different self-other interactions. For example, physiological needs are relatively more dominant in an impoverished society and in early infancy, and in both cases, need signals amplified by emotions such as distress and fear play a critical role in survival and effective adaptation. Under relatively normal biological and social conditions, however, the emotion system is the primary motivational system for human beings over the life span.

2. The six personality subsystems produce four types or classes of motivation: drives, emotions, affect-perception and affect-cognition interactions, and affective-cognitive structures and orientations. The term affect includes both emotions and drives. The drives are physiological needs such as hunger, thirst, elimination, pain-avoidance, and sex, and these assume importance for personality and social behavior as they interact with emotions. The fundamental emotions are interest, joy, surprise, distress, anger, disgust, contempt, fear, shame/shyness, and guilt. An affect-cognition interaction may be the interaction of any drive or emotion with perceptual and cognitive processes, the affect determining the selectivity and direction of these processes. Affective-cognitive structures have traitlike characteristics, and a relatively homogeneous set of affective-cognitive structures may form a basic personality orientation described by such terms as passive, aggressive, egotistical, skeptical, introverted, extraverted, anxious, or depressed.

3. An emotion has a neurophysiological, expressive, and phenomenological component. The expressive component, particularly the facial expression, has both a physiological (face-brain feedback) function, and a social (or communicative) function. At the individual physiological level expressive movements provide sensory data to the brain for the cortical-integrative activity that produces emotion experience. At the social level it provides a set of signals or messages that are particularly important in infant-caregiver and other social relationships.

4. In the case of the fundamental emotions, the neural mechanisms for emotion expression and emotion experience are innate, and the ontogenesis of a particular fundamental emotion expression is primarily a function of maturational processes.

5. The neural mechanisms for the perception of facial expressions are also innate. By this I mean that the infant does not have to learn to perceive the human face or learn to interpret the facial and vocal expressions of the fundamental emotions (Izard, 1971). As Neisser

(1976) argues, "babies are innately prepared to perceive smiles and frowns, soothing tones and harsh inflections, as indications of what others will do next" (p. 191). In Neisser's terms, infants have inborn schemata for the perception of emotion expressions, and the congenital inadequacy of these schemata and the emotion communication they capacitate may account for certain types of psychopathology such as infantile autism.

6. The innate neural programs for encoding and decoding the facial and vocal expressions of emotions and the reciprocal emotion-signaling which they capacitate form the basis for the mother-infant attachment—the first social relationship, one that is critical for survival and adaptation, and one that influences the subsequent development of relationships with significant others. As indicated in the preceding paragraph, genetic or developmental defects in this emotion communication system deprive mother and infant of critical signals that motivate social-affective interaction and may result in psychological disorders.

7. Differential emotions theory assumes that emotions emerge ontogenetically as they become adaptive in the life of the infant, with adaptiveness defined largely in terms of the success of the infant's efforts to form an emotional-social attachment to a caregiver and in terms of the quality of the infant-caregiver relationship.

8. The emotions constitute the principal organizing factors in consciousness and provide the experiential-motivational conditions and cues for cognitive-interpretive processes and action.

9. The subjective experience of each emotion is a unique quality of consciousness and has distinct motivational characteristics that tend to instigate a broad class of responses that are generally adaptive in relation to the eliciting event.

10. Each emotion adds to the complexity of consciousness, increases the capacity for processing and responding to different types of information, and increases the individual's capacity to respond appropriately to a broader set of contingencies.

11. At the neural level, emotion experience is activated by sensory feedback from the face. Once an emotion is activated, however, it typically recruits the autonomic nervous system and the physiological systems it innervates. Subsequent hormones and neurohumors influence biochemical processes that play a role in mobilizing energy and maintaining emotions over time.

12. At the conscious level, the causes of emotion range from what

Bowlby (1973) has termed "natural clues" (eliciting events that tend to act as innate releasers) to an almost infinite variety of causes that result from conditioning and social learning. Particularly after the emergence of symbolic processes, perception and cognition play a highly important role both in learning to identify emotion-eliciting events and in learning effective ways of responding to or coping with them.

13. A given stimulus situation or incentive event may elicit different emotions, depending on the stage of development in the perceptual, cognitive, emotion, and motor systems. For example, a strange nodding face will elicit a smile in the infant of 2½ to 4 months, but, depending on the context, it may elicit interest, surprise, or fear at 8 to 10 months. Similarly, the departing face of the mother will elicit interest and visual tracking in the young infant, but such separation may elicit anger, fear, and distress between about 9 months and 3 years. Of course, negative emotions in varying degrees remain a consequence of separation until the final separation of death.

14. Incentive events often activate a sequence or pattern of emotions. The first emotion that is activated influences subsequent emotions and behavior, but the overall motivational impact on the person has to be assessed in relation to the relative dominance of each emotion over time and in terms of the effects of emotions interacting with each other.

15. Each emotion helps set the stage for a particular type of learning and development. In a sense, the emergence of a particular emotion, along with correlative changes in other systems, marks the beginning of a "critical period" for certain types of experiences and for the learning of certain types of responses that are important to development at that particular stage of life.

16. The emotion process proper is a function of the somatic system, and the fact that this system is under voluntary control has important implications for the management and regulation of emotions, both in the socialization process and in psychotherapy and behavior modification (Izard, 1971; Singer, 1974). Although through learning and experience reafferent loops may come to be effective in emotion activation, the sensory feedback from the face is critical in the emotion process in infancy and early childhood. Recent research by Kleck, Vaughan, Colby, Cartwright-Smith, Vaughan, and Lanzetta (1976) and Lanzetta, Cartwright-Smith, and Kleck (1976) suggests that the simulation or dissimulation (intensification or

deintensification) of facial expression in pain and emotion amplifies or attenuates both the physiological response and the self-report of the affect.

17. The early learning of voluntary emotion expressions through imaginative play, imitation, and role assumption figures significantly in the acquisition of techniques for the self-regulation of emotion. The significance of this process is evident when we consider the importance of self-regulation of emotions for the larger domain of self-control.

II. EMOTIONS, CONSCIOUSNESS, AND ADAPTATION

Emotions are the principal organizing forces in consciousness. Their organizing and guidance functions are essential to adaptation and effective behavior.

A. Biological Processes, Emotions, and Consciousness

In his essay on the evolution of mind the geneticist Edmund Sinnott (1966) reviews the robust evidence for the innately programmed directedness in biological mechanisms and in the organism as a whole. He argues that the directedness that is an integral part of biological structures and processes is felt ("as by something like a kinesthetic sense") and that consequently "psychical life is the sense of being consciously oriented towards ends" (p. 153). He maintains that the feeling of being oriented or drawn toward some end gives rise to the sensation of desiring or wanting to achieve that end. He concludes that the subjective experiences of wants, desires, and their opposites are emotions.

The language of Sinnott, the geneticist turned philosopher, is strikingly similar here to that of Piaget, the zoologist turned epistomologist. In one of his early papers on infancy Piaget (1927/1960) explains the repetitive behaviors (circular reactions) as a function of the infant's *"desire* to have an interesting spectacle continue . . . " (p. 214). In his discussion of the growth of causal notions, Piaget maintains that phenomenologically, or from the baby's point of view, emotion is causation; it is what makes things happen. He writes: "From the very first inklings a baby has of her own power, she considers the thing on which she is acting as subject to her desire, that is, as dependent on her emotional states . . . " (p. 214).

Although Sinnott makes no effort to deal with emotion concepts in a specific or technical way, the thrust of his thinking is consistent with differential emotions theory and is supported at least in part by theorists and investigators like Piaget (1927/1960), Spitz (1959, 1965), and Emde, Gaensbauer, and Harmon (1976).

Sinnott's idea—that an emotion experience is awareness of a basic biological directedness that characterizes neurophysiological systems and the organism as a whole—has parallels not only in differential emotions theory but in various concepts relating to intrinsic motivation and psychological growth. For example, there is an easy parallel between Sinnott's concept and Elkind's (1971) notion that "intrinsic growth forces" generate seeking behavior in the infant and child. Further, Piaget and Inhelder (1969) assume that affect is the motive force for cognitive and intellectual development: "There is no behavior pattern, however intellectual, which does not involve affective factors as motives . . . " (p. 158). Thus in Piaget's theory the cognizance or consciousness of objects and their relations develops as a function of affective experience.

A central postulate of differential emotions theory is that consciousness develops and realizes its highly complex organization as a function of the emotions—their emergence, their development, and their integration with the other systems of the personality. Further, the stream of consciousness in the growing infant is often characterized by the experiences that derive from emotion responses and emotion processes in relation to some basic conditions that are universal features of human ecosystems—e.g., social interaction, attachment, separation, strangeness, pain.

B. Infant Consciousness as Affective Experiences

The development of the emotion-perception-cognition relationships of consciousness, like the development of the individual as a whole, is a function of genetically programmed structures, the maturation of biological mechanisms, and learning resulting from person-environment interactions. In early infancy preprogrammed affective responses accomplish or facilitate the information-processing and communicative functions of consciousness that are later made more sophisticated by the perceptual and cognitive systems. During this period (the first few weeks of life), internal stimulation (information) usually takes precedence over external stimulation.

Among the first contemporary scientists to recognize the predominance of affects in the newborn's consciousness was Spitz (1959, 1965), who maintained that in the early weeks of life most of the sensory data received in consciousness comes from interoceptors and proprioceptors, both internal sources of stimulation that contribute to affective experience. At this early age perceptual development has not proceeded far enough to provide consciousness with a wide array of peremptory inputs from the surround, and it will still be some months before there will be any evidence that cognitive development has resulted in acquired images or any form of memory that might compete with or modify the affective signals. Thus the first structures of consciousness are essentially affective in nature, and it is by means of affective experiences and expressions that the infant first relates to the objects and persons in the surrounding world.

A number of other investigators support the idea that consciousness in early infancy is primarily affective experience. Stechler and Carpenter (1967) maintain that it is primarily through affect that the infant derives meaning from person-environment interactions. Escalona (1968) suggests that a variety of stimulus conditions differ for 4-week-old infants only in how they make the infants feel. Sroufe (Note 1) describes the infant "not as a perceptive being, not as a cognitive being, but as a human being that experiences anxiety, joy, and anger and that is connected to its world in an emotional way" (p. 1). Taking a position on the importance of the emotions in human motivation very similar to that of Tomkins (1962) and Izard (1971), Sroufe goes on to describe affective life as "the meaning and motivational system which cognition serves" (p. 1). The empirical investigations of Emde et al. (1976) support Spitz's (1959, 1965) position that the emergence of a particular affect expression signals the appearance of a new "organizer of the psyche," describes a "new relational factor in development," and heralds a "new mode of functioning" (pp. 8–9).

Haviland (1976) has argued convincingly that users of infant intelligence scales base their assessment of awareness and comprehension in large measure on the infant's expressions of affects. More systematic use of emotion responses (e.g., changes in facial expressions) to cognitive tasks might improve the reliability and predictive validity of infant scales.

C. Emotion-Perception-Cognition Relations and Levels of Consciousness

An affect-dominated consciousness is highly adaptive for the infant, whose survival depends on attracting the attention of the caregiver. The distress cry is a compelling signal for help, and it typically communicates the need for a change in stimulation.

The emotion of interest, the activation threshold of which is relatively high in the neonate, is nevertheless crucial in gradually effecting the change from the predominantly receptive mode of consciousness structured by interoceptive and proprioceptive stimulation to a perceptive-cognizing consciousness that explores and eventually differentiates objects, persons, and relationships.

The smile of joy, evident in the early weeks of life, signals a quality of consciousness characterized by openness and receptivity to environmental inputs and to self-enhancing infant-other interactions. The behaviors motivated by this quality of consciousness tend to elicit nurturing behavior from the caregiver and to maintain a positive affective interchange.

The experiential component of interest, joy, and distress, interacting periodically (and in some measure cyclically) with the feelings initiated by drive signals, constitutes consciousness at its first level of organization. These affective-experiential modes may be considered as the predominant structures of consciousness and their expressions as the manifestations of the operations of consciousness in early infancy.

In the growing child the experiential distinctiveness and specific motivational properties of emotion experiences provide the basic selectivity, organization, and directedness that characterize consciousness. The emergence of new emotions increases the complexity of the processes in consciousness as well as the diversity of behavioral alternatives in infant-other interactions. The invariance of the fundamental emotion experiences guarantees the essential continuity of consciousness (including awareness of self) that prevails despite a number of developmental discontinuities such as those reported by Kagan (1971).

I have suggested that there are three broad overlapping levels or processes in consciousness and that these levels are a function of development or of the complexity of sensory data or information-achieving awareness. At the first level, consciousness consists primarily of sensory-affective processes. Awareness is essentially affective experience, and changes in awareness are a function of changes in the quality and intensity of affects. Affective responses occur mainly in relation to objects as global entities or to objects as a class capable of eliciting a particular quality or intensity of affect. This level characterizes much of conscious experience in the early weeks of life, when sensory feedback from physiological needs recruits the emotion of distress and the cry for help.

At level two, consciousness consists primarily of affective-perceptual processes. The differential affect-eliciting characteristics of objects differentially focuses interest and attention and facilitates the formation of images or schemata and affect-percept bonds. The images or simple schemata that obtain at this age (up to about one year) are based on relatively short-term memory. The development of sensory organs and the strengthening of the emotion of interest enables the infant to focus and maintain attention not only to objects but to their unique features. Thus awareness can now change as a function of changes in intensities or duration of affective experience in relation to specific objects within a class. The emergence of the capacity for heightened interest or surprise in response to the mis-expected and the emergence of the new emotion of anger play a critical role in the affective-perceptual processes in level two. Surprise serves a resetting function in consciousness, and the anger experience and the behavior it motivates adds a new element—self-effected changes in the environment—to the growing sense of self as causal agent.

At level three consciousness consists primarily of affect-cognition interactions. These interactions ultimately result in affective-cognitive structures, and sets of such structures may constitute an affective-cognitive orientation that tends to locate the person on dimensions such as introversion-extraversion, autonomy-dependency, or passivity-aggressiveness. The emergence of shame/shyness and fear provide the experiential/motivational conditions for level three of consciousness, which leads to a keener awareness of self, other persons, and of self-other interchanges. Shyness increases awareness of self but brings with it a sense of vulnerability; fear increases awareness of the vulnerability of the self and of the need for attachment or affiliation. The increased sensibility/awareness resulting from the emotions of shyness and fear fosters the development of additional affective-cognitive structures.

The level of consciousness achieved by the end of the first year of life offers innumerable opportunities for the development of affective-cognitive bonds that eventually become the predominant structures of adult consciousness. The increased variety of affects greatly increases sensitivity to a wider range of objects, persons, and situations, and the number of affect-image and affect-schema bonds increases rapidly. Sometime in the second half of the first year of life, affective experience in relation to an object achieves some independence of direct sensory contact with the object and by some unknown process, the object is eventually symbolized. In a similar fashion, and with much greater facility in the second year of life, symbols become associated with objects, language is acquired, and affective-cognitive development increases at an astronomical pace.

III. FACIAL EXPRESSION, EMOTION EXPERIENCE, AND BEHAVIOR

The aim of this section is to demonstrate relationships between facial expression and emotion experience and then to show that emotion experience motivates behavior (cognition, motor acts). There are two kinds of evidence that link facial expression and emotion experience. The first type of data comes from cross-cultural studies of facial expressions and their interpretation. Evidence for the universality of facial expressions supports the notion that they have an evolutionary-biological basis and makes it reasonable to infer that they play some role in motivating adaptive actions. The second type of evidence comes from psychophysiological studies that examine the relationship between emotion-related imagery, emotion experience, and facial expression. These studies demonstrate a relationship between emotion-specific cognitive processes and corresponding emotion-specific expressions.

A. Facial Expression and Emotion Experience

I maintain that facial expression is a component of naturally occurring emotion, but I recognize that voluntary facial expressions may not have a corresponding underlying emotion experience. In fact, a particular facial expression can be made in an attempt to disguise or conceal the true inner experience. Nevertheless, I assume that facial patterning is an integral part of naturally occurring emotion, and that such natural occurrences can best be observed in the developing infant during the first year or two of life.

1. *The universality of facial expression.* The early work of Darwin (1872, 1877) and the more recent work of Hass (1970), Eibl-Eibesfeldt (1971), Izard (1971), and Ekman, Friesen, and Ellsworth (1972) has shown that certain emotions, referred to in this paper as fundamental emotions, have the same expressions and experiential qualities in widely different cultures from virtually every continent, including isolated preliterate cultures having had virtually no contact with Western civilization. These cross-cultural studies, as well as studies with the born-blind, clearly point to a relationship between a particular expression and a specific emotion experience. For example, both literate and preliterate people describe the inner experience of joy and sadness or anger and fear in the same way. Further, the cross-cultural data indicate that people in widely differing sociocultural settings tend to describe similar action consequences for the various emotions. It is easy to infer that the link between facial expression and certain actions or action tendencies is a corresponding inner emotion experience that has unique motivational properties.

2. *Psychophysiological studies of facial expression and emotion.* The second type of data that links particular facial expressions to corresponding specific emotion experiences consists of electromyographic studies of the facial muscles of expression during periods of self-generated emotion imagery and emotion experience. The EMG studies were based in part on early experiments by Izard (1972) which showed a relationship between emotion-specific imagery and self-reported emotion experience.

In a more recent study, Schwartz, Fair, Greenberg, Mandel, and Klerman (1976) asked normal and depressed individuals to self-generate happy, sad, and angry thoughts and feelings—the thoughts and feelings associated with a typical day of their life. Using surface electrodes the experimenters recorded the EMG activity of the frontalis, corrugator, depressor anguli oris, and masseter muscles of the face. As in an earlier study of theirs, this experiment showed clearly different profiles of facial muscle activity while the subjects were imaging the happy, sad, and angry scenes. The EMG profiles as a group also distinguished between the normal and depressive individuals. Not surprisingly, the depressives showed an attenuated pattern in the image-happy condition. Further, the profiles for the two groups while imaging a typical day were strikingly different: For normals, the profile was rather similar to that for the happy condition, while for the depressed patients it looked like a mix of the sadness (distress) and anger profiles. The finding of a distress-anger pattern in the life of the depressed individual is consistent with both psychoanalytic theory (Abraham, 1968; Freud, 1917/1968) and differential emotions theory (Izard, 1972).

A similar experiment was conducted by Rusalova, Izard, and Simonov (1975) with Soviet actors and actresses who were trained in the method of Stanislovsky. Their rigorous four-year training program in theatrical institutes emphasizes the creation of genuine emotion as appropriate to the character and the situation. In the first condition of this study, subjects were told to experience the emotion and express it naturally. In the second condition subjects were asked to reproduce the same emotion states but in a situation where they could not reveal their feelings because of some personal or social reasons. The task was not to camouflage genuine feeling by facial expression of other emotion (e.g., joy instead of sadness) but to try to look impassive in a state of strong emotion. In the third condition the subjects were asked to show the facial expressions of the same emotion states without actually feeling any emotion.

Facial expressions were registered on videotape with simultaneous measurement of heart rate, and of EMG of four facial muscles: frontalis, corrugator, masseter, depressor anguli oris. The greatest change in heart rate was registered in condition one when subjects experienced the emotion and expressed it freely and naturally. The lowest heart rate was recorded in the third condition during voluntary expression of an absent emotion. Some subjects reported that they could not avoid emotion experience while reproducing facial expressions of an emotion. The EMG changes were generally consistent with those found by Schwartz et al.: While imaging scenes of joy, the highest degree of activity was recorded in the depressor anguli oris, in fear the frontalis, in anger the masseter, and in sadness the corrugator.

B. Emotion Experience as Motivation for Individual Action

In a study that attempted to assess the effect of emotion on altruism, Underwood, Moore, and Rosenhan (1972) instructed one group of children to think of things that made them happy and another group to think of things that made them sad. They gave no cognitive instructions to a third group. After the cognitive manipulation was finished, the children (tested individually) were asked to help themselves to pennies from a container within their field of vision, but were also told that if they wished they could leave some pennies for the children who would not have time to participate in the experiment. Cognitively induced joy made children significantly more altruistic (left more pennies for nonparticipants) than did either the cognitively induced distress (think-sad condition) or the no-instruction condition. Further, the children who experienced distress or sadness were significantly less altruistic than the control subjects.

In an experiment with 7- and 8-year-old children, Fry (1975) found that a positive affect (think-happy) condition resulted in greater resistance to temptation that did a neutral condition, while a negative affect (think-sad) condition resulted in significantly less resistance to temptation than did the neutral condition. Fry attributed the experimental effects to the imagery-induced affective (joyful, sad) states and pointed up the implications of this conclusion for child-rearing practices. He considered it reasonable to infer the conditions that made for joyful or happy experiences increase ability to resist temptation while distressful experiences have the opposite effect.

C. Emotion Expression as Motivation in Social Interaction

Long before infants can speak a single word, their facial expressions convey messages that are crucial in binding mother and infant in an affectional relationship and in the maintenance of the infant's well-being. These messages have vital importance not only because they are the infant's chief means of communication, but also because what they communicate is highly important: They indicate the emotional state of the infant. Facial expressions tell us whether infants are happy or sad, angry or frightened, surprised or shy. If we could not "read" their faces, we could not empathize with them or show them sympathy.

1. *The face as a social stimulus*. The literature on the role of the face

in the infant and child's social development has been reviewed by Charlesworth and Kreutzer (1973) and Vine (1973). Numerous studies show that the human face is an extraordinary social stimulus. The significance of face-to-face interaction between mother and infant is poignantly illustrated in the description of such an interaction by Brazelton, Tronick, Adamson, Als, and Weise (1975):

All parts of the infant's body move in smooth circular patterns as he attends to her. His face-to-face attention to her is rhythmic with approach-withdrawal cycling of extremities. The attention phase and build-up to her cues are followed by turning away and a recovery phase in a rhythm of attention–nonattention which seems to define a cyclical homeostatic curve of attention, averaging several cycles per minute.

When she violates his expectancy for rhythmic interaction by presenting a still, unresponsive face to him, he becomes visibly concerned, his movements become jerky, he averts his face, then attempts to draw her into interaction. When repeated attempts fail, he finally withdraws into an attitude of helplessness, face averted, body curled up and motionless. If she returns to her usual interactive responses, he comes alive after an initial puzzled period, and returns to his rhythmic cyclical behaviour which has previously characterized their ongoing face-to-face interaction. (p. 137)

2. *Smiling, laughing, and social interactions.* The weight of the evidence on facial expression indicates that the smile is an innate expression, preprogrammed in the human infant to help assure a strong bond with the mother and to facilitate positive social interactions with other human beings. The neonatal smile appears in the first hours of life and a responsive smile enlivens the face by the end of the third week. The fact that the infant smiles indiscriminately at all human faces from approximately 3 to 5 months of age probably testifies to the importance of smile-elicited affectionate behavior for the infant's welfare and healthy development. The effect of mutual smiling on the mother-infant relationship and infant development probably shows more clearly than any other situation the importance of emotion and emotion expression as motivational variables in human affairs.

Sroufe and Wunsch (1972) have conducted extensive research on the ontogenesis of laughing. Building on the work of Washburn and following suggestions of Spencer (1855/1890), Darwin (1872), Bergson (1911), and Hebb (1949), they developed a heterogeneous set of stimuli and proceeded to conduct a number of systematic studies on the development of laughter in infants. These studies provide further support for the hypothesis that emotion is motivational and plays a role in guiding behavior: "We have observed repeatedly that when an infant cries he pulls back in the high-chair and turns from the stimulus, whereas when laughter occurs the baby maintains an orientation towards the agent, reaches for the object, and seeks to reproduce the situation" (p. 1341).

In discussing the functions of laughter, Rothbart (1973) points out that the infant's laughing at an incongruous or strange stimulus increases the likelihood that the caregiver will reproduce the incongruous stimulus, giving the infant the opportunity to experience and explore it. Documentation of such incidents would make a good case for the adaptive value of laughing. Rothbart correctly indicates that it is the infant or child who initiates the behavior sequence involved in mother-infant interactions surrounding distress and laughter. In fact, the immediate motivating phenomena are the infant's emotion expressions. The infant's crying in distress initiates the mother's efforts to comfort and care for the child; and in the laughter game, although the mother may present the initial stimulus for arousal, if the child does not laugh, the sequence is terminated and the game does not begin.

3. *Emotion communication and mother-infant attachment*. Mother-infant attachment has been considered by many scientists as the foundation of social life, and the systems of behavior that constitute attachment are usually considered to be closely related to the emotions (Bowlby, 1969).

Attachment can be described as a set of emotion ties that create a strong bond between two individuals. In infancy the establishment and maintenance of these ties depends in large measure on emotion communication via the facial-visual system. The vocal expression of emotions (cooing, babbling, crying, screaming) also play a significant part in this special interpersonal relationship. The third important factor in developing and maintaining attachment is the sense of touch and the exercise of this sensory modality by body contact. Touching also communicates emotions.

With the emergence of language and the rapid increase in cognitive and social skills, involuntary (reflexive, spontaneous) emotion expression is no longer the only type of expressive behavior that influences the mother-infant relationship. Beginning in the first half of the second year of life the child is capable of both involuntary and voluntary facial expression. Any given emotion has an expression which occurs naturally or instinctively as a part of the normal emotion process. The same emotion can also be expressed willfully or voluntarily as in the case in which one wants to convey to another that one feels a certain emotion. Voluntary expressions may be considered a social skill, and people (from infancy to old age) vary widely in the degree to which they develop and use this skill.

4. *Expression-motivated behavior in older children and adults.* In an ingenious study in Russia with 4- to 7-year-old children, Nevrovich (Note 2) used a variety of manipulations to induce distress or concern for others and measured the subsequent effects on altruistic activity. In each condition she had a group of 4- to 5-year-old children and a group of 5- to 6-year-old children. In condition one, a child was brought into the experimental room and shown a disorderly array of toys. The child was asked to put the toys in order "so your friends can play with them later; if you do not put the toys in order your friends will not be able to play with them and they will be sad." At the end of 20 minutes the child was asked whether he/she wanted to continue working on ordering the toys or go for a walk, a diversion uniformly perceived as interesting and enjoyable by Russian children. In this condition only four out of twelve of the 4- to 5-year-old children elected to remain in the room and finish the task of placing the toys in proper order. Six out of twelve of the 5- to 6-year-olds elected to remain and complete the task for the sake of their friends. In the second condition the children were given the same verbal instructions, but in addition they were shown pictures of children with sad faces looking at the toys in disarray, unable to play with them. In this condition seven out of twelve of the 4- to 5-year-olds elected to forego the walk and remained to complete the task of ordering the toys; eleven out of twelve of the 5- to 6-year-olds did the same. In the third condition, in which the children were shown photographs of a child who was both sad and sick and unable to play with the toys because they were in disarray, almost all of the children elected to forego the walk and complete the task. Nevrovich interpreted the improvement in task performance as a function of the distress experience (induced in the subjects by a combination of verbal instructions and photographs of other children showing distress), which would be relieved by the subject's task-oriented activities.

IV. THE EMOTIONS AS THE MOTIVATIONAL THRUST IN INFANT DEVELOPMENT AND PERSONALITY INTEGRATION

There are four types of developmental processes that are associated with emotions and emotion-related behavior. The first is the ontogenesis of emotion expressions. Ontogenesis is concerned with the age of emergence of each emotion-specific expression and the sequence of the emergence of these expressions over time. The basic emotion expression ontogeny is largely a function of maturation or the biological unfolding of innate neural programs in their natural order—the order in which the capacity for each emotion expression develops. In addition, there are situation-specific ontogenies, that is, the infant's capacity to encode a particular emotion expression is activated at different ages by different incentive events. Current evidence suggests that fear is elicited in different situations at different ages—e.g., fear of heights precedes fear of strangers. Thus we are not justified in saying that fear emerges at a particular age on the basis of responses to a single stimulus situation. A more complete expression ontogeny for a particular emotion would show the age of its appearance, peaking, and decline or regulation in a number of stimulus situations, specially selected for their expected salience at different levels of cognitive and motor development.

The second type of process to be studied is the course of the development of each of the discrete emotion expressions. A number of questions arise in this area. Does each emotion expression appear full-blown at the given age of appearance, or do facial patterns in the eye region develop before those in the mouth region? Does an emotion expression develop along a continuum of intensity or control and are there predictable changes in such developments?

The third major area is the development of the emotion system as a whole. Students of emotions differ in their conceptions of how the emotions are dynamically interrelated. Some think that each emotion has a polar opposite; others hold that emotion responses are sometimes arranged in hierarchical relationships with respect to certain stimulus situations. Thus certain emotions may have complementary functions in relation to qualitatively similar stimuli that vary only in quantity or intensity. For example, a novel stimulus situation may elicit interest, surprise, or fear depending on its intensity or the degree to which it is discrepant from schemas stored in memory. Ontogenetically, the degree of discrepancy and the quality of the resulting emotion may be a function of the amount of stimulus information the infant obtains or processes and the kinds of cognitive comparisons he/she can make with existing schemas. Early emotion responses to the human face and voice may be explained in part by the existence of innate schemas for the facial and vocal expressions (Izard, 1971; Neisser, 1976).

The fourth developmental process in the emotion domain, and by far the most inclusive, is personality integration: the interrelating of the emotion system with other personality and behavioral systems—perceptual, cognitive, motor, social. We assume that the emotion system contributes directly to personality integration in two ways. First, the invariance of emotion experiences insures continuity of consciousness and self-awareness. Second, emotions provide the motivation for integrative processes that engage and interrelate other personality subsystems. The role of emotions as organizing and integrative forces in consciousness has been discussed in more detail elsewhere (Izard, 1977, 1978).

More concretely, personality integration involves development of effective interactions and interrelations between specific emotion processes and particular types of processes in the other systems. For example, it is adaptive to interrelate (and eventually integrate) the emotion of interest with the cognitive processes of attending and comparing and with the motor responses involved in exploration and the development of competencies.

A. The Ontogenesis of Emotion Expressions, Infant-Environment Interactions, and Self-Awareness

Emotion expressions that are present in the neonate include the distress cry, the neonatal smile, startle-like movements, disgust, and interest. Other expressions appear with time. The anger and surprise expressions emerge as early as 3 to 4 months of age and fear at 5 to 7 months; elements of the shame expression can be seen in the 4- to 6-month-old, components of the contempt expression in the second half of the first year, and signs of guilt in the first half of the the second year. In terms of differential emotions theory, the presence of the expression suggests that a corresponding emotion experience is also present, at least in rudimentary form.

According to Lewis (Lewis & Brooks, 1978; Lewis, Brooks, &

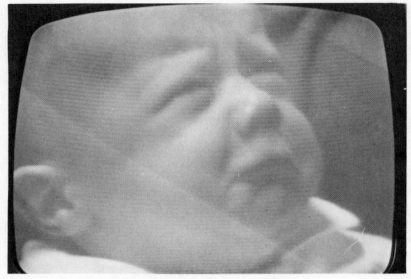

1. The Expression of Distress in a One-Month-Old Boy

Haviland, 1978), emotion cannot be inferred until the infant has achieved a level of self-awareness that occurs around 8 to 9 months of age. Lewis' position may well characterize those emotions (e.g., guilt, contempt) in which a more stable self-conception or self-awareness plays some role.

Whether or not we can agree that the very young infant has emotion experiences isomorphic to its emotion expressions, we probably can agree that it is the expressive or social aspect of emotion that is most important in the early weeks of life. The caregiver behavior that is motivated by the emotion expressions of the infant is crucial to survival and healthy development. The emotion expressions will be illustrated and their adaptive functions discussed in the following pages. The photographs illustrating the various emotion expressions were taken from videotape recordings of infants in playful and stressful situations, and they were reliably identified as to emotion category in emotion recognition and emotion labeling studies.

1. *The distress cry.* The distress cry is a peremptory social message to the caregiver for help: "Come change what is happening" (Emde et al., 1976). The caregiver's response to the infant's distress cry is the prototype of expression-motivated behavior.

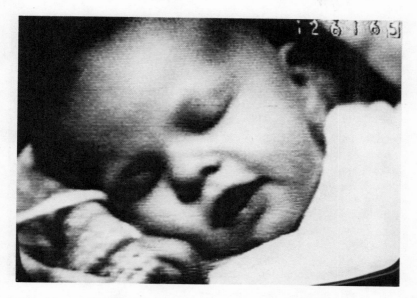

2. The Neonatal Smile During REM Sleep in a One-Month-Old Girl

This cry also serves an elemental intraindividual function. Just as the distress cry of one neonate tends to elicit a distress cry in another (Simner, 1971; Sagi & Hoffman, 1976), so does the infant's cry tend to produce further crying in himself or herself. That is, distress induces further distress until the distress cry as a social signal accomplishes its purpose.

2. *Neonatal Smiling*. The significance of the unlearned reflex we call the neonatal smile remains largely unexplained. We can infer a concomitant enjoyable experience only on the basis of a facial feedback hypothesis. The expression-motivated behavior elicited by neonatal smiling is generally positive in nature even though this smile typically occurs in rapid-eye-movement (REM) sleep and is apparently unrelated to the social surround. It has some of the same signal value as the social smile. Mothers are occasionally puzzled and mildly distressed that the neonate's smiling is not directed to them, but they generally respond positively to the smile.

3. *Startle-like movements*. Anyone who has observed a neonate's response to a loud sound or a pinprick is aware that the newborn is capable of startle-like movement patterns. The adaptive function of the startle-like movement in the neonate may reside in part in

3. The Expression of Disgust in a Five-Month-Old Boy

withdrawal from the stimulus but probably more significantly in calling the attention of the caregiver to the presence of a potentially noxious or dangerous source of stimulation.

4. *Disgust*. The disgust expression facilitates the removal or rejection of distasteful substances from the mouth. It also signals the caregiver that the infant cannot tolerate the substance and may need help in removing it.

5. *Interest*. Interest in the very young infant clearly serves both the individual and social functions of emotion. In terms of individual motivation, interest focuses and maintains attention and motivates exploratory activity. Interest is activated by novelty and change (of which movement is a prime example) and serves as the basis for the infant's first self-initiated interaction with the object world. The visual tracking that follows from movement-activated interest contributes to the development of depth perception and spatial relations.

The interest expression is also capable of motivating behavior in the perceiver. The increased alertness in the face of the infant tends to engage the caregiver's own interest in the baby and in the baby's activities.

In summary, the emotion expressions present at birth play an

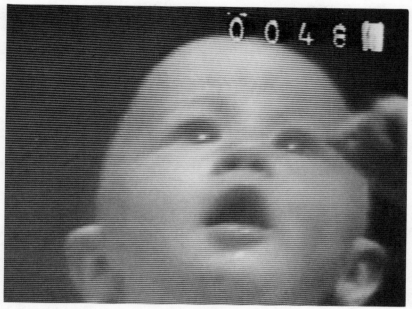

4. The Expression of Interest in a Four-Month-Old Girl

important role in the survival and the well-being of the infant, primarily through the power of the emotion expressions to attract attention and motivate helping behavior and social interchange. The neonatal smile and the interest expression motivate positive social responses from the caregiver and others in the environment. Interest plays another important role by beginning to engage the infant in the object world and the physical environment.

6. *The social smile and the strengthening of social bonds.* As suggested by Spitz (1965) and Emde et al. (1976), the advent of the social smile at 8 to 10 weeks of age signals a "biobehavioral shift," a shift to a different and more complex level of consciousness and behavior. Perhaps the principal function of the social smile is that of inviting continued social stimulation and the strengthening of interpersonal affective bonds.

Strengthening the mother's emotional tie to the infant is certainly one of the adaptive functions of the social smile. The fact that the smile is not discriminatory for several weeks after its appearance may also be adaptive in that it invites care and attention from anyone who can attend.

5. The Social Smile in a Four-Month-Old Girl

With the advent of the social smile and a new level of social interaction, the emotion of interest increases in maturity and plays an increasingly important role in the life of the infant. The infant has longer periods of alertness, during which interest focuses and sustains attention to visual and auditory stimuli and facilitates visual, tactual, and manual exploration.

7. *Shame, shyness, and self-awareness*. As Tomkins has suggested, shame or shyness can occur at any time after the infant has the capacity to discriminate self from other and familiar persons from strange persons. This can occur as early as the third or fourth month of life (Roe, 1978). Shyness at this level of development is a sensing or experiencing of a difference between a self–familiar-person relationship and a self–strange-person relationship. That is, when an infant relates to a familiar loved one, he or she experiences positive emotions of interest and joy, but the overture of a stranger may not provide the infant with the usual cues and thus may create in the infant some feeling of awkwardness or ineptness, the rudiments of the shame experience. The heightened consciousness of self that occurs in shame has motivational value for developing self-identity and self-esteem. Eventually, shame anticipation motivates the development of skills and competences that increase self-worth and decrease the likelihood of experiencing shame.

6. The Expression of Anger in a Seven-Month-Old Girl

8. *Anger, disgust, contempt, and sense of self-as-causal-agent.* The emergence of anger marks the transition of the baby from one who deals with troubles and frustrations primarily through use of the distress cry in order to obtain help from others to one who may add to the distress an anger cry and a determined effort to remove or change the frustrating condition. Between 4 and 6 months, the infant is capable of experiencing and expressing anger, and the anger experience motivates efforts to deal with frustrating restraints and barriers. Thus anger increases the infant's opportunities to sense self-as-causal-agent and, as Yarrow (1972) notes: "The differentiation of self from environment is partly dependent on the child's awareness that he can have an effect on the environment" (pp. 92–93).

During this period, the rudiments of contempt may emerge on occasions when the infant "triumphs" over a restraint or barrier. Photo 7 illustrates most of the key facial movements of the expression of contempt, but unlike the case for all the other photographic illustrations, the context from which this picture was taken offers no clues to suggest that the infant was experiencing the emotion expressed.

The full-blown experience and expression of contempt in relation to others come later.

7. Some Components of the Expression of Contempt in a Seven-Month-Old Boy

The expression of disgust, which may be seen in the first days of life in response to distasteful substances, may now be seen in response to other kinds of stimuli. That is, disgust becomes more of a psychological and somewhat less of a physiological reaction.

9. *Interest-surprise interactions, exploration, and mastery.* Beginning around the age of 5 months, the emotion of interest-excitement begins to play an increasingly significant role in the infant's development. It is during this stage that Piaget (1952) describes activity "to make interesting spectacles last," and that Hunt (1965) describes the development of intrinsic motivation, during which infants begin acting to regain perceptual contact. The net effect is an increase in the duration of the infant's contact with persons and objects in the environment. This increased contact facilitates the processes whereby novel, strange, and undifferentiated inputs become familiar and differentiated percepts. The storage of such percepts or schema make possible the phenomenon of "recognitive familiarity" (Hunt, 1965), and the emotion of joy that results from the recognitive familiarity adds the other important positive emotion-motivational force in the development and maintenance of emotion attachments.

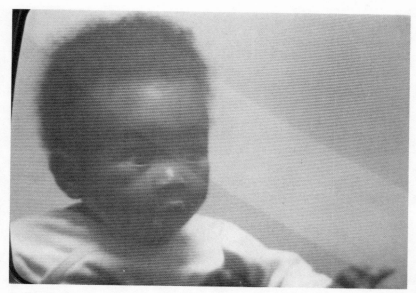

8. The Expression of Surprise in a Four-Month-Old Girl

During this period, healthy infant development depends upon opportunities to act on the increasingly strong motivational impact of the developing emotion of interest. Varying the infant's environment, providing a variety of playthings, and providing the opportunity for sustained face-to-face human interactions are critical. The infant now has an increased capability for initiating and sustaining sensorimotor activities, and healthy development requires that the infant be given varied opportunities to alter and change sources of stimulation (information input). As Hunt (1965) puts it: "Although hunger and thirst are of the essence for survival, opportunities for such informational interaction are very likely of the essence for *interest* in objects, persons, and places" (p. 234, italics added).

We now have the basis for complex emotion-perception-cognition-action sequences of a positive nature: perception of the novel activates interest, interest motivates exploration, exploration leads to surprise, surprise interacts with interest to heighten attention, and further exploration, familiarization, or mastery leads to joy. The significance of such sequences for the integration of the infant's personality subsystems is apparent.

10. *Fear and guilt facilitate self-cognitions and self-regulation*. Virtually all of the emotions play some role in the self-related perceptions and

9. The Expression of Fear in a Nine-Month-Old Boy

cognitions that lead to self-concept or self-identity and self-control. Interest and joy motivate activities that lead to a sense of positive relatedness to persons and things and to one's world. Distress provides the first opportunity for the infant to begin sensing self as causal agent; anger and disgust provide motivation for activities that strengthen the sense of self as causal agent capable of altering the relationship of self to source of stimulation; surprise facilitates the development of the sense of self as affected by sudden, unexpected (or misexpected) changes occurring in the environment.

Two new emotions emerge during this period and play a critical role in facilitating the development of self-cognitions and self-control. Fear begins to emerge sometime during the latter half of the first year of life, and the emotion of guilt as a distinct experience in consciousness and as cause of recognizable guilt-related behavior emerges at some time in the second year. The emotions of fear and guilt have in common the fact that both are associated with the establishing of behavioral limits. Both are associated with the learning of a complex set of prohibitions, or to put it more positively, these emotions motivate actions that contribute to the physical safety and psychological integrity of the individual.

Fear is the ultimate reminder of the vulnerability of the bodily and psychological self; it motivates escape from harm and danger, which may take the form of "flight to one another" (Eibl-Eibesfeldt, 1971) for mutual defense and protection. The developmental process whereby fear comes to serve adaptive functions is aptly described by Rosenblum (1978) as fear in the infant taking over some of the protective functions of the mother.

The fear experience is the experience of self endangered, and fear anticipation motivates cognitions relating to self-defense or self-protection. All of these phenomena play a role in the development of self-awareness. In particular, fear generates cognitions about self as affected by dangerous or threatening situations.

Guilt, on the other hand, motivates cognitions about self-initiated actions that cause harm to others. Guilt plays an important role in the development of self-responsibility, and it is the principal experiential motivational factor in the mature conscience.

Thus fear and guilt play distinct but complementary roles in the development of self-cognitions and self-control. Fear motivates cognition and action strategies that enable the self to navigate the world in such a way as to minimize harm and danger; guilt, on the other hand, motivates conceptions of self and cognitive and action strategies that help maintain self-integrity and the integrity of self-other relations. It is reasonable that a sense of self as causal agent would precede the capacity to experience the emotion of guilt, which involves a sense of feeling responsible for one's actions and an ability to sense that one's actions have brought psychological or physical harm to another.

Hoffman (1978) notes that empathic distress may be transformed into a feeling of guilt by the attribution of self-blame. His discussions of the development of empathy and sympathy and the process whereby thwarted altruistic activity may produce guilt suggest that this emotion may be experienced in some form as early as the latter part of the first year of life. Radke-Yarrow (Note 3) has considerable data which suggest that guilt experience occurs with some frequency during the second year of life.

Beginning about the last quarter of the first year and continuing through the second, increased differentiations of self and other, the sharpening of self-awareness and the self-concept, and the ability to form and store memories enable the infant to begin the development of affective-cognitive structures—the linking or bonding of particular affects or patterns of affects with images and symbols, including words and ideas. The type of affect or emotion associated with a particular schema, script, or cognitive map determines the motivational characteristics of a given affective-cognitive structure. The cognitive component adds specificity and aim, having the effect of giving numerous nuances to the associated emotion or pattern of emotions.

Since there is essentially an infinite variety of emotion-symbol interactions, affective-cognitive structures are far and away the predominant motivational features in consciousness soon after the acquisition of language. What I am calling an *affective-cognitive structure* here is similar to Tomkins' (1962) ideo-affective organization. It is also similar in some ways to what Kagan (1972) has defined as a *motive*, and it is not unlike Katz and Stotland's (1959) classical definition of attitude. Although Kagan's concept of *motive* emphasizes the cognitive process, he has implied that there is an affective underpinning (Kagan, 1978). The Katz-Stotland definition of attitude clearly includes affective and cognitive components and a behavioral tendency.

B. Developmental Changes in Specific Emotions

Cognitive, social, and motor development that occurs with the growth of the child appears to change the motivational characteristics of the emotions. Changes can be seen in the expressive behavior of the face, voice, and body (posture, gesture, gait) and in instrumental acts relating to the social and physical environment. The observed changes are not really changes in the quality or basic motivational properties of the specific emotion experience but in the associated cognitive, social and motor behavior (Izard, 1978).

For example, empathic distress may lead an 18-month-old girl to rub her own elbow after her mother has cried in pain from hurting her own (Hoffman, 1978; Radke-Yarrow, Note 3). When a little older, the child in this circumstance may offer her favorite toy to the mother, while later, with increased cognitive abilities and growth of physical skills, the child will bring a cold cloth or offer appropriate help. Through all these developments the experiential component of empathic distress remains invariant. The child's understanding of the causes and possible solutions to her mother's problem changes with cognitive development, and the child's willingness and ability to help increases with social development and the growth of motor skills and competencies.

Changes also occur in the repertory of emotion activators. Simple changes in environmental sights and sounds (Buechler, Izard, & Huebner, Note 4) and minimal movements of the mother's face are sufficient to capture the month-old baby's interest (Sherrod, Note 5). At 3 or 4 months the color and graspability of a toy may be important features in activating interest in the young infant. At 6 or 7 months manipulability becomes a more important activator and by the end of the first year interest is elicited by toys that serve as the basis of game-like activities (Buechler, Izard, & Huebner, Note 4).

Similarly, interest-motivated behaviors change with cognitive, social, and motor development. Toys that inspired only attention, grasping, and holding at 4 or 5 months lead to manipulation and exploratory activity in the older infant. By the age of 2 or 3 years dolls and toy utensils initiate fantasy and imaginative play that includes complex motor acts.

Changes also occur in mothers' responses to their infants' expressions of emotion. For example, the frequency of positive maternal responses to infants' anger expressions decreases and the frequency of their negative responses increases during the first year of life. The reverse is true for expressions of surprise (Buechler, Izard, & Huebner, Note 4).

CONCLUDING STATEMENT

The emotions are a part of our biosocial heritage and they served adaptive functions throughout the course of phylogeny. Emotions play an equally critical role in ontogeny. Each emotion sensitizes the infant to particular features of the environment and thus facilitates the processing of particular types of information and the learning of particular relationships. In both phylogeny and ontogeny emotions serve intraindividual as well as social functions. Emotion experience provides motivation that initiates and amplifies cognitive and motor processes. Emotion expression serves a social/communicative function, signaling the expressor's emotional state or intention.

Genetic endowment guarantees the capacities to encode and decode a set of fundamental emotions whose expressions emerge in the prelingual infant. There are also a minimal set of innate activators of emotion expressions that are biologically linked to adaptive responses or coping mechanisms. For example, the human face activates the expression of interest in the month-old baby (Sherrod, 1978), and the interest increases the amount of attention to the caregiver, the likelihood of reciprocal smiling, and the formation of a healthy caregiver-infant relationship.

Efforts to identify the hereditary capacities in the domain of emotion and to sort out the relative contributions of genetic and acquired information and competencies are important. However, there can be little doubt that most emotion experiences are a function of learned activators and most coping responses develop through individual-environment interactions. The more we know about innate emotional (motivational) capacities, the better we shall be able to predict what the infant can learn at any given age. Thus knowing what elicits interest in 2-month-olds or 12-month-olds tells us something about what will get and hold attention.

"Felt emotion," or emotion experience, is always present in ordinary states of consciousness, serving motivational and guidance functions. The emergence of each emotion ontogenetically increases motivational capacities and the complexity of the possible operations of consciousness.

A number of studies have shown that specific emotion experiences have definite action consequences. For example, cognitively induced joy and sadness have predictably different effects on such behaviors as resistance to temptation and the altruistic sharing of rewards.

Other investigations have demonstrated that emotion expression has action consequences for the observer. Even toddlers will try to comfort or help a parent who cries out in distress or pain. Older children will persist longer in a task perceived as alleviating the distress expression of another.

Each emotion contributes to a particular aspect of infant development. For example, interest focuses attention and motivates exploratory activity, and anger increases the infant's sense of self as causal agent. Finally, the emotion system is pivotal in the development of intersystem functions and the integration of the personality.

REFERENCE NOTES

1. Sroufe, L. A. *Emotional expression in infancy*. Unpublished manuscript, 1976.

2. Nevrovich, A. Personal communication, Institute of Pre-School Education, Moscow, USSR, 1974.

3. Radke-Yarrow, M. *Infants' responses to mothers' emotion expressions*. A presentation to the Committee on Social and Emotional Development of the Social Science Research Council, Cambridge, Mass., March, 1977.

4. Buechler, S., Izard, C. E., & Huebner, R. *Mothers' responses to their infants' emotion expressions*. Unpublished manuscript, 1978.

REFERENCES

Abraham, K. Notes on the psychoanalytical investigation and treatment of manic-depressive insanity and allied conditions. In W. Gaylin (Ed.), *The meaning of despair*. New York: Science House, 1968.

Bergson, H. L. *Laughter—an essay on the meaning of the comic*. (C. Brereton, Trans.). New York: Macmillan, 1911.

Bowlby, J. *Attachment and loss* (Vol. 1). New York: Basic Books, 1969.

Bowlby, J. *Attachment and loss* (Vol. 2). New York: Basic Books, 1973.

Brazelton, T. B., Tronick, E., Adamson, L., Als, H., & Weise, S. Early mother-infant reciprocity. *Parent-infant interaction*. Amsterdam: CIBA Foundation, Associated Scientific Publishers, 1975.

Breger, L. *From instinct to identity: The development of personality*. Englewood Cliffs, N.J.: Prentice-Hall, 1974.

Bruner, J. S. The organisation of early skilled action. In M. P. M. Richards (Ed.), *The integration of the child into a social world*. Cambridge: Cambridge University Press, 1974.

Charlesworth, W. R., & Kreutzer, M. A. Facial expressions of infants and children. In P. Ekman (Ed.), *Darwin and facial expression, a century of research in review*. New York: Academic Press, 1973.

Darwin, C. R. *The expression of emotions in man and animals*. London: John Murray, 1872.

Darwin, C. R. A biographical sketch of an infant. *Mind*, 1877, **2**, 286–294.

Eibl-Eibesfeldt, I. *Love and hate: The natural history of behavior patterns*. New York: Holt, Rinehart, & Winston, 1971.

Ekman, P. Universal and cultural differences in facial expressions of emotion. In J. K. Cole (Ed.), *Nebraska Symposium on Motivation 1971* (Vol. 19). Lincoln: University of Nebraska Press, 1972.

Ekman, P., Friesen, W. V., & Ellsworth, P. *Emotion in the human face: Guidelines for research and an integration of findings*. New York: Pergamon Press, 1972.

Elkind, D. Cognitive growth cycles in mental development. In J. K. Cole (Ed.), *Nebraska Symposium on Motivation 1971* (Vol. 19). Lincoln: University of Nebraska Press, 1972.

Emde, R. N. Towards a psychoanalytic theory of affect: II. Emerging models of emotional development in infancy. In S. Greenspan & G. Pollock (Eds.), *Psychoanalysis and Development, Current Perspectives*, in press.

Emde, R. N., Gaensbauer, T., & Harmon, R. J. *Emotional expression in infancy: A biobehavioral study*. New York: International Universities Press, 1976.

Escalona, S. K. *The roots of individuality*. Chicago: Aldine, 1968.

Fantz, R. L. Pattern discrimination and selective attention as determinants of perceptual development from birth. In A. H. Kidd & J. L. Rivoire (Eds.), *Perceptual development in children*. New York: International Universities Press, 1966.

Freud, S. Mourning and melancholia. In W. Gaylin (Ed.), *The meaning of despair*. New York: Science House, 1968. (Originally published, 1917. J. Riviere, Trans.)

Fry, P. S. Affect and resistance to temptation. *Developmental Psychology*, 1975, **11**, 466–472.

Harlow, H. F., & Mears, C. The nature of complex, unlearned responses. In M. Lewis & L. A. Rosenblum (Eds.), *The development of affect*. New York: Plenum, 1978.

Hass, H. *The human animal*. New York: Putnam's Sons, 1970.

Haviland, J. Looking smart: The relationship between affect and intelligence in infancy. In M. Lewis (Ed.), *Origins of intelligence*. New York: Plenum, 1976.

Hebb, D. O. *The organization of behavior*. New York: Wiley, 1949.

Hoffman, M. L. The arousal and development of empathy. In M. Lewis & L. A. Rosenblum (Eds.), *The development of affect*. New York: Plenum, 1978.

Huber, E. *Evolution of facial musculature and facial expression*. Baltimore: Johns Hopkins Press, 1931.

Hunt, J. McV. Intrinsic motivation and its role in psychological development. In D. Levine (Ed.), *Nebraska Symposium on Motivation 1965* (Vol. 13). Lincoln: University of Nebraska Press, 1966.

Izard, C. E. *The face of emotion*. New York: Appleton-Century-Crofts, 1971.

Izard, C. E. *Patterns of emotions: A new analysis of anxiety and depression*. New York: Academic Press, 1972.

Izard, C. E. *Human emotions*. New York: Plenum, 1977.

Izard, C. E. On the development of emotions and emotion-cognition relationships in infancy. In M. Lewis & L. A. Rosenblum (Eds.), *The development of affect*. New York: Plenum, 1978.

Izard, C. E., & Tomkins, S. S. Affect and behavior: Anxiety as a negative affect. In C. D. Spielberger (Ed.), *Anxiety and behavior*. New York: Academic Press, 1966.

Kagan, J. *Change and continuity in infancy*. New York: Wiley, 1971.

Kagan, J. Motives and development. *Journal of Personality and Social Psychology*, 1972, **22**, 51–66.

Kagan, J. *Infancy: Its place in human development*. Cambridge: Harvard University Press, 1978. (Monograph.)

Katz, D., & Stotland, E. A preliminary statement to a theory of attitude structure and change. In S. Koch (Ed.), *Psychology: A study of a science* (Vol. 3). New York: McGraw-Hill, 1959.

Kleck, R. E., Vaughan, R., Colby, C., Cartwright-Smith, J. E., Vaughan, K., & Lanzetta, J. T. Effects of being observed on expressive, subjective, and physiological responses to painful stimuli. *Journal of Personality and Social Psychology*, 1976, **34**, 1211–1218.

Lanzetta, J. T., Cartwright-Smith, J. E., & Kleck, R. E. Effects of nonverbal dissimulation on emotional experience and autonomic arousal. *Journal of Personality and Social Psychology*, 1976, **33**, 354–370.

Lazarus, R. S. Emotions and adaptation: Conceptual and empirical relations. In W. J. Arnold (Ed.), *Nebraska Symposium on Motivation 1968* (Vol. 16). Lincoln: University of Nebraska Press, 1969.

Lewis, M., & Brooks, J. Self knowledge and emotional development. In M. Lewis & L. A. Rosenblum (Eds.), *The development of affect*. New York: Plenum, 1978.

Lewis, M., Brooks, J., & Haviland, J. Hearts and faces: A study in the measurement of emotion. In M. Lewis & L. A. Rosenblum (Eds.), *The development of affect*. New York: Plenum, 1978.

Neisser, U. *Cognition and reality*. San Francisco: W. H. Freeman, 1976.

Piaget, J. *The origins of intelligence in children*. New York: International Universities Press, 1952.

Piaget, J. *The child's conception of physical causality*. Totowa, N.J.: Littlefield, Adams, 1960. (Originally published, 1927.)

Piaget, J., & Inhelder, B. *The psychology of the child*. New York: Basic Books, 1969.

Roe, K. V. Infants' mother-stranger discrimination at 3 months as a predictor of cognitive development at 3 and 5 years. *Developmental Psychology*, 1978, **14**, 191–192.

Rosenblum, L. A. Affective maturation and the mother-infant relationship. In M. Lewis & L. A. Rosenblum (Eds.), *The development of affect*. New York: Plenum, 1978.

Rothbart, M. K. Laughter in young children. *Psychological Bulletin*, 1973, **80**, 247–256.

Rusalova, M. N., Izard, C. E., & Simonov, P. V. Comparative analysis of mimical and autonomic components of man's emotional state. *Aviation, Space, and Environmental Medicine*, 1975, **46**, 1132–1134.

Sagi, A., & Hoffman, M. Empathic distress in the newborn. *Developmental Psychology*, 1976, **12**, 175–176.

Schwartz, G. E., Fair, P. L., Greenberg, P. S., Mandel, M. R., & Klerman, J. L. Facial muscle patterning to affective imagery in depressed and nondepressed subjects. *Science*, 1976, **192**, 489–491.

Sherrod, L. R. *Social cognition in infants: Developmental perception of the human face*. Unpublished doctoral dissertation, Yale University, 1978.

Simner, M. Newborns' responses to the cry of another infant. *Developmental Psychology*, 1971, **4**, 136–150.

Singer, J. L. *Imagery and daydream methods in psychotherapy and behavior modification*. New York: Academic Press, 1974.

Sinnott, E. W. The bridge of life. New York: Simon & Schuster, 1966.

Spencer, H. *The principles of psychology* (Vol. 1). New York: Appleton, 1890. (Originally published, 1855.)

Spitz, R. A. *A genetic field theory of ego formation: Its implications for pathology*. New York: International Universities Press, 1959.

Spitz, R. A. *The first year of life*. New York: International Universities Press, 1965.

Sroufe, L. A., & Wunsch, J. P. The development of laughter in the first year of life. *Child Development*, 1972, **43**, 1326–1344.

Stechler, G., & Carpenter, G. A viewpoint on early affective development. In J. Hellmuth (Ed.), *The exceptional infant* (Vol. 1). Seattle: Special Child Publications, 1967.

Tomkins, S. S. *Affect, imagery, consciousness* (Vol. 1). *The positive affects*. New York: Springer, 1962.

Tomkins, S. S. *Affect, imagery, consciousness* (Vol. 2). *The negative affects*. New York: Springer, 1963.

Underwood, B., Moore, B. S., & Rosenhan, D. Affect and self-gratification. *Developmental Psychology*, 1972, **8**, 209–214.

Vine, I. The role of facial-visual signalling in early social development. In M. Von Cranach & I. Vine (Eds.), *Social communication and movement*. New York: Academic Press, 1973.

Wolff, P. H. The development of attention in young infants. *Annals of the New York Academy of Sciences*, 1965, **118**, 815–830.

Yarrow, L. J. Attachment and dependency: A developmental perspective. In J. L. Gewirtz (Ed.), *Attachment and dependency*. New York: Wiley, 1972.

Script Theory: Differential Magnification of Affects

Silvan S. Tomkins, Professor Emeritus

Rutgers University

The theory of affect I first presented at the Fourteenth International Congress of Psychology at Montreal, in 1954, and later expanded in *Affect, Imagery, Consciousness* in 1962, has since been modified in four essential ways. First, the theory of affect as amplification I now specify as analogic amplification. Second, I believe now that it is the skin of the face, rather than its musculature, which is the major mechanism of analogic amplification. Third, a substantial quantity of the affect we experience as adults is psuedo, backed-up affect. Fourth, affect amplifies not only its own activator, but also the response to both that activator and to itself.

I view affect as the primary innate biological motivating mechanism, more urgent than drive deprivation and pleasure and more urgent even than physical pain. That this is so is not obvious, but it is readily demonstrated. Consider that almost any interference with breathing will immediately arouse the most desperate gasping for breath. Consider the drivenness of the tumescent, erect male. Consider the urgency of desperate hunger. These are the intractable driven states that prompted the answer to the question "What do human beings really want?" to be "The human animal is driven to breathe, to sex, to drink, and to eat." And yet this apparent urgency proves to be an illusion. It is *not* an illusion that one must have air, water, food to maintain oneself and sex to reproduce oneself. What *is* illusory is the biological and psychological source of the apparent urgency of the desperate quality of the hunger, air, and sex drives. Consider these drive states more closely. When someone puts his hand over my mouth and nose, I become terrified. But this panic, this terror, is in no way a part of the drive mechanism. I can be terrified at the possibility of losing my job, or of developing cancer, or at the possibility of the loss of my beloved. Fear or terror is an innate affect which can be triggered by a wide variety of circumstances. Not having enough air to breathe is one of many such circumstances. But if the rate of anoxic deprivation becomes slower, as, for example, in the case of wartime pilots who refused to wear oxygen masks at 30,000 feet, then there develops not a panic, but a euphoric state; and some of these men met their deaths with smiles on their lips. The smile is the affect of enjoyment, in no way specific to slow anoxic deprivation.

Consider more closely the tumescent male with an erection. He is sexually excited, we say. He is indeed excited, but no one has ever observed an excited penis. It is a man who is excited and who breathes hard, not in the penis, but in the chest, the face, in the nose and nostrils. Such excitement is in no way peculiarly sexual. The same excitement can be experienced, without the benefit of an erection, to mathematics—beauty bare—to poetry, to a rise in the stock market. Instead of these representing sublimations of sexuality, it is rather that sexuality, in order to become possible, must borrow its potency from the affect of excitement. The drive must be assisted by affect as an *amplifier* if it is to work at all. Freud, better than anyone else, knew that the blind, pushy, imperious Id was the most fragile of impulses, readily disrupted by fear, by shame, by rage, by boredom. At the first sign of affect *other* than excitement, there is impotence and frigidity. The penis proves to be a paper tiger in the absence of appropriate affective amplification.

The affect system is therefore the primary motivational system because without its amplification, nothing else matters—and with its amplification, anything else *can* matter. It thus combines *urgency* and *generality*. It lends its power to memory, to perception, to thought, and to action no less than to the drives.

This theory of affect as amplification was flawed by a serious ambiguity. I had unwittingly assumed that in both electronic amplification and affective amplification there was an increase in gain of the signal. If that were the case, what was amplified would remain essentially the same except that it would become louder. But affects are separate mechanisms, involving bodily responses quite distinct from the other bodily responses they are presumed to amplify.

How can one response of our body amplify another response? It does this by being similar to that response—but also different. It is an analog amplifier. The affect mechanism is like the pain mechanism in this respect. If we cut our hand, saw it bleeding, but had no innate pain receptors, we would know we had done something which needed repair, but there would be no urgency to it. Like our automobile which needs a tune-up, we might well let it go until next week when we had more time. But the pain mechanism, like the affect mechanism, so amplifies our awareness of the injury which activates it that we are forced to be concerned, and concerned immediately. The biological utility of such analogic amplification is self-evident. The injury, as such, in the absence of pain, simply does not hurt. The pain receptors have evolved to make us hurt and care about injury and disease. Pain is an analog of injury in its inherent similarity. Contrast pain with an orgasm, as a possible analog. If instead of pain, we always had an orgasm to injury, we would be biologically destined to bleed to death. Affect receptors are no less compelling. Our hair stands on end, and we sweat in terror. Our face reddens as our blood pressure rises in anger. Our blood vessels dilate and our face becomes pleasantly warm as we smile in enjoyment. These are compelling analogs of what arouses terror, rage, and enjoyment. These experiences constitute one form of affect amplification. A second form of affect amplification occurs by virtue of the similarity of their profile, in time, to their activating trigger. Just as a pistol shot is a stimulus which is very sudden in onset, very brief in duration, and equally sudden in decay, so its amplifying affective analog, the startle response, mimics the pistol shot by being equally sudden in onset, brief in duration, and equally sudden in decay. Affect, therefore, by being analogous in the quality of the feelings from its specific receptors, as well as in its profile of activation, maintenance, and decay, amplifies and extends the duration and impact of whatever triggers the effect. Epileptics do not startle. They experience a pistol shot as sudden but *not* startling. A world experienced without any affect would be a pallid, meaningless world. We would know *that* things happened, but we could not care whether they did or not.

By being immediately activated and thereby co-assembled with its activator, affect either makes good things better or bad things worse, by conjointly simulating its activator in its profile of neural firing and by adding a special analogic quality which is intensely rewarding or punishing. In illustrating the simulation of an activating stimulus, e.g., a pistol shot by the startle response, I somewhat exaggerated the goodness of fit between activator and affect to better illustrate the general principle. Having done so, let me now be more precise in the characterization of the degree of similarity in profile of neural firing between activator and affect activated. I have presented a model of the innate activators of the primary affects in which every possible major general neural contingency will innately activate different specific affects. Thus, increased gradients of rising neural firing will activate interest, fear, or surprise, as the slope of increasing density of neural firing becomes steeper. I assume that enjoyment is activated by a decreasing gradient of neural firing and that distress is activated by a sustained level of neural firing which exceeds an optimal level by an as yet undetermined magnitude, and that anger is also activated by a nonoptimal level of neural firing but one which is substantially higher than that which activates distress. Increase, decrease, or level of neural firing are in this model the sufficient conditions for activating specific affects. Analogic amplification, therefore, is based upon *one* of these three distinctive features rather than all of them. It so happens that the startle simulates the steepness of gradient of onset, the brief plateau of maintenance, and the equally steep gradient of decline of profile of the pistol shot and its internal neural correlate—but that is not the general case. Analogic simulation is based on the similarity to the adequate activator, not on all of its characteristics. Thus it is the decay alone of a stimulus which is stimulated in enjoyment. If one places electrodes on the wrist of a subject, permits fear to build, then removes the electrodes suddenly, we can invariably activate a smile of relief at just that moment. This amplifies (or makes more so) the declining neural stimulation from the reduction of fear. Therefore, enjoyment amplifies by simulating decreasing gradients of neural stimulation. Interest, fear, and surprise amplify by simulating increasing gradients of neural stimulation. Distress and anger amplify by simulating maintained level of stimulation.

The second modification in my theory concerns the exact loci of the rewarding and punishing amplifying analogs. From the start, I emphasized the face and voice as the major loci of the critical feedback which was experienced as affect. The voice I still regard as a major locus and will discuss its role in the next section. The face now appears to me still the central site of affect responses and their feedback, but I have now come to regard the skin, in general, and the skin of the face, in particular, as of the greatest importance in producing the feel of affect. My original observations of the intensity of infantile affect, of how an infant was, for example, seized by his or her own crying, left no doubt in my mind that what the face was doing with its muscles, and blood vessels, as well as with its accompanying vocalization, was at the heart of the matter. This seemed to me not an "expression" of anything else but rather the major phenomenon. I then spent a few years in posing professional actors and others to simulate facial affect. McCarter and I were rewarded by a correlation of +.86 between the judgments of untrained judges as to what affects they saw on the faces of these subjects as presented in still photographs, and what I had intended these sets of muscular responses to represent (Tomkins & McCarter, 1964).

This success was gratifying, after so many years of indifferent and variable findings in this field, but it was also somewhat misleading in overemphasizing the role of innately patterned facial muscular responses in the production of affect. I was further confirmed in these somewhat misleading results by the successes of Paul Ekman and Carroll Izard. Paul Ekman, using some of my photographs, was able to demonstrate a wide cultural consensus, even in very primitive and remote societies (Ekman, Sorenson, & Friesen, 1969). Carroll Izard (1969), using different photographs but the same conceptual scheme, further extended these impressive results to many other societies. The combined weight of all these investigations was most impressive, but I continued to be troubled by one small fact. The contraction of no other set of muscles in the body had *any* apparent motivational properties. Thus, if I were angry, I might clench my fist and hit someone, but if I simply clenched my fist, this would in no way guarantee I would become angry. Muscles appeared to be specialized for action and not for affect. Why then was the smile so easily and so universally responded to as an affect? Why did someone who was crying seem so distressed and so unhappy?

Further, from an evolutionary point of view, we know that different functions are piled indiscriminately on top of structures which may originally have evolved to support quite different functions. The tongue was an organ of eating before it was an organ of speech. The muscles of the face were also probably involved in eating before they were used as vehicles of affect—though we do not know this for a fact. It is, of course, possible that the complex affect displays on the human face evolved primarily as communication mechanisms rather than as sources of motivating feedback. My intuition was, and still is, that the communication of affect is a secondary spin-off function rather than the primary function. This would appear to have been the case with a closely related mechanism, that of pain. The cry of pain does communicate—but the feeling of pain does not. It powerfully motivates the person who feels it, in much the same way that affect does. That someone else is informed of this is not, however, mediated by the pain receptors themselves, but by the cry of distress which usually accompanies it. I, therefore, began to look at affect analogs such as pain and sexual sensitivity and fatigue for clues about the nature of the motivating properties of the affect mechanisms.

I soon became aware of a paradox—that three of the most compelling states to which the human being is vulnerable arise on the surface of the skin. Torture via skin stimulation has been used for centuries to shape and compel human beings to act against their own deepest wishes and values. Sexual seduction, again via skin stimulation, particularly of the genitals, has also prompted human beings on occasion to violate their own wishes and values. Finally, fatigue to the point of extreme sleepiness appears to be localized in the skin surrounding the eyes. This area will sometimes be rubbed in an effort to change the ongoing stimulation and ward off sleepiness. But in the end, it appears to be nothing but an altered responsiveness of skin receptors, especially in the eyelids, which make it impossible for sleepy people to maintain the state of wakefulness. They cannot keep their eyes open, though they may be powerfully motivated to do so.

I then found further evidence that the skin in diving animals, rather than "expressing" internal events, leads and commands widespread autonomic changes throughout the body in order to conserve oxygen for the vulnerable brain. When the beak of a diving bird is stimulated by the water as it dives for fish, this change produces profound general changes such as vasoconstriction within the body as a whole. Investigators somewhat accidentally discovered that similar changes can occur in a human being by putting a person's face in water (without total immersion of his or her body). (Elsner, Franklin, Van Citters, & Kenney, 1966). Then I examined (at the suggestion of my friend, Julian Jaynes) the work of Beach (1948) on the sexual mechanism in rats. Beach, examining the structure of the penis under a microscope, found that sensitive hair receptors of the skin of the penis were encased between what resembled the interstices of a cog wheel when the penis was flaccid. When there was a blood flow which engorged the penis, the skin was stretched smooth and then the hairs of the receptors were now no longer encased, but exposed, and their exquisite sensitivity changed the animal from a state of sexual quiescence to one of total sexual arousal.

The relevance of such a mechanism for an understanding of the affect mechanism now seemed very clear. It had been known for centuries that the face became red and engorged with blood in anger. It had been known that in terror the hair stood on end, the skin became white and cold with sweat. It had long been known that the blood vessels dilated, the skin felt warm and relaxed in enjoyment. The face as penis would be relatively insensitive in its flaccid condition, its specific receptors hidden, encased within surrounding skin. When, however, there were massive shifts in blood flow and in temperature, one should expect changes in the positioning of receptors, and pursuing the analogy to its bitter end, the patterned changes in facial muscle responses would serve as self-masturbatory stimulation to the skin and its own sensitized receptors. The feedback of this set of changes would provide the feel of specific affects. Although autonomic changes would be involved, the primary locus would now be seen to be in specific receptors, some as yet to be discovered. Changes in hotness, coldness, and warmth would undoubtedly be involved, but there may well be other, as yet unknown, specific receptors which yield varieties of experience peculiar to the affect mechanism. I would suggest that thermography would be one major avenue of investigation. I pursued this possibility about ten years ago and was disappointed at the relative inertia of the temperature of the skin. It may, however, be that advances in the state of the art in recent years may permit a more subtle mapping of the relationships between changes in skin temperature and affect. One implication of such a shift in theory is to render contemporary experimentation with the feedback of voluntarily simulated facial muscle responses as an inadequate test of the dynamics of the innate affect mechanism.

The third modification of the theory concerns the role of breathing and the vocalization of affect. I have not changed my opinion that each affect has as part of its innate program a specific cry or vocalization, subserved by specific patterns of breathing. It is rather one of the implications of this theory which took me some years to understand. The major implication which I now understand concerns the universal confusion of the experience of backed-up affect with that of biologically and psychologically authentic innate affect. An analog may help in illustrating what is at issue. Let us suppose that all over the world human beings were forbidden to exhale air but were permitted and even encouraged to inhale air, so that everyone held their breaths to the point of cyanosis and death. Biologists who studied such a phenomenon (who had also been socialized to hold their breath) would have had to conclude that the breathing mechanism represented an evolutionary monstrosity devoid of any utility. Something similar to this has, in fact, happened to the affect mechanism. Because the free expression of innate affect is extremely contagious and because these are very high-powered phenomena, all societies, in varying degrees, exercise substantial control over the unfettered expression of affect, and particularly over the free expression of the cry of affect. No societies encourage or permit each individual to cry out in rage or excitement, or distress, or terror, whenever and wherever he or she wishes. Very early on, strict control over affect expression is instituted and such control is exerted particularly over the voice in general, whether used in speech or in direct affect expression. Although there are large variations between societies, and between different classes within societies, complete unconditional freedom of affect vocalization is quite exceptional. One of the most powerful effects of alcohol is the lifting of such control so that wherever alcohol is taken by large numbers of individuals in public places, there is a typical raising of the noise level of the intoxicated, accompanying a general loosening of affect control.

There are significant differences in how much control is exerted over voice and affect from society to society: Lomax (1968) has shown a significant correlation between the degree of tightness and closure of the vocal box as revealed in song and the degree of hierarchical social control in the society. It appears that more permissive societies also produce voice and song in which the throat is characteristically more relaxed and open. If all societies, in varying degrees, suppress the free vocalization of affect, what is it which is being experienced as affect? It is what I have called pseudo, or backed-up affect. It can be seen in children who are trying to suppress laughter by swallowing a snicker, or by a stiff upper lip when trying not to cry, or by tightening their jaw trying not to cry out in anger. In all of these cases, one is truly holding one's breath as part of the technique of suppressing the vocalization of affect. Although this is not severe enough to produce cyanosis, we do not, in fact, know what are the biological and psychological prices of such suppression of the innate affective response. I would suggest that much of what is called "stress" is indeed backed-up affect and that many of the endocrine changes which Frankenhaeuser has reported in this volume are the consequence as much of backed-up affect as of affect per se. It seems at the very least that substantial psychosomatic disease might be one of the prices of such systematic suppression and transformation of the innate affective responses. Further, there could be a permanent elevation of blood pressure as a consequence of suppressed rage which would have a much longer duration than an innate momentary flash of expressed anger. Some years ago, French and the Chicago psychoanalytic group had found some evidence for the suppressed cry of distress in psychosomatic asthma (French et al., 1941).

The psychological consequences of such suppression would depend upon the severity of the suppression. I have spelled out some of these consequences elsewhere (1971, 1975). Even the least severe suppression of the vocalization of affect must result in some bleaching of the experience of affect and, therefore, some impoverishment of the quality of life. It must also produce some ambiguity about what affect feels like, since so much of the adult's affective life represents at the very least a transformation of the affective response rather than the simpler, more direct, and briefer innate affect. Such confusion, moreover, occurs even among theorists and investigators of affects, myself included.[1] The appearance of the backed up, the simulated, and the innate is by no means the same. While this may be generally recognized—so that typically we know when someone is controlling an affect, or showing a pretended affect—with anger the matter is quite confused. Because of the danger represented by this affect and the consequent enormous societal concern about the socialization of anger, what is typically seen and thought to be the innate is in actuality the backed-up. Finally, it is upon the discontinuity of vocalization of affect that the therapeutic power of primal screaming rests. One can uncover repressed affect by encouraging vocalization of affect, the more severe the suppression of vocalization has been.

1. By this reasoning the finding that observers across cultures will agree in identifying affect from facial expression does not tell us whether the faces that were used depicted innate or backed-up affect, nor whether observers recognized the difference between the two. In these studies both controlled and innate responses were used as stimuli but observers were not questioned about the difference between the two. It is my prediction that such an investigation would show a universal confusion, just about anger, in which backed-up anger would be perceived as innate and innate anger would not be recognized as such.

Fourth, I have maintained for several years that although affect has the function of amplifying its activator, I have been equally insistent that it did not influence the response to the activator or to itself. I portrayed the infant who was hungry as also distressed but in no way thereby pushed in one direction or another in behavioral response to its hunger and distress. I was concerned to preserve the independence of the response from its affective precursor. It seemed to me that to postulate a tight causal nexus between the affect and the response which followed would have been to severely limit the apparent degrees of freedom which the human being appears to enjoy and to have come dangerously close to reducing both affect and the human being to the level of tropism or instinct. It seems to me now that my concern was somewhat phobic and thereby resulted in my overlooking a powerful connection between stimulus, affect, and response. I now believe that the affect connects both its own activator and the response which follows by imprinting the latter with the same amplification it exerts on its own activator. Thus a response prompted by enjoyment will be a slow, relaxed response in contrast to a response prompted by anger, which will reflect the increased neural firing characteristic of both the activator of anger as well as the anger response itself. What we, therefore, inherit in the affect mechanism is not only an amplifier of its activator, but also an amplifier of the response which it evokes. Such a connection is in no way learned, arising as it does simply from the overlap in time of the affect with what precedes and follows it.

It should be noted that by the response to affect I do not intend any restriction to observable motor responses. The response may be in terms of retrieved memories or in constructed thoughts, which might vary in acceleration if amplified by fear or interest or in quantity if amplified by distress or anger, or in deceleration of rate of information-processing if amplified by enjoyment. Thus, in some acute schizophrenic panics, the individual is bombarded by a rapidly accelerating rush of ideas which resist ordering and organization. Such individuals will try to write down these ideas as an attempt to order them, saying upon being questioned that if they could separate and clarify all of these too fast, overwhelming ideas they could cure themselves. Responses to the blank card in the TAT by such schizophrenics imagine a hero who is trying to put half of his ideas on one half of the card and the other half on the other side of an imaginary line dividing the card into two.

The great German philosopher, Immanuel Kant (1929), likened

the human mind to a glass which imprinted its shape on whatever liquid was poured into the glass. Thus, space, time, causality, he thought, were constructions of the human mind imposing the categories of pure reason upon the outside thing-in-itself, whose ultimate nature necessarily forever escaped us. I am suggesting that he neglected a major filtering mechanism, the innate affects, which necessarily color our every experience of the world, constituting not only special categorization of every experience but producing a unique set of categorical imperatives which amplify not only what precedes and activates each affect but which also amplify the further *responses* which are prompted by affects.

This postulated set of innate linkages between stimulus, affect, and response suggests that human beings are to some extent innately endowed with the possibility of organized if primitive scenes or happenings somewhat under their own control beginning as early as the neonatal period. In script theory, I define the scene as the basic element in life as it is lived. The simplest, most primitive scene includes at least one affect and at least one object of that affect. The object may be the perceived activator, or the response to the activator or to the affect, and in a very special case the object of affect may be reflexive, i.e., affect about itself—e.g., "What am I afraid of?" "Why am I afraid?" "Will my fear abate?" In such cases, the affect of interest is generated by the affect of fear.

If our experience must be amplified in its urgency by affect in order for any scene to be experienced, but affect itself can be as brief as a startle to a pistol shot, how can scenes themselves be amplified? To extend the duration and frequency of any scene, its amplifying affect must also be extended in duration and frequency. But I will distinguish the affective amplification of a single scene from psychological *magnification*—the phenomenon of connecting one affect-laden scene with another affect-laden scene. Psychological magnification necessarily presupposes affective amplification of sets of connected scenes, but the affective amplification of a single scene does not necessarily lead to the psychological magnification of interconnected scenes.

The concept of psychological magnification can be illustrated by two contrast cases. First is what I have defined as *transient* scenes. These are scenes which may be highly amplified by affect but which remain isolated in the experience of the individual. An automobile horn is heard unexpectedly, and produces a momentary startle. It is not elaborated and has minimal consequences for any scenes which either have preceded this scene or which follow it. I may accidentally cut myself while shaving one morning. Unless I am severely neurotic, this is not experienced as a deepening sense of defensive self-mutilation in response to the threat of castration. It does not heighten a sense of helplessness and does not become a self-fulfilling prophecy. Or I listen to a very funny joke and laugh. Though the scene may be intensely rewarding because of the cleverness of the joke, it may remain a transient scene. No decisions on life work, on marriage, children, or friendship will ever be based on such an experience. The experience is unlikely to haunt me. Unless I am a professional raconteur, I am not likely even to repeat it to anyone else, or to myself. Lives are made up of large numbers of transient scenes. All experience is not necessarily interconnected with all other experience. Psychologists have not stressed such scenes because their interest is in understanding the interconnectedness of experience and the deep structures which subserve such connectedness. Nonetheless, if one were to summate the total duration of transient scenes in the lifetime of any individual, that sum might not be inconsequential. The total quantity of banality and triviality in a life may not itself be a trivial phenomenon but rather a reflection of the failure of the development of competing magnified scenes.

The second contrast to psychological magnification are scenes which are neither transient nor casual but rather are *recurrent, habitual scenes*. These are subserved by habitual skills, programs which represent much compression of information in such a way that it can be expanded effectively but with minimal consciousness, thought, and affect. Every day I shave my face in the morning. When I finish, consider how unlikely it would be for me to look in the mirror, beam at myself, and say, "What a magnificent human being you are—you have done it again!" The paradox is that it is just those achievements which are most solid, which work best, and which continue to work that excite and reward us least. The price of skill is the loss of the experience of value—and of the zest for living. The same kind of skill can impoverish the aesthetic experience too often repeated, so that a beautiful piece of music ceases to be responded to. A husband and wife who become too skilled in knowing each other can enter the same valley of perceptual skill and become hardly aware of each other. Skills may become temporarily magnified whenever they prove inadequate, or permanently magnified as a result of brain damage from a stroke, when the individual must now exert himself or herself heroically to relearn and execute what had once been an effortless skill.

Consider another type of habitual scene which I have called the *as if* scene. Everyone learns to cross streets with minimal ideation, perceptual scanning, and affect. We learn to act as if we were afraid but we do not, in fact, experience any fear once we have learned how to cope successfully with such contingencies. Despite the fact that we know there is real danger involved daily in walking across intersections and that many pedestrians are, in fact, killed, we exercise normal caution with minimal attention and no fear. It may remain a minimally magnified scene despite daily repetition over a lifetime. Such scenes do not become magnified, just because they are effective in achieving precisely what the individual intends they should achieve. Though we have said they are based on habitual skills, they are far from being simple motor habits. They are small programs for processing information with relatively simple strategies, but one may nonetheless never repeat precisely the same avoidance behaviors twice in crossing any street. These simple programs generate appropriate avoidant strategies for dealing with a variety of such situations, and caution is nicely matched to the varying demands of this class of situations, with a minimum of attention and affect. It should be noted that many highly magnified scenes are usually based upon and include habitual skills but *in addition* require intense vigilance—cognitive, perceptual, affective, and motoric—in order to transform the skilled programs to meet the ever-new demands of a constantly changing situation. Such would be the case for professional tennis players in a championship match. Their skills are almost never entirely adequate until and unless they are continually rapidly transformed to meet the novelty of each encounter. Under such conditions, there is increasing psychological magnification of their tennis scenes on and off the court in rehearsal of the past and anticipation of future encounters of the same kind.

If a life was restricted to a series of transient scenes, punctuated by habitual scenes, such a life would be fatally impoverished by virtue of insufficient psychological magnification. It would resemble the actual life of an overly domesticated cat who never ventures outdoors and by virtue of having totally explored its restricted environment spends much of its adult life in a series of cat naps.

How and when does psychological magnification begin? Let us look now at the earliest examples of psychological magnification. We are born human beings. As such we inherit all the standard vital equipment which enables us to survive. But we also inherit a complex system of mechanisms which have evolved to make it extremely probable that we will become a person. In computerese, this is the difference between the hardware and the software. In language, this is the difference between the syntax and the semantics. Psychologically, it is the difference between the innate and the learned.

Consider one of the earliest human scenes, the hungry infant in the arms of his mother. As a human being, he carries as standard equipment the rooting reflex—by which he turns his head from side to side in front of the breast—and the sucking reflex, by which he manages to get the milk from his mother's breast once his lips have found and locked on to her teat. By any conception of the good life, this is a good scene. He appears to himself, as to his mother, to be utterly competent (and that without even trying) to make the world his oyster, to reduce and appease his hunger, and at the same time to reap the rewards of drive satisfaction. As a bonus, this reward is further amplified by bursts of the positive affects of excitement followed by the positive affect of enjoyment at satiety.

Is there any reason to expect trouble in such a paradise? Everything is in the best imaginable working order. And yet the newborn infant is *not* fundamentally happy with this state of affairs. Her behavior, soon after birth, seems to tell us, "I'd rather do it myself! I may not be able to do it as well as those reflexes do it, but I might be able to do it better, and I'm going to try." The experiments of Jerome Bruner (1968) have shown that very early on, the infant will replace the reflex sucking by beginning to suck voluntarily, and this is discriminably different from reflex sucking. If she succeeds, she will continue. If it doesn't work too well, she falls back on reflex sucking. This is a prime example of what I have called *autosimulation* or imitation of one's own reflexes. The same phenomenon occurs with the orienting reflex and the several supporting ocular motor reflexes. Although the eye is innately equipped to track any moving stimulus in a reflex way, I have observed apparently voluntary moving of the head and neck very early on to bring visual tracking under voluntary control.

Psychological magnification begins, then, in earliest infancy when the infant imagines, via co-assembly, a possible improvement in what is already a rewarding scene, attempts to do what may be necessary to bring it about, and so produces and connects a set of scenes which continue to reward him with food, and its excitement and enjoyment, and also with the excitement and enjoyment of remaking the world closer to the heart's desire. He is doing what he will continue to try to do all his life—to command the scenes he wishes to play. Like Charlie Chaplin, he will try to write, direct, produce, criticize, and promote the scenes in which he casts himself as hero.

There is a deep mystery at the heart of the earliest attempts at simulation, whether that be of the other, or of the self. Meltzoff and Moore (1977) have recently shown that neonates will imitate the facial responses of others which they see for the first time. Contrary to Piagetian expectations, such early initiative in imitation and command of the earliest scenes both of others and of the self must be powered by emergents of the conjoint interactions of the several basic mechanisms which are standard equipment for the human being. It seems extremely improbable that the earliest hetero- and autosimulation could be wired in preformed software or hardware. It is also improbable that such an intention can be located either in the perceptual, cognitive, affective, or motoric mechanism. The idea of imitation, the intention to imitate, and the execution of imitation is *not* an inherited idea located in the cognitive mechanism, certainly not in the eye, certainly not in the affect programs, and certainly not in the hand and fingers. In order to imitate the other or the self, infants must somehow generate the idea that it would be something to do, generate the requisite affective interest first in the phenomenon and then in its imitation, guide the mouth, fingers, and hands in a feedback controlled manner, and stop when the intention has been achieved (which in the case of imitation of the other they cannot see). In the case of autosimulation, the idea which they must generate of doing voluntarily what they have experienced involuntarily is nowhere present as a possible model. It represents an extraordinary creative invention conjointly powered by primitive perceptual and cognitive capacities amplified by excitement in the *possibility* of improving a good actual scene by doing something oneself. These are real phenomena and they appear to be highly probable emergents from the *interaction* of several basic human capacities. This is why I have argued that we have evolved to be born as a human being who will, with a very high probability, very early attempt and succeed in becoming a person. There are some additional other assumptions which are necessarily involved in such precocious achievements, but we will not examine them here.

The most basic feature of psychological magnification appears therefore, in the first day of life—the expansion of one scene in the direction of a connected but somewhat different scene.

But if psychological magnification, as we have observed it in autosimulation, is heroic, it is not always, nor necessarily so. Even in infancy, the scenes may be more tragic than heroic. Fries (1944) experimented with infants by taking the nipple of the bottle away. Though many infants continued to struggle to recapture it, and gladly accepted it when offered again, some infants not only went to sleep, but actively resisted efforts by the experimenter to reinsert the nipple into the infant's mouth. These infants apparently judged the scene a bad one with which they wanted no more experience at that time. Negative affect proved stronger than the hunger drive. The quality of life, as these infants first encounter it, is poor.

We have contrasted transient scenes which are not magnified, whether they occur in infancy or at any time, with the earliest instances of heroic magnification on the part of the infant. This impression of the infant's readiness for initiative and magnification should now be tempered by another formidable aspect of human development—the infant's extremely limited capacity to relate experiences which occur at time intervals of any duration. Although infants are capable not only of relating scenes which follow quickly one upon the other, but even of generating new scenes in response to immediately experienced scenes, they are not capable during the first six months of their life of connecting what has happened before with what happens much later, as that interval increases.

An investigation by David Levy (1960) gives a classic account of the limited ability of the six-month-old infant to relate one scene to another even when the scenes involve intense affective amplification. Such scenes are likely to remain transient scenes, and to exercise little influence on development before six months of age. Six-month-old infants who had cried in pain to an inoculation they had received were observed on their second visit, a few months later, to the same doctor in the same clinic. Such infants show *no* sign of being afraid or distressed as they see the doctor in the white coat come at them with needle in hand. Though they *do* cry as soon as they feel the pain of the needle, they appear neither to remember what happened before nor to anticipate a repetition of the bad scene before. The pain of each inoculation is indeed amplified by the cry of distress, but nothing *new* has been added. It is presumably no worse than the first time because there has been no *anticipation* amplified by the affect. A few months later, they *will* cry at the sight of the doctor and the needle, as well as at the actual inoculation This is psychological magnification, the phenomenon of connecting one affect-laden scene with another affect-laden scene. Through memory, thought, and imagination, scenes experienced before can be coassembled with scenes presently experienced, together with scenes which are anticipated in the future. The present moment is embedded in the intersect between the past and the future in a central assembly via a constructive process we have called coassembly. It is the same process by which we communicate in speech: The meaning of any one word is enriched and magnified by sequentially coassembling it with words which preceded it and which follow it. So, too, is the meaning and impact of one affect-laden scene enriched and magnified by coassembling and relating it to another affect-laden scene. In infancy, therefore, magnification begins with immediately sequential experience but is severely limited in magnification potential whenever experience is separated in time.

In my script theory, the scene, a happening with a perceived beginning and end, is the basic unit of analysis. The whole connected set of scenes lived in sequence is called the *plot* of a life. The script, in contrast, does not deal with all the scenes or the plot of a life, but rather with the individual's rules for predicting, interpreting, responding to, and controlling a magnified set of scenes.

Although I am urging what appears to be a dramaturgic model for the study of personality, it is sufficiently different in nature from what may seem to be similar theories to warrant some brief disclaimers. By scenes, scripts, and script theory, I do not mean that the individual is inherently engaged in impression management for the benefit of an audience, after Goffman. Such scenes are not excluded as possible scenes, but they are very special cases, limited either to specific personality structures who are on stage much of their lives or to specific occasions for any human beings when they feel they are being watched and evaluated. Nor do I mean that the individual is necessarily caught in unauthentic "games," after Berne, nor are these necessarily excluded. Some individuals' scripts may indeed be well described as a game, and any and all individuals may on occasion play such games, but they are a very special kind of scene and script. Nor is script theory identical with role theory. Roles seldom completely define the personality of an individual and when this does happen, we encounter a very specialized kind of script. The several possible relationships between roles and scripts, such as their mutual support, their conflicts, as well as their relative independence of each other, provide a new important bridge between personality theory and general social science. Indeed, what sociologists have called the definition of the situation and what I am defining as the script is to some extent the same phenomenon viewed from two different but related theoretical perspectives—the scene as defined by the society or as defined by the individual. These definitions are neither necessarily, nor always, identical, but they must necessarily be related to each other rather than completely orthogonal to each other, if either the society or the individual is to remain viable. If the society is ever to change, there must be some tension sustained between the society's definition of the situation and the individual's script. If the society is to endure as a coherent entity, its definition of situations must in some measure be constructed as an integral part of the shared scripts of its individuals.

The closest affinity of my views is with the script theoretic formulation of Robert Abelson (1975) and Schank and Abelson (1977). Although their use of the concept of script is somewhat different from mine, the theoretical structure lends itself to ready mapping one on to the other, despite terminological differences which obscure important similarities of the entire two theoretical structures.

Let us examine how a set of scenes may become magnified sufficiently to prompt the generation of a script. The case we will use is that of Laura, a young girl studied by Robertson (Note 1) in connection with a study of the effects of hospitalization on young children when they are separated from their parents. Laura was hospitalized for about a week. During this week, away from her parents, she was subjected to a variety of medical examinations and procedures and also photographed by a moving picture camera near her crib. Like many young children, she missed her parents, was somewhat disturbed by the medical procedures, and cried a good deal. The quality of her life changed radically this week from good to bad. But what of the more permanent effect of these bad scenes on the quality of her life? First, the answer to such a question will depend critically on the degree of magnification which *follows* this week. How many times will she rehearse these bad scenes? Will such rehearsals coassemble them in such an order and with such spacing that they are experienced as magnifying or attenuating the negative affects connected with these scenes? Further, apart from her own imagination, what will be the quantity of good and bad scenes she experiences at home when she returns? Will her parents further frighten or reassure her, or in attempting to reassure her give her an implicit message that she has been through hell? Further, will this be the beginning of further medical problems, or will it be an isolated week in her life?

What is important from the point of view of script theory is that the effect of any set of scenes is *indeterminate* until the future happens and either further magnifies or attenuates such experience. The second point is that the consequence of any experience is not singular but plural. There is no *single* effect but rather there are *many* effects which change in time—what I have called the principle of *pluridetermincy*. Thus when Laura first returned home, she appeared to be disturbed. Therefore the effect, if we had measured it then, was deleterious. But in a few days she was her normal self again. Now if we assessed the effect, we would say that over the long term it was *not* so serious. However, some time later when Robertson visited her home to interview her parents, she became disturbed once again, so the magnification of the bad scene had now been increased. This illustrates a very important third principle of psychological magnification and script formation: Scenes are magnified not by repetition, but by repetition with a *difference*. It is, as in art, the unity in variety which engages the mind and heart of the person who is experiencing a rapid growth of punishment or reward. Sheer repetition of experience characteristically evokes adaptation which attenuates, rather than magnifies, the connected scenes. In the case of Laura, it is the very fact that Robertson now unexpectedly has invaded her home—the fortress of love and security—that has changed everything for the worse. Up to this point, the main danger appeared to be that her parents might take her from her home and leave her in an alien, dangerous environment. But now her parents appear to be either unwilling or unable to prevent the dangerous intrusion into what was, till then, safe space. Indeed, they may appear to be in collusion with the intruder. The whole matter appears to have become more problematic. Yet in a few days all is again well, and we would be tempted to think that the affair has been closed—that the long-term effects of the hospitalization are not serious.

All goes well for some time. Then Laura is taken to an art museum by her parents. They wish to see an exhibition of paintings. They leave Laura in a white crib which the museum provides. What will be the effect of this? Once before, they took her to a hospital and left her in a white crib. Will she become disturbed and cry? She does not—so we have been correct in supposing that the experience in the hospital is limited in its long-term effects. She has been left by her parents in a white crib; but the deadly parallel escapes her. A few minutes later, however, a man comes by with a camera and takes a picture of her. And now she *does* cry. The family of connected scenes has now again been critically enlarged. This man is *not* Robertson. He has a camera, not a moving picture camera. It is an art museum, not a hospital—but it smells like danger to Laura, and her own crying becomes self-validating. The scene, whether dangerous or not, has been made punishing by her own crying. Any scene which is sufficiently similar to evoke the same kind of affect is thereby *made* more similar, and increases the degree of connectedness of the whole family of scenes. Just as members of a family are not similar in all respects, yet appear to be recognized as members of the same family, so do connected scenes which are psychologically magnified become more similar as members of a family of scenes. The scene in the hospital, at home, and at the museum will now be sufficiently magnified to generate a script. What will this script be like?

First it should be noted that this series of scenes involve little action on the part of Laura. She responds affectively to the hospital and museum scenes, but is otherwise passive. There have not as yet developed action strategies for avoiding or escaping such threatening scenes. We do not know for sure that, or how much, she anticipates or rehearses these scenes. Therefore our examination of the dynamics of script formation in the case of Laura is limited to script formation which is primarily interpretive and reactive and is a simplified case of what normally includes more active reaction to and participation in the generation of scenes and scripts. It is, however, useful for us at this stage of our presentation of script theory to deal with the simplest type of script which emphasizes the attainment of understanding of what is happening in a scene, since more complex scripts necessarily always include such understanding before coping strategies can be developed.

A complete understanding of the formation of scripts must rest on a foundation of perceptual, cognitive, memory, affect, action, and feedback theory. Needless to say, none of these separate mechanisms has been entirely satisfactorily illuminated at a theoretical level and their complex modes of interaction in a feedback system is an achievement far from realization. Yet an understanding of the complexities involved in interpreting and perceptually and cognitively ordering constantly shifting information from one scene to the next requires just such a missing theory. I have elsewhere presented my theories of perception, cognition, memory and feedback mechanisms upon which I have based script theory (Tomkins, 1971, 1979). I will use some of these assumptions in an illustrative but incomplete way in the following attempts to understand script formation.

The perception of a scene, at its simplest, involves a partitioning of the scene into figure and ground. The figural part of the scene, as in any object perception, is the most salient and most differentiated part of it, separated from the ground by a sharp gradient which produces a contour or connected boundary which separates the figure from its less differentiated ground. Such a figure becomes figural characteristically as a conjoint function of sharply differentiated gradients of stimulation (of shape, texture, or color in the visual field, of loudness, pitch, or rhythm in the auditory field), internal gradients of experienced affect (so that, e.g., it is the object with contours which excites, and is experienced as "exciting," rather than the ground), correlated gradients of experienced internal images and/or thoughts and/or words so that the object is experienced as fused with recruited images or imageless compressed thoughts or is fused with a word (e.g., that is "mother"), and with actions taken or with action potentials (e.g., That object is touchable, can be put in the mouth, or dropped to make a sound). These separate sources of information, converging conjointly in what I have called the central assembly, interact intimately and produce an organization of a simple scene into a salient figure differentiated from a more diffuse background.

Differentiation of a scene involves shifting centration away from one figure to another aspect of the same scene which now becomes figural. The first figure characteristically becomes a compressed part of the ground but capable of later expansion so that it may produce a more complex awareness of the now more differentiated scene. Ultimately, the whole scene is compressed and perceived as a habitual skill so that very small alternative samplings tell individuals all they think they then want to know about a repeated scene. After achieving some knowledge of the general characteristics of a scene with respect to its beginning (what started the scene), its cast (who is in the scene), its place (where is it), its time (when did it take place), its actions (who did what), its functions (did I see it, dream it, think about it, move around in it), its events (what happened—e.g., it snowed, there was an accident), its props (what things are in the scene—e.g., trees, automobiles), its outcomes (what happened at the end of the scene) and its end (what terminated the scene), the individual through memory and thought is then in a position to compare total scenes with each other—to coassemble them and to begin to understand their several possible relationships to each other. Such comparisons between two or more scenes may go on in a third scene quite distinct from the scenes being compared, or the preceding scenes may be recruited simultaneously with another apparent repetition of one or more of the earlier scenes, in an effort to understand the similarities and differences between the present scene and its forerunners.

The human being handles the information in a family of connected scenes in ways which are not very different from the ways in which scientists handle information. They attempt to maximize the order inherent in the information in as efficient and powerful a way as is consistent with their prior knowledge and with their present channel capacity limitations. Since the efficiency and power of any theory is a function of the ratio of the number of explanation assumptions in the numerator relative to the number of phenomena explained in the denominator, human beings, like any scientist, attempt to explain as much of the variance as they can with the fewest possible assumptions. This is in part because of an enforced limitation on their ability to process information, and in part because some power to command, understand, predict, and control their scenes is urgently demanded if they are to optimize the ratio of rewarding positive and punishing negative affect in their lives.

In their attempt to order the information and produce a script from a set of scenes, they will first of all partition the variance into what they regard as the major variance and the residual variance— the big, most important features of the set of scenes—the constants of their script equation as differentiated from the related more differentiated variables of their script equation. In this respect, the procedure resembles factor analytic procedures whereby a general factor of intelligence is first extracted, followed by more specific factors which account for less and less of the variance. It resembles analysis of variance procedures in its strategy of first asking if there is a main effect, and then asking about more specific interactions.

What is the general script factor, or the main effect script question likely to be? It is characteristically determined by three conjoint criteria: (1) What is experienced with the most dense, i.e., the most intense and enduring affect? (2) What are experienced as the sharpest gradients of change of such affect? (3) What are the most frequently repeated sequences of such affect and affect changes? Whenever these three criteria are conjointly met in any series of scenes, they will constitute the first major partitioning of the variance within and between scenes. The most repeated changes in dense affect may occur either within any scene or between scenes or both. It should be noted that any one of these principles might operate in the organization of a *single* scene. An individual would, of course, pay attention to anything which deeply distressed him or her or to anything which suddenly changed, or to anything which was repeated within a scene. When, however, the task shifts to ordering a complex set of changes, both within and between scenes, his or her ability to deal with the totality of such information is sharply reduced. It is for this reason, I think, that the criteria for judging what is most important become more selective by requiring that conjoint conditions be met in a hierarchical order. The big picture must first be grasped before it can be fleshed in. An important, repeated change is the general script factor. This includes internal repetition, in past rehearsal and future anticipation.

Let us examine how this may operate in the case of Laura. The most repeated, most dense affects, which change most sharply, are those in going from home to hospital, from positive to negative affect; in going from hospital to home, a much slower change from negative to positive affect; in going from being at home with parents to the intrusion of Dr. Robertson, sharp change from positive to negative; in going from his intrusion back to being alone again with her parents, a slower change from negative to positive; and finally, in going from home to the art museum, a sharp change from positive to negative affect. The most general part of her script, therefore, can be described as a sequence of repeated dense positive affect scenes which suddenly change into dense negative affect scenes and then more slowly change back into dense positive scenes via a set of mixed positive and negative transition scenes. If we were to diagram it, it would look like this: $+ - \frac{-}{+} + - \frac{-}{+} +$. In her case the relative time of the dense positive scenes is characteristically much longer than that of the dense negative scenes. The duration of the mixed transition scenes from negative to positive we do not have enough information to describe precisely. Such a regular alternation as occurs in this case is by no means the rule in the experience of human beings. Much change within and between scenes may be perceived as random or without any sharp gradients. Many series of scenes need not invoke very intense or enduring affect. Much change within and between scenes may involve little apparent repetition. Further, the relative density of positive and negative affect and the direction of change within and between scenes need not be as they appear in this case. We will later examine some alternatives in other scripts.

Having extracted and partitioned this main variance, let us now examine the residual more specific, more differentiated variance. This script, like any processing of information, will change in time as new evidence accumulates. Based upon the first change in scenes, the residual variance would have been partitioned in the following way. There are two contrasting, correlated sets of distinctive features which account for the general variance of alternation of positive and negative affect scenes. The good, positive affect scene is characterized by *place* (at home), by *cast* (with parents), and by *action* (conversation, playing, etc.). The bad negative affect scene is also characterized by the same distinctive features—place, cast and action—but with the place in the hospital, the cast a doctor and a moving picture cameraman, and the action medical procedures. Such a neat set of contrasted correlated features could not be sustained the moment the doctor appeared in her home. In this scene, the bad member of the cast still remains the same, but place (the home) is no longer totally safe, and action (the doctor speaking to parents) is no longer the same as a medical examination or moving picture taking, but is nonetheless disturbing. In the third scene, the place is at first a good place, but eventually becomes a bad place even though it is neither home nor hospital. The cast is also not the same cast but someone like the moving picture cameraman. The action is not the same but somewhat similar, having a still picture taken.

At the end of this set of scenes, the residual variance which accounts for the general variance can be understood by the theory of the family of scenes. If we think of a set of scenes composed of features a b c d e f, and their contrasting features a^l b^l c^l d^l e^l f^l, then if a . . . f is contrasted with a^l . . . f^l as correlated variance which produces − to + affect changes, versus + to − affect changes, then in general, any contrast subsets of these two families become capable of producing the same contrasting general variance.

So, for example:

a b c	vs	a¹ b¹ c¹
	or vs	b¹ c¹
or b c d	vs	b¹ c¹ d¹
	or vs	b¹ d¹
or c d e	vs	c¹ d¹ e¹
	or vs	c¹ d¹
or a d e	vs	a¹ d¹ e¹
	or vs	d¹ e¹

would by virtue of family resemblances become capable of producing the same shifts from + to − affect, or from − to + affect as the fuller, more tightly correlated set might have done originally.

Indeed, psychological magnification would continue to grow by virtue of incremental subtractions, additions, and transformations of distinctive features which expanded the family without violating it. It is a mechanism similar to what in fact happens in the recognition of a remote member of a family one sees for the first time. One may note that he has the family chin and nose, but not the usual hair color. One now has an expanded knowledge of *that* family. When Laura can experience the same disturbance in three different places, hospital, home and museum, with two different members of the cast, Dr. Robertson and the photographer at the museum, and with three different actions—medical examinations, Dr. Robertson talking to her parents, the photographer taking a still picture—there is nonetheless enough overlap of similar contrasting subsets to account for the critical affect shifts while at the same time she learns to be disturbed by the same people in a new place, or new people in new places doing somewhat new things. As these variants grow in number yet continue to produce the more general changes in dense affect, psychological magnification increases. One should also note that such growth is at first quite discriminating. There is what I have called a critical *interscene distance* which itself changes with magnification which determines how different a scene can be and still be responded to as if it were much the same. Thus, when Laura was taken out of the home to the art museum, and left alone in a crib very similar to the one in the hospital, this was not sufficiently similar to evoke the critical general shift in affect.

I presume that each scene has a specific address in the nervous system and that such an address has one or more "names" which know that address and will retrieve that scene. I also presume the existence of names of names, i.e., messages which know or direct processing to another name. For example, most individuals have two separate programs for handwriting. One of these is for slow handwriting and one is for fast handwriting. One name for the slow handwriting is the instruction "write very slowly." Under this instruction one can recover early handwriting. But the same program can be reached by the instruction "write on the blackboard in letters two feet tall." Since this is an entirely new task, the individual ordinarily writes slowly, and such large letters are characteristically written in the early way. Magnification of scenes also grows in this fashion if the scene being experienced calls upon a unique older scene for guidance in interpretation and action by virtue of being a name of a name of a unique scene. The theory of the varieties of types of names which will know the address of unique scenes in the brain I have elaborated elsewhere (Tomkins, 1971).

Returning now to the theory of partitioning of variance into general and specific variance one may ask whether there is any evidence to support the existence of such general strategies in information-processing generally. Many years ago, long before I was involved with either affect theory or script theory, I produced some experimental evidence to support such a theory of information-processing (Tomkins, 1963). Let me present some of this evidence in support of its present application to script theory. I presented subjects with the following tasks: (1) Write as many repetitions of the capital letter N as fast as you can; (2) write as many repetitions of the capital letter M as fast as you can.

On the basis of a theory of the coassembly of the *most frequently repeated changes in direction* with a correlated set of features which were less frequently repeated, I predicted that under speed stress, errors of omission of the latter features would be produced, and this happened in the following ways:

N's were deformed as follows: (1) Either as $\mathcal{N}$ or as $\mathbf{W}$. Consider that the most general, most repeated changes of direction are up-down-up (for the letter N). The correlated *less* frequent instruction is another down in the air, following the end of each N so that the writer may again begin with an up-stroke on the next N. Because the added special instruction, to lift the pencil off the paper before you repeat the next letter, is a less frequently repeated part of the program, it is dropped under stress, and so the movement still occurs as an error on the surface of the paper, in part because by doing so there is now an increase in the number of repetitions in the letter N.

Previously, UDU was followed by D (in the air) followed by UDU. Now with the dropping of the added special instruction (D in the air), the task becomes UDUDUDU, so now there are six repetitions of alternate UD instead of two repetitions of UDU, UDU.

In the second task, we have built a differentiation of size on top of a more general and frequently repeated change of direction. The letter M can be decomposed into a general variance of Up-Down-Up-Down. The special variance, however, is less frequently repeated since the first up is a large stroke, the first down and second up are small strokes, and the last down is again a large stroke. Under speed stress, I predicted that the more special instructions of size differences would drop out and there would be regression to the mean size so that the letters would be drawn ⋀. This did happen but I did not predict something else which some subjects did. They drew the letters as /⋀, exaggerating the differences in size between the outside and inside strokes. This was in effect a defense generated against a felt pull towards a loss of differentiation.

Laura, therefore, now has a script which sensitizes her to scan for sudden possibilities of danger—but danger which will slowly subside and return her to safety and well-being for a time—the cycle to be repeated again and again, depending on how much this script is further magnified. In the early stages of magnification, it is the set of scenes which determine the script; but as magnification increases, it is the script which increasingly determines the scenes. How this can happen we will now consider.

Such a script as generated by Laura may or may not be further magnified in the future. All persons are governed by a multiplicity of scripts generated to deal with particular sets of scenes of varying degrees of magnification. Some scripts wax and wane in importance, e.g., those subserving interpersonal relationships which themselves are magnified at one time and atrophy or lie dormant at another time. Some radically magnified scripts dealing with beloved parents, mates, or children may explode in magnification upon the death of the other to become radically attenuated just by virtue of that specially intense magnification involved in mourning. Some scripts subserve habitual skills which occasionally become magnified briefly when unexpected changes tax the adequacy of the habitual skill, as when a carpenter has to deal with new building material of unusual recalcitrance to cutting. Other scripts are continually magnified by ever-changing demands on achieved skills, as in the practice of law or medicine. Even more magnified are those skills involved in competitive sports, where the peak moments of glory are few and transitory and restricted to that sector of the life span when one is in prime physical condition. Some scripts continue to be magnified even though the affects change their signs radically as when friends become enemies, or enemies friends. Some lifelong commitments become attentuated either through perceived attainment of major goals or because of erosion through intolerable cost. Some scripts show continued but intermittent growth throughout a lifetime, such as a friendship which is maintained despite spatial separation. Some scripts are highly magnified, enslaving the individual to dependencies in eating, drugs, or cigarettes which he or she cannot either control nor renounce, as in either physiological or psychological addiction. These scripts have a finite impact on the individual because they have very specific behavioral acts which, if performed, reduce the affect and consciousness of the addiction and thereby limit the degree of magnification. In the extreme instance, an individual may hoard many cartons of cigarettes in order never to encounter the experience of painful addictive deprivation. Smoking can then be treated as a habitual skill and done with minimal affect and awareness.

The major variance in most human beings cannot be understood through such scripts even though one cannot understand much of personality structure if one does not know the extent and strength of such varieties of scripts within any particular personality. The numbers and varieties of such segmental and partially stabilized scripts is an important part of the total personality structure. But the central phenomena in any human being are those scripts we define as the nuclear scripts which govern that large and ever-growing family of scenes we define as nuclear scenes. A nuclear family of scenes, and their underlying nuclear scripts, are defined by their rate and continuity of growth. They are the scripts which must continue to grow in intensity of affect, of duration of affect, and in the interconnectedness of scenes via the conjoint promise of endless, infinite, unconditional ends, of more positive affect and less negative affect, with endless conditional necessity to struggle perpetually to achieve (against lack), to maintain (against loss or threat), and to increase (against deflation and adaptation) the means to such a magnified end. They matter more than anything else and they never stop seizing the individual. They are the good scenes we can never totally or permanently achieve or possess. If they occasionally seem to be totally achieved or possessed, such possession can never be permanent. If they reward us with deep positive affect, we are forever greedy for more. If the good scenes are good, they may never be good enough and we are eager for them to be improved and perfected. If they punish us with deep negative affect, we can never entirely avoid, escape, nor renounce the attempt to master or revenge ourselves upon them despite much punishment. If they both seduce and punish us, we cannot either possess nor renounce them. If they are conflicted scenes, we can renounce neither wish, nor integrate them. If they are ambiguous scenes, we cannot simplify nor clarify the many overlapping scenes which characteristically produce pluralistic confusion. These are the conditions par excellence for unlimited magnification. These nuclear scenes and scripts are relatively few in number for any individual, but are composed of very large numbers of families of such scenes.

Let us examine some classic instances of nuclear scenes and nuclear scripts. What is it which guarantees that human beings will *neither* master the threats to which they are exposed nor avoid situations which they cannot deal with effectively? Mortality and death is one paradigm for such a state of affairs—because it cannot be mastered, nor can it be avoided. Another paradigm is the classic triangular scene (either due to the arrival of a sib, or the presence of the father) in the family romance. The male child who loves his mother excessively can neither totally possess her (given an unwanted rival) nor totally renounce her. He is often destined, however, to keep trying and characteristically to keep failing. Why does he not learn then that he would be happier to make his peace with both his mother and with his rival? Many human beings do just this, but to the extent to which the male child can neither possess nor renounce, he remains a perpetual victim.

There are many additional magnifications of the wish for possession on the one hand and the inability to renounce the wish on the other, which we will not examine here. What we will examine is the paradox of how such victimage is perpetuated by reason as well as by affect. In order to understand this, we must distinguish two different ways in which we think. One is by the principle of variants; the other is by the principle of analogs. A variant is a way of detecting change in something which in its core remains the same. Thus, if one's wife is wearing a new dress, one does not say to her, "You look very similar to my wife" but rather, "I like the new dress you're wearing." Scenes which are predominantly positive in affect tone thus become connected and grow through the classic principle of unity in variety. So a symphony is written and appreciated as a set of variations on a theme. The enjoyment and excitement of such experience depends upon the awareness of both the sameness and the difference. So an interest in any skill or in any friend can grow endlessly by increasing variations on an underlying core which does not change. It is of the essence of friendship to enjoy the rehearsal from time to time of a long shared past history.

Contrast this mode of reasoning with the principle of analog formation which, though it is used in dealing with positive affects too, is much more frequently and powerfully used in dealing with negative affect scenes. Let us first illustrate the nature of this mechanism on a neutral task. The great art historian, Gombrich (1960) demonstrated that if one asks that a series of contrasting words (e.g., "mouse" vs "elephant") be categorized as to which one would properly be called a *ping* and which one a *pong*, then it is remarkable that over 90 % of all subjects agree that a mouse is a ping and an elephant is a pong. This is an extraordinary consensus on an absurd task—without any communication or collusion among subjects. I repeated the experiment and studied it further and discovered that although most subjects agree that a mouse is a ping and an elephant is a pong, they do not, in fact, all use the identical thought processes in arriving at their conclusion. Thus, some subjects thought that since a ping seemed small, and a pong seemed large, then a mouse would be a ping since it is smaller than an elephant. However, other subjects thought that a ping sounded like a higher frequency sound and a pong sounded like a lower frequency sound—therefore, since a mouse has a squeaky voice and an elephant a low roar, a ping is a mouse and a pong is an elephant. Whichever reasons were used, however, the basic mode of thought was analogic and as often as not, somewhat unconscious. Many subjects said, "I don't know why, but a mouse just seems more like a ping to me and an elephant seems more like a pong." In fact, the individual was responding to imagined relationships between shared dimensions.

Such analogic constructions become the major mechanism whereby a negative affect scene is endlessly encountered and endlessly defeats the individual when the ratio of positive to negative affect becomes predominantly negative. Consider the following example: A man is driving his automobile on a lovely spring day on a brand new just-opened interstate highway. He looks at the lush greenery all about him and at the shiny, white new highway. An unaccustomed peace and deep enjoyment seizes him. He feels at one with beautiful nature. There is no one else. He is apparently the first to enjoy this verdant and virginal scene. Then, as from nowhere, he sees to his disgust a truck barreling down the road, coming at him and entirely destroying the beauty of the setting. "What is that truck doing here?" he asks himself. He becomes deeply depressed. He can identify the apparent reason, but he senses that there is more to it—that his response is disproportionate to the occasion, and the depression is deep and enduring.

This is an account of an individual who suffered severe sibling rivalry as a first-born, whose deep attachment to his mother was so disrupted by the birth of a sib that he became mute for six months, and who never, thereafter, forgave his mother for her apparent infidelity. This scene was one of hundreds of analogs which he constructed and imported into scenes which would have quite different significances for individuals with different nuclear scripts. It is because he can neither renounce, nor forgive, nor possess his mother that he is destined to be victimized by endless analogs which repeat the same unsolved scene—seducing him to continually try to finally settle accounts with his hated rival and his beloved but faithless mother, and to restore the Garden of Eden before the fall.

He characteristically does not know why he feels as he does (any more than why a mouse seems like a ping and an elephant like a pong). He is victimized by his own high-powered ability to synthesize ever-new repetitions of the same scene without knowing that he is doing so.

This is one of the reasons why insight psychotherapy so often fails to cure—because no amount of understanding of the past will enable this individual to become aware of his new analogs *before* they are constructed. At best, he may become more self-conscious, after the fact, that he has been unconsciously seduced into yet another ineffective attempt at a "final solution" to his nuclear script. This often may abbreviate his suffering, so that his depression will not last six months, but perhaps only six minutes. But there is no guarantee that yet another analog may not seize him within the hour.

This represents a major mechanism whereby a disproportionate ratio of negative to positive affect can become stabilized. There are other mechanisms no less powerful which serve the same purpose. Thought, like any powerful instrument, will serve any human purpose. Once enlisted in the service of powerful negative nuclear scripts, it becomes a formidable adversary which can be coped with only through the most heroic strategies. Here, insight *can* come to play a major constructive role. To the extent to which intense negative affect can be recruited *against* the repetition of self-defeating scenes, our individual may be persuaded that the suffering entailed in the renunciation of his excessive longing, and the suffering entailed in the renunciation of his excessive wish for revenge, may be less than the price he is paying for insisting on reentry into a heaven which never quite existed, and punishment for a criminal rival who was never quite so criminal.

Contrast the luxuriant growth potential of analogs compared with variants, even when both are concerned with intense negative affect. In the case of Laura, a member of the bad cast, her doctor, had to actually come into her home to produce magnification. At the museum, there was no magnification even when she was left by her parents in a crib similar to that in the hospital until a person with a camera similar to the camera in the hospital, i.e., an analog, made Laura anxious about a possible repetition of the bad scene. Variants do not lend themselves to the same rate of growth as analogs because the latter lend themselves to an increasing skill in similarity detection.

Consider another way in which a nuclear scene may grow endlessly. Any nuclear script organizes residual variance in three different ways. It may *exclude* variance as in a contrast family of scenes which by contrast and opposition heighten the nuclear script (as occurred in the case of Laura). Second, it may *satellize* other variance, using it as instrumental to the major variance. Third, it may *absorb* it and neutralize it by denying its essential quality, in order to preserve the apparent power of the nuclear scenes.

In the latter case, we are dealing not simply with analogs, but with theoretical derivations from an assumed *paradigm*. Just as any general theory of personality (e.g., psychoanalysis) has a set of constants, of assumed laws about the theoretical structure of personality, so may a nuclear script possess the characteristics of a scientific paradigm which enables the individual to extrapolate explanations for apparently remote and contradictory phenomena consistent with the paradigm.

Consider the case of a man who has suffered excessive humiliation over a lifetime, when he is confronted by unexpected praise from another man. How does his script absorb and neutralize such evidence? First, the sincerity of the judge may be questioned. Second, "He praised only this work of mine because he knows that everything else I have done is trash." Third, "He may be sincere, but he is probably a fool." Fourth, "This is a temporary lapse of his judgments. When he comes to his senses, he will have all the more contempt for me." Fifth, "What I have done is a fluke which I can never do again." Sixth, "He is trying to control me, holding out a carrot of praise. If I eat this, I am hooked and I will thenceforth have to work for his praise and to avoid his censure." Seventh, "He is exposing how hungry I am for praise and thus exposing my inferiority and my feelings of humiliation." Eighth, "He is seducing me into striving for something more which I cannot possibly achieve." So may defeat be snatched from the jaws of victory by a predominantly negative affect nuclear script. Such a script can be produced only by a long history of failures to deal effectively with negative affect scenes. It is *not* a consequence of suffering per se, but rather of suffering which again and again defeated every effort of the individual to reduce his or her suffering. Indeed, many extraordinary personalities have grown strong and full of zest for life by dealing more and more effectively with formidable misfortunes. There are many different avenues to predominantly positive or negative affect nuclear scripts. The crucial features are the repeated sequences of scenes which end either in joy or despair. These depend variously upon the different combinations of the benign or malign environments and upon the strong or weak inner resources to deal with such opportunities and constraints.

We have thus far considered the generation of families of variant scenes, families of analogs, and families of paradigms or systematic theories as generators of nuclear scripts. These are some of the more important kinds of nuclear scenes and their scripts but in no way exhaustively describe all of the varieties of possible theoretical structures.

In closing, let me briefly mention some of these alternatives. First are the systematic ideologies inherited from either the society or from parents or both. These characteristically magnify sets of contrasting scenes in which one set represents the idea of the Good, the True, and the Beautiful, what makes life worth living, and the other what makes life illusory, immoral, and ugly. It is ordinarily a conjunction of abstract theory and particularistic commands and prohibitions which may attempt to regulate both life's general direction as well as the most minute details of everyday life. Ideology includes religious ideology but is not restricted to the great historical religious ideologies. Capitalism and socialism would represent equally powerful sets of ideas for controlling the lives of those who are governed by them. Societies too are governed by both scripts and nuclear scripts. Political power, economic power, technological power, informational power, religious power tend toward endless magnification via societal nuclear scripts.

A powerful source of societal nuclear scenes and scripts arises from the ideas of transcendence and infinity, especially stressed in Western civilization, beginning with the idea of Jehovah in Judaism and the realm of Ideas in Plato. Such conceptions guarantee an irreducible distance between the particular here and now and the infinitely remote standard located out of space and time. Neither truth, goodness, nor beauty can ever, therefore, be totally or permanently possessed. I take this to be a major part of the answer to Needham's (1954) question: Why did the West, a latecomer in the development of science, so outstrip Chinese civilization which early surpassed the West? I believe that the conjunction of the affect of excitement, with its stress on novelty and transformation, together with the idea of transcendence powered an endless quest in the idea of science which approached but never attained final truth, in the idea of social and political revolution which approached but never attained Utopia, in the idea of romantic love which approached but never attained the ideal beloved, and in the idea of a God who was approached and worshipped but never possessed.

In contrast, the Chinese conjoined the affect of enjoyment with its investment of sameness, particularity, and tradition in contrast to excitement, abstraction, transformation, and change. They loved the here and now, and particularly the land which they inherited from their ancestors who had loved it before them. Their science was applied to satisfy present needs rather than pursuing a remote, never-to-be-attained final truth. Their worship of learning stressed the mastery of particular texts. Their gods were their ancestors, not remote and out of space and time. Their interpersonal relations stressed the importance of affection and piety for their parents, their mates, and their children—the experiencing of particular here-and-now individuals rather than the quest for the perfect lover and beloved and the perfect romantic love affair. Their political life included rebellions—but no revolutions in the Western sense. They would kick the rascals out, but expect no Utopia as a result. Appreciation of life as it was lived produced scripts which did not demand endless growth, productivity, mastery. It is an issue which has finally come to haunt Western civilization, now for the first time confronting the reality of limits.

This conflict between the enjoyment of the given, the particular, the finite, and the excitement of the infinite is at the heart of the basic Western religious nuclear script recorded in the old testament in Genesis. Consider that Jehovah granted Adam and Eve a life of everlasting, simple, pure enjoyment so long as they did not eat of the fruit of the tree of knowledge. Satan and Eve contested with Jehovah and for this were driven from the Garden of Eden and its perpetual bliss. Just as infants prefer to experiment with sucking on their own rather than enjoy the given particulars of their reflex endowments, so in Genesis human beings are portrayed as essentially Promethean, endlessly seeking the infinite knowledge, power, and immortality of Jehovah. The price of endless excitement are the negative affects, which appear for the first time when they are driven from the Garden. He must labor by the sweat of his brow; she must suffer distress in childbearing and rearing. They are now vulnerable to rage and murder and thus are introduced to fear for their mortality. They now know excitement not only in knowledge, but in knowledge fused with sexuality, and are thereby introduced into shame which prompts Adam and Eve to hide their genitals with fig leaves—a gesture which Jehovah recognizes as betraying their pride and sin. The price of excitement and the quest for the infinite is shame, distress, fear, and rage which power magnification without limit.

REFERENCE NOTE

1. Robertson, J. *Case history of a child undergoing short separation from mother in a hospital.* Unpublished report, Tavistock Institute, London. Undated.

REFERENCES

Abelson, R. Concepts for representing mundane reality in plans. In D. G. Bobrow & A. Collins (Eds.), *Representation and understanding.* New York: Academic Press, 1975.

Beach, F. A. *Hormones and behavior.* New York: Hoeber, 1948.

Bruner, J. *Processes of cognitive growth: Infancy.* Worcester: Clark University Press, 1968.

Elsner, R., Franklin, D. L., Van Citters, R. L., & Kenney, D. W. Cardiovascular defense against asphyxia. *Science*, 1966, **153**, 941–949.

Ekman, P., Sorenson, E. R., & Friesen, W. V. Pan-cultural elements in facial displays of emotions. *Science*, 1969, **164**, 86–88.

Frankenhaeuser, M. Psychoneuroendocrine approaches to the study of emotion as related to stress and coping. In H. E. Howe, Jr., & R. A. Dienstbier (Eds.), *Nebraska Symposium on Motivation 1978* (Vol. 26). Lincoln: University of Nebraska Press, 1979.

French, T. M., Alexander, F., et al. Psychogenic factors in bronchial asthma. *Psychosomatic Medicine*, Monograph No. 2, 1941.

Fries, M. E. Psychosomatic relationships between mother and infant. *Psychosomatic Medicine*, 1944, **6**, 159–162.

Gombrich, E. H. J. *Art and illusion*. New York: Pantheon Press, 1960.

Kant, Immanuel. *Critique of pure reason*. London: Macmillan, 1929.

Izard, C. The emotions and emotion constructs in personality and culture research. In R. B. Catell (Ed.), *Handbook of modern personality theory*. Chicago: Aldine, 1969.

Levy, D. M. The infant's earliest memory of innoculation: A contribution to public health procedures. *Journal of General Psychology*, 1960, **96**, 3–46.

Lomax, A. *Folk song style and culture*. Washington, D.C.: AAAS, 1968.

Meltzoff, A. N., & Moore, M. K. Imitation of facial and manual gestures by human neonates. *Science*, 1977, **198**, 75–78.

Needham, J. *Science and civilization in China. Volume I: Introductory orientations*. Cambridge: Cambridge University Press, 1954.

Schank, R., & Abelson, R. Scripts, plans, goals and understanding. Hillsdale, N.J.: Lawrence Erlbaum Associates, 1977.

Tomkins, S. S. Consciousness and the unconscious in a model of the human being. *Proceedings XIV International Congress of Psychology*. Montreal: I.C.P., 1955.

Tomkins, S. S. *Affect, imagery, consciousness* (Vol. 1). New York: Springer, 1962.

Tomkins, S. S. *Affect, imagery, consciousness* (Vol. 2). New York: Springer, 1963.

Tomkins, S. S. A theory of memory. In J. Antrobus (Ed.), *Cognition and affect*. Boston: Little, Brown & Co., 1971.

Tomkins, S. S. The phantasy behind the face. *Journal of Personality and Assessment*, 1975, **39**, 551–562.

Tomkins, S. S. *Affect, imagery, consciousness* (Vol. 3). New York: Springer, in press.

Tomkins, S. S., & Messick, S. (Eds.). *The computer simulation of personality*. New York: Wiley, 1963.

Tomkins, S. S., & McCarter, R. What and where are the primary affects? Some evidence for a theory. *Perceptual and Motor Skills*, 1964, **18**, 119–158.

Emotion-Attribution Theory: Establishing Roots and Exploring Future Perspectives

Richard A. Dienstbier
University of Nebraska—Lincoln

*E*motion-attribution theory depends upon the premise that some physiological arousal is a part of all experience appropriately characterized as emotional. The major thesis of emotion-attribution theory is that the quality and meaning of emotional experience is determined, in part, by the attributions made about the causes of the accompanying arousal. Since emotion-attribution processes are essentially cognitive in nature, some cognitive control is thereby attained over the nature of the emotional experience and the behavior motivated by that experience.

The present chapter represents an explication of those introductory sentences. I will attempt, on the one hand, to develop emotion-attribution principles and to demonstrate the application of those principles to appropriate areas, while on the other hand I will mention the limitations of this approach and comment on some recent criticisms of it. At the chapter's end some previously unpublished studies will be presented. Since a discussion of attributions about the cause and meaning of emotional arousal raises many issues unique to emotion, the content of this chapter will relate more to emotion theory than to attribution theory as typically considered in modern social psychology.

As emotion-attribution principles are developed within different content areas, I will apply them to three different levels. The first level concerns how emotion attributions made by the developing child (often with the guidance of a socialization agent) influence later emotional experience and emotion-motivated behavior. Consider, for example, the difference in meaning to the child when

237

emotional arousal is experienced as shame due to having been punished for a transgression as contrasted with emotional arousal experienced as guilt for having committed the transgression; in later temptation situations such diverse early attributions may motivate vastly different behaviors. Secondly, emotion-attribution principles may be invoked in understanding the contribution to emotional experience of emotional arousal which is maintained as an individual moves between different situations. It is a fascinating and potentially fruitful enterprise to delimit the rules which govern how such arousal may contribute to changing emotional experiences in new circumstances. Finally, extending these considerations to a long-term perspective, emotion-attribution principles will be applied toward understanding the ways in which emotional dispositions of long standing (i.e., mood and temperament) may result in emotional responses to cues which are salient in a current situation. Considering all three levels of analysis, a diverse set of data and observations will be brought under the theoretical umbrella provided by emotion-attribution theory.

Because emotional experience forms a central part of human life, as human beings we already know a great deal about emotion. However, emotion theory and research has been a relatively neglected area within psychology until this current decade. The young state of emotion theory and research is such that to propose approaches which relate to the experience of emotion but which fail to take into account common human observations would be premature and sterile. With this in mind, to explain and verify the theoretical approaches presented herein, this chapter will present observations which will include some mix of unsystematic (nonlaboratory) observations and observations from controlled settings.

Some perspective on emotion-attribution principles may be gained by first considering other mammalian forms, and by considering examples of human emotional learning which appear to be independent of cognitively based emotion-attribution processes. As suggested by Seligman (1970), links between specific classes of stimuli and specific emotional responses are more easily formed by members of certain species than by members of other species. Consider a classical conditioning paradigm in which an organism of unknown species is repeatedly presented with a complex conditioned stimulus consisting of a colored light, a buzzer, the smell of a flower, and a touch on the back prior to receiving an unconditioned stimulus consisting of electric shock. Whether the trained organism will respond primarily to the prior visual, auditory, olfactory, or tactile stimuli with conditioned emotionality will depend, in part, upon innate predispositions common to members of the species under study. It seems to be the case that a species member learns most easily those relationships which are important for survival in its native environment (Hamburg, Hamburg, & Barchas, 1975). Similarly, for humans, rather automatic links exist for some emotion learning, as exemplified by the situation (borrowed from Seligman & Hager, 1972) in which a person becomes violently ill following the ingestion of an unusual food or beverage: The long-term emotional reaction of disgust to the food or beverage with the unusual taste frequently shows remarkable resistance to the knowledge that the illness was more properly attributed to a brief bout of stomach flu than to unfit food. Conversely, the person from whom the flu was contracted, the restaurant in which the food was consumed, the shape of the plates and forks, the color of the "sick room," and a host of other noticeable stimuli remain free from the conditioning of any disgust reaction from that episode. In this situation the correct attributions concerning the cause of the sickness (virus or bacteria) and of the associated emotional responses are neither effective in attenuating the conditioned emotional response to the wrong cause (the specific food), nor in substantially redirecting the emotional response towards the correct cause (the sick individual from whom the flu was contracted). The individual has made cognitive attributions about the cause of the emotional response, but the emotional association is remarkably immune to any apparent influence from that cognitive attributional knowledge.

Examples of "automatic" links (or classical conditioning) between certain stimuli and certain emotional responses are not limited to food tastes and the emotion of disgust. The resistance of some "phobias" to the cognitive knowledge that the experienced fear may be elicited by stimuli which are objectively benign provides a similar example of the occasional irrelevance of cognitive or "rational" processes to emotional functioning. If these episodes described typical human reactions to situations in which emotion learning took place, we would indeed be justified in seeing our emotional responses as the primitive mechanism which many early theorists considered them to be; the stage would be set for a model of human function which would pit our "rational" capacity, allowing us to see the true meaning and origin of our emotional responses, against our emotional selves, enslaved by primitive automatic mechanisms binding powerful emotional responses to irrelevant stimuli despite "higher" knowledge to the contrary.

Fortunately for the human condition, however, experience and research (including that presented below) suggest that relationships regarding emotional learning and responding are often far more complex than that. While processes which look like the classical conditioning of emotional responses to previously neutral stimuli (or elements) apparently do occur in humans, the developing human learns to interpose a highly refined cognitive analysis between complex external situations (with many potentially emotion-stimulating elements) and emotional reactions to those situations—a cognitive capability which allows, to some extent, the association of emotional reactions with those elements which are thought to evoke the emotional reaction. With the development of that cognitive ability, automatic emotional learning such as illustrated in the illness-disgust example is apparently very limited. Through such cognitive selection, referred to here as emotion attribution, the particular "previously neutral" stimulus which comes to evoke an emotional response is not identified exclusively on the basis of innate predisposition or simple spatial or temporal contiguity. Those factors may play a role, but they must be balanced against the individual's unique attributions about the causes and meanings of the emotional experience. The degree to which cognitive control influences emotional experience, as contrasted with the more "automatic" linking resembling classical conditioning, depends upon many factors which are discussed throughout this chapter. However, the complexity of many real-world human situations and other factors, discussed below, often make it quite difficult for the individual to accurately identify those specific elements within a situation which have evoked the emotional response. The cognitively guided attribution of emotional arousal to specific elements therefore has a potential for inaccuracy similar to the more primitive automatic emotional learning as exemplified in the illness-disgust example. Furthermore, once emotional learning has occurred, the subsequent elicitation of emotional arousal by the reoccurrence of the emotion-evoking elements will result in emotional experience which will be influenced by those previous causal attributions, and by current attributions about the causes and meaning of the emotional arousal in the current situation.

As an illustration of typical situational complexity, consider the individual who becomes involved in a new love affair. The situation has the potential to elicit emotional arousal associated with the intensity and the newness of the social or sexual contact; additional emotional arousal may result from concern over possible rejection, a recognition that some bungling may occur, and from other uncertainties about whether to apply attributional labels learned during earlier socialization (e.g., negative labels which would inhibit sexual contact). When the individual is relatively inexperienced in such situations, the total arousal due to these many elements may enhance an emotional experience and emotionally motivated behaviors consonant with only one of these causal elements if one element becomes strikingly salient. For example, if the individual dwells upon the affair being a violation of some important value, then the total emotional arousal will have different implications for his or her emotional feelings and behavior than would otherwise be the case. Through this example, one can see a modern approach to understanding Freud's dictum that many behaviors are determined by multiple motivations which are not all perceived to be causal, especially when the individual is acting under some emotional arousal. (The topical area of this example is not a random choice; I will present research at the end of this chapter elaborating this issue of attraction enhancement through increasing emotional arousal.)

The major thesis of emotion-attribution theory—that emotional experience is, in part, determined by attributions about the origins of emotional arousal—depends, therefore, on assumptions that the true sources of emotional arousal may not be immediately apparent (and/or acceptable) to the individual; these assumptions, in turn, depend upon the notion that most situations which are potential emotion elicitors for humans are social and therefore quite complex, and that emotional experience does not result exclusively from "external" stimuli. (This last point will be elaborated in a later section, below.) Some research approaches support the idea of the inherent complexity of many social situations and the resultant attributional complexity—and confusion—which may result. For example, in research designed to support discrete emotion theory, Izard (1972) demonstrated that many situations result in an emotional response containing several different emotional components. Izard's research subjects were asked to imagine situations or to remember real past situations, and to indicate the degree to which they experienced the various discrete emotions from Izard's list. Invariably, significant identification was made of several emotions which were thought to be present simultaneously. Using the emotion-attribution theory approach, my interpretation would rely upon the individual's ability—not always exercised—to perceive and attribute multiple causes for emotional arousal in a given situation, so that different emotion names (related to the different attributions made) would be applied to the resultant emotional experience when those names were made salient, as was the case in Izard's procedure.

EMOTION THEORY

There are many appropriate theories of emotion, for the process of an emotional experience has subsumed within it many processes, only some of which are relevant in this paper. My approach here to emotion theory—largely a synthesis of others' ideas—is developed in order to provide a larger theoretical context in which emotion-attribution theory may be placed, and in order to make apparent the relationship of emotion-attribution approaches to the broader realm of emotion theory and research; it will therefore emphasize a level of analysis compatible with emotion-attribution theory.

Four factors are normally considered when a theory of human emotion is developed: emotional experience, physiological arousal, expressive reactions, and emotion-related (or motivated) instrumental behaviors. Of those four factors, through a developmental perspective, I shall deal mostly with emotional experience and physiological arousal, and least with expressive reactions.

Initially, early in learning, when the individual enters apparently important situations requiring significant action, the required action is usually accompanied by and apparently motivated by very noticeable emotional arousal—that is, virtually all behaviors observable in the young infant are accompanied by expressions reflecting underlying emotional states of distress, interest, or enjoyment (see also Izard, 1979). Emotion and action are therefore early concomitants. Emotion motivates behavior directed toward the perceived (attributed) cause of the emotion; the behavior is usually devoted to approach or acquisition, avoidance or rejection, or modification (as sometimes with anger) of the instigating elements in the situation. The emotion-motivated actions, when successful, change the experience of emotion, usually reducing the initial emotional state, though other emotions may then develop, as when behavior motivated by interest or excitement leads to the successful completion of a task and subsequent joy (from Izard, 1979). Emotion is motivational in a dual sense. Not only are instrumental activities and expressive behaviors motivated by emotional arousal, but the individual is also motivated to continue focusing attention toward those elements in situations which apparently elicited the emotional response.[1] Following both Tomkins (1970) and Izard (Izard & Tomkins, 1966), I see emotion as the major motivational system in the human.

In a new situation in which the young individual must react, a motivating emotion is initially elicited because the individual's knowledge of what response to make and/or the individual's ability to make a desired response is uncertain or insufficient. Either uncertainty or insufficiency may necessitate an extended search for an appropriate action sequence to modify the individual's relation with the instigating stimuli. Motivation through the emotions increases the potential for continuation of both effort related to and attention toward the instigating stimuli (even though possibly remote), since the experience of emotion depends, in part, on feedback from the body of physiological changes which may "dissipate" slowly.

A prototype example of this initial process is seen in classical avoidance experiments with animals. When an avoidance response is required, but knowledge about the effectiveness of the response and/or the skill to achieve the response are not established, a great deal of fear is evident. As suggested by Solomon's two-factor avoidance theory (Solomon & Wynne, 1954), this fear becomes a major motivator for the avoidance behavior.

Several changes occur as the individual matures. Emotional versatility or differentiation develops. With emotional differentiation, both the character and the intensity of the action potentiated by various emotions differ. For example, the amount and vigor of gross behavior motivated by even moderate levels of anger and fear (largely sympathetic emotions) tends to be greater than that motivated by sentimentality (probably largely parasympathetic). I do not imply that the motivated instrumental and expressive behaviors are always elicited, for personal and cultural restrictions, as discussed below, are imposed early. With learning and development, the individual also learns what behavioral response to make and that

---

1. A partial explanation of how attention focus is maintained is suggested by the recent work of Isen, Shalker, Clark, & Karp (1978), which shows that affect-compatible cognitive content tends to follow from the manipulation of mood.

the response normally made is effective. As a result of the learning of an efficient specific response to the perceived need, the general physiological arousal is less necessary and is reduced or inhibited. To extend the example of avoidance learning, introduced above, as the organism becomes sophisticated there is an obvious reduction in fear during avoidance responding (Solomon & Wynne, 1954). The work of Epstein (1967) with sports parachutists, and the many observations of Solomon and Corbitt (1972) in support of "opponent process theory" suggest that this reduction in the motivating emotional state is accomplished with the aid of some active inhibitory process. In Epstein's research this observation is supported by the pattern given by experienced parachutists of first increasing, then decreasing arousal responses given to increasingly relevant (to skydiving) stimuli. Similarly, Solomon and Corbitt have described a process characterized by a strong emotion of opposite tone which develops after the withdrawal of a long-standing emotion-evoking stimulus; they conclude that suppression of emotion is accomplished through the establishment of an emotion of opposite affective tone, so that the secondary emotion appears with the withdrawal of the stimulus for the primary emotion.

When important situations are mastered with appropriate instrumental responses demanding limited effort and energy, emotional arousal during such instrumental responding is practically eliminated. On the other hand, there are circumstances in which some components of physiological arousal develop without the accompanying experience of emotion. That is, even though well learned, some instrumental responses require a significant amount of energy and effort for their performance. In such instances energy mobilization may be effected through sympathetic arousal with accompanying catecholamine responses (like the arousal of active emotional states), but the experience of emotion does not usually develop, for feedback from the body concerning the arousal is attributed to the ongoing instrumental activity. These two different circumstances, of arousal eliminated due to a well-learned low-activity response and of arousal present but not contributing to the experience of emotion, will be treated separately in the following two paragraphs.

Even though reduced, emotional arousal in the sophisticated individual may continue to play a significant motivational role, and when action is blocked, appropriate emotional arousal is often quickly re-evidenced (Solomon & Wynne, 1954). In a normal "civilized" society, such action blockage is frequent, as suggested by Tomkins in this volume (1979) in his discussion of "backed-up emotion." When blockage occurs, arousal responses, including hormonal changes may develop and linger (Mason, 1975; Frankenhaeuser, 1979) for short periods (measured in hours) until metabolic processes eliminate them, or for longer periods (measured in days) if the emotion-evoking stimulus remains a part of the individual's physical reality and/or mental preoccupation (depending upon defensive style, etc.). A similar relationship has been observed between expressive style and emotional arousal with children (Buck, 1977) and with adults (Lanzetta & Kleck, 1970). More emotional expressiveness was associated with lower physiological evidence of emotional arousal.

Consider the second case, of emotional experience reduced or eliminated in the face of instrumental activity characterized by high arousal levels. Like the arousal indicated by subjects after epinephrine injections in the Schachter and Singer studies (1962, reviewed below), and the hypnosis-induced arousal of Maslach's work (in press, reviewed below), however, such arousal may be capable of adding to the experience of emotion if one's perception of the surrounding situation is that emotion is appropriate. This attribution of arousal induced in other circumstances to emotion is likely only when the arousal of the nonemotional and emotional reactions are similar, when the action is blocked or its success uncertain, and when other conditions described below in the emotion-attribution theory section are fulfilled.

Although I will leave details of the nature of the physiological arousal of emotional states to others (e.g., Frankenhaeuser, in this volume), in broad outline arousal characteristic of action-instigating emotion often involves both the sympathetic branch of the autonomic nervous system, with the subsequent release of the catecholamines of the adrenal medulla, and pituitary stimulation, with the subsequent involvement of the hormones of the adrenal cortex. The arousal of action-inhibiting emotional states such as sadness, contentment, etc., is probably better characterized by parasympathetic dominance, though the details are uncertain. The expressive responses which are also stimulated, including largely the muscles of the face, provide an additional source of short-term feedback—an issue discussed more fully below.

This approach to a theory of emotion not only fits the observation of decreases in intensity of emotional responses in situations where instrumental responses are well learned, but accounts also for the reduction in frequency and intensity of both positive and negative emotional experience which is associated with development into adulthood. Insofar as growing intelligence leads to appropriate and confidently executed instrumental responses in important encounters, emotional experiences should be attenuated by intellectual development. However, insofar as that intelligence leads to the creation or the selection of situations composed of new elements or of high complexity (so that confident and effective instrumental responses become less likely), emotional responses would increase in frequency and intensity.

EMOTION-ATTRIBUTION THEORY

This section, comprising much of the remainder of this chapter, will be divided into three subsections. The first will deal with the general principles and assumptions which are basic to my approach to emotion-attribution theory. The second will present an abbreviated outline of important factors which influence attributions about emotional arousal. The third will elaborate the outline of subsection two, sifting through a diverse psychological literature in search of supporting evidence for the outlined principles.

A brief clarification is required concerning the meaning of the constructs of "element" and "situation" as they are used in this chapter. An element is any stimulus which an individual could potentially regard as having caused an emotional response so that emotional arousal could be attributed to that element. An element could therefore be as general as the "ambiance" which is felt in a situation, or as specific as another person or the smashing of one's thumb with a hammer.

The term "situation" is used in a manner similar to its conventional use. A situation becomes a new situation when old elements are perceived to be lost or new elements are perceived to be present (as a result of the individual moving, the elements changing, or of changed perceptions of the array of elements).

Issues and Assumptions of Emotion-Attribution Theory

In order to develop a coherent approach to emotion-attribution theory, it is necessary first of all to examine the major assumptions which underlie that theory. The first assumption is that the arousal underlying emotional experience may be properly understood as at least somewhat amorphous and general, rather than unique to specific or discrete emotional states; an analysis of the evidence relating to that issue also leads to a consideration of the relative validity of discrete versus dimensional approaches to emotion. A second assumption of my approach to emotion-attribution theory relates to the relative importance of feedback from physiological arousal of the body. A related secondary issue concerns the relative importance of feedback from the body in general, rather than from only the face. As will become apparent from the following material, these issues are difficult to separate, since research evidence which relates to one is usually relevant to the others.

While it is true that some early attempts to test the general and amorphous nature of emotional arousal by inducing emotional states through epinephrine injections resulted only in subjects reporting that they felt "as if" they had experienced emotion (Maranon, 1924; Landis & Hunt, 1932), even in these early studies it was recognized that some subjects who had current emotion-relevant concerns experienced heightened—and appropriate—emotions under the epinephrine-arousal conditions. More recently, the often-cited research by Schachter and Singer (1962) lent support to the amorphous-arousal hypothesis. Schachter and Singer provided subjects with emotion-relevant environmental elements in the form of a confederate who acted angry or euphoric. They hypothesized that epinephrine-induced arousal would lead to more behavioral evidence of anger or euphoria, providing the subject had no prior knowledge of the arousal effects of the epinephrine. Indeed, subjects in the conditions described above did respond with more behavioral evidence of anger when confronted with an angry confederate, and more behavioral evidence of enjoyment in response to a euphoric confederate than did subjects who either knew of the expected arousal effects from their epinephrine injection or who were in a placebo control condition. Schachter and Wheeler (1962) subsequently demonstrated that subjects sustaining epinephrine-induced arousal would show increased behavior indicative of humor in response to a funny movie, compared to a group of subjects tranquilized with chloropromazine. Those two studies were widely accepted and cited as evidence that it is appropriate to think of the total emotional experience as consisting of two elements—general emotional arousal and cognitive labeling of that arousal induced by current environmental cues.

However, recent research and re-analyses indicate that the evidence provided by the two Schachter studies may not be as strong as previously supposed. Marshall and Zimbardo (in press) attempted and failed to replicate that part of the Schachter and Singer research which presented a euphoric confederate to the research subjects. Furthermore, when Marshall and Zimbardo increased the epinephrine dosage for some subjects beyond that given in the Schachter and Singer research, those subjects reported increased negative emotional reactions rather than the positive euphoria reported in the earlier study. In an exciting variation on the epinephrine-injection paradigm, Maslach (in press) attempted to replicate (with modifications) both the euphoric and angry conditions of the Schachter and Singer research using arousal induced by hypnosis. In a study unique in its thoroughness of manipulation checks, Maslach convincingly demonstrated both arousal and amnesia from the previously induced posthypnotic arousal suggestion. In the angry-confederate condition, the hypnotized and aroused subjects evidenced significantly increased negative emotion (compared to a hypnotized but unaroused control group). However, the impact of arousal in the euphoria conditions was also to induce negative mood, suggesting that arousal of the type induced (suggestions about heart rate, breathing rate, skin flushing, etc.) may have more of a negative than neutral quality. Coupled with analyses which show the effects in the original Schachter research to be very weak (e.g., in Schachter & Wheeler, only the tranquilized group differs from the placebo control in behavioral evidence of enjoyment) and to be dependent upon selective comparisons between groups, it must be acknowledged that evidence from the Schachter research for the general nature of epinephrine-induced arousal is uncertain. This uncertainty must be extended to those theoretical approaches which depend heavily upon a concept of undifferentiated amorphous arousal, such as Mandler's (1962) "Juke Box" theory and Schachter's emotion-attribution approach (Schachter & Singer, 1962; Schachter & Latané, 1964; Schachter, 1971). (In Mandler's version, emotional arousal is seen as comparable to putting the coin in the juke box; attribution processes are compared to the pushing of the buttons which designate the specific record to be played after arousal is achieved.) However, while these criticisms may be interpreted as indicating less evidence for an amorphous arousal approach, no strong contradictory evidence is available to refute the more supportable hypothesis that naturally induced arousal which is sustained in one situation might contribute to some other emotional states as the individual moves between situations, depending upon the nature of the arousal and the changing attributions the individual makes about the causes of the emotional arousal.

Between the approach of Mandler and Schachter, suggesting the almost completely amorphous nature of emotional arousal, and those approaches exemplified by some of the work of Tomkins (1975), Izard (1971), and Schwartz (Note 1), suggesting specific physiological response patterning (such as with facial muscles) in response to specific emotional states, there is an apparent middle ground. There are components of arousal which are similar in those emotional states which involve the stimulation of the sympathetic nervous system; emotions associated with sympathetic arousal may be either positive (e.g., excitement) or negative (e.g., fear and anger), but they are states in which an increase in activity and energy is sustained. However, there are also apparent differences in components between such emotional states—differences involving not only facial patterning and expressive responses, but also physiological patterning at the level of hormonal response (e.g., Schwartz, Note 1). Although the older research on such between-emotion differences—such as Funkenstein's (1955) observations of different epinephrine to norepinephrine ratios in anger and fear—has not been consistently replicated, approaches such as those of Mason (1975) and Frankenhaeuser (1979) with modern hormone assay techniques promise more effectiveness in demonstrating different patterns of hormones in response to different emotional stimuli and between such nonemotional stimuli as cold, exercise, heat, etc.

The relevance of these considerations is that when emotional arousal is maintained through different situations, certain misattributions about that emotional arousal are more likely to occur than others, depending upon the similarity of the pattern of arousal of the different emotional states. For example, the ease with which fear and interest seem to alternate and to contribute to each other has long been noted (e.g., Hebb, 1946); both emotions have clear sympathetic arousal components. On the other hand, anger (with largely sympathetic arousal) and sadness or depression (with a lack of sympathetic arousal) are emotional opposites, as indicated by both hormonal and behavioral evidence. Thus norepinephrine, although plentiful in anger, is deficient in depressive states; antidepressant drugs usually directly or indirectly stimulate its production. Similarly, purposeful anger induction is frequently used as an antidote to depression by both lay persons and therapists.

A related issue relevant to emotion-attribution theory concerns whether human emotions should be thought of as discrete entities or as composed of broad underlying dimensions of arousal. (An excellent review of this issue is found in Izard, 1971.) Discrete emotion theorists such as Izard (1971), Tomkins (1979), and Plutchik (1962) emphasize a finite number (usually eight or nine) discrete emotional states, often including anger, fear, disgust, interest, joy, contempt, distress, and shame (guilt). Dimensional theorists such as Lindsley (1970), Davitz (1970), and Russell and Mehrabian (1977) focus instead upon a more limited number of underlying dimensions of arousal, usually including pleasantness, potency or direction of activity, and activation level. The resolution of this issue depends upon the observation that both approaches are valid for some issues.

A close analogy exists in issues concerning verbal meaning. Just as it is apparent that both denotative and connotative meanings exist in words, implying both discrete specificity of meaning in the former case and a minimum of underlying dimensions of meaning in the latter (remarkably like those typically identified by dimensional emotion theorists—pleasantness, potency, and activity), both discrete and dimensional approaches are applicable to the study and conceptualization of emotion, with each approach having a point of focus and range of convenience (Kelly, 1955) depending upon the specific problem at issue. Emotion-attribution theory depends upon both views. While on the one hand the concept of underlying dimensions of arousal is critical to this view, on the other hand the attributions which individuals make about the causes of their emotional arousal usually result in discrete emotion labels being applied.

Consideration of the issue concerning the importance of arousal feedback to emotional experience leads directly back to the James-Lange theory of emotion, a theory which has aroused a great deal of interest in the last decade (e.g., Fehr & Stern, 1970). Reasonable direct evidence concerning the impact of feedback from the body in emotional experience is derivable from three sources—the research with spinal cord accident victims by Hohmann (1966), recent research with drugs which serve as "beta blockers," and research demonstrating central nervous system effects from hormones which originate peripherally but which cross the blood/brain barrier. Less direct but significant supporting evidence is provided by many of the emotion/attribution studies which are mentioned throughout this chapter.

In Hohmann's (1966) research with spinal accident victims, their self-reports clearly indicated very significant post-injury *reduction* in their experience of anger and fear, with this reduction correspond-ing directly with the height of the spinal cord injury—good evidence that the experience of those emotions depends upon feedback from arousal induced by the sympathetic branch of the autonomic ner-vous system. Sympathetic nerve trunks leave the spine at regular intervals down most of its length; therefore the higher the spinal injury, the less sympathetic activation would occur in the body in response to situations which would normally evoke sympathetic arousal. On the other hand, the emotion Hohmann labelled "senti-mentality" was heightened following the spinal cord accident. It may well be that this increase was due to parasympathetic domi-nance in sentimentality: A major parasympathetic nerve trunk (the vagus nerve) leaves the human spine very high in the cranial area, where spinal injury with survival is not likely; nerves descend lower into the viscera from that trunk in paths far removed from the spine, the only exception being a lesser nerve trunk from the sacral area of the spine to the genitalia, rectum, and bladder. In emotional states which may normally be associated with parasympathetic rather than sympathetic arousal, parasympathetic exaggeration is likely to result when the balance from the (somewhat) antagonistic sympa-thetic system is reduced. Whether this specific interpretation con-cerning sympathetic and parasympathetic balance is correct or not, Hohmann's observations of both the decreases in fear and anger and the increases in sentimentality support the hypothesis that arousal and arousal feedback are important in the experience of emotion.

In her discussion of the impact of environmental stressors on the level of the catecholamines in the body, Frankenhaeuser (1975, 1979) has critically reviewed the literature relating to the impact of beta blockers on emotional experience. The beta blockers prevent some neurons in the sympathetic nervous system from responding to their normal neural transmitter substance, norepinephrine, thereby substantially reducing the capability of the body to sustain sym-pathetic arousal. Frankenhaeuser concludes that basal anxiety levels are reduced in clinically healthy subjects with the infusion of such beta blockers as propranolol. Although it cannot be definitely ascertained that this effect is due to peripheral arousal reduction rather than to some unspecified central nervous system effect, the general finding of the impact of beta blockers on emotional experience is supportive of the hypothesis that arousal in the body and feedback from that arousal play a key role in emotional experience.

Several hormones which are generated peripherally during emotional arousal have an impact upon the central nervous system functioning after crossing the blood/brain barrier. For example, epinephrine acts directly upon the reticular formation and the hypothalamus (Frankenhaeuser, 1975). Hamburg, Hamburg, and Barchas (1975) have recently reviewed evidence that cortisol crosses the blood/brain barrier and influences brain function in both lower animals and humans. Similar effects have been noted for progesterone. These data provide clear evidence of the impact of peripheral physiological arousal on brain functioning—evidence which strongly suggests experiential changes from such arousal.

Even when the hypothesis that feedback from the body plays a significant role in emotional experience is accepted, however, there is sometimes disagreement concerning the importance of various body areas as sources of arousal feedback. Is feedback from the sympathetic arousal of the viscera in general or from the cardiovascular system specifically more important? Is the somatic system of skeletal muscles the source of the most important feedback, or more specifically, does feedback from certain muscles of the face account for the enhancement of emotional experience? The long-standing theoretical emphasis of Tomkins (1975, 1979) and of Izard (1971, 1979) concerning the importance of the face in emotional experience has been reiterated in their respective chapters in this volume. However, both acknowledge a lesser role for feedback from other body areas. Izard (1979) suggests that "emotion experience is activated by sensory feedback from the face. Once an emotion is activated, however, it typically recruits the autonomic nervous system and the physiological systems it innervates. Subsequent hormones and neurohumors influence biochemical processes that play a role in mobilizing energy and maintaining emotions over time" (p. 168) Tomkins (1975) has suggested that some people control all facial muscles; such an individual is "restricted to the feedback of his vascular facial responses and to the feedback of his deeper organs such as the stomach for his awareness of his own affective responses." Concerning facial feedback, there is now substantial direct evidence that feedback from facial muscles (or from skin sensations resulting from facial-muscle activity) does play a significant role in the experience of emotion (Laird, 1974; Lanzetta, Cartwright-Smith, & Kleck, 1976; Konecni, Note 2; Lanzetta, Note 3).

Both muscular and skin changes in the face during emotional experience seem to be of relatively short duration; however, many of the issues which are discussed in this chapter involve the carryover of emotional arousal across a significant time span and between emotion-evoking situations. Therefore, although feedback from the face may play a role when short-term emotion-attribution opportunities arise, a major need for many of the arguments and examples of this chapter is to establish the importance of feedback which has a long-term potential to influence emotional experience. Since no studies have been published which contrast the impact of facial versus general bodily arousal in emotional experience across different time periods, the discussion below must rely upon an analysis of a literature not specifically constructed to address this issue. To support the thesis of long-term arousal effects, the most likely area in which to search is the system mediated by the hormones of the sympathetic-adrenal medullary system (such as the catecholamines epinephrine and norepinephrine), and those of the pituitary-adrenal cortical axis (Frankenhaeuser, 1979). To illustrate the durability of such hormonal responses, in her chapter in this volume Frankenhaeuser (1979) has shown that catecholamine levels may remain elevated for the remainder of the waking day (throughout the evening) following overtime work by women employees, and that the peak of such responses corresponds with the total time (in weeks) during which overtime work had been required, rather than with the specific days on which the most work was required. Mason (1975) has demonstrated similar long-term hormonal reactions following emotional situations; he presents several human examples of three-day elevations of 17-hydroxycorticosteriod (hereafter 17-OHCS), epinephrine, and norepinephrine following emotion-evoking events, and one example of the elevation of norepinephrine for six days in a group of rhesus monkeys following an avoidance conditioning task. (Mason suggests that the human tension pattern evident in those examples would be likely to result in repressed anger, with little or no overt expression of anger and "little if any subjective awareness of anger or distress," p. 168.)

The evidence cited above concerning Hohmann's spinal accident victims, the research cited by Frankenhaeuser on beta blockers, and the work of Landis and Hunt (1932), Maranon (1924), and Schachter and Singer (1962) with injected epinephrine, and of Maslach (in press) with hypnosis suggest very strongly that a significant component of the experience of emotion is gained via feedback from areas of the body other than the face. Furthermore, it is apparent that such feedback could continue over a relatively long time span, extending potentially several days in extreme cases, allowing feedback to occur in a variety of different emotion-evoking situations.

The theoretical compromise presented here takes into account evidence of the importance of feedback from both facial (short-term) and hormonal (long-term) arousal. Whereas in the abstract the relative importance of feedback from facial versus peripheral (non-facial) areas is difficult to establish, it is expected that the importance of facial feedback will be demonstrated most easily when short-term emotional experience is at issue, while feedback from hormonal arousal will be most important when emotional experiences of longer duration are considered.

No matter how impressed one becomes with the importance of arousal feedback, the somewhat general nature of the arousal underlying different emotional states, and the other lesser tenets of emotion-attribution theory, some discomfort undoubtedly lingers from the realization that the approach seems to depend upon emotional arousal first, with a meaning analysis consisting of attributions about the cause of the arousal following. Indeed, if one attempts to abstract the basic principles from the major writings in this area, of Schachter (1971) and Mandler (1962, 1975), there appear to be two basic principles: first, that arousal which is experienced with no ready explanation for its existence will elicit a cognitive or perceptual search for its cause; and second, that once an attribution about the cause of the arousal has been made, the experience which follows will appropriately correspond with that attribution. Nothing is said about the origin of the initial arousal. Some modern critics of this approach (e.g., Averill, in press) have seen this as a most significant weakness, criticizing early theorists for failing to indicate how arousal was initiated.

There are a number of ways in which one can respond to this criticism. The first involves one's view of emotion: The primary reason for perceiving that a difficulty exists is that emotion is typically regarded as a reaction to external stimulation, or our cognitive representation of situations. This view leads to the conclusion that the individual must be almost simultaneously aware of the obvious external causal elements and of the arousal itself. On the other hand, "drives" and "motive states" such as hunger and need for achievement are usually understood as resulting from changes in states *within* the individual. However, as suggested by Bindra (1970), a continuum exists between "external" emotional states and "internal" drive or motive states, with no emotion completely externally determined and no drive or motive state completely internally determined. Arousal with the potential to contribute to a variety of emotional experiences may be due to stress from sleep deprivation, previous emotional states, menstrual or diurnal hormonal fluctuation, nutritional changes, exposure to cold, exercise, and a great variety of other sources properly characterized as being at least somewhat internal. Arousal induced by such internal sources may then be attributed to elements in a new situation, and may contribute to the experience of emotion. Of course, the arousal carried into the new situation may be arousal with some degree of specific feeling tone, rather than a general or neutral arousal as suggested by early emotion-attribution theory. (Considering the supposed internality of motive and drive states, on the other hand, exciting work by Schachter and his colleagues [Schachter, 1971] has amply demonstrated the considerable influence of external cues on the subjective experience of the "internal" drive state of hunger, especially for individuals with weight control problems.)

There are other approaches to the issue of "where the arousal comes from." As discussed above, human social situations are often so complex that unknown or unacknowledged elements in the situation elicit emotional responses. Additionally, when we consider that personal, social, and cultural demands (as discussed below) prescribe and proscribe what are appropriate emotion-evoking cues in many situations and similarly even what are appropriate emotional experiences, it is easy to appreciate that we will be motivated to acknowledge or not acknowledge certain elements as causal of emotion, and to experience or not experience certain emotional responses as acceptable. Once an emotional reaction is begun, other sources of misattribution include the influence of others who may act as socializing agents, therapists, teachers, etc.

Before outlining emotion-attribution principles in detail, it will be useful to consider what emotion-attribution theory is not. It is not an approach which is useful in the consideration of each event of human emotional experience. In even complex situations, the individual may identify and appropriately react to those salient elements responsible for the experienced emotional arousal, so that no attributional processes worthy of concern or analysis occur. Additionally, some social situations are sufficiently simple, and some individuals sufficiently sophisticated, so that although the opportunity for misattribution may be obviously available, none of significance occurs. Finally, even when misattribution occurs, either within or between situations, emotion-attribution theory provides only one of many potentially interesting levels of analysis.

Consider, for example, the system of cognitive appraisal developed by Lazarus and his colleagues (Lazarus, 1966, 1969)—a system of sufficient similarity to that outlined herein that some confusion over differences may arise. Lazarus's system relates to aspects of the emotion-experience sequence different from those at issue in emotion-attribution theory, focusing on the way in which cognitive appraisals of the situation and appraisals of one's capacity and options to respond to the situation lead to differences in the intensity of emotional experience. In that system it is assumed that the individual is correctly aware of what elements have inspired an emotional response, with the emotional experience appropriately corresponding to that knowledge. The paradigm used by Lazarus and his colleagues to explore those relationships often presented an element which would evoke an emotional response, such as a film of a bloody operation, and knowledge about the meaning of the element, such as that the operation leads to positive satisfaction for the individual sustaining it. A major interest at this level of "primary appraisal" involves how that initial information influences the individual's level of physiological responding and level of emotional experience. Contrast this emphasis with that of emotion-attribution theory, which relates to the issue of how a constant level of emotional arousal leads to different quantitative and qualitative experience, depending upon the elements in the situation to which the arousal is attributed. A secondary appraisal level in Lazarus's system relates to the question of how different appraisals of available behavioral options influence the intensity of the emotional response. Emotion-attribution theory also relates to the issue of how potential behaviors influence emotional experience, but this concern forms a starting point in a subsequent analysis of how such appraisals affect attributions about the source of emotional arousal and the quality of subsequent emotional experience. The difference between these two approaches is largely one of focus. Lazarus's emphasis on stressors and stress reactions, tends to limit the range of experimental situations explored and to direct dependent measure analysis to the intensity (rather than the quality) of the responses. Secondly, he sees emotions and emotional arousal as responses, rather than using them also as stimulus elements in dynamic processes. Whichever approach is optimal for understanding a given emotional event, Lazarus (1975) eloquently states the result of these approaches: When cognition is introduced into our thinking about emotional processes, "regulation then becomes self-regulation (p. 49)."

Outline of emotion-attribution principles

Emotion-attribution principles will be presented briefly in this section, with supporting discussion and data reserved for the following section. This is not meant to be an exhaustive list of all important or possible propositions, but is instead a beginning systematization of research and theory in the emotion-attribution area. Similarly, the research examples chosen do not represent an exhaustive review of all emotion-attribution research.

The following interplay of arousal, elements, and situations are of primary interest. Arousal developed within one situation may be misattributed to an element which did not stimulate the emotional response. Or, arousal induced in one situation (and correctly or incorrectly attributed to various elements within that situation) may be carried into another situation to influence the emotional response to an element in the second situation. Finally, arousal induced by circumstances irrelevant to emotion (e.g., exercise, temperature adaptation) may contribute to emotional experience.

Although the above division into three different patterns of emotion attribution is arbitrary, various observations and research series do seem to fall naturally into these three categories. It is, however, the middle case, involving emotion-misattribution as a result of changes between different psychological situations, which will be prototypical for this section of the chapter. In the following outline, emotion-attribution principles are usually couched in language which applies most naturally to that middle circumstance, but these principles can be extended into the other realms as well.

A. The principles of this first section relate to properties of elements or to relationships between elements or situations. Factors included in this section relate to the relative salience of the perceived emotion-causing elements or to special qualities of elements which have emotion-influencing properties. There are many levels of analysis to which this principle may be applied. For example, the maleness or femaleness of a stimulus individual will influence greatly what emotional states other individuals are likely to attribute to the presence of the stimulus individual.

1. Simpler dimensions such as element simplicity, tangibility, or concreteness also play a role, with attributions about emotional arousal more likely to be made to the more tangible or concrete elements in a situation (assuming those elements are equal in other relevant qualities to more complex elements).

2. The degree to which there is a perceived division between situations will negatively influence the likelihood of misattribution from arousal carried between situations. Interruption by arousal-influencing factors such as meditation, exercise, sleep, etc., will be particularly relevant.

3. As a special but important case of A2, above, when two situations are separated by a span of time, the longer the intervening interval, the less likely is arousal carryover between the situations and therefore the less likely are emotion misattributions of arousal from the first situation to elements within the second situation.

4. Emotion attributions are influenced by both the purposeful and the inadvertent guidance of other individuals.

B. The principles of this section relate to differences between perceiving individuals, or to factors within individuals which dispose the attribution of emotion to certain elements rather than others.

1. Cultural influences determine that certain emotional experiences, expressive behaviors, and instrumental behaviors are acceptable within certain situations while others are not. Those influences affect emotion attributions.

2. Certain roles carry with them a definition of the range of acceptable emotional experiences, expressions, and instrumental behaviors. Specific roles therefore differentially influence emotion-attribution processes.

3. Different personality or temperament types dispose different types of emotional experience, expression, and instrumental behaviors. Just as with those expectations associated with culture, socioeconomic status, and role, personality as expressed in temperament exerts an influence on emotion-attribution processes.

a. Different levels of prior experience between different emotional states will lead to different types of attributional errors within the same individual, and between individuals.

b. The defensive style of the individual will bias emotion-attribution processes.

C. The principles of this section relate to the quality and quantity of arousal experienced by the perceiving individual.

1. The amount of arousal has an impact upon emotion-attribution processes such that very high arousal is usually more difficult to misattribute, or to accurately attribute in an articulate manner.

2. The quality or pattern of arousal will influence the likelihood of misattribution to elements which induce qualitative changes in emotional experience. Misattribution of ongoing arousal will be potentiated when new elements in a situation induce an emotional experience characterized by an arousal pattern similar to the ongoing arousal.

Elaborations of emotion-attribution principles

This subsection is meant to be the heart of the chapter; I will elaborate most extensively those principles which have not been detailed previously in the literature.

A1. The most obvious interpretation of proposition A1, concerning element simplicity, is that appropriate elements must usually be present in a situation in order for current emotional arousal to be attributed to them. The earliest and most basic studies in the emotion-attribution area were successful apparently because the manipulated elements to which some emotional arousal could be attributed were presented in a simple and salient style. The following series of studies is presented here to illustrate this principle, and to provide the background for further discussion of other principles illustrated by the studies.

In a study of shock tolerance, Nisbett and Schachter (1966) administered placebo pills, giving half the subjects the expectation that the pills might induce side effects relevant to emotional arousal including faster heart rate, facial flushing, stomach butterflies, and muscle tension; control-condition subjects received information about benign (not arousal-relevant) side effects. Additionally, subjects were induced to experience either high fear of the electric shock or low fear. While the placebo manipulation did not affect subjects' abilities to feel the shock, the upper limit of shock tolerance by the subjects was significantly higher (three times the shock in amps) in those subjects who could attribute their shock-induced arousal to their placebo pills; this predicted finding held only for the low fear (of shock) condition subjects, however. (This study has been successfully replicated with modifications at least once—Nelsen, 1971.)

In a modification of the Nisbett and Schachter paradigm, I investigated the question of whether arousal induced by temptation to cheat on an exam would have less impact upon resistance to temptation if it could be attributed instead to a placebo pill. Recruited for a study on the impact of a drug on visual perception, freshmen college students were given their placebo with the expectation of either arousal or benign side effects. During a subsequent "delay" period, subjects took a vocabulary test supposedly indicative of their "future college performance" and were subjected to the autokinetic illusion which was attributed to the drug in order to validate both the visual perception cover story and the potency of the drug.

After being told to expect the onset of drug "side effects" shortly, subjects were given an opportunity to cheat on the vocabulary test in order to avoid an appointment with "the board of psychologists developing the vocabulary test" who were supposedly interested in talking with college students who evidenced "subnormal" vocabularies. It was hypothesized that all subjects would be somewhat tempted to cheat, and that the consideration of that possible course of action and the potential negative consequences would lead to emotional arousal; those students who could attribute their arousal to the placebo, in the arousal side effect condition, would be freed from the inhibition induced by that arousal and would cheat more. This hypothesis was validated in the original study with twice as many cheating in the arousal-placebo condition (Dienstbier & Munter, 1971); with modifications subsequent research has replicated these findings (Dienstbier, 1972).

A second paradigm demonstrating remarkable success with a very simple attributional manipulation was that of Ross, Rodin, and Zimbardo (1969). Subjects were told that they must make choices between receiving a reward (for solving a green puzzle) and risking a punishment from electric shock (for not solving a red puzzle) under conditions of distraction (a loud noise). Half the subjects were told to anticipate arousal side effects from the loud noise played during the puzzle-working period, while half were told to anticipate benign side effects. Those subjects who anticipated arousal from the noise apparently attributed some of their fear of shock to the noise, since they worked more on the solution to the (unsolvable) reward puzzle than the (equally unsolvable) punishment puzzle (compared to the benign placebo group). This study, too, has been replicated with extensions (Calvert-Boyanowsky & Leventhal, 1975); since that replicating study presented alternative interpretations to those of emotion-attribution, it will be discussed extensively in the final section of the chapter.

In order to verify the importance of element simplicity (or even the importance of element presence), one needs to demonstrate more than that emotion attribution seems facilitated by the presence of a simple element such as the placebo pill or noise of the procedures reviewed above. A more convincing demonstration would involve a similar procedure, but with manipulation of the presence or absence of that simple element. This control was effected in a variation of the placebo-pill cheating study described above. In the "control condition" the subjects were told they were control subjects in a drug study, and that although they would not receive any pill, they were to "look into themselves" at the same times that the "real" subjects might be experiencing the expected symptoms from the pill (Dienstbier, 1972). Half of the subjects were told of arousal side effects, and half told of benign side effects. Merely attending to the arousal or benign symptoms in the "control" conditions without the pill (in order to rate the presence of those symptoms) had *no* effect on cheating rates, but the cheating pattern of those conditions was significantly different from that of the placebo pill subjects. (In the replication conditions, arousal-condition subjects cheated significantly more than benign-condition subjects.)

A further demonstration of the role of salience relates to two contrasting findings in research on the impact of emotional arousal associated with menstruation. Rodin (1976) conducted a study in which premenstrual or menstrual symptomatology was made very salient for some of her premenstrual or menstrual subjects. (For simplicity, both the terms premenstrual and menstrual will be subsumed in the term "premenstrual" below.) In a tension-evoking study, those premenstrual women who were high in premenstrual symptomatology performed better on several tasks usually adversely affected by emotional arousal, compared with either midcycle women or premenstrual women who were low in symptomatology. The high-symptom premenstrual women also indicated less fear of shock. Apparently emotional arousal evoked by the experimental situation was attributed (in part) by the high-symptomatology premenstrual women to their premenstrual state, reducing the negative impact of that arousal on performance and on fear of shock.

A second approach, developed by Englander-Golden (Englander-Golden, Willis, & Dienstbier, 1977), studied the degree to which women at various points in their menstrual cycles attributed interpersonal pressure tactics to actors presented in videotaped vignettes. Premenstrual symptomatology and associated emotional arousal were not made salient; subjects had no idea that this variable was known to or of interest to the researchers. It was the premenstrual women who perceived the most interpersonal pressure, apparently attributing some of the emotional tension of their premenstrual state to the action presented in the videotaped vignettes.

These two studies present a striking contrast in that arousal was attributed from the external situation to the salient premenstrual element in the Rodin study, but from the *un*salient premenstrual element to the external element in the Englander-Golden et al. study. Although there are obviously many differences between the approaches used by Rodin and by Englander-Golden et al., those results are most parsimoniously explained on the basis of the intended difference in salience of premenstrual arousal as manipulated in the two studies.

Consider the next issue of element salience as achieved through element tangibility. An excellent recent review by Condry (1977) of the research on the issue of "overjustification" suggests that the evidence is very strong that unnecessary tangible reinforcers given for task performance normally reduce the quality of task performance, liking for the task, and willingness to reengage the task in the future. Even in token economies in which reinforcers are gradually phased out, performance typically returns to baseline. To understand this lack of effectiveness for stimulating long-term motivation by tangible reinforcers, I shall begin with Izard's analysis in this volume (1979) of behaviors which are motivated by the emotion of interest. According to that analysis, the successful pursuit of interesting behaviors leads to an emotional end result of joy. I have suggested previously (Dienstbier et al., 1975) that if a new and simple element (the tangible reinforcement) is introduced, it is possible that the individual will attribute a substantial part of the experienced enjoyment to that new element. In the future when no reward is offered, reduced expectations of joy will follow. Those reduced expectations will become self-fulfilling so that less pursuit of the instrumental behavior (when the behavior is independent of expected reinforcement) will occur. A number of excellent studies have been developed in the last several years to demonstrate this "overjustification" effect, beginning notably with those by Kruglanski, Alon, and Lewis (1972) and by Lepper, Greene, and Nisbett (1973); the one which best demonstrates my interpretation of the overjustification phenomenon in emotion-attribution terms is the Kruglanski et al. study. After winning a contest, a group of junior high game winners were told that "as promised," they would receive a prize for winning. In fact, subjects had received no prior (to performing and winning) information about any prize. Those winning subjects who received a tangible plastic puzzle rated their enjoyment of the games they had won lower than did those winners who received no reinforcement for their performance. According to my emotion-attribution interpretation, some of the enjoyment from the total situation was apparently attributed to the tangible reinforcer.

At least one set of findings which are difficult to explain with "conventional" approaches to overjustification can be understood through an emotion-attribution approach. The dilemma is highlighted in Condry's (1977) review. He notes that in several studies the granting of rewards to subjects who were initially *low* in interest in the task subsequently increased their task interest (Lepper et al., 1973; Greene, 1974). Additionally, Calder and Staw (1975) found that for low-interest tasks, rewards increased interest, and that the usual finding of rewards decreasing interest in initially interesting tasks also held. Overjustification theory has difficulty with this issue since when strictly cognitive approaches are used, external motivation (reward induced) of *any* task should lead to *less* interest in performing the task; according to that approach the new information about external motivation is always taken into account. Using the emotion-attribution approach, however, I would predict that when the reinforcer elicits positive affect but the low-interest task does not, the positive emotional response due to the reinforcer may be partially misattributed to the task. This emotion-misattribution effect would depend upon the relative salience (as well as the relative affective value) of the task and the reward. That is, a reward given unexpectedly with the completion of a task is not as salient an element as reward promised prior to task initiation. In the later circumstances, reward salience is enhanced by its symbolic presence during the task (in addition to its later appearance). According to Condry's review, it was only under conditions of *unexpected* reward (low reward salience) that the effect of reward increasing task interest was noted; my interpretation would suggest that affect elicited by reward would be most likely to be misattributed to the task under such circumstances.

However, certain forms of *non*tangible reinforcement seem to encourage future interest in and motivation toward instrumental tasks, independent of the expectation of future reinforcement of any kind. An emotion-attribution interpretation is based on the observation that such reinforcers usually take the various forms of attention, demonstrated pleasure at a child's accomplishments, and verbalizations such as "you did very well" or "I like that very much." Such reinforcements are not only nontangible, drawing little attention to themselves, but they are often designed to draw the child's attention back to the pleasure or joy of the instrumental activity, so that the positive emotional arousal induced by the nontangible reinforcement may be easily misattributed to the instrumental task.

Of course the "overjustification" literature should have presented no problems or startling findings for conscientious social psychologists, for various studies within the venerable literature on achievement motivation (notably Winterbottom, 1958) had convincingly established that tangible rewards tended to be associated with children low in need for achievement, while the use of nontangible rewards and the high use of affection and attention were positively associated with achievement motivation.

With respect to punishments, a similar analysis holds. Even though a certain behavior may be forbidden, its performance may lead to positive emotions, at least until an authority figure attempts to reverse these emotions. Based on an emotion-attribution approach, the most effective procedure for an authority figure to follow would be to cause the child to attribute negative emotions to the forbidden behavior. Simple and salient punishments will not usually accomplish this goal, for the negative emotional state which such punishments induce is easily attributed to those punishments, rather than to the instrumental behavior. A slap in the face, for example, is simple and as nearly psychologically "tangible" as being assigned to "time out" or made to give up a prized possession. Consider the emotion-attribution differences if, instead, the socialization agent explained to the child why the activity was wrong, explained who was hurt by the child's acts, labeled the child's behavior as worthy of negative affect (e.g., "that behavior was bad") or indicated that the child is worthy of negative labeling as long as the child is identified with such behavior (e.g., "you are bad for hurting the puppy"). In these instances, the misattribution of negative emotional responses to the instrumental behavior is far more likely than in the punishment example.

Some of my research (Dienstbier et al., 1975) has demonstrated that when the emotion-attribution messages which are implied in different types of socialization (as discussed below) are directly administered to a child who is about to be involved in a "detection-free" temptation task, the child behaves differently, depending upon emotion-attribution condition, consonant with the above predictions.

Consider the following research with second-grade children. Same-sex twins were brought to a toy-filled laboratory and asked if they would (individually) aid the researcher by watching a faulty—and boring—slotcar during the researcher's absence. During the subsequent period, when the children ceased their watching for a criterion period, the slotcar crashed (the event supposedly to be avoided through the attentions of the child) and the experimenter returned to administer emotion-attribution information to the effect that the child felt bad because of "what you have done" (internal—the message of induction techniques) or because of "my finding out what you have done" (external—the message of punishment techniques). The subsequent self-control situation of again watching the slotcar was presented to the children as detection-proof, so that the experimenter "could never find out if you did a good or a bad job this time," with the experimental situation convincingly modified to support that contention. In that second watching period, children in the internal condition transgressed half as much as their co-twins in the external conditions. (With procedural modifications and extensions, this research has been replicated several times—Dienstbier, 1978.) Thus direct attribution of emotion to the child's behavior or to the confrontation was apparently effective in changing the child's affectively motivated instrumental behavior—a result which suggests that the difference in effectiveness of those socialization procedures differing in that dimension may be due to emotion-attribution processes.

It seems possible, therefore, that emotion-attribution principles applied to reward and punishment situations may help us to develop a broader perspective on human motivation in environments with different natural or artificially constructed schedules of rein- forcement and punishment. Since negative motive development mirrors positive motive development, as analyzed through emotion-attribution principles, I will focus only on the positive. When the world is beneficent, giving reinforcement for minimal work or effort, motivation associated with the attribution of positive affect to instrumental acts is unnecessary to maintain the individu- al's pursuit of those activities; plentiful external reinforcement, with its attendant pleasures, is certainly sufficient. The apparently in- creasing apathy of American workers toward their work in an era— some would say at the end of an era—of very high reward and materialistic plenty is consistent with this analysis (see "Too many U.S. workers," 1972).

On the other hand, when the individual works in a world requir- ing far more effort and involvement in instrumental tasks for even a moderate amount of reward, the motivation of joy and interest in the task would be necessary for continued task involvement; fortu- nately, such emotions would be natural, since attribution of those emotional states to tangible reward would not be likely with incon- sistent or low frequency reinforcement. An underlying assumption is that the individual initially has interest in performing a wide variety of life's tasks independent of external reinforcement. Obser- vations of young human and nonhuman individuals playfully learn- ing the skills of adulthood, apparently motivated by little other than the interests and joys of their performance, support this beginning assumption.

A2. The analysis of moral socialization techniques presented above is similarly relevant to the proposition that clear divisions between situations discourage misattribution to elements within the different situations. Both positive induction techniques (Hoffman, 1970) applied to negative behavior and psychological rewards applied to positive behaviors prevent the child from "leaving" the psychological situation of the previous instrumental activity. That is, those socialization techniques refocus the child's attention and emotion attributions back on the previous instrumental behaviors so that new elements are not introduced. On the other hand, physical punishments or tangible rewards create a psychological division between the situation of instrumental behavior and that of the consequences of that behavior, since physical punishment and tan- gible reward introduce new elements by drawing attention and emotion attributions to themselves.

When affectively toned arousal results from factors which are not distinctive elements in unique situations but arises instead from illness, hormonal imbalance, or temperament factors with origins in genetic or early experience, then misattribution is likely to occur. These instances will be discussed more fully in section B3.

A3. Substantial evidence relates to the principle that if a significant amount of time passes between arousal generated in situation one, the dissipation of that arousal during a long delay period will attenuate the attribution of that arousal to elements of situation two.

Dutton and Aron (1974) had male subjects respond to a TAT card which was presented by an attractive female experimenter either immediately or 10 minutes after they had crossed an arousing suspension bridge over a deep gorge. Those who responded after the delay told stories with less sexual orientation, indicating that arousal from the narrow bridge which could have contributed to intensified sexual interest dissipated during the 10-minute delay period. In my research on startle and attraction presented below, it will be noted that one of the ways I have validated the relationship of arousal induced by startle contributing to attraction toward an opposite-sexed experimenter was by attenuating that effect through a similar delay-interval procedure.

A4. It appears that even mature individuals are often remarkably susceptible to the influences of others in making emotion attributions. Consider first, however, the research on self control with young children, cited briefly above. One would expect that even second-grade children would have well-established and accurate notions about what elements in temptation situations are typically responsible for their emotional reactions. Yet in several variations of the basic study the simple difference between matched scripts (matched for verbal content, phraseology, and emotional "impact") presenting emotion attribution information accounted for significant differences in dependent measures of self-control, with twins in the internal conditions typically transgressing half as much as their external-condition co-twins.

A later study with adults (Dienstbier, 1978) found similarly powerful results from a comparable internal and external labeling technique.[2] Students initially took a vocabulary test and then read a "reading comprehension" test which presented either an internal

---

2. My thanks to both Keith Willis and Lynn Kahle for help in the development and execution of the procedure used.

emotion-attribution view of conscience functioning or an external view; control-condition subjects read about memory. (These tests were presented as part of a study in "verbal testing.") Students in the internal condition read that "even if the child has never been scolded or punished by parents, the child may begin to experience emotional tension when considering the violation of moral rules about things such as lying, cheating, or stealing. . . . the individual will resist temptation to avoid the emotional tension even though no one else may ever know of the transgression . . . . research has demonstrated that often very strong feelings of emotional tension result from individuals violating their own moral values, even though other people important to them do not know of those violations." External-condition subjects read that "after being scolded or punished a number of times by parents or teachers, the child begins to experience emotional tension when considering the possibility of being found violating the moral rules about things such as lying, cheating, or stealing . . . . the individual will resist temptation to avoid the emotional tension which is tied to the risk of being found out . . . . research has demonstrated that often very strong feelings of emotional tension result when other people who are important to us discover and confront us over violations of moral values." Subsequently, students were given the correct answers to the vocabulary test and were allowed to look over their answers, giving them the opportunity to cheat on that test. Internal-condition subjects cheated significantly less (15% of 66 cheating) than either external-condition subjects (30% of 66) or control subjects (31% of 61). Although this study presented emotion-attribution information in textual form, the role of the "other" in altering emotion attributions is easily inferred from this procedure.

An area of great potential importance for the application of emotion-attribution principles in general, and for consideration of the influence of others in emotion-attribution processes specifically, is psychotherapy. The formal exploration of that potential had an unfortunately difficult beginning, however. In an attempt to demonstrate the impact of emotion-attribution principles through a laboratory procedure meant to be analogous to therapy, Davison and Valins (1969) convinced subjects that (contrived) improvement in shock tolerance which had first been attributed to a drug (a placebo pill) was really the product of their own efforts. Subsequently, those subjects tolerated more shock than did control subjects who believed that their initial "improvement" was drug induced. Bandura (1977) has recently criticized that line of research, suggesting that when replication of related research (i.e., Valins & Ray, 1967) was attempted, replication was not achieved. Indeed, the potential for successful therapy methods based upon the false feedback of emotion symptoms has never appeared to be great, for the maintenance of honest relationships between even short-term therapists and their clients is of paramount importance.

Other important avenues for the application of emotion-attribution principles in therapy are available, however. This seems particularly true for those affective disorders which have hormonal and/or neurotransmitter imbalances with a high heritance component, such as manic-depressive states. As recently demonstrated by Isen, Shalker, Clark, and Karp, (1978), cognitions which follow experimental mood induction are mood compatible. Isen et al. suggest that "our data may shed additional light . . . . the often-noted clinical observation that depressed patients do not seem to see positive aspects of even normally positive situations may reflect, in fact, the positive material's relative inaccessibility under those conditions of recall (namely, depression)" (p. 10). Under such circumstances, emotion-attribution information may be important for the client and the therapist. For example, psychotherapists (especially those with psychoanalytical orientations) often dwell upon the preoccupying thoughts and dreams of depressed clients for clues to the origins of the depression. This process is likely to reaffirm for the client the importance of that mental content. Two conclusions by the depressed client are likely: either the thoughts have some basis in reality (e.g., "I am a poor mother") or they have no basis in reality but nevertheless cause the depression and must therefore be controlled and eliminated; failure to effect such control is then a sign of significant weakness and failure. Both conclusions will tend to contribute to the ongoing negative emotional state. If, instead, the therapist were able to attribute the emotionally depressed state to its physiological origins, and if the negative mentation were attributed to the negative emotional state (the mentation being the product of, rather than the cause of the depression), the client may more easily understand the mental content to be unimportant and invalid. Such proper perspective on the depressive mentation could help the client break the spiral (of mood leading to mood-compatible thoughts which reinforce the mood) by encouraging the client to stop thinking about the depressive—and unimportant—mental content.

A similar analysis was recently suggested in a bulletin of the Alcohol, Drug Abuse, and Mental Health Administration (Note 4). An airline stewardess who survived a plane crash two years previously was described as demonstrating "a series of physical and emotional symptoms" including sleeping, eating, and motivational difficulties combined with panic when sounds reminiscent of the crash were heard. It was suggested that "if she had known her responses were normal and that she was not 'going crazy,' . . . [she] could possibly have been spared the long-term symptoms." In the terms of this chapter, attribution of emotional responses and mentation to normal processes rather than to mental dysfunction would have allowed a different interpretation of the meaning and importance of those responses, with a subsequent reduction in negative impact.

B. The principles relating to factors within and between individuals which dispose different attributions of emotion include cultural influences, role expectations, and individual differences of temperament, defensive style, and experience. These factors are not clearly separable, for often more than one of these levels of analysis may be appropriately applied to a single observation.

B1. Culture and roles prescribe certain emotional experiences, expressions, and instrumental behaviors in certain situations, while proscribing others. Additionally, culture and role expectations often prescribe the style and intensity with which emotions are to be expressed and acted upon.

In discussing the expressive dimension of emotion in his chapter in this volume, Tomkins (1979) has eloquently stated the case for the universality of cultural influence and the result of that influence on emotional expression: "Because the free expression of innate affect is extremely contagious and because these are very high-powered phenomena, all societies, in varying degrees, exercise substantial control over the unfettered expression of affect, and particularly over the free expression of the cry of affect. No societies encourage or permit each individual to cry out in rage or excitement, or distress, or terror, whenever and wherever he wishes . . . we do not, in fact, know what are the biological and psychological prices of such suppression of the innate affective response. I would suggest that much of what is called 'stress' is indeed backed-up affect and that many of the endocrine changes which Frankenhaeuser (1979) has reported are the consequence as much of back-up affect as of affect per se."

The impact which Tomkins predicts from the restrictions which culture may impose on emotional expression will be further magnified by restrictions on emotion-motivated instrumental activities; however, whereas expressive restrictions should be expected to result in short-term effects upon the individual, restrictions on activities potentiated by the arousal of the sympathetic nervous system and by hormonal changes should have long-term impact. Proscription of behavioral responses is likely to be followed by continued emotional arousal which may, in response to elements introduced later, facilitate the experience and expression of an emotional state which is either the same as the original state or similar to that original state in underlying arousal. Research by Hokanson and his colleagues (e.g., Hokanson & Burgess, 1962) relates to this phenomenon. Research subjects first indicated blood pressure increases following anger induction. Only those who could perform effective instrumental activities in the form of safe retaliation (contrasted with unsafe or no retaliation) experienced a lowering of their blood pressure to normal levels. Similar "catharsis" effects have been demonstrated through a variety of procedures (and using a variety of dependent measures, including both behavior and fantasy measures of aggression) in more recent research by others (e.g., Gambaro & Rabin, 1969; Konečni & Doob, 1972; Konečni, 1975a; Murray & Feshbach, 1978).

Not only has effective instrumental action been shown to reduce arousal, but such behavior aids in the formation of clear and definite emotion attributions, reducing the potential for later misattribution of the arousal to other elements. Attacking an offender, for example, will render later misattribution of emotional arousal to other elements less likely; the relationship of the arousal to the instigating element has been made salient. The continuation of anger-induced arousal and its reattribution to new elements is also suggested in this volume by Averill's (1979) data. Of the incidents of anger reported, 37½% were rated as "somewhat" or "very much" having served the purpose of " 'let[ting] off steam' over miscellaneous frustrations of the day which had nothing to do with the present incident" (p. 56) Averill's subjects therefore indicated that they attributed to a currently provoking element some arousal from irrelevant past incidents.

A dramatic example of this type of response (exaggerating anger through apparent misattribution of prior arousal to the current situation) is presented by the work of Magargee (1966), who noted an unusually high concentration of "overcontrolled" personality types among criminals guilty of crimes of violence (contrasted with crimes of property). Magargee's interpretation was that by refraining from mild expressions of anger and moderate instrumental activity motivated by anger, overcontrolled individuals tended to build up tension over time—tension released in an uncontrollable outburst when a significant provocation raised the overall arousal level past the point where control was possible.

These particular examples of tension buildup and release resemble Freud's "hydraulic" model of psychic energy, and they therefore appear to be subject to the same criticisms often levied against that model. Those criticisms hold, however, only when the model is applied indiscriminantly to inappropriate situations. The catharsis model breaks down when long intervals exist between arousing incidents (when even hormonally mediated arousal should have dissipated); similarly, the model is not equally applicable to all individuals, for some do not maintain arousal for very long periods because they do not use sensitizing defense patterns. Often, those who have criticized the "hydraulic" character of this model and the associated concept of catharsis (e.g., Berkowitz, Note 5) have not considered these important variables of time and individual defensive style in this manner.

Although most of the attention in this section has been devoted to anger and aggression, cultures often prescribe and proscribe emotional reactions across the full range of human emotional experiences (e.g., Rosenblatt, Walsh, & Jackson, 1976). Consider the negative emotional expressions and experiences prescribed for menstruating women in United States culture. That culture does play a role is suggested by the attributional suggestibility demonstrated in recent research by Englander-Golden (Englander-Golden, Whitmore, & Dienstbier, 1978; Englander-Golden, Chang, Whitmore, & Dienstbier, Note 6). In that research, it appears that making menstruation salient allows women to respond to culturally-induced expectations with corresponding emotion attributions. For example, under menstruation-salient conditions, women report a different cycle of sexual arousal (not consistent with the progesterone-level hypothesis) than when given daily questionnaires which do not make the menstrual cycle salient. Furthermore, when the menstrual cycle is made salient, women report emotional changes concomitant with the stages of their cycle (which they do not report on daily questionnaires). Finally, as demonstrated by the work of Rodin (1976) and that of Englander-Golden et al. (1977) reviewed in a previous section above, the momentary salience of menstruation-induced emotional arousal in combination with expectations derived from cultural influence allows emotion-attribution processes to change the impact of that emotional arousal on emotion-motivated behavior.

B2. Emotion attributions are similarly affected by role. In other writing and in his chapter in this volume, Averill (1979; Averill & Boothroyd, 1977) has suggested that a major way of appreciating the impact of emotion on behavior is through a role-metaphor approach. Averill's emotion-attribution analysis is at a slightly different level than that presented in this paper, but it is amenable to the same principles. Averill (1979) suggests, for example, that each participant in a love relationship must "play his or her role according to the relevant subset of rules" (p. 6). While Averill's reference is to *behavior*, my approach would suggest that each participant will experience emotion, in part, based upon attributions influenced by role expectations. The distinction between Averill's level of analysis and an emotion-attribution approach is highlighted by his concern with "not which cues are used in interpreting a response as emotional, but why." I would argue that it is extremely difficult to separate the "which" and the "why," since "why," in part, determines "which." However, when such separation is possible, both provide meaningful levels of analysis. (In a previous volume of this series, Simon [1974] and Gagnon [1974] presented a role and script analysis of sexual-social behavior which was compatible with the thesis that the roles one adopts affect emotional experience as well as instrumental behavior.) For example, depending upon one's chosen roles, "romantic love" may be a salient and coveted category. Under such circumstances, emotional arousal due to the many elements elicited by the presence (or absence) of an attractive other may be categorized and experienced as romantic love rather than as happiness, sexual arousal, or loneliness. Though the Walster and Berscheid (1971) expression, "adrenaline makes the heart grow fonder," gives an exaggerated weight to undifferentiated emotional arousal in contrast to more specific sexual arousal, the statement has some accuracy. (This assertion will receive more support at the chapter's end with the presentation of my research on arousal and attraction.)

Within societies derived largely from Western Europe, male roles in particular have traditionally required emotional suppression of fear. Two important examples of the reattribution of arousal following fear suppression come from studies of skydivers by Epstein and Fenz (Epstein, 1967). Even novice divers perceive that both survival and their role of skydiver require fear suppression. Epstein noted outbursts of anger which seemed quite exaggerated, given the nature of the eliciting elements, apparently resulting from fear suppression; he termed this increase in anger through misattribution of fear-induced arousal "drive displacement." Epstein made further observations by systematically asking skydivers with various levels of jumping experience to report their level of subjective emotional tension at various key temporal points during their activities before, during, and after a parachute jump. Experienced skydivers reported increased fear upon reaching the safety of the ground; various physiological indices of arousal similarly reflected that experienced increase or "afterdischarge." Apparently arousal which was previously suppressed was released from suppression when the situation was objectively safe; when that happened, however, the fear was experienced in the new, but inappropriate situation because fear-evoking elements had been recently salient.

B3. In this section, the relation of temperament and mood to emotion attribution processes is examined.

Since the concept of temperament differs significantly in usage between psychologists, a few lines will be devoted here to a discussion of that concept. Most psychologists would agree that temperament describes chronic tendencies to experience certain moods or emotional states in a variety of situations. While researchers such as Buss (1975) restrict their use of the term largely to those dispositions in which heredity plays a major role, others, including Tomkins (1975), emphasize the impact of socialization practices and early experience. Both approaches are supported by convincing research with animals (e.g., Dennenberg, 1967) and with humans (e.g., Loehlin & Nichols, 1976), and both approaches are clearly valid. Some exciting human research relating to early experience (Poe, Rose, & Mason, 1970) has indicated, for example, that early parental loss disposes differences in adult hormonal reactivity (17-OHCS) depending upon whether paternal (low 17-OHCS) or maternal (high 17-OHCS) loss was involved. That differences in concentrations of hormones (the catecholamines) correspond with differences in temperament has been shown by Frankenhaeuser (1979), who demonstrated greater happiness and liveliness in children who indicated higher catecholamine responses to school challenges than similar children with lower epinephrine and norepinephrine responses.

The concept of mood provides a means for understanding the potential ties between temperament and other personality and attitude dispositions. Mood indicates a state of emotional experience and arousal, but without a currently relevant element to which the emotional feeling is attributed. Thus, although one may be "put into a bad mood" by a specific (and identified) event or element, the concept of mood is applicable when the feeling state continues past the point when the individual focuses upon the causal element; the recognition by the individual that this point has been reached is often heralded by a warning that the individual is ready to attribute the emotional arousal to appropriate and current elements. Such warnings are often a variation of "I am in a bad mood and I shall therefore bite anyone who teases me."

To return to the temperament concept, temperament indicates a chronic tendency to experience certain moods (when specific causal elements are not identified and/or relevant) or emotions (when causal elements are identified and/or relevant). It is difficult to be specific concerning the form of the causal chain in the relationship between heredity and/or early experience and these "chronic tendencies" to experience certain emotions and/or moods. Specifically, certain early experiences and hereditary tendencies may lead to perceptual and cognitive styles which dispose one to more often perceive, for example, danger in situations which are neutral to other individuals. Those perceptions may then lead to chronic changes in physiological arousal and mood. However, those early predisposing factors may lead more directly to different patterns of emotional arousal and chronic hormonal balance—patterns which, in turn, lead to differences in threshold for certain perceptions and judgments (of danger, for example).

Emotion-attribution principles are invoked in either of the two causal chains suggested. In the first sequence (early changes leading directly to cognitive-perceptual sensitivity), the individual is likely to need to search for acceptable elements to which the resultant emotional state may be attributed, since if the individual is uniquely sensitive to danger from elements encountered in normal (e.g., family) situations, little consensual validation will be forthcoming to support attributions to such elements; that is, social, cultural, and personal dispositions may motivate the individual to conduct an attributional search among other elements. In the second causal sequence suggested above, the role of emotion-attribution is more obvious. The idea that genetic or early experience variables might lead directly to differences in the experience of moods should be considered in the context of the earlier discussion concerning the possible components of internality in emotional experience. It is appropriate to conceive of mood states arising with no apparent external stimulus, so that an emotion-attribution search may be initiated without having to first disavow a prior external emotion-instigating element.

While it seems likely that both causal chains may occur in the same individual, different individuals and different predisposing causes may relate more to one than the other of these causal sequences. In the relationships between predisposing causes, temperament, and emotion-attribution patterns discussed in the examples below, those causal patterns have been left largely unspecified. The discussion will center upon how emotion-attribution principles account for the attitude and value preoccupations associated with different temperaments in the formation of what Tomkins (1975) has referred to as "ideo-affective complexes."

Consider first the authoritarian personality syndrome. Harsh socialization practices were noted and thought to be causal of the development of authoritarianism by the early researchers (Adorno, Frenkel-Brunswik, Levinson, & Sanford, 1950). Using a psycho-analytic model, it was hypothesized that harsh parental treatment led to repression of anger and aggression (which would otherwise have been directed especially toward the parents); those repressed impulses were eventually displaced and projected toward minority groups and other weak and safe targets.

Without relying upon the intervening construct of a troubled unconscious in which hostile impulses are deposited until they may be projected and displaced, emotion-attribution principles can more simply account for the development of the major characteristics of authoritarianism. Since harsh parental treatment is often delivered unexpectedly (from the child's standpoint) for mistakes in discrimination when the child has emitted acts in one situation which were appropriate in another, the child may not be able to predict punishment, appropriately feeling insecure. Given such parental behavior the individual's confidence in his or her ability to predict and control negative outcomes may never develop sufficiently so that insecurity and anxiety may become chronic. The resultant pattern of striving to relieve anxiety by achieving security often leads to authoritarianism as manifested in an exaggerated need for social and cultural stability through extreme ethnocentrism, political and economic conservatism, militarism, harshness toward those who are different and/or offenders (authoritarian aggression), and a willingness to preserve order by submitting to higher authority with little question (authoritarian submission). Although the translation of general anxiety into specific fears through the identification of current and acceptable elements (to which the negative emotion may be attributed) should lead to a reduction in emotional arousal—as indicated in the studies of Calvert-Boyanowsky and Leventhal (1975) and Rodin (1976) reviewed below—the emotional state may not be completely eliminated; throughout life, new elements which are not completely predictable or understood may be identified as potential threats (e.g., water fluoridation, sex education, culturally exotic neighbors) so that chronic anxiety may be attributed as well to those elements. (Without using emotion-attribution language, Tomkins [1975] has presented an account of authoritarianism which is similar to that developed here.)

A similar analysis may be applied to Keniston's (1960) observations of extremely alienated personalities. Studying a group of alienated males through projective techniques, interviews, questionnaires, life histories, and observation, Keniston compared them with matched groups of typical and involved students. The most consistent difference between the alienated group and the control groups was a high incidence of sudden and severe disturbances (in late pre-puberty years) in the relationship between the alienated men and their mothers. (The findings of Poe et al. [1970] of adult hormone differences—increased 17-OHCS—among men whose mothers had died when they were children provides a suggestion for how such early events may stimulate long-term temperament differences.) Typically, the pre-alienation pattern was for the child to be an oldest or only child who had formed a very close relationship with his mother, only to have a father return from a long military absence (participation in World War II). The father typically reentered the family in a manner which abruptly and thoroughly dislodged the son from his unusually close maternal relationship. Keniston described his alienated individuals as then developing "characterological anger"—an anger which became a long-term feature of temperament and disposed negative and hostile relationships with most individuals and institutions. The pattern of development subsequent to the severe maternal-relation disturbance was characterized by a constant searching for elements within current situations to which anger could be attributed.

A parallel exists in the life of Hitler. In his biography of Adolph Hitler, Payne (1973) describes a key event in Hitler's early life which was similar to the maternal disruption event noted by Keniston— the death of a beloved brother (Edmund) when Hitler was 10 years old. Prior to his brother's death, Hitler was described as a normal and pleasant child who earned good school grades and who was liked by teachers, neighbors, and peers. "Quite suddenly something had snapped within him: a sickness of the soul or a sickness of the flesh. Exactly what caused this abrupt change in his character must remain unknown, but the death of Edmund was probably the main cause, outweighing all others . . . . the death of his brother left a deep psychological wound, which perhaps never completely healed. But it is certain that there was a dramatic change in Adolf's character during the year following his brother's death" (Payne, 1973, pp. 22–23). After his brother's death, Hitler became morose, uncommunicative, and never again performed satisfactorily in school. His later life could properly be characterized as seeking elements in current situations to which to attribute his anger. Similarly, he became a master in inducing the German people to view those elements as appropriate emotion-attribution targets by guiding their anger, born of political and economic frustration, away from himself and the National Socialists toward the German Jews and a major part of the non-German world.

In addition to the psychoanalytic orientation with its dependence upon the concept of an active unconscious, and the emotion-attribution view lovingly explicated in this chapter, there is one other major theoretical contender to explain the relationship between temperament and attitude, value, and personality complexes illustrated in the authoritarian and alienation examples. Focusing on authoritarianism, a basic or traditional learning view would suggest that through both direct and vicarious (classical) conditioning the insecure person has fewer previously neutral stimuli left untouched by some conditioned anxiety. Through conditioning, stimulus elements such as culturally different people, water fluoridation, etc., would each elicit some anxiety and be responded to appropriately, according to such a view. There are two approaches to refuting this view: The first involves an appeal to a parsimonious (and rational) approach to human behavior; the second involves an analysis of research which is easily compatible with only the emotion-attribution approach. In the two following paragraphs each approach will be presented in turn.

The apparent merit of the learning approach is the supposed simplicity of an explanation which does not involve language and other symbolic processes. Unfortunately, to exclude those obviously present processes, the view must introduce unwarranted complexity by requiring conditions of temporal contiguity, repeated trials, etc., for which there is no evidence. To paraphrase the anthropologist Washburn in his recent APA address (Note 7), approaching an understanding of human mental function without regard for human language is analogous to attempting to understand the behavior of birds while disregarding their flight; this is not parsimony.

The following research is also relevant to a choice between the traditional learning view (and the psychoanalytic view) on the one hand, and the emotion-attribution approach suggested here on the other. Sales (1972, 1973) reported that failure-induced threat increased self-reported authoritarianism, with success leading to opposite results. Citing other research indicating increased rejection of and hostility toward different others after threat, Sales predicted that insecurity spawned by the financial and social upheavals of the Great Depression during the 1930s in the U.S. (compared to the decade of the "Roaring" 1920s) would encourage authoritarianism. Sales predicted and found increased joining of authoritarian churches (compared to nonauthoritarian churches), a decline in interest in and circulation of intellectual magazines (with an increase in "macho" and escapist literature), the initiation of state loyalty oaths, heightened support of police (in comparison to fire departments), and greater punishment for rape. Most adherents to the psychoanalytic view would not predict that anger induced by the circumstances of the Great Depression would be repressed, since parental figures are not involved, etc.; the outcomes predicted and noted by Sales would therefore be difficult to reconcile with a psychoanalytical approach. A traditional learning approach would have difficulty explaining how such "previously neutral" stimuli as fear of "disloyal" employees, rapists, and intellectuals managed to achieve the temporal proximity, etc., necessary for the conditioning of anxiety from the depression to those specific stimuli. The data are, however, compatible with the emotion attribution view, suggesting a search by anxious citizens for current elements to explain their chronic anxieties. But the data also suggest a modification of those formulations suggested by other emotion-attribution theorists: rather than attributional searching ending when appropriate elements have been found to explain ongoing emotional arousal, it may be that if substantial levels of emotional tension remain for long time periods, especially when tension is felt as anxiety, the search for and identification of appropriate attributional elements is a continuous process.

B3a. The level of prior experience with emotional states, arousal sources, and situations plays a role in shaping emotion-attribution processes. The separation of this section from the following one dealing with defensive style is accomplished with some strain, since the defensive style which one assumes is determined in part by the level of past experience.

Epstein's (1967) research with skydivers provides an illustration of the natural change in the experience of emotion with increasing instrumental experience in a specific situation. On a jump day, when stimulus words were presented to *novice* skydivers in a sequence of increasing relevance to skydiving, arousal (as indicated by galvanic skin responses) increased consistently with increasing word relevancy. However, for *experienced* skydivers, increasing word relevancy corresponded with initial increases in arousal, followed by an arousal decrease for the most highly relevant words. Similarly, as *novice* skydivers approached the jump temporally through the morning of the jump day they indicated (via self-report) increasing emotional arousal until almost time to exit the aircraft; *experienced* jumpers experienced peak self-reported emotional reactions several hours before their jump—usually around breakfast time, when they finalized their decision to jump.

Epstein has characterized typical responses to new fear-evoking situations as "all or none" in defensive style. That is, the individual either denies the emotional experience as completely as possible in the early stages (by such tactics as denying the danger of skydiving), or experiences emotional arousal at an overwhelming level. With experience, the admission of danger and the experience of moderate and controllable levels of emotional response to the danger are allowed, though control is imposed by the experienced individual when the emotional reactions threaten to become overwhelming.

One way of conceptualizing such control is that with increasing experience a more articulated level of emotion attribution develops.

A likely (but speculative) explanation for this articulated defensive system is that instead of the emotional reaction being attributed to the global aspects of the situation, or to all elements within the situation, the individual learns to identify those specific elements within the system which do present danger. When that identification is made, the correct attribution of the emotional reaction to those limited threats results, while the individual simultaneously learns the instrumental responses which allow the control of danger and which lead to further emotional response reductions. This process may be accomplished by adding new knowledge, or by thinking or "worrying" about the situation, as suggested in the extensive work on stress control by Janis (1969) and by Lazarus (1969).

In developing their "opponent process" theory,[3] Solomon and Corbit (1972) suggested that positive emotional experiences are similarly controlled so that they, too, lose their all-or-none character with time. I would suggest that the lover who emits positive emotional feelings at the very mention of the name of his or her beloved learns with experience that only specific selected elements of the other are worthy of such an emotional response.

To return briefly to the skydiver example, coincident with the apparent control of fearful emotional reactions there develops a relative increase in positive excitement associated with the sport. Emotion attribution to pleasurable excitement apparently becomes easier when some control over the intensity of negative emotional experience is gained. As is illustrated in section C1, attribution to new elements is more easily accomplished at low rather than high arousal levels. Thus one important function of experience in situations with the joint potential for fear and excitement is to allow the

---

3. Opponent process theory was developed to explain an apparent paradox in the responses of organisms to new versus familiar emotion-eliciting stimuli. Although new stimuli (e.g., a lover, forced confinement, or a narcotic drug) elicit large emotional responses when they are relatively new to the individual, the permanent withdrawal of those stimuli leads to only moderate emotional and physiological responses of opposite character. On the other hand, while the emotional response elicited by familiar stimuli may be muted, the withdrawal of those stimuli (e.g., a spouse, a long prison term, or a narcotic drug) leads to a very intense and prolonged emotional response of opposite character. Solomon and Corbit have hypothesized that with the repeated presentation of the original stimulus, a strong emotional tendency of opposite character builds to attenuate the original response. The decline of emotional response to an emotion-eliciting stimulus is therefore seen as an active inhibitory process. When the original stimulus is permanently withdrawn, that strong emotion of opposite character has no counter force.

individual to reduce arousal levels so that re-attribution of arousal to the positive elements of the situation results in the development of positive emotional experience.

Elsewhere (Dienstbier, 1978) I have discussed the role of experience in the formation and development of conscience as defined above. To sketch that discussion briefly, consider the individual who matures in an environment which encourages repeated transgressions; if only some instances of a type of transgression are detected and lead to punishment, it will be mainly those which will be characterized by significant negative emotional arousal. Under such an intermittent "schedule" the individual can easily learn to make correct attributions about what elements (e.g., confrontation) elicit the negative emotional responses. Thus when an individual grows up in an environment with many irresistible temptations, even the conscientious application by socialization agents of the emotion-attribution principles suggested above may not lead to significant attribution by the individual of negative emotion to the transgression act rather than to the confrontation.

B3b. Defensive style plays a role in emotion-attribution processes. Those styles which lead to reduced emotional arousal and experience should also allow the individual to make articulated emotion-attributions to causal elements within a situation (as discussed above). (Research strongly supporting this contention will be presented in section C, below.) While it is readily conceivable that differences in defensive style may originate with different learned patterns of thinking about disturbing events, some research has suggested that defensive style may be due, in part, to physiological variables (linking it to temperament and the discussion on temperament, above). Funkenstein (1955) has demonstrated substantial individual differences in physiological recovery following stimulation by catecholamines, with individuals high in chronic anxiety slower in recovery. Thus the elevated emotional experience of the sensitizer may be tied directly to long-term emotional arousal—a pattern disposed, in part, by physiological variables. Articulated attributional processes should, therefore, be inhibited in the sensitizer, maintaining the cycle of elevated arousal inhibiting articulated defenses which, in turn, disposes continued high emotional arousal and experience. As suggested in a prior section, in combination with rigid expressive and instrumental behavior control, the sensitization style of defense may lead to the explosive behavior discussed by Magargee (1966).

This relationship between level of emotional arousal and articulated attributional searching should be curvilinear, however. With emotional reactions which are minimal, such as may be the case with psychopathy, no search for causal elements is motivated. Frankenhaeuser (1979) has presented an interesting illustration of the lack of physiological response in her study of psychopaths awaiting trial; neither epinephrine nor norepinephrine increased as the trial date approached, contrasted with more normal individuals who showed a marked increase in those catecholamines during that period. As suggested by Schachter and Latané (1964), the psychopath's failure to perceive arousal as an emotional experience may be the major reason for his or her apparent inability to avoid situations and elements which lead to punishment.

C. The principles in this section relate to the quantity and quality of emotional arousal and the impact of those variables on emotion-attribution processes.

C1. High levels of emotional arousal prevent articulated attributions of arousal to new elements or to specific elements rather than to global situations. (Since this point has been elaborated above in the sections on level of prior experience [B3a] and on defensive styles [B3b], coverage in this section will be restricted largely to the presentation of experimental evidence.) The relationship of arousal level to articulated attributions may be largely because the major function of emotion is to direct attention toward the perceived cause of the emotional arousal, and toward instrumental solutions to whatever problems are posed by the situation; therefore when arousal levels are high, attention toward certain elements is maintained more tenaciously so that internal or external induction of attention shifts to new elements is more difficult.

Several early experiments within the placebo pill paradigm using different intensities of induced arousal demonstrate this relationship. Nisbett and Schachter (1966) had subjects participate either in a low fear condition in which the consequences of shock-induced pain were not dramatized, or a high fear condition in which they were dramatized. Subjects tolerated more shock in the arousal placebo condition (i.e., were able to attribute fear of shock to the placebo pill) only in the low fear condition. Similarly, in a study with cheating as the dependent measure (Dienstbier, 1972), women were subjected to one of four different threat levels, ranging from a threat that the "board of psychologists" developing the vocabulary test would contact them if they failed to get the criterion number of items correct (at high threat), to low threat instructions which indicated that no names would be required on the answer papers, since the test was being studied rather than the students. As hypothesized, the placebo pill condition (arousal or benign symptoms) made no difference on cheating rate in the two highest levels of threat, but did differentially affect cheating with more cheating with the "arousal" placebo in the two conditions of least threat.

C2. The quality of arousal influences the likelihood and quality of emotion attributions. There are several reasons why quality differences influence emotion attribution. First, quite simply, certain emotional states are relatively unacceptable to the individual because of internalized cultural, social, or role requirements, or because of individual self-concept needs (see Section B). A second reason stems from the observation that emotional states such as anxiety and depression, which are often elicited in very complex situations (and frequently related to hormonal and/or neurotransmitter imbalances), strongly motivate a search for causes; in contrast, emotional states such as disgust or contempt are normally associated with more obvious elements in simpler situations so that attributional searching for causal elements is not as highly motivated. A discussion of this relationship was anticipated in the section above on discrete versus dimensional approaches and will be elaborated only briefly in the following paragraph of this section. Then the observation that certain emotions seem to be easily reexperienced as certain other emotions, apparently due to the similarity of underlying arousal, will be elaborated. Finally, because of the difference of exposure which individuals attempt to maintain between those situations which evoke negative versus positive emotional experiences, the reattribution of positive emotional states to new elements will often be more likely than will similar processes for negative emotions. This issue will be discussed in the final paragraph of this section.

As an example of the relationship of different emotional states to attributional searching, anxiety is an emotional state which seems to motivate more attributional searching than fear. In a sense, this statement is definitional, because anxiety is usually defined as a state similar to fear but without a specifically attributed cause. Somewhat similarly, as discussed above, depression is frequently influenced by inherited propensities toward certain hormonal imbalances (notably reduced norepinephrine) so that it may develop in individuals when no obvious causal psychological elements are apparent to which the depression may be attributed; under such circumstances, individuals are motivated to search for appropriate elements in their current situation to which to attribute those emotional states.

As noted by Hebb (1946), fear is easily reattributed to elements which are compatible with the experience of positive excitement. Two examples of modern research support that observation. The study by Dutton and Aron (1974), discussed above, noted an increase in sexual story theme responses by men to TAT pictures after those men had walked across a narrow "scenic" suspension bridge high over a gorge. My research on attraction, presented in detail in the final section, indicates that startle-induced arousal may similarly contribute to increased attraction toward an opposite-sexed other. While those examples illustrate the ease of translation of fear-induced or startle-induced arousal to sexual or interpersonal interest or excitement in a short-term sense, the thrill-seeking behavior of the psychopath discussed by Hare (1970) apparently represents a more chronic example of the same process. Apparently, because of experiencing reduced emotional arousal initially in fear-provoking situations, the psychopath is readily able to experience excitement in situations which would be experienced as fear by less psychopathic individuals with similar experience levels. With psychopaths, peer influences and the influences of older children (Yochelson & Samnow, 1976) may be significant factors in motivating and guiding such attributions.

It is in the area of anger and aggression that the most recent laboratory work has been done demonstrating the contribution of arousal generated in one situation to a different emotional experience. The general format of most studies in this group is to show that while arousal induced by circumstances irrelevant to anger will increase aggressive responding in previously angered subjects, such irrelevant arousal will not increase aggression in subjects not previously angered. Irrelevant arousal is therefore not effective in increasing anger or aggression unless salient elements justifying the anger response are present. Arousal induced by exercise has been shown to facilitate aggressive responding (Zillmann, Katcher, & Milavsky, 1972), but this contribution of exercise-induced arousal is maximized when subjects are still aroused by exercise but believe they have completely recovered, so that the element of exercise is no longer salient (Zillmann, Johnson, & Day, 1974). Arousal from listening to complex (versus simple) tones delivered in loud (rather than mild) fashion has been shown to increase aggression (Konečni, 1975b), while the possibility of attributing the anger arousal to a placebo pill with supposed arousing properties (compared to relaxation placebos) reduces aggressive responding (Younger & Doob, 1978).

Attempts to demonstrate the facilitation of anger or aggression by arousal misattribution have not been uniformly successful, however, suggesting that the nature of arousal stimulated by sexual and humorous elements may not be as similar to aggression-induced arousal as that induced by exercise, loud noise, and the other elements discussed above. Feshbach (Note 8) has suggested recently that there is no evidence for the transfer of arousal from sexual arousal to aggressive responding, arguing that in those studies which have apparently demonstrated that phenomenon, an explanation based upon the disinhibition of both behavioral systems (sexual and aggressive) by the presentation of sexually stimulating materials may account for the results. Such mixed research results should not be interpreted as indicating exclusively unique qualities in sexual excitement, however. Using a procedure similar to that of Zillmann, Johnson, and Day (1974), Cantor, Zillmann, and Bryant (1975) demonstrated increased ratings of arousal, excitement, aesthetic value, and entertainment value for erotic film materials following exercise-induced arousal, but only during the period when subjects mistakenly believed that they were no longer aroused by the prior exercise.

The examples of research in the two proceeding paragraphs provide a brief beginning for what should be learned about the potential for misattribution of arousal between different emotional states and between nonemotional arousal and emotion. The limitation of successful research demonstrations to the few areas reviewed above should not be interpreted at this early stage of interest in emotion attribution as indicating that these are the only emotion combinations between which arousal misattribution is likely.

Another factor creating attribution differences between different emotional states is that "leaving the field" in avoidance situations may prevent easy reattribution of emotional arousal to elements within that situation, with the likelihood that the original emotion attributions will stand. Articulated correct attributions which could lead to appropriate responses to the emotion-evoking elements in the negative situation are therefore not attained. In approach situations, approach leads to prolonged involvement with the elements of the situation so that more articulated and correct emotion attributions should result. The unfortunate outcome is that while phobias may be maintained for a lifetime, perhaps the only great romantic love which can survive the passage of many years is one characterized by long periods of separation.

RESEARCH ON THE SPECIAL PROBLEM OF ATTRACTION AND ROMANTIC LOVE

In his discussion of the development of romantic love, Beach (1973) suggests that romantic love blooms best in societies in which sexuality is suppressed. The emotion-attribution approach developed here leads to the hypothesis that under such circumstances attribution of sexual and emotional arousal to exclusively sexual elements is not acceptable, insofar as individuals have internalized the cultural mores. Though sexual attraction toward all or most members of the opposite sex is therefore discouraged, in such societies it usually remains permissible for attraction toward one special person to assume great significance. Since such a pattern supports monogamy, it is easy to understand why monogamous cultures would encourage this emotional and sexual attribution pattern. If this emotion-attribution hypothesis were correct, it should also be apparent that within a culture, if members of one of the sexes were required to suppress sexual interests, members of that sex should become more interested in "romance" or romantic love than members of the opposite sex. The greater focus of females of past generations in U.S. culture on romantic love (Gagnon, 1974) may be at least partially due to past cultural restraint on female sexuality. Similarly, the apparent reduction in emphasis on romantic love which seems to be characteristic of modern young people in U.S. culture may reflect the increased sexual freedom of both sexes. This analysis would suggest that either social-sexual education or experience would reduce the potential for emotional and sexual arousal to be easily misattributed, with a resultant reduced potential for the rapid or unselective development of romantic love.

The experience of attraction toward an opposite-sexed other depends upon more than the attribution of sexual feelings. The elements of close proximity, eye contact, and various social pleasures and expectations may lead to substantial emotional arousal—

arousal often experienced as positive excitement (Patterson, 1976). The research presented below relates to this latter issue.

The following research series, not previously published (Dienstbier, Note 9) relates also to the principles concerning intrinsic qualities of certain elements as influencers of emotion attribution (A1), and the role of delay in attenuating emotional misattribution (A3). The research demonstrates the misattribution of startle-induced arousal, which may contribute to increased attraction toward an attractive opposite-sexed other, but to a reduction in attraction toward a same-sexed other. The findings also illustrate the impact of individual differences (in this case, based upon sex) and cultural and role influences on emotion-attribution processes, relating to the principles of section B above. Finally, some of the unsuccessful aspects of the research relate to point C2, that the quality or type of arousal influences the individual's ability to misattribute emotional arousal to different elements.

The bases for the hypothesis of this research come largely from research in social psychology. Berscheid and Walster (1969) had suggested that general autonomic arousal facilitates attraction toward an attractive other. The false heart-rate feedback research by Valins (1966, 1967) had apparently inspired that hypothesis: In response to false feedback of heart-rate acceleration and deceleration given to his subjects while they watched slides of female nudes, those slides for which heart rate apparently changed were rated as more attractive than other slides for which false heart rate remained constant.

In an attempt to answer the question of whether real arousal changes would lead to similar rating differences, Dutton and Aron (1974) studied the sexual themes in stories told by male subjects who visited either a frightening, narrow suspension bridge or a less frightening bridge over the same scenic river. (Although one of the three studies presented by Dutton and Aron was reviewed in section A3, above, all three studies will be reviewed here.) When TAT cards were presented by an attractive female, the males who had crossed the more arousing scenic bridge told more sexually oriented stories; when the experimenter was a male, similar differences between the bridges did not occur. Since subject selection factors (interacting with sex of researcher) could have caused those differences, in a second study a female experimenter met male subjects either immediately after crossing the suspension bridge, or at least 10 minutes after leaving it. Subjects at the bridge gave more sexually oriented responses, but of course the two groups of subjects told their stories against quite different background circumstances. In a third study conducted in the lab, male subjects who thought they were to receive a painful electric shock rated a female confederate as more attractive than male subjects expecting a mild shock. My studies, presented below, were a logical extension of that and other research cited above in the emotion-attribution area.[4]

Study I was an attempt to test the hypothesis that startle-induced emotional arousal would increase the ratings of attraction given to an attractive opposite-sexed other. Sixty male subjects signed up for an experiment on "vestibular and balance function" and were given extensive supporting material to buttress that cover story. Subjects were then seated in a dental chair and blindfolded. After each turn in a sequence of circular turns of the dental chair, they were asked to identify the direction they faced. Following the ninth turn, the experiment became "unblind" as to the subjects condition and, in the arousal condition, suddenly tilted the chair backwards with an accompanying loud noise. Subjects were assured that this was a planned part of the turning sequence. Control subjects were treated identically except for this sudden tilt and loud noise.

Shortly after the chair-turning sequence, the blindfold was removed and the subject filled out two rating forms about the experiment and the experimenter. When completed, those forms were to be put into a sealed envelope "to assure confidentiality" and were dropped by the subject into a bin with many other similar envelopes. A thorough and detailed "funnel-style" post-experimental questionnaire asking very specific questions about hypothesis suspiciousness, etc., was then administered, followed by a total debriefing.

On the dependent measure questionnaire, after several dummy items, the subjects were asked, "How much do you like the experimenter personally?" Since the experimenters in all studies were very attractive, and since within each study they dressed identically for all subjects, there was little within-condition variance on the 9-point scales used to assess responses on the dependent measure. (All standard deviations in all the reported studies using this scale

4. My sincere thanks are due to the experimenters who worked in this series of studies. Specifically, my thanks to Virginia Broady for her work in Study I, to Steve Slane for his work in Studies II and III, to Nancy Kahn in Study IV, to Kathy Orr in Study V, and to Cindy Smith in Study VI.

were below 2, with most in the neighborhood of 1.) In Study I, with male subjects and a very attractive female experimenter, the liking measure and the appearance measure were both considerably higher in the startle condition as compared to the no-startle condition (8.43 vs 7.68, $t = 2.57$, $p < .05$; and 8.15 vs 7.61, $t = 1.89$, $p < .10$, respectively).

Increased liking had been predicted and was confirmed for the female experimenter–male subject combination of Study I. Since the female experimenter was an element likely to attract emotion attribution as a result of having salient interpersonal and sexual qualities, Study I was essentially an incomplete test of principle A1, that specific qualities of elements within situations lead to specific types of emotion attributions being made. A more complete test of principle A1 would be provided by changing the nature of the researcher so that a different type of emotion attribution resulted; this was accomplished in Study II.

A second problem with Study I in isolation is that alternative hypotheses may account for such results. For example, Kenrick and Cialdini (1977) recently advanced a hypothesis based upon a reinforcement explanation to account for the arousal-attraction hypothesis. They suggested that the results achieved by Dutton and Aron (and others) could have been accounted for by the subjects experiencing relief or tension reduction due to the presence of the attractive other, and that a means of discriminating between their hypothesis of reinforcement and the emotion-misattribution explanation would be to "involve the use of control groups of male subjects exposed to male confederates." This test situation, too, was effected in Study II.

In Study II, identical to Study I except for the use of the male experimenter, the aroused (startled) male subjects indicated significantly less liking for the male experimenter than control-condition subjects (6.62 vs. 7.62, $t = 2.36$, $p < .05$). No substantial differences on the appearances measure were noted. The alternative explanation advanced by Kenrick and Cialdini is weakened considerably by these results.

But of course the differences in response pattern between Study I and Study II could have been due entirely to elements of differences between the experimenters other than those based on sex. There are, therefore, alternative explanations other than the hypothesis that the male subjects of Study II who were in the arousal conditions attributed their additional arousal to a negative emotional response to the experimenter. Therefore, in Study III the same male experimenter was used in an identical procedure except that the research subjects were female. Startle-induced emotional arousal was associated with a slight increase in the ratings on the liking measure (from 6.59 to 7.11, $t = 1.33$, NS). In this study the appearance measure changed significantly in the same direction, increasing from 6.70 to 7.44 ($t = 2.02$, $p < .05$).

This change in the pattern of responses between Studies II and III presents a rather dramatic illustration of principle B, that individual differences will determine how attributions of emotional arousal are made. Male and female subjects made dramatically different attributions of their arousal in the presence of the same attractive male in the two studies.

Two additional studies were done to demonstrate a different kind of emotion attribution process, but those studies were not wholly successful. They are presented here because the lack of positive answers to some of the experimentally asked questions illustrates some of the issues developed in the A portion of the outline above. These studies do, however, replicate the findings of Studies I and III above.

In Study IV the research was elaborated by introducing a placebo pill manipulation. Half the aroused (startled) subjects and half the control subjects were given a placebo and led to expect arousal side effects from their pill. The other half of the subjects anticipated benign side effects. It was hypothesized that if the male subject could attribute emotional arousal to both the placebo pill (in the arousal-pill conditions) and to the attractive female experimenter, the effect of increased attraction from the startle-induced arousal would be attenuated. Although the placebo pill manipulation led to no significant or suggestive trends, aroused subjects (from the startle) liked the researcher considerably more (8.19 vs. 7.37, $F = 4.02$, $p < .05$), and rated the appearance of the researcher somewhat higher (8.30 vs. 7.90, $F = 2.21$, NS), replicating Studies I and III.

Since the pill manipulation results in the expectation of gradual symptom onset, and since startle-induced arousal is characterized by sudden onset of arousal, it may be that the failure to achieve significant placebo pill effects in this research was due to those differences in real and expected emotional-arousal onset patterns. It must be acknowledged, however, that the arousal pattern which one would expect from the continued presence of the attractive opposite-sexed experimenter would also differ from that induced by startle from the quick tilt of the chair; at the time of the research I hypothesized that the presence of an attractive opposite-sexed other was an extremely salient element in the situation—much more salient than the previously ingested placebo pill, despite the timely reminder of the expected "side effects" of that placebo.

To attempt to increase the salience of a competing element in Study V, the noise procedure developed by Ross, Rodin, and Zimbardo (1969) was substituted for the placebo pill. I assumed that a continuous loud noise, from which half the subjects would expect arousal symptoms and half benign symptoms, would be a more salient stimulus than the placebo pill of Study IV had been. At the point in the experiment when the startle was administered to the arousal subjects, the loud noise was played through a speaker over the subjects' heads. Half the subjects in each of the startle conditions were told to anticipate arousal side effects from the loud noise, whereas the remaining subjects were told to anticipate benign side effects from the noise.

While no noise symptom effects were noted (all F's less than 1.0), a near replication of the startle-arousal effects of Studies I, III, and IV was achieved. Male subjects who were startled liked the female experimenter somewhat more (7.79 vs. 7.50, $F < 1.0$, NS), and rated her as more attractive (8.36 vs. 7.79, $F = 3.77$, $p < .06$). Obviously, no substantial advantage in increased salience was gained between Studies IV and V by the substitution of noise for the placebo pill approach.

Studies IV and V together suggest that the emotion attributions which may be made are limited, in part, by the form of the arousal and by the salience of the elements to which emotion attributions might be directed.

The final study in the series was done to further verify that the pattern of results in Studies I through III was due to the attribution of emotional arousal. It should be expected that the startle-induced emotional arousal would decay over time, as was apparently the case in the Dutton and Aron (1974) study, whereas if the increased attraction effect were due to a cognitive process, the passage of time would not have a similar large impact. In Study VI, all the male subjects were subjected to the startle-induced arousal. As previously, the subjects were assured before the startle that this was a normal part of the research procedure—That is, they were told to anticipate being moved in a different manner than previously. Subjects were then told that there would be a delay in the middle of the experiment to ascertain whether relaxation induced by sitting quietly and listening to quiet music would change their vestibular ability. This 10-minute delay during which the experimenter was not present in the room (but during which the subjects remained blindfolded) was presented either immediately before the arousal (late arousal condition) or immediately after the arousal (early arousal condition). It was hypothesized that subjects in the early arousal condition would experience some reduction in emotional arousal during the 10-minute delay, rating the experimenter less highly at the end of the experiment by virtue of having less autonomic arousal to attribute to her at the time of the rating procedure.

A different type of dependent measure scale was introduced in Study VI, replacing the 9-point scale of the first five studies with a 20-cm line like that used by Valins (1966) in his nude-rating studies. It was anticipated that this response format would allow more response flexibility and therefore might be more sensitive to between-condition differences. Subjects were to make a pencil mark through the line. As predicted, subjects in the late arousal condition rated the experimenter considerably more attractive, drawing their line 1.17 cm from the high end on the attraction line, while subjects in the early arousal condition drew theirs 2.01 cm from the end (t 1.74, $p < .05$, one-tailed). On the liking variable, however, the results actually tended to be nonsignificantly in the opposite direction from that predicted—that is, subjects in the late arousal condition drew their line 3.02 cm from the high end, while those in the early arousal condition drew theirs 2.46 cm from that end point ($t = .83$, NS).

Whereas it appears that the subjects in this research are responding differently, depending upon when they attain their arousal from the startle, the pattern of their difference does not correspond as well to the previous results as had been hoped. It is surprising that the liking measure does not show the pattern of results which was predicted and which was found on the attraction measure. While the study offers some support for principle A3, that the time span between situations would negatively influence one's ability to misattribute arousal, the support for that proposition is somewhat mixed. It is possible that exposure to the attractive female and arousal prior to the delay period may have left the subjects of Study VI with all the necessary ingredients to attribute increased attraction toward the experimenter during the delay despite her leaving the room during that period and their remaining blindfolded. Why only one of the dependent measure scales should fall victim to this explanation is not obvious, however.

CRITICISMS AND CONCLUSIONS

Emotion-attribution principles have been demonstrated through a wide variety of procedures and studies, forming a system of converging observations sufficient to be convincing to a growing group of researchers. Yet interpretations of emotion-attribution principles and of the studies themselves have not gone unchallenged. Some modern emotion theorists have been critical of emotion-attribution theory as oversimplified and as inappropriate for some of the areas to which it has been applied. There are several reasons for distrust of the approach. In the past the theory has not been adequately placed within the realm of general emotion theory. Additionally, some of the specific studies in the early tradition have failed to replicate (e.g., see Kellogg & Baron, 1975; Marshall & Zimbardo, in press; Maslach, in press). Finally, an interpretation with some appeal has been advanced by Calvert-Boyanowsky and Leventhal (1975) to account for some of the data of emotion-attribution research without using emotion-attribution principles. Except for the Calvert-Boyanowsky and Leventhal criticisms, directed specifically toward the study (reviewed above) by Ross, Rodin, and Zimbardo (1969), I believe that the other major criticisms have been answered throughout this chapter. Attention will, therefore, be turned to the Calvert-Boyanowsky and Leventhal criticism.

Ross et al. had subjects attribute arousal or benign symptoms to a loud noise played while the subjects worked on reward puzzles or shock-avoidance puzzles; subjects who could attribute their arousal to the noise worked less to avoid shock, indicated reduced fear as a result of their misattribution of emotional arousal to the noise. Calvert-Boyanowsky and Leventhal added the two new conditions of either arousal or benign symptoms being attributed to the "threat of shock" (rather than to the loud noise). (In a study reviewed in part above, Rodin [1976] performed a similar manipulation of attributing arousal symptoms to "fear of shock" with results similar to those achieved by Calvert-Boyanowsky and Leventhal.) Results in the "threat of shock" conditions essentially replicated the noise attribution condition; that is, subjects who could attribute arousal symptoms to the "threat of shock" evidenced less fear of shock than benign-symptom subjects, as indicated by spending less time working on a puzzle which supposedly led to shock avoidance. The authors suggested that an alternative hypothesis to an emotion-attribution explanation could be applied to their research and to other emotion-attribution studies: Information consonant with reality results in lowest levels of emotion. That is, since all subjects experienced emotional arousal from the anticipation of shock, whenever those subjects were told to anticipate arousal from some source, the good fit of their expectations of arousal and reality (the experience of that arousal) relaxed them. Unfortunately, even though the data of the second study in the Calvert-Boyanowsky and Leventhal paper were correctly predicted, those data fit poorly with that explanation. In that second study, when noise intensity was very low, arousal symptoms attributed (by the manipulation) to the noise did *not* relieve the fear of shock compared to arousal symptoms attributed to a louder noise or to the "threat of shock." Although the low intensity noise is obviously an unlikely source for the attribution of emotional arousal, the requirements which underlie the Calvert-Boyanowsky and Leventhal explanation are met in that condition—subjects have been told to anticipate arousal symptoms and they experience them (from the fear of shock). The problem is that since the low intensity noise did not provide the subjects with a plausible or salient element to which they could *attribute their emotional arousal*, the manipulation failed, with no fear (of shock) reduction resulting. But the failure is more consonant with predictions of emotion-attribution theory than with the suggested alternative hypothesis.

The explanation advanced by Calvert-Boyanowsky and Leventhal also fits poorly with other emotion-attribution literature. Consider both the Nisbett and Schachter (1966) study and one of the cheating studies discussed above (Dienstbier, 1972). In both studies, under high fear conditions the attribution manipulations failed to have an effect, while the attribution of arousal to the arousal placebo was effective under low fear conditions in allowing subjects to experience more shock (in the Nisbett & Schachter study) and to cheat more (in my study). From an emotion-attribution standpoint, it is easy to understand why the manipulation failed under high arousal conditions—emotional arousal due to fear of intense pain from shock or harsh consequences from failure was attributed to those true sources, since those sources were very salient under intense threat conditions. But *strongly* positive results would have been predicted by the Calvert-Boyanowsky and Leventhal hypothesis under high-fear conditions since an expectation for arousal symptoms is given in the arousal conditions and high arousal is present (more so than in low-threat conditions). My work with self-control in children, discussed above, provides a second type of study in which only the emotion attribution predictions are consonant with the data (Dienstbier et al., 1975). Children were told to anticipate emotional arousal ("you will feel bad") under one of two contingency conditions ("if you transgress" or "if you are caught transgressing"). Both groups were put in "detection-proof" situations in which some transgression almost always followed, leading (apparently) to some emotional reactions. Since expectation of arousal and real emotional arousal are equally present in both conditions, the Calvert-Boyanowsky and Leventhal explanation would not predict between-group differences. Strong and consistent replicated differences were clearly obtained, however, with more self-control (indicating more emotional inhibition) from the group told they would feel bad if they transgressed.

Nor could that explanation account for any of the emotion-attribution research which adds arousal to increase emotional responding. Their hypothesis simply has no relevance to the research discussed above indicating increases in anger (Zillmann, Johnson, & Day, 1974), or heightened sexual interest, esthetic rating, entertainment value, and excitement ratings of erotic materials (Cantor, Zillmann, & Bryant, 1975). Similarly, their explanation does not fit with the "bridge" research by Dutton and Aron (1974) with increased sexual themes at the scenic bridge following exercise, nor with my research presented above on increased (or decreased) attraction following startle-induced arousal.

With the Calvert-Boyanowsky and Leventhal explanation for the emotion-attribution phenomenon fitting well with their own data from their first study and fitting quite poorly with their own second study and much of the remaining emotion-attribution literature, only one problem of significance remains: In the first study of the Calvert-Boyanowsky and Leventhal paper (and in a similar study by Rodin, 1976), why did the attribution of arousal symptoms to the "threat of shock" reduce the impact of emotional arousal on behaviors relevant to shock avoidance (in the case of the former study). A proper analysis of this issue will require a more detailed consideration of the Rodin study. (Two studies were presented in the Rodin paper cited; the second study, focusing upon the misattribution of menstrual arousal, was reviewed in a prior section of this chapter.)

Rodin used a placebo pill procedure, with subjects divided into high and low arousal conditions. The high arousal subjects were told that their performance, indicative of intelligence, would be timed; they were also warned to anticipate a painful electric shock as part of a test of skin sensitivity. Since the three attribution conditions did not influence the low arousal group, only the high arousal procedures will be reviewed. In the pill-attribution condition, subjects were told that the pill could make them feel "much more nervous and upset than usual" and would produce arousal-relevant physiological symptoms. A "correct attribution" group was told that "people sometimes become anxious when they anticipate receiving shock and when their performance is being measured"; they, too, were presented with the physiological symptom list and informed that if such changes were felt "it is probably because you are worried about the timed test and probably somewhat afraid of the shock." Control subjects were given the placebo pill with no information about possible side effects. Controls performed most poorly on two (of three) dependent-measure tasks which are normally adversely influenced by anxiety (digit symbol substitution and anagrams); additionally, control subjects worked much less on a frustrating unsolvable puzzle than either subjects in the low arousal conditions or than pill- or "correct"-attribution subjects, again indicating the highest level of negative emotional arousal in the control condition.

It is likely that subjects in both the Calvert-Boyanowsky and Leventhal (1975) and the Rodin (1976) studies were anxious initially because of many aspects of the situation, including fear of failure (on the puzzles and tasks), general evaluation apprehension, the newness of the experimental situation, the potential for embarrassment, and the potential for receiving shock (the certainty of shock, in the Rodin research). The "correct attribution" instructions directed the subjects to attribute arousal from those many diverse elements to the single element of shock (plus evaluation apprehension in the Rodin study).

The Rodin study presents no issue for emotion-attribution principles; since receiving shock is not contingent upon performance in that study, it should be expected that the attribution of emotional arousal to the fear of shock (and evaluation apprehension) should reduce the overall level of negative emotional arousal, allowing better performance on tasks usually adversely influenced by negative arousal. However, in the Calvert-Boyanowsky and Leventhal study, the results suggest that under some circumstances fear-motivated behavior may be reduced toward even the element to which emotional arousal is attributed. The work of Janis (1969) in improving the postoperative prognosis of surgery patients is relevant in understanding this finding. Janis has achieved significant success by focusing patients' attention upon those elements of the surgery which will pose the most significant hazard and discomfort. Like the subjects in the Calvert-Boyanowsky and Leventhal study, Janis's surgery patients do not need to physically practice any instrumental responses to reduce the impact of their negative emotional arousal. They have reasoning and defensive skills to invoke if only the specific elements posing the danger are identified and therefore isolated from the rest of the situation. Once that is accomplished, instrumental and/or cognitive activities can be directed to the simultaneous elimination of the danger and control of the emotional arousal and experience. The demonstration that the reduction of emotion-motivated avoidance of even the "target" element may happen within a very brief time period is the valuable contribution of the Calvert-Boyanowsky and Leventhal research, adding a new quantitative temporal dimension to emotion-attribution theory.

Reapplying this principle to one of the areas of discussion in another section of this chapter, it is suggested that a way in which a skydiver may eliminate the fear of skydiving, in general, and fear of the parachute not opening, specifically, is to realize that it is that specific element which should be the focus of attention, since significant danger does exist at that point. Then some combination of mental rehearsal, instrumental practice, and direct emotional control will occur, limiting the negative emotional response to skydiving and to the danger posed at the moment when the parachute must open.

In summary, emotion-attribution processes may allow the reduction of emotional experience and arousal in two ways. First, if causal attribution processes lead to emotional arousal being attributed to other elements (rather than the target element), the target element will evoke less emotional arousal and will be the focus of reduced emotional experience; secondly, in complex situations with many potential elements "competing" for emotion-attribution attention, the identification of a few elements as causal will allow even those elements to eventually evoke reduced emotional arousal, for the identification of specific elements will allow the individual to bring cognitive, rational, or defensive reactions to bear, and/or to select, execute, and practice instrumental behaviors which will change the individual's relationship to the target element. The Calvert-Boyanowsky and Leventhal study has apparently demonstrated the second option.

Although the limitations of emotion-attribution theory are not dramatized by the Calvert-Boyanowsky and Leventhal study, such limitations do exist. Not every instance of evoked emotion occurs with sufficient ambiguity so that a significant search is undertaken for elements to which emotion might be attributed; nor do influences such as socialization agents continuously barrage us with new emotion-attribution information when we have not initiated our own search for causal elements. Certainly as we become more experienced in life generally and in various specific situations, we more easily identify those elements responsible for our emotional reactions, precluding substantial misattribution of emotional arousal. In some of my research on the impact of temperature adaptation on emotional experience (presently unpublished), I have repeatedly observed the apparent accuracy with which individuals can sometimes apportion components of their total arousal to the various contributing causes, including temperature and emotional elements. Some of the studies cited above similarly include conditions in which minimal misattribution of exercise-induced arousal occurs, while subjects remain aware of the true origins of that arousal (Cantor, Zillmann, & Bryant, 1975; Zillmann, Johnson, & Day, 1974). Misattribution of arousal is not universal; it may even be the exception to the way in which some mature adults respond to most emotion-evoking stimuli, depending upon their openness to experiences which may be contrary to cultural and role expectations, the salience of the arousing elements, etc.

Even in those circumstances where emotion-attribution principles do provide relevant insight, such as in the attraction research detailed above, I would be quite disappointed if the approach accounted for all of the interesting variance in an episode involving attraction. But in those many instances where emotion-attribution theory is relevant and useful, the framework of principles provided in this chapter should prove useful for understanding diverse observations of some of the most fascinating areas of human experience.

REFERENCE NOTES

1. Schwartz, G. E. Physiological patterning and emotion revisited: Hemispheric-facial-autonomic interactions. In H. Leventhal (Chair), *New perspectives in the research on emotion*. Symposium presented at the meeting of the American Psychological Association, Toronto, August 1978.

2. Konecni, J. J. Perception and labeling of emotional states in oneself and others. In H. Leventhal (Chair), *New perspectives in the research on emotion*. Symposium presented at the meeting of the American Psychological Association, Toronto, August 1978.

3. Lanzetta, J. T. Facial expressive behavior and the regulation of emotional experience. In H. Leventhal (Chair), *New perspectives in the research on emotion*. Symposium presented at the meeting of the American Psychological Association, Toronto, August 1978.

4. *Aircraft disasters and mental health*. News feature service bulletin of Alcohol, Drug Abuse, and Mental Health Administration, 5/1/78.

5. Berkowitz, L. *Two cultures of violence: Some opposing views of aggression in therapy*. Presidential address to Division of Social and Personality Psychology at the meeting of the American Psychological Association, Honolulu, September 1972.

6. Englander-Golden, P., Chang, H. S., Whitmore, M. R., & Dienstbier, R. A. *Female sexual arousal and the menstrual cycle*. Paper presented at the meeting of the American Psychological Association, Toronto, August 1978.

7. Washburn, S. L. *Human behavior and the behavior of other animals*. Invited address presented at the meeting of the American Psychological Association, San Francisco, August 1977.

8. Feshbach, S. Sex and aggression: Some social implications. In L. Berkowitz (Chair), *Aggression and violence*. Symposium presented at the meeting of the American Psychological Association, Toronto, August 1978.

9. Dienstbier, R. A. *Attraction and repulsion as a function of natural arousal and appropriate social cues*. Unpublished manuscript, University of Nebraska at Lincoln, 1977.

REFERENCES

Adorno, T. W., Frenkel-Brunswik, E., Levinston, D. J., & Sanford, R. N. *The authoritarian personality*. New York: Wiley, 1950.

Averill, J. R. The emotions. In E. Staub (Ed.), *Personality: Basic issues and current research*. Englewood Cliffs, N.J.: Prentice Hall, in press.

Averill, J. R. Anger. In H. E. Howe, Jr., & R. A. Dienstbier (Eds.), *Nebraska Symposium on Motivation 1978* (Vol. 27). Lincoln: University of Nebraska Press, 1979.

Averill, J. R., & Boothroyd, P. On falling in love in conformance with the romantic ideal. *Motivation and Emotion*, 1977, **1**, 235–247.

Bandura, A. Self-efficacy: Toward a unifying theory of behavioral change. *Psychological Review*, 1977, **84**, 191–215.

Beach, L. R. *Psychology: Core concepts and special topics*. New York: Holt, Rinehart & Winston, 1973.

Berscheid, E., & Walster, E. H. *Interpersonal attraction*. Reading, Mass.: Addison-Wesley, 1969.

Bindra, D. Emotion and behavior theory: Current research in historical perspective. In P. Black (Ed.), *Physiological correlates of emotion*. New York: Academic Press, 1970.

Buck, R. Nonverbal communication of affect in preschool children: Relationships with personality and skin conductance. *Journal of Personality and Social Psychology*, 1977, **35**, 225–236.

Buss, A. H. *A temperament theory of personality development*. New York: Wiley, 1975.

Calder, B. J., & Staw, B. M. Self-perception of intrinsic and extrinsic motivation. *Journal of Personality and Social Psychology*, 1975, **31**, 599–605.

Calvert-Boyanowsky, J., & Leventhal, H. The role of information in attenuating behavioral responses to stress: A reinterpretation of the misattribution phenomenon. *Journal of Personality and Social Psychology*, 1975, **32**, 214–221.

Cantor, J. R., Zillmann, D., & Bryant, J. Enhancement of experienced sexual arousal in response to erotic stimuli through misattribution of unrelated residual excitation. *Journal of Personality and Social Psychology*, 1975, **32**, 69–75.

Condry, J. Enemies of exploration: Self-initiated versus other-initiated learning. *Journal of Personality and Social Psychology*, 1977, **35**, 459–477.

Davison, G. C., & Valins, S. Maintenance of self-attributed and drug-induced behavior change. *Journal of Personality and Social Psychology*, 1969, **11**, 25–33.

Davitz, J. R. A dictionary and grammar of emotion. In M. B. Arnold (Ed.), *Feelings and emotions: The Loyola Symposium*. New York: Academic Press, 1970.

Dennenberg, V. H. Stimulation in infancy, emotional reactivity, and exploratory behavior. In D. C. Glass (Ed.), *Neurophysiology and emotion*. New York: Rockefeller University Press, 1967.

Dienstbier, R. A. The role of anxiety and arousal attribution in cheating. *Journal of Experimental Social Psychology*, 1972, **8**, 168–179.

Dienstbier, R. A. Attribution, socialization, and moral decision making. In J. H. Harvey, W. Ickes, & R. F. Kidd (Eds.), *New directions in attribution research* (Vol. 2). Hillsdale, N.J.: Lawrence Erlbaum Associates, 1978.

Dienstbier, R. A., Hillman, D., Lehnhoff, J., Hillman, J., & Valkenaar, M. C. An emotion-attribution approach to moral behavior: Interfacing cognitive and avoidance theories of moral development. *Psychological Review*, 1975, **82**, 299–315.

Dienstbier, R. A., & Munter, P. O. Cheating as a function of the labeling of natural arousal. *Journal of Personality and Social Psychology*, 1971, **17**, 208–213.

Dutton, D. G., & Aron, A. P. Some evidence for heightened sexual attraction under conditions of high anxiety. *Journal of Personality and Social Psychology*, 1974, **30**, 510–517.

Englander-Golden, P., Whitmore, R., & Dienstbier, R. A. Menstrual cycle as focus of study and self-reports of moods and behaviors. *Motivation and Emotion*, 1978, **2**, 75–86.

Englander-Golden, P., Willis, K. A., & Dienstbier, R. A. Stability of perceived tension as a function of the menstrual cycle. *Journal of Human Stress*, 1977, **3**, 14–21.

Epstein, S. M. Toward a unified theory of anxiety. In B. A. Haher (Ed.), *Progress in experimental personality research* (Vol. 4). New York: Academic Press, 1967.

Fehr, F. S., & Stern, J. A. Peripheral physiological variables and emotion: The James-Lange theory revisited. *Psychological Bulletin*, 1970, **74**, 411–424.

Frankenhaeuser, M. Experimental approaches to the study of catecholamines and emotion. In L. Levi (Ed.), *Emotions: Their parameters and measurement*. New York: Raven Press, 1975.

Frankenhaeuser, M. Psychoneuroendocrine approaches to the study of emotion as related to stress and coping. In H. E. Howe, Jr., & R. A. Dienstbier (Eds.), *Nebraska Symposium on Motivation 1978* (Vol. 27). Lincoln: University of Nebraska Press, 1979.

Funkenstein, D. H. The physiology of fear and anger. *Scientific American*, 1955, **192**, 74–80.

Gagnon, J. H. Scripts and the coordination of sexual conduct. In J. K. Cole & R. A. Dienstbier (Eds.), *Nebraska Symposium on Motivation 1973*. Lincoln: University of Nebraska Press, 1974.

Gambaro, S., & Rabin, A. I. Diastolic blood pressure responses following direct and displaced aggression after anger arousal in high- and low-guilt subjects. *Journal of Personality and Social Psychology*, 1969, **12**, 87–94.

Greene, D. *Immediate and subsequent effects of differential reward systems on intrinsic motivation in public school classrooms*. Unpublished doctoral dissertation, Stanford University, 1974. Cited in J. Condry, Enemies of exploration: Self-initiated versus other-initiated learning (*Journal of Personality and Social Psychology*, 1977, **35**, 459–477).

Hamburg, D. A., Hamburg, B. A., & Barchas, J. D. Anger and depression in perspective of behavioral biology. In L. Levi (Ed.), *Emotions: Their parameters and measurement*. New York: Raven Press, 1975.

Hare, R. D. *Psychopathy: Theory and research*. New York: Wiley, 1970.

Hebb, D. O. On the nature of fear. *Psychological Review*, 1946, **53**, 259–276.

Hoffman, M. L. Moral development. In P. H. Mussen (Ed.), *Carmichael's manual of child development* (Vol. 2; 3rd ed.). New York: Wiley, 1970.

Hohmann, G. W. Some effects of spinal cord lesions on experienced emotional feelings. *Psychophysiology*, 1966, **3**, 143–156.

Hokanson, J. E., & Burgess, M. Effects of status, type of frustration, and aggression on vascular processes. *Journal of Abnormal and Social Psychology*, 1962, **65**, 232–237.

Isen, A. M., Shalker, T. E., Clark, M., & Karp, L. Affect, accessibility of material in memory, and behavior: A cognitive loop? *Journal of Social and Personality Psychology*, 1978, **36**, 1–12.

Izard, C. E. *The face of emotion*. New York: Appleton-Century-Crofts, 1971.

Izard, C. E. *Patterns of emotions*. New York: Academic Press, 1972.

Izard, C. E. Emotions as motivations: An evolutionary-developmental perspective. In H. E. Howe, Jr., & R. A. Dienstbier (Eds.), *Nebraska Symposium on Motivation 1978* (Vol. 27). Lincoln: University of Nebraska Press, 1979.

Izard, C. E., & Tomkins, S. S. Affect and behavior: Anxiety as a negative affect. In C. D. Spielberger (Ed.), *Anxiety and behavior*. New York: Academic Press. 1966.

Janis, I. L. *Stress and frustration*. New York: Harcourt, Brace & World, 1969.

Kellogg, R., & Baron, R. Attribution theory, insomnia, and the reverse placebo effect: A reversal of Storms and Nisbett's findings. *Journal of Personality and Social Psychology*, 1975, **32**, 231–236.

Kelly, G. A. *A theory of personality: The psychology of personal constructs*. New York: Norton, 1955.

Keniston, K. *The uncommitted: Alienated youth in American society*. New York: Dell, 1960.

Kenrick, D. T., & Cialdini, R. B. Romantic attraction: Misattribution versus reinforcement explanations. *Journal of Personality and Social Psychology*, 1977, **35**, 381–391.

Konečni, V. J. Annoyance, type and duration of postannoyance activity, and aggression: The "cathartic effect." *Journal of Experimental Psychology: General*, 1975, **104**, 796–802. (a)

Konečni, V. J. The mediation of aggressive behavior: Arousal level versus anger and cognitive labeling. *Journal of Personality and Social Psychology*, 1975, **32**, 706–712. (b)

Konečni, V. J., & Doob, A. N. Catharsis through displacement of aggression. *Journal of Personality and Social Psychology*, 1972, **23**, 379–387.

Kruglanski, A. W., Alon, S., & Lewis, T. Retrospective misattribution and task enjoyment. *Journal of Experimental Social Psychology*, 1972, **8**, 493–501.

Laird, J. D. Self-attribution of emotion: The effects of expressive behavior on the quality of emotional experience. *Journal of Personality and Social*

Psychology, 1974, **29**, 475–486.

Landis, C., & Hunt, W. A. Adrenalin and emotion. *Psychological Review*, 1932, **39**, 467–485.

Lanzetta, J. T., Cartwright-Smith, J., & Kleck, R. E. Effects of nonverbal dissimulation on emotional experience and autonomic arousal. *Journal of Personality and Social Psychology*, 1976, **33**, 354–370.

Lanzetta, J. T., & Kleck, R. E. Encoding and decoding of nonverbal affect in humans. *Journal of Personality and Social Psychology*, 1970, **16**, 12–19.

Lazarus, R. S. *Psychological stress and the coping process*. New York: McGraw Hill, 1966.

Lazarus, R. S. Emotions and adaptation: Conceptual and empirical relations. In W. J. Arnold (Ed.), *Nebraska Symposium on Motivation 1968* (Vol. 16). Lincoln: University of Nebraska Press, 1969.

Lazarus, R. S. The self regulation of emotion. In L. Levi (Ed.), *Emotions: Their parameters and measurement*. New York: Raven Press, 1975.

Lepper, M. R., Greene, D., & Nisbett, R. E. Undermining children's intrinsic interest with extrinsic reward: A test of the "overjustification" hypothesis. *Journal of Personality and Social Psychology*, 1973, **28**, 129–138.

Lindsley, D. B. The role of nonspecific reticulo-thalamo-cortical systems in emotion. In P. Black (Ed.), *Physiological correlates of emotion*. New York: Academic Press, 1970.

Loehlin, J. C., & Nichols, R. C. *Heredity, environment, and personality: A study of 850 sets of twins*. Austin: University of Texas Press, 1976.

Magargee, E. I. Undercontrolled and overcontrolled personality types in extreme antisocial aggression. *Psychological monographs*, 1966, **80**, No. 3 (Whole No. 611).

Mandler, G. Emotion. In R. Brown, E. Galanter, E. H. Hess, & G. Mandler, *New directions in psychology*. New York: Holt, Rinehart & Winston, 1962.

Mandler, G. *Mind and emotion*. New York: Wiley, 1975.

Maranon, G. Contribution a l'etude de l'action emotive de d'adrenalin. *Revue Francais D'endocrinologie*, 1924, **2**, 301–325. Cited in S. Schachter and J. E. Singer, Cognitive, social, and physiological determinants of emotional state (*Psychological Review*, 1962, **69**, 379–399).

Marshall, G., & Zimbardo, P. G. The affective consequences of inadequately explained physiological arousal. *Journal of Personality and Social Psychology*, in press.

Maslach, C. Negative emotional biasing of unexplained arousal. *Journal of Personality and Social Psychology*, in press.

Mason, J. W. Emotion as reflected in patterns of endocrine integration. In L. Levi (Ed.), *Emotions: Their parameters and measurement*. New York: Raven Press, 1975.

Murray, J., & Feshbach, S. Let's not throw the baby out with the bath water: The catharsis hypothesis revisited. *Journal of Personality*, 1978, **46**, 462–473.

Nelson, M. R., Jr. *Manipulation of pain by reattribution of symptoms and cognitive dissonance.* Unpublished doctoral dissertation, University of Nebraska–Lincoln, 1971.

Nisbett, R. E., & Schachter, S. Cognitive manipulation of pain. *Journal of Experimental Social Psychology*, 1966, **2**, 227–236.

Patterson, M. L. An arousal model of interpersonal intimacy. *Psychological Review*, 1976, **83**, 235–245.

Payne, R. *The life and death of Adolf Hitler.* New York: Popular Library, 1973.

Plutchik, R. *The emotions: Facts, theories, and a new model.* New York: Random House, 1962.

Poe, R. O., Rose, R. M., & Mason, J. W. Multiple determinants of 17-hydro-xycorticosteroid excretion in recruits during basic training. *Psychosomatic Medicine*, 1970, **32**, 369–378.

Rodin, J. Menstruation, reattribution, and competence. *Journal of Personality and Social Psychology*, 1976, **33**, 345–353.

Rosenblatt, P. C., Walsh, R., & Jackson, D. A. *Grief and mourning in cross-cultural perspective.* Human Relations Area Files, 1976.

Ross, L., Rodin, J., & Zimbardo, P. G. Toward an attribution therapy: The reduction of fear through induced cognitive emotional misattribution. *Journal of Personality and Social Psychology*, 1969, **12**, 279–288.

Russell, J. A., & Mehrabian, A. Evidence for a three-factor theory of emotions. *Journal of Research in Personality*, 1977, **11**, 273–294.

Sales, S. M. Economic threat as a determinant of conversion rates in authoritarian and nonauthoritarian churches. *Journal of Personality and Social Psychology*, 1972, **23**, 420–428.

Sales, S. M. Threat as a factor in authoritarianism: An analysis of archival data. *Journal of Personality and Social Psychology*, 1973, **28**, 44–57.

Schachter, S. *Emotion, obesity, and crime.* New York: Academic Press, 1971.

Schachter, S., & Latané, B. Crime, cognition, and the autonomic nervous system. In D. Levine (Ed.), *Nebraska Symposium on Motivation 1964.* Lincoln: University of Nebraska Press, 1964.

Schachter, S., & Singer, J. E. Cognitive, social, and physiological determinants of emotional state. *Psychological Review*, 1962, **69**, 379–399.

Schachter, S., & Wheeler, L. Epinephrine, chlorpromazine, and amusement. *Journal of Abnormal and Social Psychology*, 1962, **65**, 121–128.

Seligman, M. E. P. On the generality of the laws of learning. *Psychological Review*, 1970, **77**, 406–418.

Seligman, M. E. P., & Hager, J. L. Biological boundaries of learning (The Sauce-Bearnaise syndrome). *Psychology Today*, 1972, **6**, 59–61, 84–87.

Simon, W. The social, the erotic, and the sensual: The complexities of sexual scripts. In J. K. Cole & R. A. Dienstbier (Eds.), *Nebraska Symposium on Motivation 1973.* Lincoln: University of Nebraska Press, 1974.

Solomon, R. L., & Corbit, J. D. An opponent-process theory of motivation: I. Temporal dynamics of affect. *Psychological Review*, 1972, **81**, 119–145.

Solomon, R. L., & Wynne, L. C. Traumatic avoidance learning: The principles of anxiety conservation and partial irreversibility. *Psychological Review*, 1954, **61**, 353–385.

Tomkins, S. S. *Affect, imagery, consciousness. Vol. 2: The negative affects*. New York: Springer, 1963.

Tomkins, S. S. Affect as the primary motivational system. In M. B. Arnold (Ed.), *Feelings and emotions: The Loyola Symposium*. New York: Academic Press, 1970.

Tomkins, S. S. The phantasy behind the face. *Journal of Personality Assessment*, 1975, **39**, 551–560.

Tomkins, S. S. Script theory: Differential magnification of affects. In H. E. Howe, Jr., & R. A. Dienstbier (Eds.), *Nebraska Symposium on Motivation 1978* (Vol. 27). Lincoln: University of Nebraska Press, 1979. Too many U.S. workers no longer give a damn. *Newsweek*, April 24, 1972, p. 65.

Valins, S. Cognitive effects of false heart-rate feedback. *Journal of Personality and Social Psychology*, 1966, **4**, 400–408.

Valins, S. Emotionality and information concerning internal reactions. *Journal of Personality and Social Psychology*, 1967, **6**, 458–463.

Valins, S., & Ray, A. Effects of cognitive desensitization on avoidance behavior. *Journal of Personality and Social Psychology*, 1967, **7**, 345–350.

Walster, E. H., & Berscheid, E. Adrenaline makes the heart grow fonder. *Psychology Today*, 1971, **5**, 46–50, 62.

Winterbottom, M. R. The relation of need for achievement to learning experiences in independence and mastery. In J. W. Atkinson (Ed.), *Motives in fantasy, action, and society*. Princeton: Van Nostrand, 1958.

Yochelson, S., & Samnow, S. E. *The criminal personality. Vol. 1: A profile for change*. New York: Jason Aronson, 1976.

Younger, J. C., & Doob, A. N. Attribution and aggression: The misattribution of anger. *Journal of Research in Personality*, 1978, **12**, 164–171.

Zillmann, D., Johnson, R. C., & Day, K. D. Attribution of apparent arousal and proficiency of recovery from sympathetic activation affecting excitation transfer to aggressive behavior. *Journal of Experimental Social Psychology*, 1974, **10**, 503–515.

Zillmann, D., Katcher, A. H., & Milavsky, B. Excitation transfer from physical exercise to subsequent aggressive behavior. *Journal of Experimental Social Psychology*, 1972, **8**, 247–259.

Subject Index

Author Index

315

81
83
86
88